'G   ' ' '

D1355718

The Later Middle Ages

THE CONTEXT OF
ENGLISH LITERATURE

The Later Middle Ages

EDITED BY
STEPHEN MEDCALF

METHUEN & CO LTD
LONDON

First published in 1981 by
Methuen & Co. Ltd
11 New Fetter Lane, London EC4P 4EE

© *1981 Stephen Medcalf, Nicola Coldstream,*
Marjorie Reeves, David Starkey

Typeset in Great Britain by
Scarborough Typesetting Services
Printed in the United States of America

British Library Cataloguing in Publication Data

The context of English literature.
The later Middle Ages.
  1. English literature – History and criticism
  2. Literature and society
I. Medcalf, Stephen   II. The later Middle Ages
  820'.9   PR83

ISBN 0-416-85990-0
ISBN 0-416-86000-1 Pbk (University paperbacks 702)

Contents

Illustrations

Preface

As the writing of this book has been collaborative and inter-disciplinary, it may be useful to have a record of the kinds and degrees of collaboration that went into each part. Most parts of the book have been heard and criticized by several or all four of the collaborators. Chapter 1 is mine predominantly: it was written partly before the rest as an introduction to what would be useful from the point of view of a student of English literature, partly at the end of all as a drawing together of themes. The second chapter, on intellectual history, is predominantly by Marjorie Reeves, except for the section entitled 'The philosophy of the world', which is mine. Here the principle of work was that Marjorie Reeves designed and wrote the first draft, and I added portions which did not alter her text. The third chapter, which devotes itself to lesser literature on the whole as a guide to the way in which medieval people describe themselves, was written like the first. The fourth, by Nicola Coldstream, was kept deliberately within the bounds of one discipline: it describes the development of art and architecture in parallel with that of English literature, with the intent that literature should be introduced only to illustrate art and architecture here, and the background given by the chapter be used elsewhere to illustrate the other disciplines. The fifth chapter is the most thoroughgoingly collaborative: the draft by David Starkey was discussed and agreed on sentence by sentence and word by word between him and myself, and read over by the other two contributors. Over all, the book represents fairly, I think, the fullest possible range not of disciplines but of kinds of interdisciplinary collaboration.

Our thanks are due to a number of readers who tried to induce some coherence and comprehensibility into the result: to Gabriel Josipovici, Clare Hawkins, Tony Nuttall, Malcolm Kitch, Veronica Bruce-Gardner, Josey Acres, Neil Warren, John Burrow, Ben Gibbs, Tamar Miller, and the members of the South-Eastern Universities Medieval Seminar.

I fear the final product is still pervaded by a fund of eccentricity and error due to me and not to the other contributors. In particular, I am uneasy about the kind of modernization given to the quotations: it is frankly inconsistent. In verse and in the more literary passages of this book, a slightly regularized Middle English is preserved. But it is my experience that even quite conscientious readers become less attentive, and persuade themselves that they have understood more than they have done, in reading expository Middle English prose and verse. Here I have adopted a compromise between making the quotations intelligible to readers who have never encountered Middle English before and preserving their true sound and quality. It should not be relied on as a scholarly guide to the texts.

We can only hope that the reader will obtain one-tenth as much enjoyment and instruction as we obtained in the writing.

A note about the cover illustration: On the cover is one of the wall paintings of Miracles of the Virgin, by William Baker and Gilbert, in Eton Chapel (1479–88). It depicts a story from the *Golden Legend* (translated into English by Caxton in 1483). A lady who could not attend mass at Candlemas, because she had given her mantle to a poor man, dreamed that she was at a mass celebrated by Christ, and sung by Our Lady with a great company of virgins. She was given a candle, which she refused to offer even when an angel dragged it from her. It broke, and at once she woke to find the piece of the candle in her hand. This candle was preserved and venerated at Arras.

One might set the story in varying ways not only with *Pearl* and the story of the Grail, and the visions of Margery Kempe, but with what Coleridge said of imagination: 'If a man could pass through Paradise in a dream, and have a flower presented to him as a pledge that his soul had really been there, and if he found that flower in his hand when he awoke – Ay, and what then?' (*Anima Poetae*). The variety of late medieval attitudes to vision and imagination in art and religion, and their contrast with those of the Romantics, are discussed in the text.

Stephen Medcalf

1 On reading books from a half-alien culture

STEPHEN MEDCALF

. . . it is a real book: i.e., it's not like a book at all, but like
a thunder-clap.[1]   (C. S. Lewis)

Difficulties in understanding

Reading a book is a complex thing to do; giving a true reading of a
book illimitably complex. Even now as I am writing, I am trying to
talk about our common world; but you are trying to understand me,
to put yourself at the centre from which a cobweb of language half-
creates my world. There is a gap between the two meanings, mine
and yours; but it can be to all intents and purposes closed, because
we are contemporaries, sharing a common language, and because I
am not writing an ambitious work of art or self-expression.

But in this book we are dealing with *Piers Plowman*, *Troilus and
Criseyde*, *Morte Darthur*, Skelton's poems. In reading these great
and ancient works, the gap between author's and reader's meaning
may be very wide, and ways of closing it are various and unsatisfying.
One school of thought might let the author's side be lost, arguing
that a poem is a public work and should be read as what it means to
us, the only permissible discussion being critical discussion of the
structure and internal relations of the words as we hear and understand them. An opposite school would devote its time to transport-
ing the modern reader across the gap, arguing that the medium of a
poem is the meaning of its words in the context in which it was
written, its subject matter is the life of its own period, its structure is

something governed by the aesthetic criteria of its own age, and its purpose is its author's speaking as he intended to the audience he designed.

These are extreme views, both despairing of closing the gap. Less extreme practitioners may try to bring one side or the other closer in; either rendering the poem into its modern equivalent (as Dryden did with Chaucer) or calling up scholarship to make the modern reader acquire medieval reading habits.

In this book, trying to set both medieval literature and its modern readers in the context of the medieval world (both inner and outer) and its values, its notion of the arts and its social organization, we tend towards the last approach. But, as this first chapter will try to show, we think that the dispute can be transcended. And, although both medieval studies and the co-operation between disciplines are at such a point that we hope what we shall have to say is novel and interesting at any level of scholarship, in trying to resolve the dispute we have primarily in mind not the professional medievalist but the common reader who inhabits all of us. We should like to move at the level of such annotated texts appealing to a wide range of readers as John Burrow's *English Verse 1300–1500*, A. C. Cawley's *Canterbury Tales*, Cawley and Anderson's *Pearl, Cleanness, Patience and Sir Gawain and the Green Knight*, A. V. C. Schmidt's *Piers Plowman*, and R. T. Davies's *Mediaeval English Lyrics* and *Corpus Christi Play of the English Middle Ages*. In particular, we remember H. G. Wells's Mr Polly, the person who has little or no experience of medieval English, who has encountered medieval culture and found it distant and mysterious, yet 'had the strangest sense of being at home – far more than he had ever been at home before.'[2]

Those differences of approach, which we hope to transcend, and which seem scholarly or critical, rest on two profounder disagreements, about personality and about words.

What is it, first, for a word to mean something? It is not a question that much troubles us (though perhaps it ought) as long as we stay within the borders of our native language and culture. It is when we move outside – or as in the case of England between 1330 and 1550, half-outside – when we find ourselves making implausible, or suspect we are making plausible but false, interpretations of books that the questions begin. To understand a word, must one know the whole structure of the language, even of the culture, of which it is a part? Or does one begin with single words, with mysterious particular flashes of intuition about their relation to our common world? How far, indeed, is our common world itself composed of atoms that we can be sure of reaching, put together in different constructions by different cultures, and how far is it made visible only by the projections of our forming consciousness?

We know, at least, that we notice things by naming them. But what should we notice in using unfamiliar names? In reading from the *General Prologue* to *The Canterbury Tales* the description of April, when

>. . . the yonge sonne
>Hath in the Ram his half cours yronne[3]

we may have help from the picture for April in the Duc de Berry's *Très Riches Heures*, in which above the duke's castle of Dourdan the blue sky merges with no particular break (that might indicate a different world) through clouds to a king in a chariot holding the sun: then beyond a space marked for a calendar are the heavens, spangled with stars and divided into sections of the zodiac with the Ram and the Bull. But should we refer the words primarily to some such representation? Or to our own knowledge of the stars and the young spring sun? Or to a date in the calendar, rhetorically decorated? Or to something more conceptual, only to be understood in a whole structure of alien ideas, experiences and symbols? Or to something mysteriously between all these? How much weight should we give to the fact that Chaucer's contemporaries believed that each of the heavenly bodies was guided – not indeed by any physical being, nor by a god, but by an intelligence? In what way should we take the not quite formulable sense that much medieval poetry gives, of an outer world alive, active, and yourself a living part of it?

The second fundamental question is: what is it to be a person? Are we atomic individuals, independent substances only externally related, communicating by constructions and works of art placed between us? In that case, reading a book is like contemplating an artefact designed to elicit such and such responses in the reader, and if the artefact does not work we legitimately adjust it. Or are we beings who exist partly in terms of each other, capable of and needing radical empathy, so that our languages, even over a gap of time, are relations partly internal to ourselves, intuitively understood? In that case, reading a book is entering the truth of someone else's mind, and, if we cannot enter, it is we ourselves who must change.

But these profound disagreements are complicated by a matter of history: namely, that different ages tend to take different sides on them, and the Middle Ages in particular probably felt less sense than we now do of individual isolation, had a different sense of inner and outer, and a greater sense of a common way of thinking in a shared and stable world. But does that make the gap that separates them from us narrower (if in fact they wrote with a certain assumption of givenness and community) or wider (if in fact we cannot share their assumptions)?

Chaucer, for example, in writing as he did about the sun, was not creating a personal image but drawing on an inherited language. In fact, he was following closely Guido delle Colonne's Latin *History of the Destruction of Troy*: 'sol maturans sub obliquo zodiaci circulo cursum suum sub signo iam intraverat arietis'[4] ('the hastening [or, ripening] sun in the sloping circle of the zodiac had already entered his course under the sign of the ram'). But evidently Chaucer has altered it: he has done something extremely characteristic of his age, by having given (as it was put then) a new *sense* to an old *matter*. How much, then, of the effect we receive – the effect of a stately dance, of gorgeousness and assurance in an objectively meaningful and stably recurrent world – is our general and alien reaction to medieval rhetoric, how much what is specifically meant in this passage? How much relates to the matter Chaucer draws from his culture, how much to the sense, the bloom he has created as a particular craftsman? When, as often in Chaucer, there is a contrast between the original and the new version, when we know or suspect irony, then it becomes imperative to know (as with Betjeman's poetry in our time) what and how many levels there are. In this case Chaucer seems, by translating or changing *maturans* into 'young', bringing out of *cursum*, 'course', its latent sense of 'run', and shortening the whole phrase, to have enhanced the sun's speed, increased our sense of its personality, and added to the eagerness of the passage. If this is a right account, there is no irony or distancing: everything he has done has enhanced the original meaning, and indeed made vivid to us a sense of the world we only barely receive from Guido delle Colonne. But it does not seem to be so when he writes, one can scarcely but think in parody,

> . . . the brighte sonne loste his hewe;
> For th'orisonte hath reft the sonne his light;
> This is as much to seye as it was night.[5]

orisonte] horizon

How, then, do we decipher? How much do we need to decipher?

When the business of deciphering ancient scripts was first seriously undertaken, it was thought that Egyptian hieroglyphics would give up their meaning if you traced your own train of associations from what they seemed naturally to present to you, on the general assumption that they were presenting wisdom. This was in fact in the late fifteenth century, so that the general difficulty of decipherment was complicated by a culture still enmeshed, as Chaucer's had been, in visual allegories and emblems. The Italian humanist Ficino accordingly wrote:

> Our way of thinking about *time* is complex and shifting. For example, 'time goes quickly', 'time revolves and ends where it began', 'time teaches prudence', 'time gives and takes away'. This whole range of thought was comprehended in a single firm figure by the Egyptians when they drew a winged serpent with its tail in its mouth.[6]

Ficino was intelligent but wrong. No advance was made – even by the discovery of a bilingual inscription like the Rosetta Stone – until decipherers worked on the principle that inscriptions in alien symbols have a latent structure, not apparent to free association, but to be determined by observing the relations of the symbols to each other. Nevertheless, the later and successful decipherers from Champollion to Ventris could still work only from intuitions and discoveries of meaning which were as immediate as Ficino's, as much based on man's general instinct for creating and understanding symbols, but better placed and based, and less assured that the sounds or ideas to be discovered would conform to expectation.

We are always somewhat in the position of decipherers when we try to understand the productions of a different culture: even when listening to the conversation of someone from a different part of our own country; even, perhaps, when individual talks to individual, however nearly identical their backgrounds; even, finally, in recalling our individual pasts. Within the limits of my own time and consciousness, within the single decade 1960–70, my awareness of the phrase 'make love' changed, so that while about 1960 I read it naturally as 'talk lovingly' and had to decipher it in novels where it meant 'have sexual intercourse', by 1970 it was the second meaning that I found normal while the first struck oddly. It was a shared and public shift; but I doubt if anyone could describe exactly what happened. Certainly it was not that the phrase corresponded at one time to one evident feature of the world and then moved, as if a needle passed from one track on a record to the next: yet there was a time when a great number of sentences existed in which the phrase naturally had the old meaning for a person accustomed principally to the old ways of life, and the new for someone acquainted with both the traditional and the new. Something reactive happened: there was a change in how and when people used the actual phrase but there was also a change in the pattern of customs to which it referred, and the meaning of the things done, which themselves are in a sense symbolic. For some people the phrase changed meaning simply in that it denoted different things being done, sexual intercourse in place of words, but things expressing the same emotions. Presumably that was why it was possible to continue using the same phrase, 'make love', which after all takes its meaning primarily from the emotion. Yet, for others, the difference in what was done implied or created a change in the emotion too.

Something similar probably happens with all semantic changes: the analogy with hieroglyphics holds not only for words but for habits, gestures, rituals, psychologies, philosophies and religions, for all the symbolic activities of man. How much do human emotions change, how far do we understand them, when they are expressed by changed customs, languages and concepts?

For our comfort, we recognize at the centre of the complex otherness of medieval civilization the friendly face of Chaucer, assuring us in the opening of Book 2 of *Troilus and Criseyde* that he understands our difficulties perfectly. He may have been the first man to do so. He had preparation: Lucretius, Horace, Seneca and Boethius among the ancients, Dante and Petrarch among the moderns, gave him precedent for awareness of change in custom and language. He had probably read the observation in Sir John Mandeville's *Travels* that, whereas Mandeville wondered at what was to be seen in the ends of Asia, the inhabitants of those parts thought what he had to tell them of western Europe equally impossible; if he had read that, then he knew Mandeville's assumption that both sides were right, for 'God is marvellous in His works'.[7] He must have encountered the question of understanding between two cultures when he travelled between Edward III's, Langland's and the Gawain poet's England, and Boccaccio's and Petrarch's Italy. But, all the same, no one before him had dealt with change in custom and language as a problem in understanding the feelings of the past. No one had gone on to observe, first, that what is expressed in custom and language need not change though they do, and, secondly, that differences between epochs are not fundamentally different from the differences one can observe between one's friends and contemporaries:

> Ye know eke that in form of speech is change
> Within a thousand year, and wordes tho
> That hadden price, now wonder nice and strange
> Us thinketh hem, and yet they spake hem so,
> And sped as well in love as men now do.
> Eke for to winnen love in sundry ages,
> In sundry landes, sundry ben usages.
>
> Eke scarcely ben there in this place three
> That have in love said like, and done in all.[8]

It was not to be an isolated observation: Thomas Usk copied it from him within a year or two in his *Testament of Love*.[9]

But though he offers us his ironic sympathy, Chaucer characteristically leaves the mystery intact. His Troilus, a Trojan of 2000 years before, is a medieval lover, and so far as we can judge any strangeness in his way of love is medieval too – just as, when in *The House of Fame* and *The Legend of Good Women* Chaucer tells the story of Dido and another Trojan, Aeneas, although he claims to follow Virgil's *Aeneid* closely, he makes Aeneas a typical faithless chivalric lover of the fourteenth century. And though he translates fragments of the Aeneid as delightfully as it has ever been done – such as Venus 'Venatrix, dederatque comam' diffundere ventis'[10]

> Going in a queint array
> As she had been an hunteresse
> With wind blowing upon her tresse[11]

queint] graceful, artful, cunning

– still he does this where classical and medieval coincide. In those lines Venus might be one of the faery hunt, such as the classical King of Hades became when the story of Orpheus was retold in the first part of the fourteenth century as *Sir Orfeo*:

> The king o fairy with his rout
> Come to hunt him al about
> With dim cry and blowing.[12]

Chaucer was praised from France as 'grant translateur,[13] by Eustache Deschamps. And indeed he was fascinated by the idea of translation, even in fantasy. He loves to wonder about the meaning of birdsong, as of the May birds who in his dream in the *Legend of Good Women* sing variously 'The fowler we defy', or of love, 'Blessed be Saint Valentine', or 'Welcome, summer'.[14] But when he imagines understanding the language of birds, it is sheerly by dream or magic, as by Canace's ring in the *Squire's Tale*; and, although the tale does not intend it as such, it is an emblem of the way magic comprehends the universe that what Canace hears from a falcon is nearly all an imposition of human ways on a little understanding of the bird's world. In Canace's language or the Squire's, the falcon laments that her lover, though gentle-born and seeming to keep all the observances of 'gentilesse' in love, deserted her for a kite. What Chaucer doubtless did intend is that this usage of 'gentilesse' by the Squire, himself gentle-born, sets off a display of how the Host and the Franklin use and understand the word, detachedly observed in their conversation, seen through the Franklin's very eyes and instincts in his *Tale*. Chaucer spares no subtlety of observation to understand the ways and words of people within his own world; as for birds and Trojans, he uses their distance from us only to see in them ourselves from an imagined viewpoint. He is a great translator in the medieval way: not because he tries to render different worlds, but because he has a perfect instinct for the affinities between what we might think are different worlds, which he treats as all continuous, and because where he finds no affinity he transforms what he sees into what is native to the world he knows, like Ficino deciphering the hieroglyphics.

Part of the story of the period 1330–1550 is that of how people began to conceive the classical world – not, like Chaucer, as something with which they had a continuous tradition, but as something past of which there might be a renaissance. Later involutions of the senses of history and of cultural strangeness provided the decipherers of alien scripts with the interplay of intuition and study of alien structures of which we have spoken, and made it harder for us to read Chaucer as Chaucer seems to have read Virgil.

The fact of understanding: 'I sing of a maiden'

In two respects, however, we have advantage over decipherers of alien symbols when we read medieval literature. First, medieval culture is not utterly alien to us but continuous, ancestral, familial. We may speak a language descended from theirs, worship in their churches, share some of their presuppositions, religion and rituals – and all this without self-consciousness. We do not *translate*:

> I sing of a maiden
>   That is makeles
> King of alle kinges
>   To here sone she ches.
> He cam also stille
>   Ther his moder was
> As dew in Aprille
>   That falleth on the gras.
> He cam also stille
>   To his moderes bowr
> As dew in Aprille
>   That falleth on the flowr.
> He cam also stille
>   Ther his moder lay
> As dew in Aprille
>   That falleth on the spray.
> Moder and maiden
>   Was never none but she
> Wel may swich a lady
>   Godes moder be.[15]

What we are doing, since we cannot call it translation, is hard to see. It is not quite like reading a book of our own century, at any rate a popular book. Yet it is more like reading a book of our own age in which certain idioms and words escape us than it is like reading a deliberately obscure twentieth-century book such as *Finnegans*

Wake. We inhabit these words, and we inhabit them more naturally than we inhabit James Joyce's.

Secondly, in spite of all there is to be said about the necessity and difficulty of correct reading, W. H. Auden was right in saying that you should never ask 'Have you read any good books lately?' but 'Have you been read by any good books lately?' Books break in on us, judge us, break and reform our responses. But this breaking in, this judging and reforming, happens with books five times deeper in the past than Chaucer's – with the *Iliad* and the Old Testament. And over all this irruption makes a way for truth, whatever particular misreadings and misunderstandings may occur. On the one hand it is true that, even from the purest aesthete's point of view, we disregard the meanings of alien words and ways at our peril. A colour-blind man, however sensitive he may be to drawing and line, cannot assess the mass and balance of a painting. He is blind not only to its colour but to its form. He may contrive to see it as partly perfect, and the whole of it is as having a kind of consistency, but a perverse and unsatisfying one. If he received the gift of seeing colours, what he would see would no longer be marked by oddness but by a shock of strangeness and life. But the analogy is in the end hopeful. For it is with a shock of strangeness and life that we do receive *Troilus and Criseyde*, *Sir Gawain and the Green Knight* or 'I sing of a maiden'. And with structures as complex as these, in which every word sparks off a new set of responses, it is not credible that our continued delight is based on substantial misunderstandings. Our naïve response is the primary datum: it is sometimes totally mistaken, but any hypothesis that suggests this – as by suggesting that medieval society imposed different emotions, or medieval ethics and aesthetics different literary responses – has a burden of proof laid on it. But if against all the difficulties of communication from culture to culture 'I sing of a maiden' does succeed in communicating something close to its original meaning, how does it do it?

A poem is a closely interlocking pattern of words and meanings, and what happens in reading 'I sing of a maiden' seems to have to do with interlocking contexts. Of the meaning of a word which a reader begins by inhabiting, some areas are denied to him by its context in a sentence, while in some other areas he is gestured towards rooms in experience that he did not know even existed; he may even find previously unknown, still hardly knowable, demands laid upon him.

One word will illustrate the point. We have in our common usage a direction of meaning for the word 'lady', even though the direction is towards something old-fashioned, muted, not more than delicately affecting and perhaps less: a polite elderly woman with a particular way of handling teacups. It liberates, but scarcely helps, to know that the original meaning of the word, seven centuries the other side of this lyric and wholly alien, wholly to be translated, is likely to have been 'loaf-kneader' (*hlaef-dige*) for the household. But in this lyric the direction that we bring for the word is limited and deepened by every key word from 'sing' and 'maiden' to 'moder' and 'king', even though some of these words, removed from the whole figure, would be as faded as 'lady' itself; and when we finally come upon 'lady' placed at a point in the verse where we have three times encountered the connotations of 'Aprille' – the spring, new life. fair and fertile weather, love – we are given such a meaning for it as we could not gain from volumes on social custom and religious belief, because we intuitively seize on and inhabit it. And what is happening is, as semantic change tends to be, reactive: from 'lady' we further understand, looking back, what was implied in 'maiden', 'moder', 'Aprille' and the rest.

But it is easy enough to go wrong; and before or after or with 'the felt change of consciousness'[16] in reading poetry, we do desire not only aesthetic impact but truth. We want our responses to be correct. But what truth is it we want, and what correct meanings of words do we have in mind? Not our own, apparently, else we should not be so anxious for correction. What truth or meaning can we have in mind, other than those of the author as author? – the book's meaning in the time when he uttered it, excluding, no doubt, meanings he intended but failed clearly to express, including nevertheless meanings of which he was not directly conscious himself, meanings governed by his unknown, subliminal self, by customs he took for granted in his own culture, and by the depth of meaning that words acquire from their birth onwards by their uses on indefinitely many occasions. For the great writer is, it seems, intimate with his depths.

Accordingly, although reading 'I sing of a maiden' lets one in not only to the poem but to the culture it grows from, still to know more of the culture can only enrich the poem. One's first intuitions are corrected, confirmed, deepened. Other poetry may provide the first context: for example, the word 'lady', since it is now for us associated

with April, may be further enriched by the lines from the prologue
to the *Canterbury Tales* which we began this chapter by discussing,
and by the April scene in the *Très Riches Heures*, with its enchanting
betrothal – curiously enriched by the hypothesis that the young
man in that picture is the poet Charles d'Orléans, and Bonne, the
Duc de Berry's granddaughter, is the 'lady'. A poem from the
Nativity play of the thirteenth-century Bavarian *Carmina Burana*
suggests that April is not only the month of love and new life but
also

> Of all things the beginning
>   Was on an April morn
> In the spring the earth remembereth
>   The day that she was born.[17]

But wider knowledge of the culture will provide the idea of the
'lady' with its background in social hierarchy, in the secular
devotion of courtly love, and in the adoration of the Virgin Mary,
'Our Lady' herself. Behind that is both the context of medieval
kingship, with its combination of sacredness and power, and the
tender contemplativeness of late medieval piety, concrete and visual
yet also elusive and recessive. One learns how Old Testament events
and images were read in the light of the New Testament, so that
Gideon's fleece in Judges, on which as a sign from God dew lay
while the ground about was dry, is a type of Mary with the Son of
God descending on her through the Spirit; wisdom, which in the
Book of Wisdom comes down from God in the silence of the night,
is an adumbration of Christ as the word of God; and both the flower
of the field which is an image of the beloved in the Song of Songs,
and the rod from the stem of Jesse from which Isaiah says a saviour
will come, foreshadow Our Lady. Moreover, one use of an image in
the Old Testament suggests others, so that the dew on Gideon's
fleece suggests other foreshadowings of Christ: the dew that Isaiah
calls on to come down from heaven as an image of God's righteousness, and again the drop of morning dew that falls on the earth,
which the Book of Wisdom uses as an image of the insignificance
before God of the whole earth, which nevertheless he loves, preserves
and will show his mercy to.[18] Someone has converted all this into an
intense simplicity, opening the way into it for readers never brought
up to it. And one may justify one's emotions before this symbolism
that has, so to speak, brightened into a fresh naturalism by what is

said of the almost contemporaneous (*c.* 1427–8) Flemish painting of the Annunciation, by the Master of Flémalle in the Mérode altarpiece, 'that God, no longer present as a visible figure, seems to be diffused in all the visible objects'.[19]

Reader, writer, book

However, the fixing on what the author meant as author is complicated by further variations in the relation of reader, writer and work. The distinction between original writer, adapter and translator is one not much made before the sixteenth century, and particularly little by religious dramatists and lyrists. The balance, the cadency, the riches in simplicity of 'I sing of a maiden', encourage one to believe that in the form that affects us it was the outcome of a single act of making – and this is only emphasized when one discovers that part of it exists in a thirteenth-century poem which has no such impact:

> . . . of on ic wille singen that is makeles
> the king of alle kinges to moder he hire ches
> . . . Maiden and moder nas never non wimon but he
> wel mitte he berigge of Godes sune be.[20]

But its simplicity sits well with its anonymity: like most medieval lyrics, it was probably written for *use*, as meditation, prayer or song – it survives, in fact, in a fifteenth-century book of songs (MS Sloane 2593); and even today the authorship of such things is not greatly insisted on. Medieval anthologies exist (for example, John Audelay's) in which the compiler has put his favourite poems, some clearly by himself, some clearly not, and some uncertain, but has not distinguished them. Indeed, a fair amount of late medieval writing comes to us in large manuscripts that constitute personal commonplace books or booksellers' anthologies so that one's attention is concentrated on the compiler's taste rather than on the writer's idiosyncrasy: this encourages us to include the poem's meaning to those who read it in our canon of significance. We should be much less ready than is our habit with later books to read as if the author has put himself into our hands as a being of uniquely interesting struggles and idiosyncrasies, or as if we were committing ourselves into his hands.

Nevertheless, Chaucer's ironies often seem like playing with the reader in a way that the reader has come to expect from Chaucer, and his disciple Thomas Hoccleve diverts us by recounting his own nervous breakdown: so neither of these ways of reading may be excluded. But 'ways of reading' is also often a misleading phrase, if we think of reading by the eye rather than listening. Medieval literature was certainly more oral than our own, and differences in the importance of physical sound, of tempo and of attention, make this a distinction almost as great as that between two art forms – say, books and paintings. It may not always matter. In the case of song, some lyrics, and those among the greatest, seem to carry their own music with them over and above the ordinary music of words – 'I sing of a maiden' itself, or Dunbar's hymn of the nativity of Christ,

> Sing, hevin imperial, most of hicht,
> Regions of air mak armony . . .[21]

Nor do we know how often poet and composer were the same person, nor by any means certainly what proportion of lyrics were set to music. Yet where we have the music, the rather flat and home-spun melancholy of lyrics like some of Wyatt's or the fifteenth-century 'Now wolde I fain som merthes make'[22] will start out of two dimensions into the depth, the light and shade appropriate to the 'courtly makers' their authors were later called. And inconsiderable verses – 'Rutterkin is come to town' and 'Go, hert, hurt with adversite' –[23] become, in the former instance, a remarkable comic miming of drunkenness, in the latter the heart of something ravishing.

As for story, we scarcely know how to assess the differences, adults have so lost the habit of listening at length. But (as will appear in later chapters) our period was one of sharply increasing literacy. Some literature, notably ballads, was surely meant primarily to be listened to and gained some of its effect from this; it was after our period that Sidney found his 'heart moved more than with a trumpet' when he 'heard the old song of Percy and Douglas'.[24] Some of the greatest poems of our period, such as *Troilus and Criseyde* or *Gawain and the Green Knight*, show signs of having been written for both kinds of audience, combining the powerful ever-moving narrative needed by listeners with minute local effects that suggest a reader pausing to think or turning pages back to compare an earlier passage. But as the classic novel addresses itself to its 'Reader!' sometimes explicitly and sometimes to important aesthetic effect, so *Gawain* is addressed to those who will *listen* awhile, and *Troilus* to the lovers in the same place as the narrator, of whom not three have behaved the same way in love. A famous frontispiece to a copy of *Troilus* made not long after Chaucer's death illustrates just the audience he evokes – a poet reading to a gaily dressed court. Once, however, in *Troilus* he does address his 'redere';[25] and since this manuscript was designed to be lavishly illustrated, as the manuscript of *Gawain* actually is, both are evidently meant at least partly for private perusal, and the evidence to the contrary need not be taken literally.

Private perusal need not imply abandonment of an oral feeling for literature. One of the humorous idiosyncrasies in himself that Chaucer diverts us with is that he reads 'also domb as any stoon'.[26] Is that only opposed to conversation, or does it suggest that silent reading, reading in the head (which children still learn as an added accomplishment to simple reading), was still unusual – that we are still not far from 'that almost unimaginable period' when even reading alone was reading aloud, in which C. S. Lewis thinks Augustine lived, 'so relentlessly objective that in it even "reading" (in our sense) did not yet exist'?[27]

But perhaps these differences – about how public literature may be, how much like talk and song – are less important than the other differences about use that we touched on in connection with 'I sing of a maiden': the differences between reading to be instructed, reading with various degrees of detachment and commitment, reading aesthetically to enjoy form in all its variety, reading empathetically for enjoyment or understanding of character and emotion, and reading existentially, involved in a net of religious and ethical judgement and demand. Some of these differences involve difficulties about actual belief. One medieval book, *The Cloud of Unknowing*, explicitly challenges you not to read it unless you already intend to follow its teaching: its uncompromisingness in this is bound up with its tremendous impact, both empathetic and aesthetic. This is equally, though implicitly, true of much medieval lyric and drama. How far can I read such books if I do not share all their authors' beliefs? Can one, while standing outside a culture, understand its depth and complexity? Is poetry divorced from belief? A person so committed to cultural relativism that the beliefs of different cultures are equally valuable to him surely loses the very thrust of belief that makes most poems what they are.

Such a poem as 'I sing of a maiden', in addition to making its reader understand an unfamiliar symbol like the word 'lady', can also present before him (as if real) symbols in which he may have little lively, or no belief – such as the Incarnation, Annunciation and virgin birth. 'That suspension of disbelief for the moment which constitutes the poetic faith'[28] makes a bridge for us. But it is always mixed with real belief; and the proportion of one to the other varies from age to age and from individual to individual. When we read that in 1940 people in precisely the *Gawain* poet's district 'still believed' that ' "a man on an 'oss without a yed on, an awful gory sight" ' rode on the hill of Morridge,[29] does our degree of belief in that prepare us for the Green Knight's riding headless out of Arthur's court, in the same way as the kind of belief of the poem's first audience prepared them? Part of the answer is that the great poem does not need that preparation: it enforces the suspension of disbelief so that we understand and believe in the Green Knight as we never could in the man at Morridge.

But can the poem do all the work?

One wonders, too, considering the beliefs of other cultures – perhaps one should be considering one's own – how much 'poetic faith' entered into their real belief. When Sir John Mandeville told his audience about the marvels and monsters of Asia – when the Bestiary told them that the pelican feeds her young with her blood as Christ feeds us – what proportion of their response was belief and what suspension of disbelief? Such explicit answers as one can find suggest that there was even a third element in their belief, a suspension of disbelief not because of the aesthetic power of a story but because of its moral weight. Caxton, for example, having raised the problem of the historicity of King Arthur, concludes 'And for to pass the time this book shall be pleasant to read in, but for to give faith and believe that all is true that is contained herein, ye be at your liberty.' Then he appeals to a quotation from St Paul's Epistle to the Romans much used by medieval literary theorists, namely:

> But all is written for our doctrine, and for to beware that we
> fall not to vice ne sin, but to exercise and follow virtue, by
> which we may come and attain to good fame and renommé

in this life, and after this short and transitory life to come
unto everlasting bliss in heaven; the which He grant us that
reigneth in heaven, the blessed Trinity. Amen.[30]

The implication of such passages is that Caxton and many of his
contemporaries were so much aware of the transcendent world that
they were willing to accept, as possible history and certain symbol,
points where it conspicuously shows through the fabric of this world
– in stories, for example, of notable vice or saintly virtue: they cared
relatively little for a story's harmony or discrepancy with fact and
history. They valued, as they said, the *kernel* more than the *shell*,
the *grain* more than the *chaff*.

The convention, then, seems to be of easy half-belief in story, and
of real belief in the inner meaning of story, as a revelation not of the
personal world of its author but of the transcendent world. But there
are always writers for whom convention exists to be played with. No
one has ever surpassed some of the medieval writers, and above all
Chaucer, in the delicate irony with which they pick up and drop
these and other conventions and attitudes.

Artists and craftsmen

If we turn from the relation of reader and writer to notions of the
writer in himself, we find them somewhat ambiguous. Poetry and
music, in contrast with the other and socially inferior arts, possess a
body of theoretical literature that made both of them proper
(though lowly) subjects of study at universities, and possible
occupations for men of high birth. The social status of poetry is
exceedingly variable. Kings like James I of Scotland might write or
be supposed to have written poetry, and professional poets might be
praised in poetry during their lifetime by dukes, as the Duke of
Suffolk appears to have praised Lydgate:

> For thy coming is such and eke thy grace
> After Chaucer to occupy his place.[31]

These are poets of the courtly tradition. Among the poets of the
more provincial alliterative tradition, the author of *Winner and
Waster* says that lords used to love to hear original poets but prefer
minstrels now (1352),[32] implying perhaps a traditional place in the
household going back to that of the Anglo-Saxon bard. Langland,

on the other hand, places himself distinctly lower when he says of the angel who announced the birth of Christ, 'To pastors and to poets appered that angel'.[33] We are apt to read that with a romantic exaltation of shepherds and poets alike. But the line makes no sense unless poets are fairly lowly people, like shepherds.

Poetry, then, may be a highly regarded craft, practised by men of any station. But it is still a craft, not the inspiration or overflow of a special kind of man in the classical or the romantic way. Chaucer knew of the semi-divine status of the poet from classical models, and Eustache Deschamps praised him on such models during his life-time, Hoccleve after his death. But the nearest he comes to the idea himself is as a joke, when he wonders whether the Eagle in the *House of Fame* may not have come to 'stellify' him.[34] Humility was a great virtue to Chaucer as to many of his contemporaries: it was less natural for them than for many of the moderns to cultivate the ego, to think in terms of self-expression, to be interested in the artist as Artist. If, as is common enough, a poem has the form of a vision or a dream, it comes to the great fourteenth-century poets (or so they say) – to Chaucer, Gower, Langland or the *Pearl* poet because they are unusually weak, ignorant or delinquent. The words 'imagina-tion' and its synonym 'fantasy' are purely neutral terms for the capacity for creating mental images. It is only at the end of our period that Chaucer is praised by Stephen Hawes for his 'imagina-tion',[35] a word only then first used in its laudatory sense of the poet's power of creation; and it is in the same generation that Skelton boasts in the new Renaissance fashion of his own importance as a poet. It is much more characteristic of Chaucer's time that the classical tag *Ars longa, vita brevis est* – easily read by us in accord-ance with the exalted notion that art outlasts life – is correctly translated by him as 'The lyf so short, the craft so long to lerne'[36] – a workman's reflection on any job with its own rules.

To a large extent, though not wholly, poetry fits with the general situation of the arts. Painting or sculpture or building, in all or nearly all our period, were merely craft skills, and therefore the province of inferior social groups. Their affinities lay not with the ruling class of landed gentry or with the learned clerks but with the urban artisans. Among the livery companies of London, painter-stainers, goldsmiths and embroiderers rubbed shoulders with grocers, mercers and barber-surgeons.

In other words, the aspect of art that may seem least important to us now – the technical: the hammer, the chisel and the workshop – was then the most important. The history of medieval art is not a history of abstracts – of self-consciousness, imagination, self-expression – but is a history of concretes: of developing technical skills, of changing fashions, of shifting patterns of wealth. The craftsman normally worked to the wishes of a patron, and therefore definite limitations were laid on free inspiration. It may be partly for this reason that the history of the subject matter of medieval art tends to be the record of an established iconography of scenes, whether sacred, as from the Bible or from the great mass of legendary and historical matter assembled in apocryphal biblical literature and in saints' lives, or secular, as especially in the scenes of the activities of the months, arranged in a way traditional over several centuries.

This picture does not, of course, imply that the craftsman found no delight or meaning in the forms, matter and technique of his craft. On the contrary, the late medieval world was one not only of established iconography but of an expectation that what one sees and handles will have its own meaning in God's purposes; and in this world an expression of delight and felt significance might have the support of being thought to be much more than personal and subjective. And if an architect, for example, is commonly referred to in some such phrase as *builder*, *mason* or *constructor*, this need not mean an absence of the delight and creativity we think of as 'art'; rather, it implies an absence of distinction between that and the delights of 'craftmanship'. Nicolaus Pevsner, for example, observes of the work done at Lincoln Cathedral around 1200 under St Hugh that 'The passion for Purbeck shafting and for detached shafts [the architect Geoffrey de Noiers] had caught at Canterbury'.[37] Some twenty or so years later the writer of a Latin verse biography of St Hugh displayed a craftsman's delight, whether or not he was himself experienced in building, in these shafts and their Purbeck marble,

> . . . not content with a single colour; instead of having a rough grain, these shine with a high polish, strongly built in stiff positions, by no means deigning to be tamed by iron [tools], were it not softened by special skill: when the surface is ground down by the manifold rubbing of sand, and the solid marble permeated with strong vinegar. On

examining the stone, the mind might doubt whether it were of jade or marble; if of jade, then a dull jade; but if marble, one exceptionally fine. As for the slender shafts themselves, which thus surround the columns, they look like [maidens] in a round dance. Their outer surface, more polished than the growing fingernail, reflects a sparkling brilliance to the view: for nature has there painted so many different forms that, if art by long persistence laboured to get the likeness exact, it could hardly equal the reality.

Later he observes that the three qualities of this stone, 'smooth, shining, dark', express three qualities of the Bride of Christ, the church, 'frank, virtuous, afflicted': 'Thus the insentient stones conceal the mysteries of stones that live.'[38] One could hardly conceive a more inclusive delight – sensuous, technical, allegorizing, traditional in its significations, but personal. And an examination of Lincoln or any other complex medieval work of art surely suggests that patron, architect-craftsman and critic shared just such an inclusive delight.

This picture of crafts, including poetry – performed (1) on preconceived patterns, (2) which are often, though not necessarily, traditional, (3) to ends outside the crafts themselves, economic, religious and moral, (4) delighted in, in a way appropriate to these characteristics, (5) by men of not very high status, (6) valued not for their own inspired characters' sake but for their skills – might be made clearer by comparison with the romantic view of the artist. This is crystallized by Collingwood in his *Principles of Art*: the pure artist, he maintains, does not know when he begins his work what he is composing, not even its genre, much less its substance, because the work of art is his self-expression, and he cannot express his self-discovery better than in the growth of the work itself. It is tempting to find in medieval works of art the diametric opposite of this view, and to say that in this subjective aspect there were no artists in the fourteenth century, only craftsmen – even among poets.

In a standard handbook of that very body of theoretic literature we have referred to as distinguishing poetry from other crafts, Geoffrey de Vinsauf's *Poetria Nova*, we find the analogy between the poet's composing his book and the architect's planning his building, drawn to show that the poet should plan his work before he begins:

If a man has to lay the foundations of a house, he does not set rash hand to the work; the inward line of the heart measures forth the work in advance and the inner man prescribes a definite order of action; the hand of the heart designs the whole before that of the body does so: its state of being is first the prototype, then sensible. . . . The inner compasses of the mind must encircle the whole quantity of material beforehand.[39]

It is possible to make this the beginning of a general Gothic aesthetics, of what has been called 'inorganic form': not of course to describe what every craftsman had in mind, but to give a rationale of what every craftsman did and some had in mind. The analogy between such a work as the *Canterbury Tales* and a great church is particularly suggestive here, planned out beforehand but conceived and executed in bays, so that the building will still stand even if work has to be brought to a halt before formal completion. The detail of the *Tales*, too, is easily read as being like the illuminations of such manuscripts as the St Omer Psalter, with their 'mixture of seriousness and anecdote, artificial pattern and attention to details of life'.[40] What we shall say of mid-fourteenth-century decorative arts in general, that 'a world in miniature envelops the spectator and shuts him away from the world outside',[41] fits one's first impressions of medieval romances, or of *Pearl*. What we have already said of the persistence of a traditional iconography in painting and sculpture has its reflection in medieval poems, thought of not as self-expression nor as creation, but as old 'matter' handled with a novel 'sense' – what Malory did with the Arthurian stories, or what Chaucer did with delle Colonne's description of spring or on a larger scale with Boccaccio's *Il Filostrato* in *Troilus and Criseyde*. Quite frequently the connection goes beyond analogy in that poets may actually follow traditional iconography in their stories or in pieces of word-painting. Chaucer's description of January in the *Franklin's Tale* suggests exactly the pictures that decorate calendars in books of hours. Again, there is a moral fable of a woman who neglected feeding the poor for her dogs and was eaten to death by a dog-faced demon, which appears in wall paintings (e.g. probably at Chaldon in Surrey) and may give a grim overtone to Chaucer's description of the Prioress and her little hounds.

In such a context, when all the arts are complementary and

interdependent, it may be useful to attend to categories that obviously relate to technique but cross the borders of the crafts – even to analogies that might appear frivolous in modern times. Thus one might apply to modern taste in poetry Hugh Johnson's observation of the early nineteenth-century practice of adding other wines, or brandy, to claret: 'Today's preoccupation with authenticity even at the expense of quality makes these practices seem abusive'.[42] We tend to look for authenticity in word, rhythm and emotion. The exact converse, very much in conformity with the general picture we have been developing, is suggested by the cookery book compiled for Richard II, 'best and royallest viander of all Christian kings'.[43] Its recipes are at a far remove from authenticity: the native flavour of food is not to be retained, but overlaid, mixed and decorated with spices, herbs and poignant sauces, with probably a usual effect of sweet-and-sour. Colour, shape and symbolism, however, are admired as much as flavour (as when, to take an extreme example, by sewing half-capons and half-pigs together, stuffing as for pork, roasting and gilding with egg yolks, ginger, saffron and parsley juice, the cooks served up cockatrices). And a feature of the table would be 'sotelties', edible set-pieces on chivalric and religious subjects, for which a poet like Lydgate might write accompanying poems. Thus the whole table would provide not merely an analogy but an example of the abundance of symbolism, gorgeousness, decorated surface and deliberately artificial art common in the fifteenth century.

Of course, this is not the whole story: this gorgeousness and display are represented by the high style adorned with 'colours of rhetoric', 'as when that men to kinges write',[44] which Chaucer's Franklin and Host both contrast with the 'plain' style. Medieval art of any kind – perhaps all art – is certainly at its finest when gorgeousness and authenticity interplay. And in medieval culture the two corresponding ethical values, magnanimity with its corollary magnificence, and humility with its corollary simplicity, are both recognized. One can see both poles architecturally expressed by standing in King's College Chapel at Cambridge and looking east at Henry VI's simplicity and west at the Tudor magnificence; and at the beginning of our period they are partly represented by the two styles, the richness and bulk of Decorated, the more austere and insubstantial early Perpendicular. Both are consistent with the dominance of craft rather than art and of inorganic rather than expressive form.

Chaucer states three medieval commonplaces that seem to support this total picture. At the end of Book 1 of *Troilus and Criseyde* he quotes Geoffrey de Vinsauf's analogy of the architect:

> For every wight that hath an hous to founde
> Ne runneth nought the werk for to biginne
> With rakel hand, but he wol bide a stounde,
> And sende his hertes line out fro withinne,
> Alderfirst his purpos for to winne.[45]

> *rakel*] hasty   *stounde*] time   *Alderfirst*] First of all

In the Prologue to the *Legend of Good Women* he tells us to look to the authority of books for the doctrines and stories that we should believe, for

> . . . if that olde bookes were awaye
> Yloren were of remembrance the keye.[46]

> *Yloren*] Lost

And the Nun's Priest tells us (for a comic equivalent of Caxton's Preface to Malory) to look for the morality of a story:

> But ye that holden this tale a folye
> As of a fox, or of a cok and hen,
> Taketh the moralite, goode men.
> For Saint Paul saith that al that writen is
> To oure doctrine it is ywrit, ywis:
> Taketh the fruit, and lat the chaf be stille.[47]

> *ywis*] indeed

There is little doubt that these are commonplaces which Chaucer can assume are generally accepted. But Chaucer is not to be easily pinned down. And, in fact, he quotes Geoffrey de Vinsauf's dictum, not with regard to poetry, nor with entire approval: he applies it to the plans of Pandarus to gain Criseyde for Troilus – to plots, that is, whose very success lays the foundations for ultimate ruin. As for the praise of books as authorities, we do not have to look further than the *House of Fame* to find Chaucer – after his fears that may be made a star have been laid to rest – making further mock of himself for trusting to the authority of books for his knowledge of stars, rather than accepting the Eagle's offer to show them to him close at hand. And in *Troilus and Criseyde* he burlesques the whole notion of authority by ignoring his real debt to Boccaccio's *Il Filostrato* in order to lament his need to keep close to his authority Lollius, a writer whom he never read, for he never existed.

At the end of his writing, furthermore, when Chaucer retracted his 'worldly vanities' including *Troilus and Criseyde* and most of the *Canterbury Tales* that make for sin, he used St Paul's text with uncharacteristic absence of ambiguity with the implication that it fits only his devout and virtuous books. In the *Nun's Priest's Tale*, by contrast, he leaves it open to us to interpret: 'if you're the sort of person who cannot enjoy a good story, then content yourself with the moral'. And the natural meaning of his moral statements is not usually dogmatic. We can, as we did earlier, suggest that he draws on traditional iconography, with its strait system of ethics, to provide an overtone for the Prioress's care for her dogs; but we must in honesty note too that it is with a gentle irony that he describes her foible, concluding, 'And al was conscience and tender herte.'[48] There is no ground for assuming that the irony that plays off stern moral judgement against indulgent praise supports either tone at the expense of the other. Both in overt references to authority and in his natural style, irony is the means by which Chaucer liberates himself from the authority he exploits and the tradition he follows.

Most significant, perhaps, is the attitude to craft and technique which he shows in the continuation of

> The lyf so short, the craft so long to lerne,
> Th'assay so hard, so sharp the conquerynge,
> The dredful joye, alwey that slit so yerne:
> Al this mene I by Love, that my felynge
> Astonyeth with his wonderful werkynge
> So sore, i wis, that whan I on hym thynke
> Nat wot I wel wher that I flete or synke.[49]

slit so yerne] slides away so quickly

The craft he means is the craft of passionate love: he has no sense of any antithesis between technique and passion. Probably, too, both he and Geoffrey de Vinsauf would be happy to stress the emotion associated with 'heart' when they speak of sending out the heart's line.

To sum up, then, because a man is not wholly free in his inspiration, it does not follow that he has no inspiration, and an artist can put his heart into a commissioned work, whether made in glass, stone or words. A deliberate regard for authority, tradition, craft and ends for art outside art may as in 'I sing of a maiden' provide the matter, the tree on which the maker works. A preconceived plan, moreover, may be modified in obedience to the demands of material and circumstance; the wisdom derived from authority be modified by experience; the story be told for the story's sake; and the morality be modified by compassionate understanding. In all these ways, the work of art will turn out different in the execution from the conception, and an element of the Collingwoodian picture of the artist must enter in.

This would not be worth saying, but that modern feeling is apt, where it finds conformity to tradition, to regard it as a proof of absence of inspiration and, where it finds inspiration, to look for evidence of alienation. This is particularly tempting when as with Langland and Chaucer at the beginning of our period or Wyatt at the end the great artist is among other things a great satirist. But a great satirist is not necessarily fundamentally at issue with his culture, particularly if that culture embodies, as the medieval did, in its religion a tradition of radical moral criticism, and in its morality an emphasis on contrition. In our period, the most obvious way to construct a sense of the self was by open or secret confession; and this, as we shall see, has left a pervasive mark on literature. It is not surprising, therefore, if, not only in Chaucer's case but in that of Langland, the *Gawain* poet and others, a kind of freeing play of self-awareness is the principal means of bringing life to traditional motifs and structures which their authors continue to enjoy. It is as a result of moral criticism and contrition that these poets perform the function that Collingwood attributes to the expressive artist: to purge the corrupt consciousness of their society. But it is when contrition itself becomes a formula, and the authenticity that is on the whole associated with it becomes (as in Lydgate) overweighted by magnificence, that medieval art goes wrong. To these points we shall return.

Underlying these questions about the artist is the general one we began with. What is it to be a person? Is a person valuable or interesting in virtue of the essential singularity of his being? Or in virtue of what is universalizable in him, of his relation to a general

type or to the categories of a code of ethics? Or in virtue of his
relation to other people, or to one other person, or to God? As with
the idea of an artist, so with that of a person, one hypothesis would
define the medieval view as the exact opposite of the romantic
view. Kierkegaard in the nineteenth century maintained that a
man's essential singularity and his relation to God are the same,
essentially private thing: the hypothesis I refer to would say that the
medievals identified the point of a person's being with his place in
a public ethical scheme or social hierarchy. Similar is the theory
epigrammatized by Henry Adams in the titles of his two books
Mont-St Michel and Chartres: A Study in Thirteenth Century Unity
and *The Education of Henry Adams: A Study in Twentieth
Century Diversity*. Evidence may be found in both literature and
art to support such theories, and they are powerfully advocated in
D. W. Robertson's *A Preface to Chaucer*. They are undoubtedly
useful in formulating general cultural differences, and help one to
notice, to ask the questions that lead to understanding in reading
particular books. But the exactness of the contrast with modern
instincts suggests that the theories have a mythical element,
generated by modern psychological needs. And they cannot be
reconciled with the ironies of Chaucer or with the subtleties of
Gawain's temptations in *Gawain and the Green Knight*. The hero
who represents the uniqueness of human personalities can be seen
in Gawain and other figures; and the author of the *Cloud of Unknowing* recalls even Kierkegaard when in his *Epistle of Discretion
of Stirrings* he guards against thinking that any 'man knoweth
which ben the privy dispositions of man but the spirit of the same
man which is in himself'.[50] Nor is it surprising that he should recall
Kierkegaard; for he is quoting the First Epistle to the Corinthians of
St Paul, the father in all ages of people sensitively or painfully
aware of their irreducible individuality. What is surprising to
modern feeling is that someone may have as sensitive an awareness
and convey as strong an impression of his individuality as does the
author of the *Cloud*, while in no way insisting on his own
idiosyncrasy, and remaining anonymous in much more than the
simple sense of being unnamed. Since in this he is only the most
conspicuous case of a quality almost universal among medieval
writers in one way or another – but for a very few exceptions
like Margery Kempe – this is a point to which we shall return
frequently.

History, personality, literature

In many ways, reading a medieval book cannot be entirely distinguished from understanding medieval people. The reader's and the historian's interests begin to merge. This is to their mutual advantage. G. K. Chesterton well observes that while we neglect 'the inside of history' – that is, 'the consideration of what things meant in the mind of a man, especially an ordinary man, as distinct from what is defined or deduced merely from official forms or political pronouncements'[51] – there is a limitation on history that can be better transcended by art. But if the historian gains from literature its special authority about what experience meant, the reader can take advantage of the guides and checks of fact. The illumination that either gains is reactive. History illumined by literature illumines history and literature alike, as does literature illumined by history: 'ogni parte ad ogni parte splende'.[52]

But when we are looking not only to history to provide context and elucidation for reading literature, but conversely to literature to provide 'innerness' and evidence for constructing history, further questions ensue, questions about relating books to the general run of events in their time. What causes affect the degree of truth or distortion of truth with which writers describe their age? The answers still to some extent have to do with the way in which we regard personality.

We tend to assume both a great individuality and a great typicality about the characters of fiction and their environment, unless clear signs say 'This is fantasy'. Often enough this is just: one of the attributes of great writers is an eye for reality, though the reality on which their eye is directed may not be very much like the sociologist's statistical verity. The author may be aiming at actuality, with varying stress on the individual and the general, or he may be aiming at persuasion, at moral truth, or at fantasy.

One indication of the kind of reality the authors of an age have in mind is the favourite forms of literature of their age – epic, novel, tragedy and comedy, etc. – and particularly forms that are not only favourite but more or less peculiar to the age. An author may not use those forms, but their ghosts may haunt his work: he may share their spirit. Two medieval forms are suggestive in this way: allegory of the life of man (whether of love, like the *Romance of the Rose*, or of death, like *Everyman*, or of the moral life of choices and salvation, like *The Castle of Perseverance*) and the debate, such as one of the first notable poems of our period, *Winner and Waster*, in which two principles (neither of them normally wholly right nor wholly wrong, though one perhaps apparently the better) argue the case between them with as much art and elegance as the author can command (and normally in the end are not so much judged as transcended). These two forms represent a pervasive tendency in the Middle Ages to be interested in characters that embody whole classes of people, aspects of a man, or principles. It is not only an English but a European tendency, dating back long before our period: the two forms, allegory and debate, come into English from French and Latin. Why it should exist is a subject to which we shall return. Here we have only to say that it existed and was continually modified by intention to portray concrete particular individuals. The results are complex – when humour and irony come in, as with Chaucer, almost unassessably complex. Blake said of the Canterbury Pilgrims: 'As Newton numbered the stars, and as Linnaeus numbered the plants, so Chaucer numbered the classes of men . . . nor can a child be born who is not one of these characters of Chaucer.'[53]

Blake may have hit on a truth here: the *Canterbury Tales* does have moral, social and psychological typicality. But the kind of typicality varies. The poor Parson is probably an ideal of good living, the Wife of Bath, whatever she is, probably not that. What Chaucer intended by Criseyde and Troilus, or Malory by Guinevere and Lancelot, is much more complex. We do not even know, can scarcely know by internal evidence, how far the courtly love which binds these couples was matter of life, story or moral object-lesson. The overtones of the word 'lady' as we have sketched them are probably more reliable in understanding courtly love than is any single story.

Explicitly moral, legal and political statements and stories are dangerous in this regard. We easily suppose that, because some person or culture is firmly persuaded that a thing is or ought to be so, therefore it was so. Yet an ideal is often asserted with particular vehemence just because it is not much fulfilled: that is, it is asserted in a compensatory spirit.

Fortunately we have for medieval England Chaucer, who seems to be aware of this as of other complexities. Thus, for example, the *Clerk's Tale* and the *Man of Law's Tale* and Chaucer's own *Tale of Melibee* suggest that there was a frequently asserted ideal of womanly submissiveness. But it does not at all follow that women were often or usually submissive, or that people generally expected or wanted them to be; for Chaucer hints that the ideal is only a fancy appropriate to scholars, lawyers and, perhaps, himself. He makes his Parson attempt to uphold the ideal by observing rather hopelessly, 'thereas the woman hath the mastery, she maketh too much disarray: there needen none ensamples of this. The experience of day by day ought suffice.'[54] He creates a complex balance in the whole number of stories that have to do with relations between the sexes, including haughty wives and lecherous girls among his characters. Above all he creates something of the density of individuality and reality in the Wife of Bath, attractive and seven times married, who triumphantly quarrels over wifely submissiveness with her last husband, significantly a clerk. We shall see how close she comes to nature when we look at Margery Kempe in Chapter 3. Of course, the ideal of submissiveness affected both the Wife's character and Margery Kempe's; but in no simple way. The limitations that even Chaucer has are significant – he has not, as Shakespeare has, any heroines who are both virtuous and actively adventurous, more at any rate than the Man of Law's Constance or the Franklin's Dorigen. It would probably be fair to infer that he found no occasion to suppose they existed. But once again the overtones of the word 'lady' may be most helpful here, if we may learn to use it properly, to respond to its curious blend of rule and submissiveness. And if the historian can advise on the likelihoods of life, and therefore on the degree of convention in portrayal, and on the relation of ideals to what have been called 'real ideals', ideals worked out in everyday custom and practice, he can help us to read. Conversely the reader can show the historian what social forms meant – what, for example, love may have felt like, or marriage – through the stories of Chaucer or the fulminations of Langland.

To map out the context of 'I sing of a maiden', of the *Canterbury Tales* or of other great literature may only be to take conscious possession of an inwardness the poem has already offered us. But this identity of particular intuitions with admission to the total structure is perhaps characteristic only of poetry at its heights. In lower ranges of poetry one has to place oneself more deliberately. John Lydgate provides examples of both processes. If one takes him at his heights, the lines that appeal as much to modern as to medieval taste, he is great when he deals with mutability –

> Fresshnesse of floures, of braunchis the beaute
> Have ay on chaung a tremblyng attendaunce[55]

– displays marvellous auditory imagination in the rhythms when his musician is drawn into the Dance of Death –

> This newe daunce is to me so straunge –
> Wondir diverse and passingly contrarye –
> The dredful fotyng doth so ofte chaunge . . .[56]

– is moving when he renders Christ's call to leave both mutability and death –

> Thy place is bygged above the sterres clere,
> Noon erthly palys wrought in so statly wyse,
> Come on my frend, my brother most entere –
> For the I offered my blood in sacryfice[57]

bygged] built

– and beyond criticism when he combines all three of these themes in *Midsummer Rose* as Christ, sharing in mutability by his Passion, makes mortality put on immortality. The evidence of art and other literature shows that those are the deepest concerns of his time, of the period that Huizinga called the 'Waning of the Middle Ages'; so that one has been admitted to the heart of an age almost without noticing it.

But this is to be admitted to only a part of Lydgate. If one wants to go on to read him in bulk, one must acquire medieval reading habits, recognize how well he was thought of for his long poems in his own century, learn to love diffuseness and appreciate generality, and take a certain dullness for granted if it serves didactic moralism and rhetorical magnificence. In this way, too, one will learn much about medieval values – in particular, as we shall see in Chapter 5, about the way in which magnificence is built into social life among the 'real ideals'.

The whole age

The common quest of reader and historian has many byproducts in the way of theory and general understanding. The civilization, the literature and the people one studies become on the one hand more familiarly human and, on the other, founded on more radically other presuppositions than one had ever dreamed. Auden called this conversation 'breaking bread with the dead'. But the end to which it is directed is too elusive, too perennially qualified, too often living only in particular understandings to be easily named. Would the right word be poise? Poise, as in the successive discussions of this book, within the late medieval world of ideas, between the medieval senses of inner and outer, among medieval aesthetic expectations, within the household, in the whole age. The most obvious example is poise in space and time. One should move with Pandarus through the geography of a fourteenth-century house, and know into how much and how novel a privacy this takes us, when reading how, having asked of her folk where Criseyde is,

> . . . he forth in gan pace
> And fond two othere ladys sete, and she,
> Withinne a paved parlour . . .[58]

One should be aware that, for poorer people than Criseyde, bed-rooms 'were the only places where one could get any privacy; Chaucer's Clerk of Oxford seems to have read in bed, and that, no doubt, is the reason why'.[59]

And one should certainly be able to move at ease through the medieval year to read almost any fourteenth-century poet. Their April we have already touched on, but it should take its place in the sequence that includes the ringing of the bells on Easter Day in *Piers Plowman* and the faery associations of the May morning on which Langland looked into the waters of the burn on Malvern Hills and fell into his dream; the long June day on which the Corpus Christi plays were held; and the high season in August, probably Lammas when the first loaf made from the new-cut corn is baked, that sets the scene for the meditation in the garden at the beginning of *Pearl* on the death and rising again of the grain, and probably contributes to the closing scene of the poem when the priest shows us Christ 'in the forme of bred and wyne'.[60] Two verses at the beginning of the second part of *Gawain and the Green Knight* carry us through the year from the festivities of New Year by a union of agricultural, folklore and Christian cycles: Lent tests people with fasting, the trees put on green leaves, and

> Wrothe wynde of the welkyn wrasteles with the sunne,
> The leves lancen fro the lynde and lyghten on the
>   grounde,

And al grayes the gres that grene watz ere;
Then al rypes and rotes that ros upon fyrst[61]

– with overtones of mythic combat of the seasons and of the inter-
change of life and death as Gawain anxiously waits until he must
leave Arthur's court to seek out his combat with the Green Knight
– on All Hallows' Day, the beginning of the bad part of the year
and, perhaps in consequence (as we shall see), of the court's festive
season.

These examples are late fourteenth-century. But they remain
fairly constant until the close of our period. The years 1330–1550 do
form a recognizably unitary climate of culture. There are even two
literary forms, over and above the more universally medieval
allegory and debate, which are virtually peculiar to them. These are
the religious carol and the cycle of mystery plays, which have as their
background a constellation of religious habits that do not otherwise
occur together in England: public pageantry, personal devotion, the
confessional.

The mystery plays have their root and archetype in Christ's
command to 'do this . . . in remembrance of me' at the Last
Supper. The idea of remembrance haunts Christianity with something more than the English word 'remembrance' connotes:
anamnesis, the acting out of Christ's breaking bread and blessing
wine, with a sense, such as Langland powerfully conveys, that time is
rolled up and that we stand in the presence of Christ himself at the
Last Supper and on the cross, no longer only in time but with a
symbol of eternity before us. An attempt to extend this sense was
made in the development of the commemoration of Christ's life in
the Christian year, though this was bound to be more a ritual
commemoration, less a mystical re-presentation, than the mass. In
the tenth century this took a dramatic form in a chant written for
Easter, a dialogue between the women who came to find Christ's
body and the angels at the tomb, beginning 'Whom do you seek in
the tomb, people of Christ?'[62]

Perhaps on the inspiration and model of this, liturgical plays
began to be written. It is not clear how those became the great cycles
of plays performed outside the church, nor why this should have
happened particularly in England in the late fourteenth century.
The most likely explanation is that the establishment in the
thirteenth century of the new Feast of the Body of Christ, Corpus

Christi, gave occasion for a procession in which the consecrated host, the body of Christ itself, was carried; and that, in turn, gave occasion for a pageant to describe the whole history of salvation, from Creation and Fall to Judgement, centring on the Passion. Certainly this kind of procession, with a wagon for each play stopping in succession at fixed points, as it made its way round a city like York or Coventry, was one mode of performance for the plays; but they were also performed in an open place with the audience surrounding them, giving precedent for the Elizabethan 'wooden O'. The latter kind of production must have offered, as it proceeded through a midsummer day from the creation of light at the dawn to the doom at sunset, a remarkable sense of the stage as world: the former must have curiously articulated and even hallowed men's sense of the streets of their town. Either way, each play was the responsibility of one of the trade guilds of the town and in this way also hallowed the whole community. As pageants and processions performed by the guilds and other lay or ecclesiastical organizations, the plays were far from unique: throughout the year, though predominantly in the half-year from Christmas to Corpus Christi when the Christian year is concentrated, public acts (both sacred and secular and normally both) filled the streets and towns with colour, pattern and significance. The whole age is one of what the Greeks called, from the same root as *drama*, the *dromenon*, the 'thing acted out', story, symbol, ritual, pageant and sacrament.

Personal piety, as well as these public acts, influenced the mystery plays. The mass had become more and more something done by the priests, acted out in their part of the church, beyond the great screens that were becoming prevalent, and in Latin, the language specially of the clergy. Someone, perhaps from among the friars whose preaching came to fill this gap, brought a share in the acting out of Christ's life to the laity in the plays, and the laity's own instinct for this *anamnesis* was embodied in them. In this the mysteries take their part with the proliferation of handbooks for meditation and books of devotion for the laity at this time – books of hours for private prayer through the day, and manuals like the *Layfolk's Massbook* to be used during mass.

The plays also presented a challenge and a demand, like the sermon. The rolling up of time that occurred in them so that the audience might feel themselves present at Bethlehem and Calvary (to the degree that, when the plays had been going for a generation or two, the Wakefield Master can afford to make a joke of it, alternating his place references between Wakefield and Bethlehem in a deliberately dizzying manner) was not only for contemplation and worship and spiritual strengthening; it represented the dreadful doctrine of the time of salvation, the time that will soon be over, perhaps at death, perhaps sooner, when alone it is possible to take possession of the grace of God, to be moved to a new life by Christ's Passion. Bitter moral doctrine, therefore, and, as in the sermons, biting social satire were part of the plays.

The mysteries vanished during the sixteenth century. In London and the South-East they may simply have dropped out of favour. From the beginning they had been ill received by those who, like the Lollards, laid stress on authenticity and inwardness against ritual and church: the Reformation, in so far as it was the victory of those ideas, was likely to disfavour the plays. Cranmer's new Book of Common Prayer gave drama and lay participation a form more agreeable to the new age in its service of Holy Communion. In the Midlands and the North, attempts were made to adapt them to Protestant taste, but Queen Elizabeth's government thought them an occasion of strife between Papist and Protestant and actively discouraged them. All the same, they went on long enough to affect the Elizabethan stage – Shakespeare's quite frequent allusions to them suggest that he may have watched some – while in Cornwall and the North-West they were probably last played in James I's time.

The carol, a combination of dance, music and song performed by a group, has a parallel history. Although it existed earlier as a secular form – the round dance of which St Hugh's biographer was reminded by the shafts at Lincoln – it seems to have been turned to pious uses from about 1350. It was peculiarly appropriate to the communal festivities of the medieval year, and to the lay and ecclesiastic households that were the normal social units, filling the great halls, which were their gathering places, with formal movement. The dance was probably an integral part of the form at the beginning of our period, but we do not know how long this lasted. Gavin Douglas in Scotland in 1513 finds it natural to translate Virgil's 'circum . . . sacra canunt'[63] ('round about they sing holy things') as 'syngand karrellis and dansand in a ryng'.[64] The whole form went out of fashion probably during the sixteenth century from changes in musical and religious expression, along with other celebrations like the election of a boy bishop to rule religious households at some point during the Christmas festivities, which did not fit new senses of religious decorum, and new insistences on inwardness and solemnity. Yet, of course, the carol has its descendants in the songs we sing now only at Christmas.

In fact, one can best approach fourteenth- and fifteenth-century culture through hearing or singing a carol with its contemporary music (e.g. Audelay's 'What tidings bring you' in the *Oxford Book of Carols*[65]). One discovers thus a language that is not a distorted modern English but something with its own consistent organization and sound pattern, with a suggestion of the culture it expressed: broader and more open vowels and clearer and more guttural consonants, pronounced with mouths more open. At the beginning and richest part of our period there is a more liquid flow, caused partly by the frequent light 'e' at the close of words. Text and music suggest, though it can hardly be proved, a more staccato motion in speaking, a tune in ordinary conversation by which the voice lifts at the end of sentences rather than falling, as ours does – altogether in fact something that moves more like a modern Romance language than like modern English. The Burgundian poet Jean Regnier heard it as 'God and oul Lady helpemy'[66] in the 1420s. Even two or three generations after the loss of final 'e', this Romance tune is perhaps suggested by Andrea Trevisano of Venice in 1497: he says that English, 'although it is as well as the Flemish derived from the German, has lost its natural harshness, and is pleasing enough as they pronounce it'.[67] In the music itself, notes are sounded separately, without *legato*, and in the carols there is a time that suggests, as Eliot wrote, that

> . . . you can hear the music
> Of the weak pipe and the little drum . . .
> Earth feet, loam feet, lifted in country mirth.[68]

It is easy to feel that one is hearing something analogous to the way in which Chaucer handles a language until recently spoken mainly by artisans and 'uplandish men',[69] handles it with grace, irony and cosmopolitan sophistication: the echo of a culture in which a number of things abstracted from each other by us – movement, poetry, music, formal social pattern – exist undivided.

Eliot seems also to suggest, in the poem I have quoted, that this dance, music and song reflect something about the relation, at that period, of man, through ritual, sacrament and the rhythm of the seasons, to an ordered cosmos. Whether this is a full picture is perhaps the central question of this book.

The sketch of a history

It is hard not to beg this central question. One of the difficulties about dealing with a culture so distant is to know how much it changed within itself. The apparent differences from ourselves bulk so large that, as in the landscapes of another planet, the features of different times and places within the culture seem more uniform than they are. It is particularly difficult with the late Middle Ages because on the one hand a sense of eternity, stability and community does hang about its works, its sense of personality was different and in a way less marked than ours, its habits of art and thought were in some respects conservative; on the other, we lack information to a degree that promotes a quite spurious sense of anonymity and changelessness. So a picture true in itself is apt to be exaggerated, and the whole difficult question of individual, artist and society distorted. This is particularly important in setting literature in its context, above all of the arts. Analogies between literature and the arts are distorted if we do not distinguish between analogies that reveal general Gothic principles and analogies that reveal something of the cultural weather of the decade when a poem was written. In letters as in art and architecture one can recognize a medieval, a Gothic style, or more particularly a late Gothic style. But in art and architecture it is often possible to localize, as we shall see, the fashions of particular decades or less; and, hampered though we are by the paucity of what survives and by the difficulty of ascertaining exact dates, it is comparably possible with the fashions of literature. At times in the Middle Ages fashions changed slowly; in most of our period they changed rather fast, and one ought to be able to feel Malory and Chaucer as perhaps as different in the cultural atmosphere they presume as, say, Thomas Hardy and William Golding.

What follows is conditioned by this need to outline the transformation of the time. It is a tentative scaffold and a mnemonic. Its seven or eight periods are merely a sketch at something preferable to phrases like 'the fifteenth century'. Its chronology is not to be relied on in detail, and it is deliberately speculative. But it is (I think) indispensable to this book, particularly when we deal with the arts.

*   *   *

Before 1373   This is an experimental period, which, as it roughly coincides with the long reign of Edward III (1327–77), we could call Edwardian. About 1330 two collections suggest what English literature was then, a provincial offshoot of French: the Auchinleck manuscript in which are collected along with religious and didactic matter romances like the rich and marvellous *Sir Orfeo*, an English version of a French poem, telling the classical story of Orpheus and Eurydice; and MS Harley 2253, a varied collection of English verse with some Anglo-Norman and Latin material, probably from Herefordshire. This is just about at the end of the long winter of English after the Norman Conquest, and just as at the end of winter almost everything seems at its most dead, so English must have seemed nearest to becoming the language only of 'uplandish men',[70] who themselves would rather talk French, as Ralph Higden thought in 1327 when he wrote his chronicle *Polychronicon*: just when, if one only knew where to look, its spring flowers were appearing – kinds of literature independent of France, and new beginnings. Between 1333 and 1352, for example, Laurence Minot, probably from Yorkshire, wrote kinds of ballad in traditional alliterative forms, celebrating the early victories of the Hundred Years War. Also in Yorkshire and up till his death in 1349, Richard Rolle was writing English verse and prose, picking up a devotional style that went back to Anglo-Saxon literature, but turning it to his own intoxicating mystical emotions, which seem to have raised in many people the thirst for religious experience. In the new colleges at Oxford, and particularly at Merton College, there was the beginning, though only the beginning, of a scientific revolution, and much more than the beginning of philosophical and theological revolutions which, though expressed in the international language, Latin, were soon to get into English. Bradwardine's *De Causa Dei* in 1344 set off new thoughts on God's grace, free will and pre-destination. It is a time, too, of experiment in the arts, especially architecture, with the conflict of the styles called Decorated and Perpendicular. At the beginning of our period English architecture was immensely more sophisticated and influential than literature in

English: even the French accepted the influence of the Decorated style. By the end of the century literature had fully caught up in sophistication.

At the end of the century John Trevisa, revising Higden's *Polychronicon*, looked back to the years immediately following the Black Death of 1348–9 as the time when the whole linguistic situation changed. English spread suddenly as a literary language, and there seem to be a series of decisive new beginnings. In 1352 *Winner and Waster* turned the alliterative metre inherited from the Anglo-Saxons to brilliantly conceived social satire: it was perhaps the inspiration, ten years or so later, of a still greater poetic or rather prophetic social satire, Langland's first version of *Piers Plowman* (the A text). Quite suddenly, so far as we know, the alliterative metre took to itself such wonders as two poems on Alexander the Great, the less good recounting his meeting with the Brahmins in India, and the romance of William of Palerne who was carried off and aided by a werewolf. Drama apparently flowered – the earlier biblical mystery cycles probably go back to this time, and the earliest surviving morality play, *The Pride of Life*. At the end of the period Chaucer began his career, translating the *Roman de la Rose* and writing the *Book of the Duchess* in 1369 – still following the French tradition but decisively new in that a favourite court poet – and, as it proved, so great a one – chose to write in English. And in 1372 a Franciscan friar, Johan de Grimestone, compiled a handbook for preachers wonderfully adorned with fragments of verse; these were probably enough written by himself, but inspired by the piety, poignant, immediate and personal, and the turning of secular-love expressions to the love of Christ which the Franciscan order seem to have learnt from St Francis himself, and which gave the impulse to much medieval lyric and other art and writing:

> Lovely tear of lovely eye
> Why dostu me so wo?[71]

1373–1400   John Burrow has called the literature characteristic of the last years of Edward III and of the reign of Richard II (1377–99) Ricardian. One might date such a period from the second week of May 1373, in which Chaucer returned from a long diplomatic sojourn in Italy full of the writings of Boccaccio and Petrarch and of Dante's *Divine Comedy*, and Julian, an anchoress at Norwich, had revelations of divine love. In the following years Chaucer translated his favourite philosophical text, Boethius' *De Consolatione Philosophiae*, out of Latin into English, and under its influence and that of Boccaccio and Dante wrote such poems of love and fate as *The Parliament of Fowls* and above all *Troilus and Criseyde*. During the earlier part of the period a court circle seems to have formed round Chaucer, dedicated to English writing, as is evidenced by Sir John Clanvowe's *Book of Cupid* and *Two Ways* and Henry Scogan's *Moral Ballade*: it was possibly dispersed by the events leading up to the taking of control over both the country and the young King Richard by the lords appellant, and to the Merciless Parliament of 1388. In these events Chaucer's most ardent early disciple was executed, the city clerk Thomas Usk who gives in his *Confession* and *Testament of Love* access to the allegoric-symbolic habit of mind of an intelligent average man of the time. All this literature seems beautifully epitomized if we set Chaucer's exhortation to the audience of *Troilus and Criseyde*

. . . yonge fresshe folke, he or she
In whom that love upgroweth with your age

to

. . . thinketh all nis but a faire
This world, that passeth soon as floures faire[72]

alongside 'I sing of a maiden' (which, however, may belong to the early fifteenth century), and Julian of Norwich, who may have had in mind that verse from Wisdom comparing the world to a drop of dew, when she saw the whole universe little and perishable as a hazelnut that 'lasts and ever shall, for God loves it'.[73] Julian was one of several mystics who wrote about this time; these include a priest in the East Midlands who, apparently anxious to redirect the mystical enthusiasm of such people as the followers of Richard Rolle, wrote the *Cloud of Unknowing*, and Walter Hilton of Thurgarton in Nottinghamshire, who tried to hold a middle way between Rolle and the *Cloud* in his *Ladder of Perfection*.

The vision of the world as God's design from creation to doom was offered to all kinds and classes of men by the drafting of the York and Chester cycles of mystery plays, which probably continued in these years. And Langland's social and political prophecy intensified into the mystical when he rewrote *Piers Plowman* around 1377 (the B text). But in 1381 the leaders of the Peasants' Revolt seem to have found in his poem a store of inspiring doctrine and slogans, and thereafter it is likely that Langland intended to remove this revolutionary misconstruction by producing his final version, the C text, perhaps completed by 1388. Wyclif preached other revolutionary opinions, and under his influence the first Lollard English Bible was produced; his opinions were condemned in 1382.

Religious literature, drawing on the fertile variety of the Bible, comprehended surprising extremes, including (in one manuscript, the Vernon) the gaily told legend of *Susannah*, and meditative verse, in which the vision of God's design is altogether clouded by a sombre scepticism based on Ecclesiastes. There must have been a considerable reading market: notable translations besides biblical ones are made about this time – of Sir John Mandeville's *Travels*, previously existing in French and Latin, and in 1387 by John Trevisa of Higden's *Polychronicon*. Romances were now and later produced in great profusion, chivalrous like Thomas Chestre's *Sir Launfal* or simply adventurous like *Gamelyn*. And a considerable body of alliterative verse, splendid in diction, heroic, flamboyant or exotic in subject, loving such themes as the battles and adventures of Arthur and his knights (*Morte Arthure*, *The Awntyrs of Arthure*, *Golagros and Gawane*) and the *Destruction of Troy*; and the *Siege of Jerusalem* was composed now and into the fifteenth century, in England and in Scotland. Its crown came when somewhere near Staffordshire, somewhere about this time, the third great poet of the age (with Chaucer and Langland) brought a subtle, ironic and profound moral and religious sense to re-create old romance and the old alliterative metre, all the gallantry and beauty that he loved finding its consummation in contrition, in *Patience*, *Cleanness*, *Gawain and the Green Knight* and the Dantesque *Pearl*. Saints' lives too abounded, and one of the finest of these, *St Erkenwald* (probably of 1386), has suggested to some by its metre, diction and moral intelligence that it too is the work of the *Gawain* poet.

This intensely exciting period moves into a culmination late in the 1380s with something that it is tempting to call High Ricardian. The general pattern does not change, and some books already mentioned may belong to this time (Walter Hilton's, for example). But it is worth making the distinction, for English has now become an assured literary language. Chaucer's friend John Gower, who previously wrote his *Mirour de l'homme* in Anglo-Norman and his

Speculum Meditantis in Latin, now adds himself to the greater English poets with *Confessio Amantis*. We have seen Langland revising *Piers Plowman* probably in the mid-1380s; probably in 1393 Julian extended her *Revelations* and about 1395 John Purvey made a freer and more idiomatic version of the Lollard Bible, some of which resembles and perhaps was incorporated in the Authorized Version. *Piers Plowman* also begot more alliterative poetry, social-satirical like *Pierce the Plowman's Creed* and *Mum and the Soth-segger*, and perhaps rather later the exclusively religious *Death and Life*. Another massive prose translation, whose popularity endured till the seventeenth century, was John Trevisa's of Bartholomaeus' encyclopedia *De Proprietatibus Rerum*, finished on 6 February 1399 at Berkeley in Gloucestershire.

But the true encyclopedia of the decade, which along with Gower's *Confessio* makes one imagine a new expansiveness in English literature, is of course Chaucer's *Canterbury Tales*, so near to 'God's plenty'[74] that its incompleteness seems only a tribute to its indefinite variety. Chaucer died (a year after the usurpation of the throne by Henry IV) in October 1400, almost exactly closing one of those thirty-year periods like the Elizabethan/Jacobean which are so fecund with great literature as to defy explanation. One can only add to the wonder by noting that painting also developed extra-ordinarily, with the coming to England during the 1390s, the 'High Ricardian' decade, of the rich, graceful, newly naturalistic International Gothic style whose English crown is the Wilton Diptych. Foreign influence had much to do with the development in painting; court culture, spreading through Europe and centring in England on Richard II, influenced all the arts and no doubt contributed something to the literary miracle: but only a fraction.

1400–1449 But the falling off of literature in the reigns of Henry IV, V and VI, which we may fairly call the Lancastrian period, is not nearly so great as is often said. It is true that skill in metre becomes uncertain: Chaucer had handled with assurance the double inheritance of the Old English alliterative metre that counted stresses and the French metre that rhymed and counted syllables; but it seems merely to have confused Lydgate and others of Chaucer's successors who make use of Chaucer's metrical licences without understanding what justifies them. And some sort of assurance in handling symbolism and allegory does wane. But in its place comes something striking that is to do with the author's presence in his works. In the earlier generation Gower, Chaucer, Langland and the *Gawain* poet, Usk, Julian or the author of the *Cloud* are present in their works for the most part obliquely or comically, idealized or allegorized: the self not felt as flowing out, but seen as from outside. This sense continues in, for example, the morality plays, one of the greatest of which, *The Castle of Perseverance*, dates from early in the new period. But Thomas Hoccleve, Margery Kempe, James I of Scotland, John Audelay and even those who add to the cycle plays in this age seem much more present in their own selves and emotions. We shall draw on the *Book* of Margery Kempe (*c.* 1375 – *c.* 1450) in our chapter on how medieval people described themselves, and on Hoccleve's (1378–1426) handling of himself: except perhaps in Langland's last additions to *Piers Plowman* there is nothing earlier quite like them. But somewhere in the decade or so about 1425 the narrator of *The Kingis Quair*, probably the most beautiful poem in all the following of Chaucer, models himself on the *Book of the Duchess*, the *Parliament of Fowls* and the *Knight's Tale*; yet if, as is likely, the writer is James I of Scotland he was writing genuine though stylized autobiography. John Audelay again, who put together a book of principally devotional poems at Haughmond Abbey in Shropshire about 1426, includes not only the traditional verse narrative of *The Three Living and the Three Dead Kings* but a poem with a certain insistence on himself:

> Learn this lesson of blind Audlay
> When bale is highest, then bot may be.[75]

In drama, too, the 'Wakefield Master' in the 1420s and the 'York Realist' ten years or so earlier wrote, comically or horrifically, like personalities, as the first writers, servants of the biblical word, had not. Indeed, in one still-used distinction between the Middle Ages and the Renaissance, the turn to individualism and self-expression, one finds with surprise that the English Middle Ages began to fade into the Renaissance about the time of Richard II's deposition, though the kind of individualism remained penitential and what Burrow calls petitionary in relation to God and man. In another sense, too, something of the Renaissance penetrates this country in the personality of Humphrey, Duke of Gloucester (d. 1447), a magnificent prince like his contemporaries in Italy, who looked for models for himself in Plato's *Republic* and Plutarch's *Lives*, and who acted as patron for much, though not much good, English poetry, including Robert Parke's translation *Palladius on Husbandrie*, which the duke corrected himself, and Lydgate's *Fall of Princes*. Lydgate is the dominant writer of this whole half-century; and (in opposition to any sense that this was the Renaissance) we have already noted how much the diffuseness and generality of one side of his writing represents the duller aspect of medieval taste. Only by conscious paradox can one argue that his shambling metre, thickly studded with the Latin polysyllables that constitute the 'aureate' style, parodying rather than following Chaucer, represents personal idiosyncrasy. What most affected his writing was probably the spread of private reading. As often with advances in technology, the appetite that printing was to satisfy pre-existed it – an appetite for large masses of verse which should be not too heavy on the attention (as it might be, the equivalent of Georgette Heyer) – and in his *Troy Book* (1412–20), *The Pilgrimage of the Life of Man* (1426–8), *The Fall of Princes* (1431–9), *The Life of our Lady* (1434), and so on, Lydgate responded to it, not to our taste. Didactic writing in verse was in demand, too, and Lydgate gave advice on how to live in his immensely popular *Dietary*, while John Walton translated Boethius' *Consolation* into elegant verse (1410) and someone, said to be Adam Moleyns, offered shrewd political verse in the *Libel of English Policy* (1436): there is a wealth of other examples.

But we have also seen that Lydgate is more to our taste, and equally typical of his time, in poignant lyric, and this is indeed a great age of lyric, above all of the carol. Much of the finest lyric is anonymous – 'In the vaile of restless mind'[76] and, preserved in a manuscript possibly from Lydgate's monastery of Bury St Edmunds, 'I sing of a maiden'[77] and 'Adam lay i bounden'.[78]

The English language can probably claim even a Frenchman, Charles d'Orléans, who wrote and translated in both languages as a prisoner from Agincourt (1415) till 1440. This wealth of song is probably connected with the fact that the second quarter of the century was one of the greatest ages of English music, when a Burgundian could praise Burgundian musicians by saying that 'merveilleuse plaisance' makes their music 'joyeux et notable'[79] because they follow the Englishman John Dunstable. So that besides being an age of nascent self-expression and of bulk reading-matter, it was a singing time.

1449–1476   The next twenty-five years, from the death of Lydgate to the setting up of Caxton's press at Westminster, carry on the same tendencies. Possibly because they were disturbed years, coinciding roughly with the Wars of the Roses, there is a shortage in named writers, and the greatest was notoriously a knight-prisoner (though we do not know whether he was imprisoned in England or in France), Sir Thomas Malory. His *Morte Darthur* (finished 1469–70) (in which the interlacing episodes of traditional Arthurian story, arranged like a modern radio or television serial for listening over a long period, are disentangled into longer stretches such as readers prefer) carries on the adaptation to solitary reading. So does the N-town cycle of mystery plays, whose manuscript of 1468 is elaborately written and annotated as if for private study. Private letters – those of the Pastons, above all – are much more often written with an eye to entertaining the recipient. And expository prose develops in the hands of Reginald Pecock and of Sir John Fortescue (*The Governance of England*). But traditional writing goes on unchanged in carols, allegories (*The Court of Sapience*), morality plays (*Wisdom*) and *La Belle Dame sans Merci*, which Sir Richard Roos (*c.* 1410–82) translated from Alain Chartier, an excellent poem for the reader who (as a reader of love allegory should) can take as much interest in the rights and wrongs of un-requited love under the code of love as in the psychology and fortunes of lovers. The Renaissance tradition begins to take heart in the translation by John Tiptoft, Earl of Worcester (d. 1470), of Buonaccorso's *Declamation of Noblesse*, which Caxton printed in 1481.

1476–1497   However, partly because Caxton's own taste and the tastes he judged would buy the books from his printing press were conservative, this next quarter-century was the period of consolida-tion of the medieval literature that was to be passed on to later times – in Caxton's own translations, as of *Reynard the Fox*, and in his choice of the works of others, as the *Canterbury Tales*, which seems to have been his first large piece of printing in England. But in general it was perhaps the last age when it was easy to feel secure in the possession of medieval culture: probably *The Assembly of Ladies* belongs here, and *The Flower and the Leaf* – the last pure, un-troubled inheritors of the tradition of love allegory that goes back through Chaucer to the *Romance of the Rose*. And in the year of the discovery of America, another friar, James Ryman, made one of the great collections of English carols (1492). Love allegory and lyric devotion are both related to the tradition triumphantly summed up in August 1484 by Richard Methley in the opening sentence of his mystical *Scola Amoris Languidi*: 'The final concern of everything that is made is to love and be loved.'

But Caxton himself declared in the Epilogue to the *Order of Chivalry* that an age was over, and in Scotland Henryson's poems have a kind of violence and harshness that it is hard to think assured – conspicuous in the way in which he transforms Chaucer's 'sorry', 'sliding'[80] Criseyde into the 'maculate', 'giglot-like'[81] cruelly punished leper of *The Testament of Cresseid*.

Printing made subtle differences to the nature of books, making a text a stabilized thing independent of the vagaries of scribes, solidifying the concept of publication, and making more definite even an author's idea of himself and of his responsibility for what he has written. Altogether new things are coming.

1497–c. 1525 One of the first of these new things was Henry Medwall's *Fulgens and Lucrece*. Medwall was capable of writing a traditional morality play (*Nature*), but in *Fulgens and Lucrece*, based on Tiptoft's *Declamation* and like that under the influence of the new self-conscious modelling of one's writing on the classics called 'humanism', he wrote a moral entertainment whose atmosphere was secular and whose setting classical – the first Tudor interlude.

Contemporaneously with this spreading of humanism came a new literary attitude to politics. John Skelton reveals in the *Bouge of Court* secular worries about position and security in the Tudor court which are in marked contrast to the moral, religious dealings of Langland with Lady Meed at the Plantagenet court. C. S. Lewis, who once described Malory as 'a Kafka who enjoyed the labyrinth',[82] comments on the *Bouge*'s 'Kafka-like uneasiness',[83] as if between 1469 and 1499 we pass to a literature that has a real affinity with the pressures and uncertainties of the twentieth century.

It looks as if this were a period in which one might alternately feel enormously excited by the variety of literature – part medieval, part Renaissance – and then dejected, wandering as Matthew Arnold was to wander 'between two worlds': 'One dead, the other powerless to be born'.[84] The most powerful writing is a pure, intense

crystallization of the Middle Ages – of the medieval sense of death
in the finest of the moralities, *Everyman*, of medieval mystery in the
Corpus Christi carol

> Lully, lulley, lully, lulley
> The fawcon hath born my mak away.[85]

mak] mate

and of courtly love longing in the four lines

> Westron wind, when will thou blow,
> The small rain down can rain?
> Christ if my love were in my arms
> And I in my bed again.[86]

– while the lyric 'Yet if His Majesty, our sovereign lord'[87] offers a
devotion which might have been the work of anyone from Walter
Hilton to Vaughan. This intense working-out of medieval themes is
most conspicuous in the North. The very last alliterative poem,
Scottish Field, was written with a primitive energy by the knight of
Baguley Hall in Cheshire to commemorate the defeat of the Scots at
Flodden (1513); and the chivalry terribly injured at Flodden had for
Scottish poetry the magnificent piety, the 'terrible . . , genial and
friendly rankness'[88] and dazzling beauty of William Dunbar, and
the exuberant allegory of *King Hart* and Gavin Douglas's *Palice of
Honour* (1501). But in southern England too, Sir Thomas More's
finest poem is the purely medieval lament for Queen Elizabeth
(1503). More's most notable work of this period, however, is
Utopia, typical of the humanists in that it was written in Latin
(1516) and only translated into English in 1551, and typical of the
period in its veiled humour, such a humour as is also in Erasmus'
Encomium Moriae (*Praise of Folly*), sketched out at More's
suggestion at Chelsea in 1509 and punning on his name in the title:
a humour that in both books makes it finally uncertain what the
authors are aiming at. In Erasmus and More's Latin this uncertainty
is transmuted into urbanity; it seems very different in the helter-
skelter English of John Skelton – in *Philip Sparrow* (1504?), in the
interlude *Magnificence* (1516) or in the farragos, like the *Garland of
Laurel*, *Colin Clout* and *Speak, Parrot*. E. M. Forster comments, I
think rightly, that Skelton himself does not always know how comic,
ironic or serious he wants to be: again perhaps it is only in a

hyperbolically energetic medievalism that he is assured, in the comedy of *The Tunning of Elinor Rumming*, some of the lyric addresses to ladies or the macabre attacks on Cardinal Wolsey's 'wolf's head wan, blo as lead'[89] and the court. There is a similar uncertainty in Stephen Hawes's *Example of Virtue* (1504) and *Pastime of Pleasure* (1505), which read like Rabelais as read by H. G. Wells's Mr Polly – a medievalized Rabelais, great fun but with nothing like the Frenchman's assurance. They are already revivals rather than continuations of medieval allegory, delighting in colour, obscurity and romantic wandering in a mode that was only to find itself in Spenser's *Faerie Queene*. Similar in flavour is the anonymous chronicle play about *St Mary Magdalen* whose Brechtianly broken-backed mixture of allegory and realism, heaven and earth, finds its proper fulfilment only in Shakespeare's last plays.

The situation in literature has a kind of parallel in the architecture of Henry VII's chapel at Westminster and of King's College Chapel at Cambridge, where Gothic structure is driven to exciting extremes of illusionism on which Renaissance detail is imposed, scarcely absorbed. But in literature the structural elements (allegory and metre, except for song metres) are less certain, and one is more aware of the conflict of detail. There is one magnificent exception, not surprisingly from Scotland, Gavin Douglas's translation of the *Aeneid* (1513); this, making an uncompromising choice in the dilemma about how to transpose cultures, devoted good humanist learning to elicit everything in Virgil that found an answering chord in the intense extreme of late Scots medievalism. (The wildest example, the 'nuns of Bacchus'[90] who make Mount Cithaeron resound all night with their clamour, perhaps as much suggests that Douglas found ecstatic piety congruous with the word 'nun' as that he recognized dedication and ritual in Bacchus' Thyiads.) The magnificent prologues that Douglas adds to each book draw him to our attention as inspired scholar and creator of the whole poem; and their nature poetry, in which, as W. P. Ker put it, one finds 'convention and long tradition leading to a sudden stroke of genius',[91] looks so far forward as to have a flavour of Tennyson ('The wynd maid wayfe the reid weid on the dyk').[92] Ker said of the description of midsummer dawn following close on sunset in the last prologue, that Douglas 'sees a new thing in the life of the world . . . and in naming it he gives the interpretation also, the spirit of poetry: *pleasance and half wonder.*'[93] But, aside from this example, perhaps he was no more or less capable of seeing nature than the *Gawain* poet, but only records it with more self-awareness, and at length.

By contrast, in the 1520s Sir John Berners's translation of Froissart's chronicles of the chivalric world gives a sense of catching back at something that is only just vanishing over the horizon; and his other translation, of *Huon of Bordeaux*, a faery tale which he seems uncertain whether to take as history, has a claim to be the last purely medieval book (printed posthumously in 1534). But he translated more humanistic works too.

In music and song, however, tradition goes on developing, especially in the courts of Henry VII and VIII. Henry VIII and his musician William Cornish are probably responsible for some delightful lyrics: and the pure tradition of Charles d'Orléans in love song is taken up in the mid-1520s by Sir Thomas Wyatt.

c. 1525–1549   These years might be counted the purging of the Middle Ages. The period is more or less what C. S. Lewis (who did not care for it) called the Drab Age, of the poetry of Wyatt ('lean and sinewy and a little sad'[94]) and of the Earl of Surrey: a period of reaction and avoidance of the medieval richness lately abused. At court it is the sad and dangerous period of the last years of Henry VIII; in religion it is the first stage of the influence of Luther's ideas and of the ensuing spiritual conflicts. For all these reasons it is an age that looks for authenticity – in Wyatt's verse, in Tyndale's and Coverdale's translations of the Bible, in controversial and devotional writings both reforming (Tyndale) and traditional (More), in the valiant, vivid sermons of Hugh Latimer. Humanist writing displays further reaction against the medieval in the name of classicism – Elyot's *Book called the Governor* (1531), Ascham's *Toxophilus* (1545) and cheerful interludes like John Heywood's *Play of the Weather* (1533) based on Lucian, and John Bedford's *Wit and Science*. That medieval literature was now felt as *past* is fairly demonstrated by the smooth and witty *Court of Love*, imitating the love allegory of Chaucer, Hoccleve, Lydgate and Roos in deliberately archaic English.

But Surrey, using Gavin Douglas's translation, yet producing a severer, more alien and literal version of part of the *Aeneid*, created for it, presumably to represent Virgil's hexameters, what the title page of the first edition in 1557 called 'a strange metre': blank verse. Stiff as he writes it, this was to be the structure that would naturalize the humanist version of Latin and Greek image and thought in English and in Shakespeare's plays harmonize it with medieval tradition.

Wyatt's lyrics and Latimer's sermons draw heavily on medieval tradition: Wyatt's satire, like Sir David Lindsay's in Scotland at the very end of our period (*Ane Satire of the Three Estates*), draws on medieval as well as classical precedent, as comedy was to do in the mid-century in Nicholas Udall's *Ralph Roister-Doister* and in *Gammer Gurton's Needle*. John Bale did his best to write Protestant morality plays and to find in King John a medieval reformer; in his *King John* (performed at Thomas Cranmer's house in 1539), in which John is confronted by emblematic figures such as Clergy and Usurped Power, he produced something that seems to link the morality with the Elizabethan history play. The typical product of the age is Thomas Cranmer's first Book of Common Prayer (1549); with his humanist, melodious balance of latinate and English words ('create and make in us new and contrite hearts'[95]), his temperate modifying of all richness ('whose service is perfect freedom' for the Latin *cui servire regnare est*, 'whom to serve is to be a king'[96]), terse, purged metaphor ('lighten our darkness'[97]), response to drama (his translation of the consecration prayer in the mass to include St Paul's 'who in the same night in which he was betrayed' for the Latin *pridie quam pateretur*, 'the day before he suffered', and his resetting of the traditional act of breaking bread so as to accompany the words 'brake it') and passionate authenticity, Cranmer displays precisely the qualities which are most distinctive in Wyatt's poems. Thus he made available for a religiously austere age the richness of medieval devotion. Along with Bale's publication in the same year of John Leland's *Journey*, introducing a deliberate quest for antiquity, Cranmer's Book of Common Prayer offers a significant transition point on which to close. In other arts, as we shall see, Reformation and Renaissance mark radical changes: in literature, tradition, in spite of graftings and prunings, puts itself forth from the old roots. Spenser and Shakespeare remained the heirs of Langland, Gower and Chaucer.

Notes

These notes have been compiled with the interests of further reading in mind. References to Chaucer here and throughout are to *The Works of Geoffrey Chaucer*, ed. F. N. Robinson, 2nd edn (Oxford, 1966).

1   C. S. Lewis, *They Stand Together*, ed. W. Hooper (London, 1979), p. 328.
2   *English Verse 1300–1500*, ed. J. A. Burrow, Longman's Annotated Anthologies of English Verse, vol. 1 (London and New York, 1977); Chaucer, *The Canterbury Tales*, ed. A. C. Cawley, Everyman Library (London, 1958); *Pearl, Cleanness, Patience and Gawain and the Green Knight*, ed. A. C. Cawley and J. J. Anderson, Everyman Library (London, 1976); Langland, *The Vision of Piers Plowman*, ed. A. V. C. Schmidt, Everyman Library (London and New York, 1978); *Mediaeval English Lyrics*, ed. R. T. Davies (London, 1963); *The Corpus Christi Play of the English Middle Ages*, ed. R. T. Davies (London, 1972). H. G. Wells, *The History of Mr Polly* (London, 1910), ch. 3, p. 68.
3   *Canterbury Tales, General Prologue*, ll. 7–8; *The Très Riches Heures of Jean, Duke of Berry*, ed. J. Longnon *et al.* (New York, 1969), f. 4v.
4   Guido delle Colonne, *Historia Destructionis Troiae*, Bk 4; quoted in M. Bowden, *A Commentary on the General Prologue to the Canterbury Tales*, 2nd edn (London, 1967), pp. 20, 40.
5   *Canterbury Tales, Franklin's Tale*, ll. 1016–18.
6   Ficino, *Plotini omnia opera*; quoted in M. Pope, *The Story of Decipherment* (London, 1975), p. 21.
7   *Mandeville's Travels*, ed. M. C. Seymour (Oxford, 1967), ch. 29, p. 191.
8   *Troilus and Criseyde*, Bk 2, ll. 22–8, 43–4.
9   Thomas Usk, *The Testament of Love*; in *Chaucerian and Other Pieces*, ed. W. W. Skeat (Oxford, 1897), Bk 1, ch. 5, pp. 38–70.
10 *Aeneid*, Bk 1, l. 319.
11 *The House of Fame*, Bk 1, ll. 228–30.
12 *Sir Orfeo*, ed. A. J. Bliss, 2nd edn (Oxford, 1966), ll. 283–5.
13 Eustache Deschamps, 'Ballade' addressed to Geoffrey Chaucer, in D. Brewer (ed.), *Chaucer: The Critical Heritage* (London, 1978), vol. 1, pp. 39–42.
14 *Legend of Good Women*, F version, ll. 138–48.
15 In *Mediaeval English Lyrics*, ed. Davies, p. 155; cf. pp. 17–18.
16 Owen Barfield, *Poetic Diction* (London, 1928), ch. 2 and *passim*.
17 In *Mediaeval Latin Lyrics*, ed. Helen Waddell, rev. edn (London, 1933), pp. 218–19 (MS. of Benediktbeuern).
18 I take most of this from *Mediaeval English Lyrics*, ed. Davies; also Book of Wisdom 2:23–6.
19 E. Panofsky, *Early Netherlandish Painting* (Harvard, 1966), vol. 1, p. 142.
20 In *English Lyrics of the XIIIth Century*, ed. Carleton Brown (Oxford, 1932), p. 55.
21 William Dunbar, '*Rorate celi desuper*', in *Poems*, ed. W. M. Mackenzie (London, 1932).
22 Recorded on *Medieval English Lyrics*, Argo RG 443.
23 Recorded on *Altenglische Lieder: Liebe, Lust, und Frömmigkeit*,

Stereo 25 22286-1 BASS, and on *Medieval English Lyrics* (see n. 22 above), respectively.

24 Sir Philip Sidney, *Apology for Poetry*, ed. G. Shepherd (Manchester, 1973), p. 118.
25 *Troilus and Criseyde*, Bk 5, l. 270.
26 *House of Fame*, Bk 1, l. 656.
27 C. S. Lewis, *The Allegory of Love* (Oxford, 1936), p. 64.
28 S. T. Coleridge, *Biographia Literaria* (London, 1817), ch. 14.
29 W. P. Witcutt, *Return to Reality* (London, 1955), p. 33.
30 William Caxton, Preface to Sir Thomas Malory, *Morte Darthur*, quoting St Paul's Second Epistle to Timothy 3:16; in *Works of Sir Thomas Malory*, ed. E. Vinaver, 2nd edn (Oxford, 1967).
31 Attributed to the Duke of Suffolk, though uncertain, in *English Verse between Chaucer and Surrey*, ed. Eleanor P. Hammond (New York, 1965), pp. 198-201, ll. 27-8.
32 *Winner and Waster*, ed. I. Gollancz and M. Day (London, 1931), ll. 20-30.
33 *Piers Plowman*, B text, ed. A. V. C. Schmidt (London, 1978), Passus XII, l. 149.
34 *House of Fame*, Bk 2, l. 586.
35 Stephen Hawes, *The Pastime of Pleasure*, ed. W. E. Mead, EETS (Oxford, 1928), l. 1328.
36 *The Parliament of Fowls*, l. 1.
37 N. Pevsner and J. Harris, *Lincolnshire* (Harmondsworth, 1964), p. 88.
38 *Metrical Life of St Hugh*, extract trans. in John Harvey, *The Mediaeval Architect* (London, 1972), pp. 236-9.
39 Geoffrey de Vinsauf, *Poetria Nova* (translation based on Harvey, op. cit.), in *Les Arts poétiques du XIIe et du XIIIe siècles*, ed. E. Faral (Paris, 1924), ll. 43 ff.
40 See p. 187 below.
41 See p. 188 below.
42 Hugh Johnson, *World Atlas of Wine* (London, 1972), p. 16.
43 *The Forme of Cury*, prologue; see the version edited by Lorna H. Sass, *To the King's Taste* (London, 1978).
44 *Clerk's Prologue*, l. 18; cf. *Franklin's Prologue*, l. 726.
45 *Troilus and Criseyde*, Bk 1, ll. 1065-9.
46 *Legend of Good Women*, Fuersion, ll. 25-6.
47 *Nun's Priest's Tale*, ll. 3438-43.
48 *General Prologue*, l. 150.
49 *Parliament of Fowls*, ll. 1-7.
50 *A Pistle of Discrecioun of Stirings*, in *Deonise Hid Divinite and Other Treatises*, ed. P. Hodgson, EETS (Oxford, 1958), p. 63.
51 G. K. Chesterton, *The Everlasting Man* (London, 1925), pp. 156-7.
52 Dante, *Inferno*, VII, l. 75.
53 William Blake, *A Descriptive Catalogue* (1809).
54 *Parson's Tale*, ll. 927-31.

55 Lydgate, *Fall of Princes*, ed. H. Bergen, EETS (Oxford, 1924–7), Bk 3, ll. 2201–2.

56 Lydgate, *The Dance Macabre*, st. 64; in *English Verse between Chaucer and Surrey*, ed. E. P. Hammond (Duke University, 1927), p. 139.

57 *The Testament of Dan John Lydgate*, final stanza; in *Minor Poems*, ed. H. MacCracken, EETS (Oxford, 1911), p. 362.

58 *Troilus and Criseyde*, Bk 2, ll. 80–3.

59 Arnold Fellows, *The Wayfarer's Companion* (Oxford, 1937 and often reprinted), p. 181.

60 *Pearl*, ed. Cawley and Anderson, l. 1209.

61 *Gawain and the Green Knight*, edited with *Pearl*, ed. Cawley and Anderson, ll. 525–8.

62 E. K. Chambers, *The Mediaeval Stage* (Oxford, 1903), vol. 2.

63 *Aeneid*, Bk 2, ll. 238–9.

64 Douglas, *Eneados*, IV, 70; in *Selections from Gavin Douglas*, ed. D. Coldwell (Oxford, 1964).

65 *Oxford Book of Carols*, ed. P. Dearmer *et al.*, new edn (Oxford, 1964), pp. 78–9.

66 *Les Fortunes et Adversitez de Jean Regnier*, ed. E. Droz (Paris, 1923), pp. 85 ff., ll. 2364–91.

67 *English Historical Documents 1485–1558*, ed. C. H. Williams (London, 1967), p. 195.

68 T. S. Eliot, 'East Coker', I.

69 Higden's *Polychronicon*, trans. Trevisa, Rolls Series (London, 1969), Bk 1, ch. 38.

70 Ibid.

71 In *Mediaeval English Lyrics*, ed. Davies, p. 111.

72 *Troilus and Criseyde*, Bk 5, ll. 1835–41.

73 Julian of Norwich, *Revelations of Divine Love*, in *A Book of Showings to the Anchoress Julian of Norwich*, ed. E. Colledge and J. Walsh (Toronto, 1978), pp. 212–13, 300.

74 Dryden, Preface to *Fables, Ancient and Modern* (London, 1700); in *Geoffrey Chaucer: A Critical Anthology*, ed. J. A. Burrow (Harmondsworth, 1969), p. 66.

75 John Audelay, 'Lady, helpe! Jesu, merce!', ll. 43–4, in *Mediaeval English Lyrics*, ed. Davies, pp. 170–1.

76 'Quia amore langueo', *Oxford Book of Medieval English Verse*, ed. C. and K. Sisam (Oxford, 1970), p. 357.

77 See n. 15 above.

78 In *Mediaeval English Lyrics*, ed. Davies, p. 160.

79 Martin Le Franc, *Le Champion des dames*, quoted in F. L. Harrison, *Music in Medieval Britain* (London, 1958), p. 250.

80 *Troilus and Criseyde*, Bk 5, ll. 1098, 825.

81 Robert Henryson, *The Testament of Cresseid*, in *Poems and Fables of Robert Henryson*, ed. H. Harvey Wood (Edinburgh, 1933), ll. 81–3.

82 C. S. Lewis, 'The anthropological approach', in *Literary Essays*

(Cambridge, 1969), p. 310.

83 C. S. Lewis, *English Literature in the Sixteenth Century* (Oxford, 1954), p. 135.

84 Matthew Arnold, *Stanzas from the Grande Chartreuse*, stanza 15.

85 In *Mediaeval English Lyrics*, ed. Davies, p. 272.

86 Ibid., p. 291.

87 In *Poetry of the English Renaissance*, ed. J. W. Hebel and H. H. Hudson (New York, 1947), p. 441.

88 Edith Sitwell, *The Atlantic Book of British and American Poetry* (London, 1959), vol. 1, p. 59.

89 John Skelton, *Speak, Parrot*, in *Complete Poems of John Skelton*, ed. P. Henderson, rev. edn (London, 1964), p. 304.

90 Douglas, *Eneados*, IV, vi, 41; in *Selections*, ed. Coldwell.

91 W. P. Ker, *The Art of Poetry* (Oxford, 1923), p. 24.

92 Douglas, *Eneados*, VII, prol., 59; in *Selections*, ed. Coldwell.

93 Ker, op. cit., p. 26.

94 C. S. Lewis, *English Literature in the Sixteenth Century*, p. 230.

95 Collect for Ash Wednesday.

96 Collect at Morning Prayer, for Peace.

97 Collect at Evening Prayer, for Aid.

Select bibliography

This bibliography is suggestive and incomplete; it should be supplemented by the particularly useful bibliographies in the books marked with an asterisk (*).

Theory of interpretation
Barfield, O. *Poetic Diction*, London, 1928.
Hirsch, E. D. *Validity in Interpretation*, New Haven, Conn., 1967. (Expresses more sophisticatedly a position like that of this chapter, whose text was, however, complete before Professor J. A. Burrow told me of Hirsch.)
Lewis, C. S. *An Experiment in Criticism*, Cambridge, 1961.
—— *Studies in Words*, 2nd edn, Cambridge, 1967.

Literary history
Bennett, H. S. *Chaucer and the Fifteenth Century*, Oxford History of English Literature, Oxford, 1947.
*Bolton, W. F. (ed.) *The Middle Ages*, Sphere History of Literature in the English Language, vol. 1, London, 1970.
Burrow, J. A. *Introduction to Middle English Literature*, Oxford, in press. (Most useful in relation to the concerns of this book.)
Chambers, E. K. *The Close of the Middle Ages*, Oxford History of English Literature, Oxford, 1946.

*Lewis, C. S. *English Literature in the Sixteenth Century*, Oxford History of English Literature, Oxford, 1954.

*Malone, K., and Baugh, A. D. *A Literary History of England*, vol. 1: *The Middle Ages*, 2nd edn, London, 1967.

*Pearsall, D. *Old English and Middle English Poetry*, Routledge History of English Poetry, vol. 1, London, 1977.

Contexts of particular writers
By far the most useful book in providing contexts for medieval literature is that in the series 'Writers and their Background' on *Geoffrey Chaucer,** ed. Derek Brewer (London, 1974). But discussion of Chaucer has generally included much context, for example:

Brewer, D. *Chaucer*, 3rd edn, London, 1973.

Curry, W. C. *Chaucer and the Mediaeval Sciences*, New York, 1960.

Schoeck, R. J., and Taylor, J. (eds) *Chaucer Criticism*, 2 vols, Notre Dame, Indiana, 1960.

More recent special studies are:

Burnley, J. D. *Chaucer's Language and the Philosophers' Tradition*, Cambridge, 1979.

Wilkins, N. *Music in the Age of Chaucer*, Cambridge, 1979.

Examples of works on other writers providing ways into late medieval culture are:

Bishop, I. *Pearl in its Setting*, Oxford, 1968.

Burrow, J. A. *A Reading of Gawain and the Green Knight*, London, 1965.

Kolve, V. A. *The Play Called Corpus Christi*, Stanford, Cal., 1966.

Pearsall, D. *John Lydgate*, London, 1970.

Iconography and the commonplaces shared by literature and the other arts

Curtius, E. R. *European Literature and the Latin Middle Ages*, trans. W. R. Trask, New York, 1953. (This is the fundamental guide from the point of view of literature, though it perhaps mishandles the idea of the traditional theme or *topos* – a most important concept, which nevertheless produces havoc in the understanding of medieval culture when it comes into contact with the frequent modern dislike of stock responses.)

Gray, D. *Themes and Images in the Medieval English Religious Lyric*, London, 1972.

Pearsall, D., and Salter, E. *Landscapes and Seasons of the Medieval World*. London, 1973.

Tristram, P. *Figures of Life and Death in Medieval English Literature*, London, 1976.

(Both these last two are enchantingly illustrated.)

A really fundamental study in the relation of medieval literature to the visual arts, of which his essay in D. Brewer (ed.), *Geoffrey Chaucer* (London, 1974), was a foretaste, is coming from V. A. Kolve.

The whole context
Cottle, B. *The Triumph of English 1350–1400*, 'History and Literature', London, 1969.
Daiches, D., and Thorlby, A. K. (eds) *The Medieval World*, London, 1973.
Evans, J. (ed.) *The Flowering of the Middle Ages*, London and New York, 1966. (Very finely illustrated.)
Kinghorn, A. M. *The Chorus of History 1485–1558*, 'History and Literature', London, 1971.
Loomis, R. S. *A Mirror of Chaucer's World*, Princeton, NJ, 1965. (Very finely illustrated.)
Mason, H. A. *Humanism and Poetry in the Early Tudor Period*, London, 1959.
Mathew, G. *The Court of Richard II*, London, 1968.
Myers, A. R. *England in the Late Middle Ages*, rev. edn, Harmondsworth, 1980. (A good summary of the whole period.)
Scattergood, V. G. *Politics and Poetry in the Fifteenth Century*, 'History and Literature', London, 1971.
Stevens, J. *Music and Poetry in the Early Tudor Court*, London, 1971.

Particularly ambitious to engage the problems of the quality of the cultures they discuss are:
Aers, D. *Chaucer, Langland and the Creative Imagination*, London, 1980.
Auerbach, E. *Mimesis*, trans. W. R. Trask, New York, 1957.
Burrow, J. A. *Ricardian Poetry*, London, 1971.
Green, R. F. *Poets and Princepleasers*, Toronto, 1980.
Lewis, C. S. *The Discarded Image*, Cambridge, 1964.
Muscatine, C. *Chaucer and the French Tradition*, Berkeley, Cal., 1957.
____ *Poetry and Crisis in the Age of Chaucer*, Notre Dame, Indiana, 1972.
Robertson, D. W. *A Preface to Chaucer*, Princeton, NJ, 1963.

No one will be convinced by all these, and the books by Aers and Robertson seem to me profoundly wrongheaded; but no one even slightly interested in things medieval could fail to be excited and illuminated by any of them.

Most useful will be the proceedings of the Colston Research Society symposium, 1981, on *English Court Culture in the Later Middle Ages*, ed. J. A. Burrow (Bristol, forthcoming).

2 The ideal, the real and the quest for perfection

MARJORIE REEVES and STEPHEN MEDCALF

At the beginning of the fourteenth century, Dante mourned the cupidity that drove men after that which was not their own, and so disrupted a God-given pattern of social relationships. He saw human society as the reflection of a divine idea laid up in heaven which gave each man his place in an appointed hierarchy. In the *Paradiso*[1] he makes his ancestor, Cacciaguida, bewail the expansion and social change taking place in Florence, and look nostalgically back to a mythical age when each man was content with his own, and Florence was so small that everyone could hear the Badia bell. Yet about the same time Giovanni Villani described the Florence of 1300 as 'in the greatest and happiest state which had ever been since it was rebuilt, or before, alike in greatness and power and in number of people, for as much as there were more than 30,000 citizens in the city, and more than 70,000 men capable of arms in the country within her territory'.[2] He took pride in recording how the old, constricting circuit of city walls had been thrown down and a more expansive one built. 'His chronicle is essentially a success story.'[3] Villani was a member of the great banking house of Peruzzi. For such there was no standing still. Thus Dante's static, idealized concept of society stands in sharp contrast with the dynamic, changing actuality.

The philosophy of the world

Dante and his contemporaries inherited a world-view built up through the centuries during which Christian doctrine had gradually

permeated European society. Though stubborn elements of pagan-
ism remained, the church had embraced the world within its realm.
The Jewish doctrine of creation, as set forth at the beginning of the
Bible and expounded in the Christian church, placed the whole
universe under the dominion of God. The universe was seen then
through a Judaeo-Christian glass; but Graeco-Roman thought had
supplied its philosphical framework. Within the cosmos thus conceived, God had assigned to every living creature its due place in the
order of being and the law under which it should live. So Chaucer
says in the *Knight's Tale*, quoting the sixth-century philosopher
Boethius, that nature takes its beginning

> . . . of a thing that parfit is and stable,
> Descendynge so til it be corrumpable.[4]

corrumpable] corruptible

For, as Boethius went on to say, perfect things obviously exist before
less perfect things. It is an axiom to him, and one that goes flatly
against the evolutionary assumptions we tend to take for granted.
Where you see anything that might be better, you can be sure that
the standard by which you judge it, the good that it might be,
already exists. The world does not move towards better things that as
yet do not exist: it exists as a hierarchy, with perfection at the top.
This hierarchy of beings is fixed eternally; it unites in a chain of
relationships all parts of the created universe. By Dante's time the
order of higher beings had been elaborated into a celestial hierarchy
of nine angelic choirs, with man next below them. But though man
was made 'a little lower than the angels', God had given him
dominion over the animals and all lower orders of being. This did
not, however, mean that man could do as he liked. Within human
society itself there was also a clear hierarchy of function and
authority, and divine rule required that every man should observe
his due relationship, not only with those above him, but also with
lower orders, extending down through the natural world. Every man
stood under the law of God and the law of nature which he had
ordained. The interpretation of human duty in all spheres – even
economic – was given to the church. Its sources of authority were
the Bible and tradition, especially the teachings of the church
fathers.

One important consequence of the hierarchical concept was that the significance of human beings was more often measured in terms of their functioning within given relationships than of their individual gifts or 'potential'. Moral teaching was mostly addressed to 'types', as broadly distinguished, for instance, in the formula 'The cleric prays, the knight fights, the peasant tills the soil', or dissected in more detail in Last Judgement scenes, where particular dooms were allotted to kings, bishops, merchants, and so on. Because the divine cosmic order was the all-embracing and benevolent 'given' element in the human situation, men could realize their true natures only by working joyfully within the role assigned to them. Similarly, the architect, artist or musician, seeking to express perfection, must attend to the proportion and harmony of the universe – the faintly caught music of the spheres – rather than to his own inspiration or inner feelings. Not surprisingly, the question 'How free, then, is man?' was anxiously and often debated, but because the debate tended to start from the premiss of God's order, the answers reached usually approximated to that which Dante expressed with passion: the earthly beatitude of man lay in building a society that sought to express – albeit imperfectly – the harmony of the divine order. The true freedom of individuals and societies lay in embracing God's will: 'in His will is our peace'.[5]

Through Boethius, and through the search for a satisfactory theory of knowledge of St Augustine of Hippo (AD 354–430), the philosophy of Plato and his followers, the Neoplatonists, filtered through to the Middle Ages. If behind this changing world there was the changeless reality of the creator, then the human mind must seek beyond sensory experience a correspondingly immutable realm of knowledge. Augustine and others found this affirmed in the Platonic concept of forms, thought of as the ideas of God. Among these forms great emphasis was placed on mathematical ideas and the principles of order, rhythm, symmetry and harmony derived from them. From the eternal ideas the objects of our sensory perception draw their being, and our knowledge is true only in so far as it discerns these realities.

This in outline is the medieval philosophy of realism, which provided the philosophical counterpart to the doctrine of creation: out of the absolute, supra-individual realities existing in his mind, God the artist had fashioned the particulars known to sensory perception. The end of knowledge was to pass through corporeal phenomena to arrive at the changeless originals of this changing world of experience.

Even social ideas were coloured by realism: corporations were prior
to individuals, as universals were prior to particulars.

But there was always the question to be faced: might not general
terms or universals be merely the names we use, not independent
entities at all? In the twelfth century there flared up a controversy
between the traditional realists and the nominalists, who asserted
that universals were not real but nominal: not things but words.
Most famous of those taking part in this argument was Peter Abelard
(1079–1142), who sought to hold a middle position: radical
nominalism was too destructive of the way in which we do in fact
understand the universe, yet realism, pushed to its limit, implied
that the particulars known to our senses were unreal and the manifest
variety of things an illusion. Abelard showed signs of the coming
influence of Aristotle, in that he insisted that human knowledge
begins with particular perception, but his theology would not allow
him to abandon the over-arching reality of eternal verities.
'Theological thought was too deeply based upon Augustine for
Abelard to offer no acknowledgements to the Platonic Ideas. Ideas
exist as patterns of things in the divine mind.'[6] Abelard's position
pointed forward to the great work of synthesis which became
necessary in the thirteenth century when most of Aristotle's works
had been translated from Greek and Arabic into Latin, and their
weight felt. The desire for coherent unity in all things inspired not
only the harmonizing of Aristotelian principles and Christian faith
but the bringing of all knowledge into one intelligible structure. St
Thomas Aquinas (*c.* 1225–74) was the final architect of this great
Summa in which the Aristotelian understanding of human
knowledge was incorporated, without forgetting the Platonism of
the Augustinians, into the Christian view of the universe.

The heart of this system is given us in the moment described by
Plato in the *Phaedo* when Socrates, waiting for execution, says that a
man who only gives physical, mechanical explanations of the world
is making the same mistake as if he said that Socrates was sitting in
the condemned cell because certain muscles had driven certain
bones in his legs and then stopped doing so rather than because he
had thought it better to obey the laws of Athens; whereas, in fact, if
Socrates had not thought in that way, his muscles and bones would
long ago have been off to the nearest foreign country, following a
mistaken opinion. Such people, Socrates says, confuse conditions
without which something cannot happen with true causes.

That particular story was unlikely to be quoted in the Middle Ages; but most people assumed the attitude it enforces – that explanations of how things happen, which Aristotelians called material and efficient causes, are less important than final causes, the reasons why things happen: ends are more important than means. The result was a picture of the universe that has one great advantage, that man and his values make sense within it. Even in terms of physics and astronomy, the universe is arranged in a hierarchy of values. At the centre is the place of change and decay, our earth. Even within that sphere, of the four states of matter experienced by us, the basest thing, solid matter (earth) is lowest: above it things become lighter, swifter, nobler – from liquid (water) through gaseous (air) to fire.

Beyond fire begin the heavens, and the fifth element, or quintessence. Things are corruptible this side of the moon: from the moon outwards the seven planets move, themselves unchangeable, the moon, Mercury, Venus, the sun, Mars, Jupiter, Saturn, in a perpetual dance of the noblest form, the circle, making music together by the spheres in which they are set touching each other, till we come to the sphere of the fixed stars. In that heaven, an unthinkable distance away, Dante looked down and saw 'the threshing-floor',[7] the little round thing with the turbulent chaff flying across it which waited for our own time to be photographed.

Dante's extraordinary intuition rests on the assumption that the Middle Ages took from Boethius, that the true view of the universe is perceived not from where we are but from where God is. The universe of space and time itself vanishes, in Dante's vision, when he passes beyond the fixed stars and the Primum Mobile (the 'first movable' thing through which all the universe is moved). In Thomist–Aristotelian thought, space was purely relative, only existing as the relation of physical bodies. At the edge of the universe Dante stands in the heaven which, having no further physical object enclosing it, and therefore no space to be in, has no *where* but the mind of God.[8]

Time suffers the same change. Aquinas tells us that delight as such is not in time. It sounds like a comment on our actual sensation of time, on what ecstasy feels like, and so it is. But it is also a deduction from the concept that, like space, time is relative, being only the measurement of change. Delight implies the possession of what we had wanted: to possess a thing is to have no need to change in relation to it any more: our relation to it, therefore, being something that does not change, is itself not in time.

Change, and time with it, imply the end of change and time. For the Aristotelian, change is the making actual of what is now only possible: time being the measure of change, the future is all simply possibility, and the present is the moment when the possible becomes actual. As E. A. Burtt puts it, 'the present exists unmoved and draws the future into it';[9] this has further implications.

For it is an Aristotelian position that nothing can change itself or cause its own existence. There must always be an impulse from some other thing to cause change, and there must be support from some other thing to maintain existence. Moreover, everything we ordinarily experience is contingent, might not exist, unless caused to exist by its relation with other things.

But this is difficult; for it is also contrary to Aristotelian thought to imagine a universe which has no bottom, which is only a set of things circularly causing each other's existence and each other's change: only a hole inside a hole inside a hole. There must be a base which causes without being caused, changes without being changed: and this, the first cause, we call God. Since the most important kind of cause is the final cause, the end, the reason why, God must be the perfect end. This explains a further difficulty: by what means can God cause or change the world? The perfect, unmoving end cannot be affected by anything else, or he too would be changed, which is absurd. But if we think of God as the goal of the universe, then we can say, as Aristotle does, that he moves the world by being loved. The beloved does not need to do anything to cause her lover to seek her; and the perfection at which we aim likewise does not need to act.

It is in the present moment that God, unchanged and self-existent, causes existence and change. The thought on time already sketched had been brought to its crown by Boethius, who said that to God all time must be unchangingly present. He defined eternity, therefore, as the possession of past, present and future together, in one moment of time. He pointed out too that true happiness must be the same as the possession of the perfect good. But the perfect good simply is God. To be happy, then, we must possess some part in the eternal, and in God. Any happiness that is not a participation in God is only a mistake – like that of a drunken man trying to find his way home. As Chaucer renders it:

> A dronke man woot wel he hath an hous,
> But he noot which the righte wey is thider,
> And to a dronke man the wey is slider.[10]

There is or may be, then, a continuity between our ordinary experiences of delight, themselves out of time, and the perfect vision of God.

To all this, the Christians added that the final good is love: somewhat paradoxically, because God as the final good is unalterable, while love seems to imply being affected by something. One can indeed use the analogy of the artist (a familiar one in the Middle Ages, when God was sometimes portrayed in the act of creation as an architect with a pair of compasses). Not because he is constrained by his creation, but only out of the love with which he creates it, wholly self-moved, the artist loves what he makes: so with God. But the love of God does not fit happily into the Aristotelian scheme; nor does its validation in the Incarnation and Crucifixion, nor the moment in the mass when the Crucifixion is made present in the consecration of bread and wine. The bread and wine, apparently retaining all their physical attributes, are said in Aristotelian language to have changed their substance in the miracle of transubstantiation when they became the body and blood of Christ. The love of God, the Incarnation and Passion of Christ and the sacrament of the mass were at the heart of medieval thinking. The scheme had to accommodate them, and it did so, as exceptions to itself, as miracle and paradox. But it does seem to creak in the attempt.

The religious aspect of this vision of the world is better expressed by beginning at the other end, with the active love of God. Julian of Norwich expresses the contingency of 'all that is made' in her *Revelations of Divine Love* (1373) when she says that it seemed so small, 'like a hazelnut in the palm of my hand', that it might have 'fallen to nothing for very littleness'. She was answered that 'it lasts and ever shall, for God loves it'.[11] Dante saw everything in the universe, things and qualities and all the relation between them, gathered up, like pages that in our experience of them are scattered through the world, into a book bound together by love: and all nevertheless the same as the simple light which is God.[12] As Julian says at the end of her book, 'Love is His meaning.'

In spite, then, of their sense of contingency, there has never been more trust in the fact, in the thing created, than we find in Dante, Julian or Thomas Aquinas. But the fact must be read as part of a book written by God, with his meaning running through it. Their sense of the world is deeply symbolic: what Auerbach calls the 'figural' sense of the world. When God allegorizes, says St Thomas, he does it with facts.[13]

Conversely, although what we perceive is in a sense symbolic, there is here a trust in human perception. Indeed, in Aristotelian theory, what men perceive is an actual aspect of the thing perceived, not a mere decoding of impressions received from it. When one sees or understands a thing one participates in the thing itself by means of its sensible or intelligible species, whether that thing be a twig or God. For many generations, the doubts that arose about the system were doubts about the relation between what we perceive (the appearances of the world) and thought (transcendental reality): in particular, the doubts of realism versus nominalism as to what we know of transcendental reality. It was not till towards Descartes's time that doubt was raised about whether our perceptions correspond to external reality. The very word 'objective' implies in medieval philosophical language an object as it is presented to our consciousness; it was not till after Descartes that it acquired its characteristic modern connotation of object as it would be if it were not presented to our consciousness, as if the right way of imagining a thing is to think of it as it would exist if we were not imagining it. Everything in the world, on this side of God, says Thomas Usk, is made 'buxom' (responsive) to man's thought.[14]

The strength of this system lies where it is nearest to dealing with consciousness. The example embodied in any medieval ghost story compared with any modern one – that a medieval man encountering a ghost would, although frightened, know what to do by way of righting a wrong or offering a mass, to give its disturbed and unhappy existence rest, while a modern man would stand at a loss before something utterly undealable with[15] – points to a truth. Such things as the phenomenon of consciousness, confidence in values and the existence of mystical states, which threaten the modern and mechanical system, were the foundation of the medieval one.

Conversely, the weakness of the medieval system, apart from those religious paradoxes already mentioned, lay in areas where mechanical explanations and measurement in discrete, inorganic units are most appropriate, first of all in dynamics and in physics. The analogy with man's awareness of himself which pervades the medieval model of the world breaks down when the planets are described as moving by the guidance of intelligences, and when stones are described as moving towards the earth because that is their natural place of rest in the hierarchy of beings. Paradoxically, then, what Chaucer would have thought of as metaphor drawn from physics when he says of the eagle in the *Parliament of Fowls*, 'In hire was everi vertu at his reste',[16] seems to us to fit nature more closely in its transferred application to psychology. For the whole system seems today like a gigantic metaphor derived from the pattern of man's being.

Some of these cracks, as we shall see, were to appear very soon; and Aquinas stood on the verge of an intellectual and social change that was to undermine harmony and coherence.

The clerk's world

Paradox is always present in history, but the paradoxes of the fourteenth century are particularly evident. Our example from Dante and Villani is a symbol of one of these; for the idea of the hierarchically ordered society stood over and against the reality of rapid social change. Education still presupposed a unified structure of knowledge that could be systematically taught, yet, within the schools, this very system was breaking up under attack, while, outside, the clerical monopoly of learning was being challenged by an increasingly articulate and literate laity.

In 1300 formal education was still virtually a monopoly of the church, designed to serve chiefly religious ends. 'Cleric' and 'clerk' began as one word, meaning one thing. In ABC schools – where they existed – the parish priest aimed at a basic literacy to support religious teaching, while cathedral song schools were geared to the liturgical requirements of cathedral services. The foundations of this system were, as for the boys in the *Prioress's Tale*, 'to syngen and to rede'.[17] The signs of the future were already present in the beginnings of grammar schools, yet the early grammar schools were all linked with ecclesiastical institutions, and none could be started without the consent of the cathedral chancellor. In London, for instance, there were schools in connection with St Paul's and the larger parish churches. Chantry schools were scattered over the country, a new crop being founded after the Black Death. There was a grammar school in Cambridge, and in Oxford several schools appear in the fourteenth century. The most important of these developments was that of William of Wykeham in founding (1373–9) his school for ninety-six scholars, choristers and commoners at Winchester as a feeder for his foundation, New College at Oxford. The foundation of university colleges was quickly followed by a spate of collegiate churches in places as scattered as Ottery St Mary, Warwick and Stamford, each with its grammar and song school.

But a lay interest in schooling is already seen in some of the founders and benefactors of these schools, and it increases as we move into the fifteenth century. Many benefactors were noble or royal – for example, Isabel of Pembroke, who founded a collegiate church and school at Tong in Staffordshire around 1410, and Henry VI, who founded Eton in connection with King's College, Cambridge, in 1440–3. More significant is the spread of educational interest among the middle classes, seen in the development of schools connected with town guilds, such as the grammar school established at Stratford-upon-Avon by the Guild of the Holy Cross just after 1400. And a new note – almost an anticlerical one – was struck in 1432 when William Sevenoaks, a grocer of London, pro-vided in his will for 'a master, an honest man, sufficiently advanced and expert in the science of grammar and a Bachelor of Arts, but by no means in Holy Orders, to keep a grammar school in Sevenoaks and to teach and instruct all boys whatsoever coming there for learning.'[18] This secular trend is also seen in an increasing number of married schoolmasters. Moreover, townspeople wanted education to be more relevant to practical needs. In 1459 Simon Eyre, a London draper, left his fortune to promote 'the earliest attempt to endow a commercial school':[19] it proved abortive, but others followed. Grandest of lay-controlled schools was St Paul's, founded by Dean Colet in 1509, and deliberately put into the hands of the Mercers' Company because 'while there can be no absolute certainty in human affairs he found less corruption in a body of lay married men like the Mercers than in any other order or degree of mankind'.[20] Thus within our period we see the movement from an ecclesiastically oriented and controlled education to the beginnings of secular management.

But in content change was slow. In early fourteenth-century

Oxford the boys in the university grammar school had to compose verses and letters, 'not in six-foot-long words and swelling phrases, but in succinct clauses, apt metaphors, clear sentences and as far as may be, full of good sense'.[21] In his *Polychronicon* (1327) Ralph Higden complained that the corruption of the English language comes because 'boys abandoning their native tongue, are compelled to construe in French, and . . . noblemen's sons from their very cradles are taught the French idioms . . . [while others wishing to] appear more respectable, endeavour to Frenchify themselves with all their might.'[22] Thus the century begins with French well ensconced as the vernacular of cultivated people, but it was soon to be unseated. John Trevisa, who translated the *Polychronicon* into English in 1385, comments that, since Higden wrote, John Cornwall, master of the grammar school attached to Merton College at Oxford, had substituted Latin-into-English translation for the customary Latin-into-French, about the time of the Black Death (1348), and others had followed him:

> so that now . . . in all the grammar schools of England children leaveth French and construeth and learneth on English, and habbeth thereby avauntage in one side, and dis-avauntage in another. Here avauntage is that a learneth here grammar in less time than children were ywoned to do. Dis-avauntage is that now children of grammar school conneth no more French than can here left heel, and that is harm for ham and a shall pass these and travel in strange lands.[23]

There is almost a modern note in this dilemma. In the 1360s the Lord Chancellor began to open parliament with an English speech, and in 1362 a parliamentary petition urged that pleading in the law courts should be in English, since French was too little known. Parliament rolls, law yearbooks and wills continued to be written in French and Latin, but change was on the way. English rapidly gained ground as the main literary and commercial language. By the fifteenth century French was being taught as a foreign language necessary for law and trade.

But otherwise education remained traditional: it was literary to the core. William of Wykeham saw grammar as the foundation, gate and source of all the other liberal arts. Grammar (including construing and writing in prose and verse) and manners were his twin pillars of education.

Conditions in some ways seem perennial. Langland thought school to be heaven on earth,[24] but at Magdalen College School around 1500 a master laments that 'as soon as I am come into the school, this fellow goeth to make water. . . . Soon after another asketh licence that he may go drink. Another calleth upon me that he may have licence to go home'; and a boy complains that before he went to school he could lie happily between the sheets when the sun was up 'to behold the roof, the beams and the rafters of my chamber, and look on the clothes that the chamber was hanged with', but 'now at five of the clock by the moonlight I must go to my book', and 'breakfasts that were sometime brought at my bidding is driven out of country and never shall come again'.[25] The author of the vivid translation pieces from which these complaints come speaks slightingly of the new attempts by humanists, such as Dean Colet, to reform the teaching of grammar and rhetorical composition, and the selection of authors taught. But, although the 'new authors doth rebuke the noble deeds of them that ben before hem',[26] the changes they made were not great. School education was long to remain predominantly literary and Latin.

Many school foundation deeds state that anyone who comes is to be educated free; some specify 'poor scholars', some 'gentlemen's children'. Who, in fact, benefited from these foundations? In the fourteenth century it is fairly clear that the children of villeins (unfree peasants) only exceptionally benefited, for manorial court rolls still show fines for sending such children to school without the lord's licence. William of Wykeham's poor and needy scholars were mostly sons of the landed gentry, farmers and burgesses. In 1406 the Statute of Labourers stated that, while peasants were forbidden to apprentice their children unless they owned land worth more than £1 p.a., any man or woman of any estate should be free to send a son or daughter to 'learn literature', that is, Latin, in any school they pleased. This has been thought to constitute a significant advance, but Dr Orme, a recent authority on medieval education, believes it was not intended to end restrictions on villein education. In any case, it is unlikely to have made any significant difference to the literacy of the lower orders. It may, perhaps, be a pointer towards the gradual erosion of a society rightly ordered in 'estates'. We shall return to the general question of literacy.

On the literary basis of the schools 'higher education' was built. The first stage remained – theoretically at least – patterned on the traditional *trivium*, that is, grammar, rhetoric and logic (or dialectic), and *quadrivium*, arithmetic, geometry, music and astronomy. After this bachelor's degree in the seven liberal arts, the master's course expanded into areas of philosophy and theology, while the three doctorates were in law, medicine and theology. Dante well represents the unified structure of knowledge when he likens these various stages to the hierarchy of the heavens: the seven liberal arts are the heavens of the planets, the natural and metaphysical philosophies correspond to the heaven of the fixed stars, ethics belongs to the heaven of the Primum Mobile, and theology to the empyrean, the still centre of the universe.

It is strange that in the later Middle Ages, when universities were proliferating in western Europe and Scotland produced three, no new universities were founded in England. Oxford and Cambridge held the monopoly. From an intellectual point of view the relative autonomy of both was a vital factor. Whereas Paris University was closely under the control of the cathedral chancellor, Oxford – far from the bishop's seat in the vast diocese of Lincoln – had escaped from this supervision in the thirteenth century, while Cambridge was also not an episcopal seat. The internal structure of these universities evolved in a way that buttressed a position of autonomy and privilege. The fourteenth century is famous for the bitter disputes between town and gown in Oxford – that is, between laity and clerks. The university always won because it was supported by the crown, and steadily its privileges and immunities, as against the townsmen, were built up. Tension reached a climax in the famous riots on St Scholastica's Day in 1355, from which the university emerged with increased jurisdictional powers which in many ways put the town at its mercy. Though violence was never far away, the privileged scholar-clerks could live within a circle of immunity that marked them off decisively from the lay community. From the other side, the hierarchy of the church left them free to pursue the burning intellectual issues of the fourteenth century until, in the 1380s, Wyclif and his disciples overstepped the bounds of orthodoxy and the university was made sharply aware that its intellectual autonomy could never be absolute.

Oxford was the centre of tremendous controversy in philosophy and theology throughout the fourteenth century, but, together with Cambridge, it was also the place where the succession of those 'duly qualified for the service of God in Church and State'[27] was trained.

One of the most distinctive educational ideas in the medieval English university was that of the hall, or later college, arising in the first instance out of practical needs but becoming a society that exercised some discipline over boisterous undergraduates and sometimes produced brilliant circles of academic discussion. Residence together became a feature of university education. From Oxford and Cambridge went forth those who serviced the realm and staffed the church as administrators, lawyers and diplomats, judges and political advisers. Though much of the curriculum appears quite irrelevant to such vocations, the universities were professional schools. Abstract intellectual enquiry and career preparation were interlocked, since the leading thinkers held teaching roles: a great master would not wrestle with problems purely for the satisfaction of his own mind, but also because he had a duty to the generation that must be taught.

The strength of this tradition of inherited learning was astonishing. The literary education inherited from classical times embodied the knowledge felt to be necessary for a civilized society. Knowledge was not something to be found out *de novo*: it was an inherited corpus to be handed on. Unless it was fully and faithfully passed on, society would be in danger of reverting to barbarism. Education, therefore, was the understanding of an inheritance, and the search for truth was largely seen as the comprehension of texts. Though, as we shall see, advance in scientific thinking marked the English university in the fourteenth century, 'research' in the modern sense of increasing knowledge by direct observation and experiment was largely lacking, and the idea that investigation could lead to discoveries with a technical application was, we think, absent. Technical advances were made by people who used their hands to construct things, and learning was divorced from the manual arts. This is clearly seen in the distinction between medicine, a traditional university subject studied mainly through the classical texts of Galen and Hippocrates, and surgery, which was still a clumsy craft.

But however firmly the view was entrenched that civilization meant the understanding of an inheritance, a changing society was beginning to demand more professional training. A flourishing school of business studies, including letter writing and accountancy, developed in Oxford in the later Middle Ages, but, significantly, it was not part of the university. Again, the development of the law schools in London points up the failure of Oxford and Cambridge universities, wedded to Roman civil and canon law and excluding the study of common law, to respond to new needs in society. The growing demand for common lawyers is evident not only in the needs of government but in the increasing litigiousness of a period when property was changing hands more quickly, trade was posing new legal problems, and old sanctions and forms of medieval life were dissolving. In 1340 Edward III appointed the first lay chancellor, and only a few years later the Temple was leased to professors and students of law who migrated from an already established inn at Holborn. Within ten years the four great inns of court and their cluster of contributory hostels had formed what was in essence the first lay institution of higher education in England. More aristocratic than the universities because the fees were high, it attracted upper- and middle-class families because it provided them with the one professional skill (apart from fighting) that they most needed.

A parallel development took place in medicine. John Arderne, the first great English surgeon, gained his experience on fourteenth-century battlefields and in private practice. His works, though widely circulated, owed nothing to an academic background. A new consciousness of importance led the master surgeons to form a guild in 1386, but they never sought a university context. About 1421, allied momentarily with the physicians, they petitioned the king for professional recognition and the right to have a teaching centre in London. In the end it was with the barbers that the surgeons united in the Company of Barber-Surgeons, set up in 1540 with a monopoly of practice and teaching. As with law, we see here a striking example of a profession brought to a new status by the independent initiative of its lay members. Clerical monopoly and traditional learning were being challenged.

Again, for all the highly traditional matrix of the universities, there was a remarkable breakthrough in thought among fourteenth-century academics. The intellectual structure of the late thirteenth century had begun to disintegrate almost as soon as it was built. Gordon Leff sees a parallel here between intellectual and social change: 'There is a growing distrust of an ordered hierarchy between the tenets of revelation and rational demonstration at a time of mounting discontent with a fixed social order.'[28] The synthesis that Aquinas had attempted between Aristotelian cosmology and Christian revelation produced a reaction against what was felt to be an implicit determinism. God could not be tied down to a description in terms of first cause. There was a swing over to a new emphasis on God's infinite freedom of action which denied that we can define by reason constant modes of divine operation, since this attempt infringed God's absolute sovereignty. St Thomas had distinguished between faith and reason, yet seen them as a continuum, but now a divide appeared. There was no meeting-place between reason and faith, the natural order and the supernatural. On the one hand, this freed the reason to study the natural order more experimentally, uninhibited by metaphysical assumptions. On the other hand, in emphasizing the indeterminism of the supernatural order, the impossibility of knowing God at the natural level, the door was opened to mystical, non-rational approaches.

The two thinkers who, above all, were responsible for this revolutionary change in intellectual atmosphere were Duns Scotus and William Ockham. Yet in many ways they stood opposed to each other. Duns Scotus, who died in 1308, embodied the Augustinian revolt against the attempt to bring God into relationship with the physical universe through the Aristotelian concept of first cause. Towards the end of the thirteenth century a group of thinkers went back to the traditional Augustinian view that God's self-revelation came through immediate personal illumination rather than through sensory experience or analogies from the created world. It was impossible to work back from observable effects in the natural order to causes, and finally to a first cause in the supernatural order, for – recalling the Platonic element in Augustinian thought – the ideas that existed in the supernatural order were prior to, and more real than, their objects or effects accessible to the sense in the natural realm. Thus real knowledge was possible only through ideas implanted in the soul by God. Duns Scotus took this general hostility to the Aristotelian thinking used by St Thomas much further. Since it was impossible to reach a cause through its effects, human reason could hardly establish a relationship between the created world and its creator. God was infinitely free: his ways were incalculable. One had to postulate a complete distinction between theological and scientific knowledge and limit the action of human reason to the latter. Yet Duns did his best not to step outside the accepted framework of metaphysics. He still believed that by reason one could arrive at general propositions about existence and made a last great effort to adapt the realist tradition to the new sense of God.

Ockham, who died in 1349, took the radical dissociation between theology and metaphysics, between divine and human knowledge, to its limit. In commenting on the *Sentences* of Peter Lombard, one of the traditional university textbooks, he made the new division between faith and reason quite explicit: revealed truth, which was outside sensory experience, was not accessible to the methods of reason because it could not be verified; it could be 'known' only by divine illumination. This cut at the heart of the scholastic method of the previous century, to which the belief that by reason the mind could rise through the hierarchy of knowledge until it was enabled to mount the last step by faith to revealed truth had been fundamental. Now whole tracts of academic thought in the physical sciences, in logic, in philosophy, were cut loose from the guidance of revelation. Not only was the Christian–Aristotelian synthesis of Aquinas under attack, but Augustinian Neoplatonism was also criticized for confounding God and man in a single metaphysical system. A totally new intellectual atmosphere was engendered. Knowledge, deprived of an ordered hierarchy or framework, was fragmented, questions were discussed piecemeal and reduced to the scope of practical experience, and the focus intensified on logic and on the precise ordering of concepts, rather than on metaphysical systems.

This new atmosphere was disturbing, but also exciting. Problems in natural knowledge could be pursued with uninhibited questioning. Here the English scientists could reap the fruits of pioneer work in Oxford in the thirteenth century of Grosseteste, Roger Bacon and others. They took from Grosseteste the method of verification by experiment, though their work remained mainly theoretical, and there was a great quickening of interest in mathematics, physics and astronomy, now freed from theological implications. Jean Buridan at Paris, Walter Burley and Thomas Bradwardine at Oxford, although not Ockhamist in their theology, represented the new scientific advances.

Bradwardine began something very like a scientific revolution with his *Treatise on Proportions* (1328) by mathematizing the notion of motion through space. This seems familiar enough today; but Aristotle had treated motion through space purely as a kind of change. As with all change, he thought, everything that is moved must be moved by something else for as long as motion continues; and motion had to be proportional to the force of what was causing it, although it would be inversely proportional to the resistance of any medium through which the moving thing passed. By natural motion, as we have seen, a thing proceeded to its goal, as a stone does to its natural place the earth, or as a heavenly body does, which must be guided by a living principle, which the Middle Ages called an 'intelligence'. Unnatural motion needed constant interference by some outside agent. If a stone continues to move about the earth after it leaves the hand that has thrown it, then this must be because the air is pushing it as an intermediate agent.

There are many ways in which this is an unsatisfactory account of motion, notably in its dealing with acceleration and the varying speed of a body; but it is hard to discuss them until a mathematical account of speed is given. However, that involves treating speed as a ratio between space and time – that is, treating space and time as commensurable in a way highly unnatural to Aristotelian philosophy. Now Bradwardine did treat speed quantitatively. Moreover, he generalized this so far as to declare that it is mathematics 'which reveals every genuine truth', and even when he plunged into the controversy about the relation between God and man he sought to establish his argument by mathematical proof. His followers at Merton College, especially William Heytesbury, made further discoveries in dynamics on which Galileo was to build: some of them, in particular John Dumbleton, attempted to extend mathematical method by assigning numerical values to such qualities as truth, faith and perfection. Jean Buridan, in Paris but still under Bradwardine's influence, denied Aristotle's belief that motion requires the continued action of a mover, by substituting the notion of impetus, and realized that this might imply a mechanical universe:

> One does not find in the Bible that there are Intelligences charged to communicate to the celestial spheres their proper motions: it is permissible then to show that it is not necessary to suppose the existence of such Intelligences. One could say, in fact, that God, when he created the universe, set each of the celestial spheres in motion as it pleased him impressing on each of them an impetus which has moved it ever since. God has therefore no longer to move these spheres, except in exerting a general influence similar to that by which he gives his concurrence to all phenomena. Thus he could rest on the seventh day from

the work he had achieved, confiding to created things their mutual causes and effects.[29]

It is the mechanical model that Buridan is putting forward as a daring speculation, the personal that he takes for granted: it suggests that his contemporary, Chaucer, although he will not have meant a literal truth in his portrayals in the *Knight's Tale* of Mars, Venus and Saturn, will there, and in his usual identification of the pagan gods with the planetary powers or astrology, have had in mind literal realities behind his fictions quite different from, and much more personal than, those we assume. But already in Chaucer's lifetime the whole Aristotelian universe of value, of a hierarchy of perfection, of space and time conceived relatively, of a first mover – first not by having been a beginner in time but by being at every moment the primal source of change – is endangered; and a quantitative, mechanical, Newtonian universe extended in absolute space and time can be, if only distantly, intuited.

On the other side of the division between religion and science, the way in which the inaccessible God impinged on man was the subject of burning controversy. Questioning, even scepticism, was freely indulged in at the natural level, but, at the supernatural, authority was absolute. What, then, was the relation of divine will to man's will? Since unity between God and his creatures could no longer be assumed, they had to be reconciled by new efforts of thought. For Ockham, God's absolute freedom made him utterly unpredictable. He could not be bound by any rules or known by any process of ratiocination. There was an absolute hiatus between intuitive knowledge of God by revelation and processes of rational deduction. Ockham rejected Aristotle's metaphysics completely, denying that universals had any existence outside the mind and holding that human knowledge began with experience of particular entities. The singularity of the real was one of his basic assumptions. Concepts such as motion, time and place had no separate existence; they were only words. Here Ockham was certainly a 'nominalist', as opposed to the 'realists', but the fourteenth-century intellectual conflict was far wider than the nominalist–realist controversy. The omnipotence and authority of God were to Ockham unquestionable; none the less, since God was unknowable by human effort, Ockham virtually shut him out of his universe.

Against this position Bradwardine reacted violently in his *De Causa Dei* of 1344. In some ways he stood on the same ground as the Ockhamists. Both refused to argue from the created to the creator, or to attempt the description of God in terms of reason. Both agreed that the only point of contact between God and man lay in the action of God's will. But when the Ockhamists pushed God out of their system on the grounds that he is unverifiable and unknowable, Bradwardine accused them of being the new Pelagians, of making man the centre of attention and assuming his self-sufficiency within the natural order. Bradwardine begins *De Causa Dei* by describing his own experience in the schools, where he revolted against the emphasis on man's mastery over his own free acts. This assertion of man's free will denied God's omnipotence. Against it Bradwardine set up the grace of God, denying any merit to the creature. God is the immediate cause of all men's actions: the whole world is an extension of God's will; it interpenetrates all activities in the natural order. Because God cannot permit without acting, argues Bradwardine, he is included in every human action, which cannot be autonomous in any sense.

Thus the issues that beat so fiercely through fourteenth-century minds concerned, not broad speculative problems such as the nature of the godhead, but precise questions about God's will and activity in relation to man's. Bradwardine tackled this crucial issue in the same style as his opponents, by a narrow concentration on a tightly reasoned argument advanced with an almost mathematical sequence of propositions and proofs. The so-called Pelagians on the other side – Ockham himself and men such as Robert Holcot and Thomas Buckingham – fought with equal seriousness for a position that was vital to them. Ockham's theory of knowledge, which denied an independent reality to anything not perceived by the senses, placed a barrier between practical knowledge and the realm of the super-sensory. Beyond the barrier was the *potentia absoluta* of the godhead, outside time and space, and not immediately active in sustaining the universe. No chain of cause and effect could be established between God and his creatures, for God was conceived in terms of infinite possibility rather than intelligible order. In Leff's words, 'His attributes dissolved before the blaze of His glory.'[30] If this concept freed God from the limits of human reason, it also freed reason from the domination of theology. Thus the sceptics used an absolute beyond reason as a means of asserting the autonomy of reason.

Unlike modern sceptics, these never doubted God's existence and sovereignty. Their dispute with Bradwardine was over man's freedom. Against their assumption of virtual independence for man's rational activity, Bradwardine reasserted the complete subjection of man to God. This was no logic-chopping scholasticism: it was a real and urgent dispute which split faith and reason apart like a hatchet cleaving wood, destroying the whole basis of metaphysics as a mode of establishing contact between the divine and the created. It was the end of the traditional scholastic framework, yet this turbulent area of thought was still contained within the shores of the academic system. The curriculum retained its accustomed structure; methods of lecturing and disputing remained traditional; scholars proceeded up the established ladder. 'The effect on scholasticism was to polarize form and content; the disputations in the schools became largely divorced from the substance of knowledge.'[31]

This intellectual ferment had repercussions far beyond the schools. Ockham complained that laymen and old women used to badger university lecturers on questions such as necessity and the limits of God's power. The controversy is reflected in *Pearl*, the poem of around 1350–1400 whose core of some 300 lines is an argument on the reality of divine grace. As we shall see, the swing towards mysticism was the obverse side of the coin whose reverse was the new scepticism about the knowability of God in rational terms. The academic doctrines of divine omnipotence and unpredictability became for the mystic the inner, individual search for the ineffable. It is true that the mystic, in rejecting the external world, moved far from the Ockhamist interest in studying the natural world on its own terms, but both had the effect of separating the realm of sensory experience from that of faith. At Oxford itself, in the 1360s, Wyclif joined the argument, casting into the academic pool extreme views whose consequences spread outwards like ripples from a stone.

Wyclif reacted violently against the nominalism of the Ockhamists. As an extreme realist, he postulated the self-subsistence of universal concepts, endowing every being with an essence that existed eternally in its archetype. This – the *esse intelligibile* – was located in God. Thus he reaffirmed a chain of being from the archetype in God to the individual in the material world. Clearly Wyclif had returned to a Platonic metaphysic in strong reaction against the intellectual revolution of his contemporaries. In the obstinacy with which he stuck to his position, he was probably not a match for some of his opponents, but the importance of his metaphysical view lies in the fact that from it he derived the views on the Bible and the sacraments, the church and the state, which stirred up the Lollard protest. The Bible was sovereign and timeless. Its literal words embodied unchanging truth, for 'God and his word is all one and they may not be separated'; 'Not to know Scripture is not to know Christ, since Christ is the Scripture we ought to know.'[32] Nothing could be added to it or subtracted from it; it was the touchstone of all knowledge. Reason could be used in elucidating its meaning, but the approach must be from metaphysical assumptions – the eternal meaning God had implanted in it. To understand biblical truth an awareness of the nature of being was more important than a logical study of verbal consistency. Wyclif's view of the church was closely bound in the same system of thought. The eternal reality of the archetypal church led to an absolute separation of the elect from the damned. The only true church was that of the saved, bound together by predestined election, not to be recognized physically but present wherever the elect were. Equally absolute was the body of the damned, the congregation of Antichrist. Since men remain totally ignorant of whether they are elected or damned, the visible church has no reality in truth. This was one of Wyclif's most disruptive doctrines, for it struck at the root of authority in the visible, institutional church: institutions, religious practices, offices, could all be questioned, for Wyclif looked beyond the existing hierarchy to the unchanging source of authority in the realm of eternal verities. The word of God in the Bible was the only certain guide by which all doctrines and practices should be judged. The onus of understanding its message was laid on the individual, who by a combination of faith and reason – not denying the support of the church fathers – could reach that inner conviction which was his responsibility to attain. He was to be his own theologian, to the exclusion of the institutional church as a mediating body. God's word 'constituted the *sensus catholicus* in contradistinction to the visible church'.[33] The consequence of this position was, of course, to exalt the preaching of the word and to play down the importance of the sacraments. On the position of the priest Wyclif was ambivalent, never wholly denying his authority, yet denouncing the sinful priest as devoid of power. The layman who was a member of the true church could exercise priestly powers, but who knew his position?

Wyclif's theology led him straight to a rejection of the ecclesiastical hierarchy. The word of God spelled material poverty and spiritual humility. He therefore increasingly attacked the wealth, civil power and pride of the contemporary church. In the primitive church, which was his model, there had been no popes, hierarchy or juris-dictional rights. Finally, he called for disendowment of the church, and rejected popes, cardinals and bishops on the authority of Scripture. The implication was that the whole visible church had virtually lost its purpose. This rejection is crystallized in one of Wyclif's later works, *De Potestate Pape* (written in 1379 or 1380), where he did not, however, wholly dismiss the papal office, but argued that the contemporary holders of this and other ecclesiastical offices were obviously not chosen of God and therefore not true holders. In the last analysis he virtually identified the papacy and the hierarchy with Antichrist, calling for their overthrow. The Bible alone was the standard of truth, and power not founded on the Bible was that of Antichrist. To manifest again the true church, civic powers must expropriate the church and destroy its jurisdictional powers. In *De Civili Dominio* and *De Officio Regis* he expounded the role of the secular authority, exalting the king into a vicar of God. The power that Wyclif denied to the church he handed to the secular ruler whose position, under God, demanded universal sub-mission from clergy and laity alike. Finally, in his teaching on the Eucharist, starting from the metaphysical position of a realist that there is no attribute (accident) without a substance and that substances are indestructible, he substituted for the orthodox doctrine of transubstantiation the postulate that the bread and wine continued to coexist with the body and blood of Christ whose presence made the sacrament. Wyclif did not attempt to explain how this miracle happened: it was a spiritual coming and presence of Christ. The significant point was that the role of the priest was diminished: his words of consecration no longer performed a change from bread and wine into Christ's body and blood. Rather they were a recognition of Christ's coming which was independent of human agency or physical change.

Wyclif was a scholastic drawing conclusions from metaphysical and theological principles. But he was also a passionate reformer, deeply moved by the evils of the contemporary scene. Academic reasoning and living experience fused in a system of thought which, for all its philosophical refinements, ultimately made an impact on his contemporaries in terms of two almost simple propositions: the sovereignty of the Bible as interpreted by the individual Christian and the rejection of the existing ecclesiastical hierarchy. This was a new and vital element in the outlook of a country that had produced no heresiarch since Pelagius and only a handful of heretics. We must return to the consequences later.

There was no complete gulf between the intellectual preoccupations of the academic clerisy and the interests of the laity. One of the notable developments of this period was the interaction between the thoughts of clerks and of laymen who were educated or half-educated. Chaucer himself forms a good 'bridge' example. We know nothing about his formal education, but he probably went to a London grammar school. A list of books left in 1358 by a schoolmaster of St Paul's Almonry School closely parallels a hypothetical list of books that Chaucer would seem, from internal evidence, to have read in his youth. But he was soon receiving another sort of education, as a page in the household of the Duke of Clarence, whence, probably after studying at the Temple, he passed to the service of John of Gaunt and King Edward III. Here he learnt the accomplishments of a courtier, was introduced to courtly literature, and began to translate and write poems for himself. For translating he turned to that great model of courtly love poetry, the *Roman de la Rose*. He had acquired Latin, as well as the obvious French. By about 1370 he had read Virgil and Ovid, the medieval Alain de Lille's *De Planctu Naturae* and other Latin works. In the following years, sent on various missions to France and Italy, he widened his literary experiences, learning Italian and discovering the works of Dante, Petrarch and Boccaccio. But alongside this education through the life and literature of the court and of the early Italian Renaissance there must also have been contact with philosophers and scholastic thought. Those burning debates on free will and determinism reached Chaucer as well as the author of *Pearl*. They are reflected in the *Nun's Priest's Tale* and in *Troilus and Criseyde*. Thoughtful laymen in Chaucer's day were interested in this great debate, much as in this century they have been in dialectical materialism.

The layman's philosopher was still the ancient Boethius. One of the striking features of medieval thought is the influence exercised by Boethius, particularly over laymen. The story of this Roman senator, struck down by a suspicious barbarian king and, while awaiting execution, extolling the power of the human spirit to triumph over all misfortune, had inspired many medieval minds. Chaucer also fell under its spell, translating it and constantly making use of its ideas on *fortuna*, on nobility, on the role of Lady Philosophy in strengthening the human will to bear the buffets of fate. Boethius' message – that men can achieve tranquillity in any situation since they are endowed with reason and choice – struck home in a restless, unstable world. His 'consolation' was more stoic than Christian, and it is significant that he should still have been revered by moderate men in an age that witnessed a flight into determinist thought on the one hand, and into mystical experience on the other.

Chaucer also acquired knowledge on the natural sciences of his time. In *Troilus and Criseyde*, the *Knight's Tale* and the *Man of Law's Tale* his Boethian dealings with fate and free will merge with his interest in astrology and the possible influences of the stars. But he always seems to have thought astrology a dangerous pursuit: the most natural way of reading the *Knight's Tale* contrasts the disasters that follow Arcite's attempt to manipulate the influences of the stars with Theseus' Boethian advice to recognize both the power of fate and its subservience to the will of God, and so to rise above it. Chaucer even wrote a technical *Treatise on the Astrolabe*: it has been plausibly conjectured that it represents a turning away from predictive astrology, in which, he says, 'my spirit hath no faith'. In another later story, the *Canon's Yeoman's Prologue and Tale*, he mocks alchemy. The sciences he most makes use of are the psychological ones, physiognomy and the doctrine of the humours, which offer him the same possibilities of quick character drawing as Freudianism did for W. H. Auden. Wonder at the natural world is often expressed in his works – as, for example, that it is 'Wonder to maken of fern-asshen glass'.[34] This is common in writers of his time – such as Langland or the *Gawain* poet – but their wonder does not take a scientific form: in this Chaucer may be less typical than they of the ordinary literate person.

But how widely spread was literacy? One can do little more than collect examples. For the early fourteenth century Miss Smalley cites a knight, Sir Thomas de la Mare, who could write a report in French of the proceedings when a deputation demanded Edward II's abdication in 1327. In 1330 we have the first evidence that a king could write in a letter of Edward III to the Pope, while proofs of royal literacy grow fuller with Richard II and the Lancastrian kings.

By mid-century we meet the first chronicle written by an English layman, the Latin *Scalacronica* of the Northumbrian Sir Thomas Gray of Heaton, who was inspired to write it by reading Latin, French and English chronicles while imprisoned by the Scots. Knights had to be literate to undertake all the business of local government, able to use French and English at least, in a society where 'illiterate' was coming to mean lack of Latin. As for the nobles, many in the fourteenth and fifteenth centuries were semi-professional soldiers who found that the business both of soldiering and of estate management demanded some literacy. But the court of Edward III, and still more that of Richard II, was a centre of culture, and many nobles went far beyond the minimum of literacy. Two of Edward III's sons were authors; Henry of Grosmont, first Duke of Lancaster (1310–61), wrote a remarkable book of devotion; John Montagu, Earl of Salisbury, was also an author; while Henry of Derby (later Henry IV) composed music. Among Chaucer's friends was Sir John Clanvowe, one of Richard II's knights, who probably wrote the love poem *The Cuckoo and the Nightingale* as well as a devotional tract, *The Two Ways*.

Picture books were always needed in the households of the provincial nobility and gentry. Of these the only outstanding example is the Holkham Bible Picture Book of *c.* 1326–31, with its patterning and interpretation of biblical events, and possible reminiscences of contemporary drama and contemporary affairs, probably 'intended for a comfortable and educated but not high-brow audience of laymen and ladies'.[35] The private chapels of great nobles were equipped with missals, psalters and books of hours, of which we shall see more when we deal with art. What is notable is the evidence for private, individual devotions expressed in special prayers and liturgical additions.[36] The sumptuous books of hours were not just picture books: the taste of the owner often seems to dictate the selection of contents. In the Bohun family the last Earl of Hereford had his own additions in his psalter, while his daughter Mary, Countess of Derby, introduced a more intimate note into the prayers she chose for herself, revealing the influence of the mystic Richard Rolle. Rolle's English works circulated among nobility and gentry: Sir William Beauchamp had some, and the collection in the Tanfield manuscript belonged to Lord Fitzhugh. Evidence of books possessed by laymen comes mainly from wills. Some had quite large libraries: Thomas of Gloucester had eighty-three books, and Sir

Simon Burley nineteen. Not all books owned would necessarily appear in wills; and it must be remembered that a 'book' might often be a collection of works bound together, including romances, practical treatises and lyrics, and forming a little library on its own. Most lyrics that survive come from apparently personal compilations, above all, MS Harley 2253 of *c.* 1330–40. History and myth were also popular among lay readers, and we shall return to them.

The swing from French to English books was gradual. Robert Mannynge of Bourne, Lincolnshire, translated William of Wadington's *Manuel des pechiez* into English as *Handlyng Sinne* in 1303. Henry of Grosmont chose French for his *Livre de Seyntz Medicines*, but apologized for it, since he was an Englishman. Humphrey de Bohun (d. 1361) seems to have commissioned the translation of *William de Palerne* from French into English alliterative verse for the benefit of his household, and Elizabeth Salter has associated the whole alliterative revival with a group of magnates – Bohuns, Beauchamps and others – who were patrons of literature. T. Turville-Petre, however, argues for rather lesser gentry as the patrons of alliterative poetry: *Winner and Waster* (1352) and *Mum and the Sothsegger* (*c.* 1400) mark political self-expression in this style. Richard II's mother tongue was probably English, and he patronized Chaucer and Gower. At the foot of the reading scale, the *Lay Folks' Mass Book* was already in English around 1300, instructing in behaviour and devotion at mass, and during the fourteenth century there were various translations of works on moral advice to the laity.

The turn of the century must have marked a noticeable advance in literacy since, as Miss Deanesley has observed, between *c.* 1390 and 1415 papal and episcopal registers are speaking of a new class of 'literate laymen', a phrase found neither earlier nor later. We may fairly date the emergence of a general reading public from John Shirley's anthologies and lending library (*c.* 1420–50) in London. The fifteenth century sees the library of Humphrey, Duke of Gloucester (d. 1461) – some 500 books – and his patronage of Lydgate and others: a deliberate attempt to enrich English letters. There is a vast increase in the production of literature of various kinds. The seven poetical works of which more than fifty manuscripts survive make a striking balance of attention to health spiritual and physical, entertainment, devotion and the quest for perfection. They are *The Prick of Conscience*, the *Canterbury Tales*,

Lydgate's *Dietary*, *Piers Plowman*, a verse prayer to Mary, the *South English Legendary* of the saints, and Gower's *Confessio Amantis*.[37] The century is, of course, also the source of the first surviving collections of private letters, the Paston, Stonor and Cely letters. Among the Paston Letters, Professor Davis has shown that the men write their own, the women employ secretaries – even in the two touching valentines of Margery Brews in 1477 to her husband-to-be John Paston. The style is often stiff, as befitting a new art, yet not always: among the Stonor Letters we have Thomas Betson's letter to his child bride-to-be, irresistibly recalling Lewis Carroll.

By 1533, Sir Thomas More observes that more than four-tenths of the people of England 'could never read English yet'[38] – implying presumably that over half could.

The knight's world

'The clerk prays, the knight fights . . .' With all their piety and growth in intellectual interests, soldiering remained a major vocation for the nobility and many of the knightly class; and war rumbled in the distance or broke in direct storm continuously through our period until 1485. Its concepts and rules dominated their minds and moulded their attitudes. To understand those attitudes we have to grasp the fact that, though embryonic nation-states were just emerging, Christendom as one society was still a living idea. The profession of a knight was to defend the right and put down injustice within the borders of Christendom and to destroy its pagan enemies outside. Soldiering was a Christian profession and a highly honourable one, for 'arms ennoble a man whoever he may be'.[39] This rested on the assumption that all legitimate fighting was against evil in some form. The only true war was one which, in the eyes of the combatants, was a just war, whose object was the restoration of harmony, destroyed by some act of aggression or cupidity. The unjust war, Isidore of Seville had said, was that which resulted from passion, not reason. It was, said Augustine, no more than robbery or brigandage on a grand scale, whereas, 'for those who really follow God, wars may themselves be peaceful, since they are not fought out of a desire for gain or cruelty, but out of a longing for peace, so as to correct the wicked and relieve the good'.[40] For Christine de Pisan, whose *Le Livre des faits d'armes et de chevalerie* (1408–9) was a textbook of knighthood at this time, 'The holy scripture saith of God that he is fierce and governor of hosts and battles. And war and battle which is made by just quarrel is none other thing but right execution of justice.'[41] The satisfaction of being able to marry a sense of righteousness to warlike instincts is eloquently conveyed in Jean de Bueil's *Le Jouvencel*, where the hero at a merrymaking extols war thus:

> What a gratifying thing war is, for many are the splendid things heard and seen in the course of it. . . . And I believe that God favours those who risk their bodies by their willingness to make war to bring the wicked . . . and all who act against true equity, to justice. . . . When one feels that one's cause is just and one's blood is ready for the fight, tears come to the eye. A warm feeling of loyalty and pity comes into the heart on seeing one's friend expose his body, with such courage to . . . accomplish the will of our Creator; and one makes up one's mind to go and die or live with him, and, out of love, not to abandon him. No man who has not experienced it knows how to speak of the satisfaction which comes from this sort of action. . . . I think that he who serves in arms in this way as the true agent of God is equally blessed both in this world and the next.[42]

Whatever motives of cupidity or aggression lay underneath, no medieval lord would go to war without some kind of 'legal' claim, real or trumped up, in the name of which he would seek justice. Ideally, fighting was righteousness in action and therefore, for the knightly caste, it was governed by a code built up over the centuries and recognized as a law of arms, applicable anywhere in Christendom and enforceable in any military court. It concerned allegiances, keeping of oaths, conduct in battle, treatment of prisoners, ransoms, and so on, and presupposed a web of personal attachments; for the military man was bound in a series of solemn relationships, with a vocation to uphold his obligations by individual exploits. Thus the knight himself was often less concerned with the justice of the war as a whole than with his own 'just' fulfilment of chivalric duty, which would earn the salvation of his soul if he died in battle. There were two curious consequences of this outlook: the outcome of the contest often mattered less to those who appraised it than whether it was fought in true chivalric style, and mass fighting – increasingly important in actuality – gained less attention than acts of individual daring.

Because the realities of battle, devastation, siege and sack in the Hundred Years War were so brutal, some historians have written off the chivalric code as by this time a mere posturing, providing occasion for lavish display but exercising no real influence on the actualities of war. Certainly the professional soldier's code appears simpler than the idealized image held up by either clergy or romancers, but rules of conduct are still recognizable, if we remember that attitudes could be held together which would be regarded as quite incompatible today, because the underlying assumptions were different. The pursuit of honour could be accompanied by horrifying slaughter, and gallantry in battle with an avid grasp at ransoms. Above all, the code of chivalry applied only to the élite within the charmed circle: the lower orders were excluded alike from its duty and its mercy. When in 1370 the Black Prince, in a fury at the disloyalty of its bishop, put all the inhabitants of Limoges to the sword, the common mass who expiated the crime of their lord were outside any pity. The English lords could ride un-moved through women and children begging for their lives, but John of Gaunt had to grant life to three gallant French knights who surrendered to him under 'the law of arms'. At the sack of Caen in 1346 nobles rode about trying to save 'those worthy to be saved'.[43] The two opening lines of *Gawain and the Green Knight* contrast the two worlds:

> Sithen the sege and the assaut was sesed at Troy,
> The borg brittened and brent to brondes and askes.

Sithen] After   *The borg . . . askes*] The town destroyed and burnt to charcoal and ashes

In the first line the stressed words 'siege', 'assault' and 'ceased' are Norman French and the whole line suggests the chivalric, aristo-cratic, mythic world; in the second, every word is Old English with an overlay of Norse: does it not suggest the bitter underside of war?

Honour permitted the ruthless treatment of those outside the code, but it could force a commander to act against the interests of his cause, as when the Black Prince released the great French general Du Guesclin, who was soon to be his undoing: Froissart comments admiringly that Edward was 'always a wise and loyal knight'.

The pattern heroes of chivalry revealed its paradoxes. The Black Prince was acclaimed internationally as the 'flower of earthly chivalry', one who always fought by the chivalric principles. Yet his ferocity was famous. Gower celebrates it in his *Vox Clamantis*: 'his sword was often drunk with the blood of his enemies. . . . His sword point refused to go back into the sheath dry. . . . His broadsword was unwilling to drowse within the scabbard, it disgorged itself out of its mouth.' As John Barnie says, 'The ultimate vindication of honour lies in physical violence.'[44]

Compare this with Henry of Grosmont who, a generation before the Black Prince, was likewise regarded as a model of Christian chivalry: young knights flocked to his standard. He fought as a crusader for the faith on the frontiers of Christendom; he was famed for his prowess and largesse; he delighted in sensual pleasures, in the splendid style, in the powers of an aristocrat, while his acts of charity lived alongside the occasions of ruthlessness permitted by the laws of war. Yet a deep ascetic strain led Henry in late life (1354) to a searching self-analysis in his *Livre de Seyntz Medicines*, where he classifies his transgressions under the Seven Deadly Sins. Here a gulf opens between the standards of worldly chivalry and the ideals of a perfect Christian knight. Sir John Clanvowe, Chaucer's friend, followed the same course in his *Two Ways*, and although such hypersensitivity may not have been common it is striking that Henry was acclaimed as a model as much for his deep piety as for his conventional knightly deeds. Chaucer's knight (who seems to have overgone Henry in fighting *only* against the heathen) is of the same pattern: the sieges and battles in which he engaged were bloody, but this serves only to underline the paradox of the code even in its most Christian followers.

Froissart's life and chronicles reflect this code – its internationalism, for instance. He was born at Valenciennes in 1337 and one of his first patrons, who suggested the idea of the chronicle to him, was Robert of Namur. Yet at an early stage we find him at the English court of Edward III, with a particular attachment to the queen, Philippa of Hainault, also a native of Valenciennes. In the early years of the Hundred Years War he moved between France and England, getting eye-witness accounts of battles, sieges and deeds of valour. It is often difficult to see where his loyalty lay, for all deeds of honour were recorded with equal admiration. It was the way the game was played rather than its outcome that was of chief significance to Froissart. When he assessed battles by the code, Poitiers (1356) was judged superior to Crécy (1346) on four counts: first,

Crécy was fought in the evening 'without order', whereas Poitiers was a morning action and well conducted; secondly, better feats of arms were performed at Poitiers, so that fewer great men were killed; thirdly, those who fought at Poitiers acquitted themselves loyally, so that it was no dishonour to have fought there; fourthly, unlike his father at Crécy, King John of France did not flee the field but fought alongside his knights to the end. The famous scene after Poitiers in which the Black Prince entertains his prisoner, King John, is as important as the victory itself, and the words in which Froissart makes his prince address the disconsolate king display the code splendidly:

> Sir, for God's sake make none evil nor heavy cheer, though God this day did not consent to follow your will; for, sir, surely the king my father shall bear you as much honour and amity as he may do, and shall accord with you so reasonably that ye shall ever be friends together after. And sir, methink ye ought to rejoice, though the journée be not as ye would have had it, for this day ye have won the high renown of prowess and have passed this day in valiantness all other of your party. Sir, I say not this to mock you, for all that be on our party, that saw every man's deeds, are plainly accorded by true sentence to give you the prize and chaplet.[45]

Again, the individualism of combat stands out. Froissart admits that the massed archers played a decisive part in winning Crécy, but his tale is all of personal exploits, even when they are tangential to the main course of the war. The sally out of besieged Hennebaut by Sir Walter Manny and his friends is typical. They had a great desire to destroy a particular siege engine which was harassing the castle. So they dashed out, destroyed the engine and burnt many enemy tents. As they withdrew, the enemy came galloping after them like madmen. Then Sir Walter said: 'Let me never be beloved with my lady, without I have a course with one of these followers.' Then 'there might well a been seen on both parties many noble deeds, taking and rescuing.' When the gallant band returned, 'the countess descended down from the castle with a glad cheer and came and kissed [Sir Walter Manny] and his companions one after another two or three times, like a valiant lady.'[46]

With admiration for style in fighting went response to the sheer beauty of a great army arrayed for battle. Chaucer's knight says that

Theseus' banner shone so 'that alle the feeldes glyteren up and down'; Chandos Herald says of the Dauphin's host marshalling at Poitiers: 'Then you might see banners and pennons unfurled to the wind, where on fine gold and azure shone purple, gules and ermine. Trumpets, tabors, horns and clarions – you might hear sounding through the camp; the Dauphin's great battle made the earth ring.'[47] Froissart repeatedly says such things as this (of the Flemish army): 'It was great beauty to behold shining against the sun the banners, pennons, and clear bassinets, and so great number of people, that the eye of man could not number them; their spears seemed a great thick wood.'[48] It is significant that the two latter enthusiastic descriptions are of *enemy* forces: the more beautiful and terrible the opponents, the more exhilarating the contest.

Paradoxically, it is within this international framework of knightly honour that what may have been one of the first deliberate attempts to foster national feeling was made. In 1344 Edward III held a 'round table' or series of jousts at which he planned to inaugurate a fellowship of 300 knights after the pattern of King Arthur. (It was perhaps as part of this endeavour that the round table in the other sense, the wooden table called Arthur's at Winchester, was made.) Heralds proclaimed the tournament in Scotland, France, Germany, the Low Countries and elsewhere; anyone could be elected who did not support the king's enemies; indeed, the French were offered a safe conduct to attend. Thus the Order of the Garter, which came into being a few years later, was conceived within the international order of chivalry, yet, in evoking the myth of Arthur, Edward seems to have been consciously adopting the role of a second Arthur as a focus for patriotic loyalty. Miss McKisack argues that he 'harnessed the idealism of chivalry to his cause and linked to himself under an obligation of honour some of the greatest names in the land'.[49] This was, however, still couched in personal terms, for the language of patriotism was lacking. Barnie maintains that the slow growth of national sentiment was related to the continuing use of the French language, and that the development of a sense of Englishness by the beginning of the fifteenth century should be associated with that of the English language. But already in 1344 land and language go together, for Edward, putting his case against Philip of France, asserted that the latter intends to 'destroy the English language and to occupy the land of England'.[50] Although Edward conceives of his war with the French in dynastic terms, government propaganda links it with the welfare of the country. In 1355, for instance, a government speech to the Commons speaks of Edward's 'great labour . . . for the defence and salvation of his kingdom'. 'We sleep securely, while he rarely sleeps,' says a war poem.[51]

Perhaps a more genuine patriotism was developing at the grass-roots, gathering round the defence of the English–Scottish border by northern knights, and of the south coast by combinations of knights, clergy and merchants. Thus in 1360 John of Reading reported: 'clergy and laity came together in arms to resist the afore-said enemies and, if it were granted, to fight for their native land.'[52] John Philpot, an important London merchant, equipped a fleet to patrol the Channel 'for the salvation of my own countrymen and the liberty of my native land'.[53] By the end of the fourteenth century, disillusionment over a failing war and a disrupted society was generating a feeling for 'country' which was no longer wholly focused on deeds of kings and princes. Gower rededicated his *Confessio Amantis* to England rather than to King Richard, while in his *Vox Clamantis* he wrote: 'above all I love my own land, in which my family took its origin.'[54]

One factor keeping the attitudes of chivalry alive was the strong sense of history which lay behind them. The law of arms itself was believed to descend from the Romans: 'the valour and warlike skill of the votaries of chivalry had won the *imperium* for the Roman people.'[55] Of Henry V, Waurin, in his *Chroniques*, says (like Shakespeare's Fluellen): 'Well he kept the discipline of chivalry as did the Romans in former times.'[56] Constables and marshals who enforced the code of chivalry were held to be descended from the *magistri militum* of the Roman army. The basis for this sense of con-tinuity lay in the survival of the strange concept of the 'Roman people' through which many medieval thinkers claimed their kin-ship with Rome. The law of arms applied between all those nations who were part of the Roman people, while its authority was based on the civil and canon law of the Roman Empire and Church. By this time the secular authority of Rome was to all intents and purposes divided between kings and princes who were 'emperors' in their own realms, but any one of their constables was a *magister militum* with authority among all the Roman peoples, who remained, in theory, one. It was not only Dante who believed that the unity of Christendom lay in a divinely ordained *populus Romanus*, nor was

Henry V's pious intention to lead this people on a final crusade entirely hypocritical.

This leads us back to the myths on which the age was nourished. The chronicler wanted to provide his audience with a 'plausible and splendid past for a great people. . . . He wanted to find a long succession of early dynasties . . . . he wanted to trace them back to Japhet or Aeneas; he wanted his heroes of the distant past to be adventurous princes with armed followers, who founded empires and built towns.'[57] This past had been supplied in the twelfth century by the famous *Historia Britonum* of Geoffrey of Monmouth, and its vernacular derivatives, commonly known as the Brut. Brutus, grandson of Aeneas of Troy, reached Britain and founded its dynasty of kings around 1170 BC. Under Rome it produced the great Constantine, and finally Arthur, last of the Romans. In one form or another this was the basis from which most later chronicles of England started. *Gawain and the Green Knight* begins and ends with the line of adventures that have happened here since Brutus came from Troy; Chaucer hails Henry IV as 'conqueror of Brutes Albion'.[58] It was living history, for the medieval knight felt himself to be the heir of Greece and Rome. When, at the funeral of Edward I in 1307, his exploits were praised, the knights were made to say:

> Once with Alexander, king of Macedon, we defeated the kings of the Medes and the Persians. . . . Now at the end of time, with great King Edward we have borne a ten-year war with Philip, famous king of France . . . we have got Wales by slaughter; we have invaded Scotland.[59]

Besides Alexander and Aeneas, Edward I was also compared, to his advantage, with Brutus, King Arthur, King Edgar and Richard Cœur de Lion. Henry Percy's deeds at Neville's Cross (1346) earned him comparison with Gideon, Samson, Joab, Solomon and Gawain. Froissart thought some deeds of arms in the French wars worthy of Charlemagne, and the Black Prince's knights were compared to Roland and Oliver. Humphrey Bohun, Earl of Hereford, actually called one of his sons Aeneas.

The inception of Sir Thomas Gray's *Scalacronica*, already mentioned, vividly illustrates this inheritance of history. While imprisoned by the Scots he reads the 'histories' in Latin, French and English. Then in imagination the Sibyl appears who leads him to a wall with a scaling ladder, such as was used in the siege warfare, leaning against it. The ladder has five rungs and rests on two books, the Bible and the story of Troy. The wall – that is, the structure of history – has windows into the past. Gray climbs the first rung and sees a great city and a master in a fur-trimmed gown who is Walter the archdeacon, supposed to have translated the Brut into Latin. On the next rung he sees through the window a black monk, Bede, in a study, writing his history. On the third is the monk of Chester, Higden, writing his *Polychronicon* and, on the fourth, another historian, John of Tynemouth. Gray cannot climb higher but the Sibyl tells him that at the top of the building are Henry of Huntingdon and Merlin, wise men who foretold the future. There is a fine mix-up of chronology here but the element of myth is clear. Yet in chronicling his own times Gray does not romanticize: he tells a plain tale vigorously.

History for lay people comes into its own in the fourteenth and fifteenth centuries. While its readers could identify themselves with great heroes, it was also a vehicle for moral teaching. History was 'not only pleasant but praiseworthy'.[60] Peter Langtoft, an Austin canon of Bridlington, wrote a verse chronicle in Norman French which begins when 'le duk sire Eneas' escapes from Troy and works up to the glorious wars of Edward I. In 1338 Robert Mannyng translated this into English, with additions, because, he said, Englishmen ought to know their history. People had begged him to turn this story into easy rhyme, so he writes for those who do not know Latin or French, to entertain them when they gather for games or amusement. By 1400 English-speaking audiences had the story of *Alexander* and the *Destruction of Troy* in alliterative verse; Lydgate gave them his *Troy Book* (commissioned by Henry V) in 1412–20 and the *Siege of Thebes* in 1421–2. The appetite of half-lettered country gentry and townsmen for historical stories was being met.

How did the more scholarly historians of the later Middle Ages view the legendary 'matter of Britain'? Ralph Higden of Chester was prepared in his *Polychronicon* to accept Brutus and the line of British kings descended from him but was sceptical about some of Geoffrey of Monmouth's tall stories. John Trevisa, his Cornish translator, criticizes him severely for his unbelief. In the fifteenth century we meet the beginnings of an argument that was to go on right into the seventeenth century. On the one hand, emotional attachment to British antiquity produces a devotee as passionate as John Rous; on the other, there are signs of a new critical attitude in the little group of early humanists. Rous (1411–91) became chaplain of the Beauchamp Chantry in Warwick and lived all his life under the patronage of the Earls of Warwick. His devotion found its focus in gathering materials to endow them with a glorious past, out of which came his two Warwick Rolls (one Latin, one English), which form a pictorial history of the Warwick ancestry. Then he wrote the *Historia Regum Angliae*, which plunges us into a forest of early legend, with much on eponymous founders of cities and kingdoms, such as King Westmer of Westmoreland. Warwick, which he identified with Caerleon, had been the residence of an Arthurian king. He embroiders the Beauchamp story of Guy of Warwick, a famous Saxon giantkiller, and declares that he sees daily Guy's sword and hauberk in the castle, and that he has drunk from a gold cup connected with another legendary figure, Sir Enyas, Knight of the Swan. Guy of Warwick takes Rous on an excursion into the history of giants in Britain and their origin in a monstrous marriage of the exiled daughters of the Greek Danaus to the devils they found in the island. Rous sees that there are problems of inconsistency in this story, but with a certain insouciance he brushes this aside: 'Hanc ambiguitatem non determino, totum relinquens Deo'[61] ('I do not settle this doubt, leaving all to God'). He also takes a hand in the furious controversy over the origins of Oxford and Cambridge. Oxford, he believes, had originated with Greek scholars who came to Britain with Brutus, but had really been set on its feet by King Alfred in 873. Cambridge claimed foundation in the days of the British kings by a Spanish exile, named Cantaber, who married King Gurgentius' daughter, but Rous – an Oxford man – is sceptical about this. John Rous is, in fact, a curious mixture. He displays some notion of historical development in his visual representations of the Warwick ancestors, depicted right back to a mythical antiquity in the Warwick Rolls. Clothes he renders happily in the fifteenth-century style, but in the armour he is groping for some principles of evolution. Thus he draws Arthurian and Saxon earls in the long mail hauberks almost to the ankles and then shows how later armour evolves. But he cannot apply critical principles to the myths in which he is absorbed.

A later contemporary of Rous, William of Worcester, has been called the first practising lay antiquary. At Oxford he concentrated on medicine and astronomy; later he learnt French and some Greek; he collected a good library and his notes also show knowledge of mathematics and Hebrew. As Sir John Fastolf's secretary until 1459, he travelled often between East Anglia and his native West country. His great achievement lies in the antiquarian notes he made on a journey from Norwich to St Michael's Mount, Cornwall, in 1478. He had a passion for concrete information of all kinds, measuring and describing buildings in detail and talking to anyone whom he could buttonhole. He could respond with acute observation to what lay around him, but when it came to writing history, like Rous, he accepted quite uncritically the inherited myth and legend.

Yet signs of a critical sense were appearing. About 1435 Abbot John Whethamstede of St Albans gave in his *Granarium* four reasons for not believing in Brutus as the founder of British kingship. Kendrick suggests that his view reflected that of the small humanist group around Humphrey, Duke of Gloucester, who may have been the first member of the royal house to discount the tradition that the line was descended from Troy. John Capgrave, patronized by Humphrey, was also unenthusiastic about Brutus and Arthur. The humanists' new critical approach to texts seemed likely to erode belief in the myth by degrees. Yet this did not happen at all rapidly. The romances, above all Malory's *Morte Darthur*, continued to flourish in popularity, while the legendary histories received a great boost at the end of the fifteenth century, just when one might have thought humanist scepticism would prevail, for a Welsh king took the crown at Bosworth Field in 1485, and the prophecy made by Cadwallader, the last British king in the legend, seemed to be fulfilled. Rous cut up his Latin Roll – for his sympathies had been Yorkist – and re-edited it to suit the new dynasty. Henry VII called his eldest son Arthur, and this was the start of an Arthurian cult that ran right through the Tudor period. Fanciful designs for Tudor arms included so-called quarterings of Brutus, Belinus, Arthur and others. The Round Table at Winchester was painted (*c.* 1522) with a portrait of Arthur distinctly resembling Henry VIII. Polydore Vergil, the Italian historian in England, was unkindly sceptical, but nothing could yet kill the enthusiasm for this longlived myth.

Caxton accepted the historicity of Arthur, giving sensible reasons in the Preface to *Morte Darthur*, and fostered the cult. It is striking how medieval was Caxton's choice of material for his new medium of communication. His first effort, in 1471, was the *Recuyell of the Histories of Troy*. In 1480 he printed *Chronicles of England* with all the 'matter of Britain', and in 1485 Malory. His imagination was still in the world of chivalry: he translated and printed Christine de Pisan's work as *The Book of Fayttes of Armes and of Chyvalrye*, and Ramon Lull's *Book of the Ordre of Chyvalry*. In an epilogue to Lull he eloquently mourned the decay of chivalry:

> in ancient time . . . the noble acts of the knights of England that used chivalry were renomed through the universal world, as for to speak to-fore the incarnation of Jesu Christ, where were there ever any like to Brennius and Belinus, that from the great Britain, now called England, unto Rome and far beyond conquered many Royaumes and lands whose noble acts remain in th'old histories and the Romayns. And sith the Incarnation of Our Lord, behold that noble king of Britain, king Arthur, with all the noble knights of the round table. . . .
>
> O ye knights of England, where is the custom and wage of noble chivalry that was used in tho days? What do you now but go to the baynes [baths] and play at dice? . . . Leave this, leave it and read the noble volumes of Saint Graal, of Lancelot, Galahad. . . . There shall ye see man-hood, courtesy and gentleness. And look in latter days of the noble acts sith the conquest, as in king Richard days Cœur de lion; Edward the first and the third. . . . And also behold that victorious and noble king Harry the fifth . . . how many knights ben there now in England that have . . . the exercise of a knight, that is to say, that he knoweth his horse, and his horse him. . . . I would it pleased our sovereign lord that twice or thrice in a year . . . he would cry jousts of peace, to th'end that every knight should have horse and harness and also the use and craft of a knight. . . . This should cause gentlemen to resort to th'ancient customs of chivalry, to great fame and renome, and also to be allway ready to serve their prince when he shall call them or have need. Then let every man that is come of noble blood and intendeth to come to the noble order of chivalry read this little book.[62]

It sums up the traditional attitudes with which the Tudor period started, and which underlie Malory.

The quest for perfection and the end of the world

Idealized chivalry was, from one point of view, the search for perfection in this age. 'Salute me unto my lord sir Lancelot my father,
and . . . bid him remember of this world unstable' were the last
words Malory gave Galahad after he had achieved the Grail. We
have seen how far the transcendent world and the world of experience were cloven apart by Malory's time. Auerbach in his
Mimesis has suggested that this sense of the mutability of this world
and the far-awayness of the transcendent world underlies what he
calls the 'creatural' style of the fifteenth century, following
Huizinga's picture of 'the waning of the Middle Ages'. Huizinga
observed that, the deeper the inherent pessimism of an age, the
more strongly the vision of a sublime life will haunt men. A
pessimism accompanied the 'waning of the Middle Ages' in
northern Europe[63] and tinged even the harbingers of the Renaissance
in Italy. The end of the age seemed not far off, and while there was
yet time the quest for perfection must be pursued, even under the
imminent judgement of God.

In this sense Morton Bloomfield sees *Piers Plowman* as a
'fourteenth-century Apocalypse'.[64] To meet the spiritual crisis of the
age, he argues, Langland presented the search for an ideal society in
terms of a return to an older view, one he calls 'monastic perfection'.
Only so could Langland 'relieve the contending tensions of his age
– the competing claims of society and the individual, of grace and
freewill, of piety and learning, of this world and the next'.[65] He has
turned back to the static concepts of status and hierarchy, in which
each status has its own perfection, yet he combines this with quest,
with progression through grades of attainment. On the topmost
rung of the earthly hierarchy is the life of 'monks' (i.e. all religious)
who are, in Bloomfield's interpretation, 'the key to the establishment of a just and loving society'.[66] This is why Langland lays such
emphasis on the reform of the friars, which is crucial to the reform of
the whole world, since corruption of the best brings disaster on the
whole society. On the highest rung of the ladder, monks are 'the
foremost exponents of Christian perfection'; their dwelling is the
most perfect habitation on earth and closest to heaven; 'their
communal life reflects that of the angels and their silence the peace
of heaven'; they are 'the living eschatological element in history'.[67]
Accompanying this concept of a perfect state was the notion of

progression through grades. Bloomfield points out that in medieval thought these often went in triads: beginner, progressor and perfect; marriage, widowhood, virginity; laymen, priests, monks. One of the most famous of these progressions was the apocalyptic scheme of history evolved by Joachim of Fiore, a twelfth-century monk of Calabria whose pattern of three successive *status* characterized respectively by the work of the Father, the Son and the Holy Spirit exercised a powerful influence in the centuries that followed him. He saw these three ages symbolized in the orders of married men, clergy and monks. Langland's three grades, Do-well, Do-better, Do-best, exemplify this way of thinking, but closer to the Joachimist vision is Langland's use of three grades in the Tree of Perfection. In the C text, when Liberum Arbitrium is describing the Tree to Will, he says that the fruits are married men, widows and virgins (or hermits), the last being the topmost fruits which receive heat from the Holy Ghost, as from the sun.[68] There are difficulties in linking Langland's imagery with Joachimist expectation, which Langland could, however, have known, since it was widely disseminated in England. The pilgrimage of the poem is both that of the individual soul and of society towards perfection. Bloomfield links the ideal leader who appears in the B and C texts with the angelic pope and saviour-emperor of late medieval prophecy, who fulfil the Joachimist vision of a final blessed age of history. When Conscience goes in quest of Piers he is seeking 'the ideal pope, or by extension, ideal cleric or religious, or Christ himself', for 'Piers is to be the model for the reconstitution of society'.[69] Whether it is Joachim's third *status* (age) that Langland envisages cannot be proven, but the quest for the holy society which will transform the life of this age places Piers Plowman within the same range of prophetic expectation.

If Bloomfield is right, Langland was drawing on a renewed monastic philosophy which was one of the answers to the intellectual and spiritual confusion of the age. The religious orders were on the defensive against radical attack; they were also, to some extent, in reaction against the intellectual trends among academics. Dr Pantin has shown in these centuries a series of writings defending the monastic concept – both for its antiquity, deriving, it was claimed, from Samuel, Elijah, Elisha and the Sons of the Prophets, and because it embodied the final perfection towards which the whole of history was moving. An outstanding example is a work by a monk of Bury St Edmunds, written before 1360, historical in approach, but with a sense of expectancy towards the future; for monks bear the supreme role in history. Other treatises and sermons follow the same thinking. For instance, a fifteenth-century sermon preached before the Benedictine monks – after the Mass of the Holy Ghost, which might suggest Joachim's last age – emphasizes the high calling of the monks, the order that will endure until the end of time. Thus monastic thinking was placed within an apocalyptic context. The *Eulogium Historiarum* of a Malmesbury monk (*c.* 1366) expects a climax shortly in history and a worldwide renewal. This sense of imminent crisis in society also characterizes the famous sermon of Thomas of Wimbledon at Paul's Cross in 1388, popularized in numerous editions in the fifteenth century and later printed. Everyone, says the preacher, will have to give an account of his stewardship in respect of his particular *status* in society, whether religious, knight or peasant. It was not only the dissolution of the individual that haunted the imagination but the dissolution of society itself before the oncoming of Antichrist and Doomsday. In literature and visual art these themes recur throughout western Europe. Yet pessimism and optimism rub shoulders: the quest for individual and social perfection leads towards a *renovatio mundi* on the horizon, whether or not this was seen in the Joachimist terms of an Age of the Holy Ghost. The pull between this world and the next is an essential element in the intellectual climate of the later Middle Ages.

Throughout the Middle Ages there was eager debate about the antithesis of the active life (*all* activity, including intellectual, properly speaking) and the contemplative, about the possibility of their combination in the 'mixed life', and about the question as to which of the three was best. Aquinas thought the mixed life the most perfect, since Christ followed it. These questions assumed a new urgency with the growth of lay piety and, particularly, with the movement towards mysticism. This movement can be seen as a reaction, like the intellectual movement of the Ockhamists, against the effort to reach God through natural theology and revelation. Both the mystics and the Ockhamists, says Leff, emphasized God's unpredictability in terms of external wisdom – ineffability for the mystic, unpredictability for the Ockhamist. 'If the one tended to militate against an ecclesiastical regime of worship, the other did so against a natural theology.'[70] Both preferred to do without intermediaries. The mystic sought perfection through the pilgrimage of the individual soul rather than through a movement in history towards the final holy society. Yet the two quests were never really separated. *Piers Plowman* is surely concerned with both. Joachim had found the quintessence of his Third Age in the order of hermits who were to mediate for the whole society through contemplation on the mountain top. The appropriateness of this model for the late Middle Ages is seen in the growth of the contemplative order of Carthusians at this time. Six of the nine English 'charterhouses', whose plan of separate houses for each monk arranged round a great cloister demonstrates their reconsideration of solitariness and community, were founded between 1340 and 1400. 'It is a world', says David Knowles, 'in which personal, individual problems and values are supreme, a world in which the kinds and degrees of love, divine and human, are matters of earnest debate, together with a search for clarity of conscience.' And, speaking of the Carthusian houses, 'those who joined and the bishops and magnates who founded them, show by their choice of order what was most esteemed. The religious climate of the age was sympathetic to a personal and mystical approach to the way of perfection.'[71]

Whereas Rhineland and Netherlandish mystics mostly belonged to religious communities, in England they tended to retire into the solitary life either of *hermits*, who retired into wilderness (Greek *eremia*) far from towns, or of anchorites and anchoresses, who lived in 'anchorholds' within towns. They were 'freelances' in their spiritual life, yet these recluses were also set in the midst of the community's activities, revered by all and consulted by many. The anchorite of Westminster, John of London, counselled Richard II and probably Henry V. Some wrote in English for the growing class of literate laymen and women. The Carthusians of London and Sheen and the Brigittines of Syon multiplied copies of their works and, when the era of printing began, mystical works, both European and English, were among the first to be published. They were chiefly works of spiritual direction for the bands of disciples who gathered round the mystics. There was no set form, and so we get simple, direct writing, non-schematic in its approach and vivid in its use of words and images to convey personal experiences. Richard Rolle, who died at Hampole in Yorkshire in 1349, the first of these writers, had a great following, and it is claimed that there are more manuscripts of his works extant than of any other medieval English writer. The *Cloud of Unknowing*, of which we shall see more later, is careful to counsel against the too easily deceptive ecstasies and visions that Richard Rolle had evidently widely inspired. Walter Hilton's *Ladder of Perfection* may in its turn have been written to modify the *Cloud*'s austerity, by describing possibilities open to many rather than calling on a few to follow a total vocation. Julian of Norwich (1343–after 1413) calls herself 'unlettered', but her most recent editors argue that her writing exhibits not only a good grounding, and between her short and her long texts an increasing mastery, in rhetoric, but signs that she made her own translations from the Vulgate. 'Her mind', says Knowles, 'can wrestle with the deepest mysteries of theology and has absorbed much of the abstruse technical phraseology of the Schools.'[72] Langland is closest in temper to Hilton and Julian, though there is no certainty that he read them. Do-well, Do-better and Do-best parallel (though they are not identical with) Hilton's active, contemplative and mixed lives, the third uniting the first two. Langland's sense of Christ's closeness to us, and of the combination of physical agony and thirst for souls in the cry 'I thirst' – a thirst that seems to imply ultimate universal salvation, too mysterious to be more than hinted at – are closely similar to Julian's *Shewings*. In the next generation Margery Kempe, to some extent a disciple of Julian, was certainly unlettered, and dictated her *Book* to at least two people: she will be discussed at length later.

The history of the anonymous *Mirror of Simple Souls* illustrates how closely orthodox mystical experience bordered on that of sects like the heretical Brethren of the Free Spirit, and how ambiguous was the line between them. In its original form it has been convincingly attributed to a Beguine heresiarch, Margareta Poreta, condemned as a lapsed heretic at Paris in 1310. The condemned tenets are clearly set forth in the *Mirror*. Repeated attempts were made to suppress it, as emanating from the Brethren of the Free Spirit; yet historians still argue about whether it is a heterodox work, preaching the deification of man and a libertinism dispensing with moral law, or orthodox late medieval mysticism. The desire for an immediate, all-absorbing experience of God which consumes outward forms became so urgent that works like the *Mirror* were eagerly seized on. A translation from French into Latin was made in England in the fifteenth century, and this in turn was translated into English around 1451 by Richard Methley. The first English translator added extensive glosses to guard against dangerous tendencies, and it became an acceptable manual of lay devotion. Among the more orthodox mystical writings, Margaret Beaufort, the mother of Henry VII, promoted the publication of Hilton's *Ladder of Perfection* and the *Imitatio Christi* of Thomas à Kempis, translated and published in 1503. These and similar works, printed by Caxton, Wynkyn de Worde and Pynson, went through many editions. For nearly two centuries, down to the Henrician Reformation, these works provided the spiritual food on which many devout people were nourished.

If the line between orthodoxy and heresy was sometimes blurred in the case of mystics, the Lollards, on the opposite wing of radical religion, were soon placed outside the pale. While intellectually the mystics had closest affinities with the Ockhamists, the intellectual roots of Lollardy lay in Wyclif's realism. But in practical terms they represented a backward-looking quest for perfection in the simplicity and purity of apostolic times. Wyclif laid on each individual Christian the responsibility for knowing God's law personally. In feudal terms, all dominion derived from God and every man was his tenant-in-chief; thus the focus of the Lollard movement lay in the Lollard Bible. So far as we know, no other complete English translation had yet been made; it coincided with the new demand for vernacular literature. Wyclif's theology required that it should be as faithful a copy of God's 'real' word as possible; hence it is literal, scholarly (within the limits of its age) and without obvious bias. Because of their reverence for the integrity of the text, Lollards advocated the use of unglossed texts: 'Let the Church of England now approve the true and whole translation of simple men,' says Purvey in his General Prologue.[73] The Lollard translations were made while Lollardy was still mainly an Oxford movement (1380–4), and around 1395 they were revised to follow letter a little less, and thought rather more. They were deliberately aimed at a lower stratum of literacy – knights, bourgeoisie, even labourers – than that of the aristocratic owners of French Bibles. Behind the translations was Wyclif's belief that none of the questions of ecclesiastical and social reform that troubled the age could be solved except by the direct authority of God, illuminating the individual conscience through his word. There was at first no ban on the Lollard translations. In fact, Wycliffites inserted some of their texts into Rolle's translation of the Psalms – which was not forbidden. But ecclesiastical authorities soon recognized the centrality of the Bible

in the Lollard movement. At the trial of the Lollard Thorpe, Archbishop Arundel said that the Lollard aim was 'to pick out such sharp
sentences of holy scriptures and of doctors to maintain their sect and
lore against the ordinances of Holy Church'.[74]

A group of nobles and courtiers, knights of Richard II's chamber
in some cases, gave protection for a time to Lollard preachers. These
'Lollard knights', friends of Chaucer and members of a literary
group, read religious writings, not only Rolle's, but also Lollard
works. Sir William Beauchamp possessed, as well as Clanvowe's *Two
Ways*, Wyclif's Latin works. Even outside the court circle, that
'rough soldier' Thomas of Woodstock had in his library a rich Wyclif
Bible, books of prayers and meditations and some theological works.
He also staged a debate between Lollards and their opponents.
These men do not fall into nice categories: hard-bitten soldiers and
careerists, yet susceptible both to the new devotion of the mystics
and to Lollardy; open to radical religious ideas, yet often conventional in their piety.

Chaucer himself shows something of their range in the moments
when he is most likely to having been giving his creed straightforwardly. Some have fancied a connection between his usual impenetrable irony and Ockhamism, though he never mentions any
contemporary philosopher by name except Bradwardine and his
own friend Ralph Strode. Boethius was, as we have seen, his
favourite philosopher: in *Troilus and Criseyde* he seems to pass from
the Boethian statement of relation between God's love and all the
loves in the world in the Prologue to Book 3, to the direct contrast
between the unstable love of man and woman and Christ's unchanging love at the end of the poem (*c.* 1383–5). In the 'Balade de
bon conseil', addressed to an associate of the Lollard knights, Sir
Philip de la Vache, probably around 1386–9, and also Boethian in
flavour, he calls on Vache to remember that this world is not our
home but a wilderness, and to go on pilgrimage to God, protected
by truth. The sentiment and image are like those of *Piers Plowman*,
and come too in Hilton's *Ladder*; but presumably the vision of life as
pilgrimage was much in Chaucer's mind at this time, when he was
beginning the *Canterbury Tales*. In the *Tales* themselves, though
there is nothing specifically Wycliffite, it is striking that the ideal
poor parson, accused of being a Lollard, does not reject the
accusation: together with Chaucer's association with the Lollard
knights, this does suggest even a little more than a general sympathy

with the Lollard moral earnestness and zeal for church reform in Chaucer. Total scepticism of human integrity, consistency and, perhaps, knowledge, and a huge gap between man and God, are suggested when he says in the winter of 1396–7 in the *Envoy to Bukton* that

> . . . whan of Crist our kyng
> Was axed what is truth or sooth fastnesse
> He nat a word answered to that axinge
> As who saith: 'no man is al trewe', I gesse

At the end of his life there remains a self-abnegation like that at the end of *The Tempest*, when at the close of the *Parson's Tale*, retracting anything he has written that may 'sounen into sin', he says:

> Now pray I to them all that hearken this little treatise or read, that if there be anything in it that liketh them, that thereof they thank our lord Jesu Christ, of whom proceedeth all wit and all goodness. And if there be any thing that displease them, I pray them also that they arrette [impute] it to the default of my uncunning and not to my will, that would fain have said better if I had had cunning.

For a time Wyclif's works and the Lollard Bible circulated freely. But the condemnation of the Oxford Wycliffites, the statute for burning heretics (1401), the prohibition in 1408 of any translations from the Bible except authorized ones, and the Lollard rising of Sir John Oldcastle (1414) ended this period of openness. For a time the intelligentsia seem to have avoided possessing any books associated with Lollardy. Miss Deanesley's researches suggested that in the first half of the fifteenth century English Bibles were less frequent than the French *Bibles historiales* in the fourteenth century. No English biblical books are mentioned in monastic library catalogues except Rolle's psalter or Anglo-Saxon Gospel books. From the wills of clergy only five cases of priests owning English translations have come to light, of whom two possessed Wycliffite texts. In the most dangerous Lollard days there is no evidence that either Henry IV or Henry V had an English Bible, though both Henry VI and Henry VII had one. The nuns of the house of Syon and Barking were specifically licensed to have English translations for their offices. These were houses containing some of the most aristocratic and best-educated women: only those of high rank were safe with such works. For the masses, Archbishop Arundel licensed a translation of the *Meditationes Vitae Christi* which concentrated on the beginning and end of Christ's life, reducing the ministry and teaching to small compass. As the *Mirror of the Blessed Life of Jesus*, translated by the Carthusian Nicholas Love, this was very popular with the laity.

It was not scholars at Oxford, aristocrats, courtiers or gentry (except Oldcastle) who finally carried the Lollard faith to martyrdom and persisted in persecuted groups throughout the fifteenth century, but much humbler people, semi-literate or illiterate craftsmen or peasants. Their theology became strangely confused, straying far from Wyclif's scholastic position, but they clung with tenacity to the general principle that men hold, not mediately, but immediately from God and that therefore each man must attend to God's law for himself. In this they formed part of the current of medieval heterodoxy most clearly exemplified by the Waldensians. This represents the simple, lay approach to the quest for perfection, not through monastic vows, the life of the ascetic or mystic, but through a direct and naïve attention to the Scriptures. When arraigned before the ecclesiastical authorities, these humble, little-educated people astonished their inquisitors by their power to quote and use the Bible. Waldensians and Lollards both stood fully within a medieval context, but it is significant that the former became the one medieval sect outside the official church to survive to the present day, while, though no institutional links can be proved, Lollard groups must almost certainly be connected with Protestant beginnings in the first half of the sixteenth century.

The fourteenth and fifteenth centuries had been a period in which the medieval world-view had largely disintegrated, though surviving in large pieces. Uncertainty had led, on the one hand, to sharp intellectual questioning and, on the other, to spiritual questing. Yet the search for perfection, juxtaposed to the expectation of Doomsday, focused aspiration on a future that still took a medieval shape, even while prophetically all the medieval foundations were shaking. When we pass into the Tudor period we find that its intellectual framework still incorporated many medieval elements. A hierarchical bond was still presumed to bind all classes in one commonweal. Education remained traditional. Chivalric cults still evoked romantic responses and history itself could still be read as romance and myth. The legacy of medieval mysticism enriched personal piety and kept alive devotion to old practices. Lollardy, with its roots in medieval radical protest, was renewed in the new protest. Similar attitudes can be traced in Quattrocento Italy, but by 1500 humanism, as a new kind of response to the legacy of the past, was in full flower there. England was much slower in reorienting its intellectual outlook. It needed the visits of Italian scholars, such as the Florentine Poggio Bracciolini (1418–22) and the papal commissioner Piero del Monte (1435–40), the new elegance of Latin style in communication from the Roman Curia, the collection of manuscripts and commissioning of translations, the enthusiasm of patrons such as Humphrey, Duke of Gloucester, William Gray and John Tiptoft, Earl of Worcester, and, finally, the visits of English scholars to Italy, to nourish English humanism into a flourishing plant. Until 1500 England lacked the conditions for creating influential literary circles. Solitary patrons were no substitute for the continuing patronage of scholars at Rome, for instance, or the stimulus of the Florentine Platonic Academy, or the literary circles at Mantua or Urbino. Oxford and Cambridge were in the doldrums in the fifteenth century, the former, in particular, suffering from the results of the suppression of Lollardy. It was not until the two universities were ready at the end of the fifteenth century to entertain the new ideas and the new scholars and, still later, when Sir Thomas More's house in Chelsea became their meeting-place, that the new humanism found really congenial ground in England. Yet More had intended to become a Carthusian in youth, and to his end as a martyr for the old religion united in himself both the older and the newer ways to perfection.

Notes

1 Dante, *Divina Commedia, Paradiso*, XV, ll. 97–133; XVI, ll. 46–154. See also *Paradiso*, XXVII, ll. 121–41; *Purgatorio*, VI; *Monarchia*, I, l. 11.
2 G. Villani, *Cronica*, VIII, 39.
3 C. T. Davis 'Il buon tempo antico', in N. Rubenstein (ed.), *Florentine Studies* (London, 1968), p. 46.
4 *Knight's Tale*, ll. 3009–10.
5 Dante, *Paradiso*, III, l. 85.
6 M. H. Carré, *Realists and Nominalists* (Oxford, 1946), p. 61.
7 Dante, *Paradiso*, XXII, l. 151.
8 Dante, *Paradiso*, XXVII, l. 109.

9 E. A. Burtt, *The Metaphysical Foundations of Modern Physical Science* (London, 1932).
10 *Knight's Tale*, ll. 1262–4.
11 Julian of Norwich, *Revelations of Divine Love*, in *A Book of Showings to the Anchoress*, ed. E. Colledge and J. Walsh (Toronto, 1978), pp. 212–13, 300.
12 Dante, *Paradiso*, XXXIII, ll. 85–7.
13 Aquinas, *VII Quodlibets*, VI, 14 ff.; in *Theological Texts*, ed. T. Gilby (Oxford, 1955), pp. 17 ff.
14 Thomas Usk, *The Testament of Love*; in *Chaucerian and Other Pieces*, ed. W. W. Skeat (Oxford, 1897), Bk 1, ch. 9, pp. 39–40.
15 C. Erickson, *The Medieval Vision* (Oxford, 1976), pp. 13–17; M. R. James, 'Twelve mediaeval ghost stories', *English Historical Review*, 38 (1922), pp. 413–22.
16 *Parliament of Fowls*, l. 376.
17 *Prioress's Tale*, l. 500.
18 A. F. Leach, *The Schools of Medieval England* (London, 1915), p. 244.
19 N. Orme, *English Schools in the Middle Ages* (London, 1973), p. 78.
20 Leach, op. cit., pp. 244–5.
21 Regulations of the faculty of grammar, quoted in Leach, ibid., p. 181.
22 Quoted in Leach, ibid.
23 Trevisa's translation of Higden's *Polychronicon* (see Chapter 1, n. 68); quoted in ibid., pp. 196 ff.
24 *Piers Plowman*, B text, ed. A. V. C. Schmidt (London, 1978), Passus X, ll. 297 ff.
25 Magdalen College School, *Vulgaria*, quoted in Orme, op. cit., pp. 138 ff.
26 Ibid., p. 110.
27 Bidding Prayer of Oxford University.
28 G. Leff, *Medieval Thought* (London, 1959), p. 258.
29 Quoted in A. C. Crombie, *Augustine to Galileo*, vol. 2 (Harmondsworth, 1969), p. 82.
30 G. Leff, *Paris and Oxford Universities in the Thirteenth and Fourteenth Centuries* (New York, 1968), p. 309.
31 G. Leff, *Bradwardine and the Pelagians* (Cambridge, 1957), p. 13.
32 Quoted by G. Shepherd in D. Brewer (ed.), *Geoffrey Chaucer*, 'Writers and their Background' (London, 1974), p. 286.
33 G. Leff, *Heresy in the Later Middle Ages* (Manchester, 1967), pp. 523 ff.
34 *Squire's Tale*, l. 254.
35 B. Smalley, *English Friars and Antiquity* (Oxford, 1960), p. 24.
36 For material in this paragraph I am indebted to Dr Jeremy Catto for permission to use his unpublished paper 'The religion of the English nobility in the second half of the fourteenth century'.
37 C. Brown, R. H. Robbins and J. L. Cutler, *Supplement to the Index of Middle English Verse* (Lexington, 1965), p. 521.

38 *The Workes of Sir Thomas More* (London, 1557), p. 850; quoted in M. B. Parkes, 'The literacy of the laity', in D. Daiches and A. K. Thorlby (eds), *The Mediaeval World* (London, 1973), p. 571.
39 Jean de Bueil, *Le Jouvencel*, quoted in M. H. Keen, *The Laws of War in the Late Middle Ages* (London, 1965), p. 3.
40 Augustine, *De Civitate Dei*, XIX, 12.
41 Christine de Pisan, *Book of Fayttes of Armes and of Chyvalrye*, trans. W. Caxton, quoted in C. T. Allmand, *Society at War* (Edinburgh, 1973), p. 19.
42 Quoted in Allmand, op. cit., pp. 27–8.
43 J. Barnie, *War in Medieval Society* (London, 1974), p. 81.
44 Ibid., p. 75.
45 Froissart, *Chronicles*, trans. Sir John Berners, Bk 1, ch. 168.
46 Ibid., Bk 1, ch. 81.
47 Barnie, op. cit., p. 73; Chandos Herald, *The Life of the Black Prince*, ed. and trans. M. K. Pope and E. C. Lodge (Oxford, 1910), ll. 984 ff.
48 Barnie, op. cit., p. 73; Froissart, op. cit., Bk 10, ch. 249.
49 M. McKisack, *The Fourteenth Century* (Oxford, 1959), p. 252.
50 Barnie, op. cit., p. 102.
51 Ibid., p. 113.
52 Ibid., p. 108.
53 Ibid.
54 Ibid., p. 109.
55 Monstrelet, *Chronique*, quoted in Keen, op. cit., p. 57.
56 Waurin, quoted in ibid.
57 T. Kendrick, *British Antiquity* (London, 1950), pp. 1 ff.
58 *The Complaint of Chaucer to his Purse*, l. 22.
59 Smalley, op. cit., p. 9.
60 Ibid., p. 19.
61 Quoted in Kendrick, op. cit., p. 25.
62 Epilogue to the *Order of Chivalry* (1484), in N. F. Blake (ed.), *William Caxton* (Oxford, 1973), p. 111.
63 J. Huizinga, *The Waning of the Middle Ages* (New York, 1954), pp. 31 ff.
64 M. Bloomfield, *Piers Plowman as a Fourteenth-Century Apocalypse* (New Brunswick, 1961).
65 Ibid., p. 6.
66 Ibid., p. 46.
67 Ibid., p. 62.
68 *Piers Plowman*, C text, ed. W. W. Skeat (Oxford, 1886, etc.), Passus XIX, ll. 71 ff.; ed. D. Pearsall (London, 1978), Passus XVIII, ll. 71 ff.
69 Bloomfield, op. cit., p. 148.
70 G. Leff, *Heresy in the Later Middle Ages*, p. 26.
71 D. Knowles, *The English Mystical Tradition* (London, 1961), p. 43.
72 Julian of Norwich, *Revelations of Divine Love*, pp. 45–52, 735–48; Knowles, op. cit., p. 135.

73 Quoted in M. Deanesley, *The Lollard Bible* (Cambridge, 1920), p. 304.
74 Ibid., p. 228.

Select bibliography

Education
Leach, A. T. *The Schools of Medieval England*, London, 1915.
Orme, N. *English Schools in the Middle Ages*, London, 1973.

Universities and academic thought
Leff, G. *Bradwardine and the Pelagians*, Cambridge, 1957.
_____ *Medieval Thought*, London, 1959.
_____ *Paris and Oxford Universities in the Thirteenth and Fourteenth Centuries*, New York, 1968.
Robson, J. A. *Wyclif and the Oxford Schools*, Cambridge, 1961.

Religion
Deanesley, M. *The Lollard Bible*, Cambridge, 1920.
Knowles, D. *The English Mystical Tradition*, London, 1961.
Leff, G. *Heresy in the Later Middle Ages*, Manchester, 1967.
Smalley, B. *English Friars and Antiquity*, Oxford, 1960.

War and chivalry
Allmand, C. T. *Society at War*, Edinburgh, 1973.
Barnie, J. *War in Medieval Society*, London, 1974.
Keen, M. H. *The Laws of War in the Late Middle Ages*, London, 1965.
Kendrick, T. *British Antiquity*, London, 1950.

Society and literature
Bennett, H. S. *Chaucer and the Fifteenth Century*, Oxford, 1947.
Bloomfield, M. *Piers Plowman as a Fourteenth-Century Apocalypse*, New Brunswick, 1961.
Cottle, B. *The Triumph of English 1350–1400*, London, 1969.

Cosmology
Burtt, E. A. *The Metaphysical Foundations of Modern Physical Science*, London, 1932.
Crombie, A. C. *Augustine to Galileo*, 2 vols, Harmondsworth, 1969.
Lewis, C. S. *The Discarded Image*, Cambridge, 1964.
On the Properties of Things, trans. John Trevisa from Bartholomaeus Anglicus, eds M. C. Seymour *et al.*, Oxford, 1975.
Thomas Aquinas, *Philosophical Texts*, ed. T. Gilby, Oxford, 1951.
_____ *Theological Texts*, ed. T. Gilby, Oxford, 1955.

General
Huizinga, J. *The Waning of the Middle Ages*, New York, 1954.

3 Inner and outer

STEPHEN MEDCALF

A kind of objectivity

The key to the culture of the Middle Ages is often said to be symbol or allegory; and indeed many medievals thought it was the key – not, of course, of their age but of the world as it is. Bartholomaeus Anglicus' encyclopedia *On the Properties of Things* (translated into English in 1399 by John Trevisa, and widely used till after Shakespeare's time) begins by saying that the point of knowing the nature of things is to understand the 'riddles and meanings' of the Bible and other writings which the Holy Spirit has given 'darkly hid and wrapped under likeness and figures'. 'The beam of God giveth to us no light but veiled', because our intelligences rise to the 'contemplation immaterial of the hierarchies of heaven' only if, as St Paul says in the first chapter of Romans, they are led by consideration of things that are seen.[1]

Symbol and allegory, however, are ideas with many tones and variations and perhaps should be approached from a little further off. I want now to look at something with which they overlap, the way in which men describe themselves and their inner lives. In particular, I want to look at four late medieval English people – Margery Kempe, Thomas Hoccleve, Thomas Usk and the author of the *Cloud of Unknowing* – at their ways of describing themselves, and their use of allegory and symbol in connection with those ways.

For what first strikes one in very many medieval books is not allegory but rather a kind of objectivity. I do not mean that medieval writers avoid the subjective as we understand it, only that, whether their styles be simple or gorgeous, there is to our tastes something direct, impersonal and even solid in their exploration of what seems to us broken, private and elusive. In them, moreover, the division between inner and outer does not run deep.

For example, perhaps the very first thing one notices in medieval descriptions of character is the classification by humours. Two things take longer to notice. First, it is a very good classification. Pavlov rediscovered it through the two kinds of response that people show to stress – active dealing with the situation (aggression) and simple ignoring of it (inhibition) – in two degrees, controlledly or uncontrolledly. There are then four character types: controlledly inhibitory, which the medievals called phlegmatic; controlledly aggressive, or sanguine; uncontrolledly aggressive, or choleric; and finally what in both systems is either a native character type, or else the state to which anyone will be reduced in the end by stress – that is, uncontrolled inhibition, melancholy.

Secondly, the medieval classification is psychophysical. Blood, sanguine; phlegm, phlegmatic; yellow bile, choler; black bile, melancholy – these may not be accurate correlations. But the principle of relating moods to secretions of the body is sound (biochemistry is leading us back to it) and for literature very advantageous, in that a man's character and his body may be seen at the same glance. Our word 'complexion', which we have reduced to the visual aspect, implied in its original meaning of 'mixture' that both facial colour and character are manifestations of the mixture of humours. Thus we both understand and visualize Chaucer's Franklin – 'Of his complexioun he was sangwyn'.[2]

This narrowing of the gap between inner and outer is congruous with what we have seen of medieval philosophers in the last chapter: that they assume meaning to be inherent in the world, are less bothered than later philosophers by any gap between subjectivity and the external world, and concerned rather with the relation of the transcendent and the immediate.

It fits, too, with what we have suggested of their artists, that their self-expression, in so far as it happens, is either indistinguishable from, or subsidiary to, or comes into being as an ironic variation on craft and preconceived, commonly traditional pattern.

Something like this could be said of style. Virginia Woolf says that Chaucer shows us 'common things so arranged that they affect us as poetry affects us, and are yet bright, sober, precise as we see them out of doors', and connects this with the stiff, matter-of-fact language of the Paston Letters, which she thinks 'far better fitted for narrative than analysis'.[3] There is something in this. True soliloquy – for example, soliloquy such as Hamlet's or Iago's that explores inward – occurs scarcely if at all in English medieval writing. What soliloquy there is will take the form of a prayer, as Dorigen's brooding on the rocks in the *Franklin's Tale*,[4] or be indistinguishable from a formal argument, as Criseyde's paired soliloquies: 'Now sette a cas . . .', then

> What shall I don? to what fin live I thus?
> Shall I nat love, in cas that if me leste?

> *fin*] end   *me leste*] I wish

against 'To what fin is swich love I can nat see'.[5]

Of course, Virginia Woolf goes too far. Her statement omits the way in which medieval narrative, like the biblical and Latin narratives from which it learnt, can imply more depth and subtlety than analysis can reach, as in *Gawain and the Green Knight*. It omits the delicacy and passion of medieval lyric. And it ignores Chaucer's narrative devices – that preternaturally innocent 'china-blue eye'[6] and deferential suspension of judgement that enable him to give a finely open description of judgement, constantly suggesting an awareness of the indeterminacy of human perception and motivation.

But, conversely, these devices that are so strange to twentieth-century usage – the extreme directness of a narrative that eschews analysis for implication, the way in which even the love lyrics tend to float free of the private and personal situations that gave rise to them and become simply songs, and the odd humour that lurks in Chaucer's irony even at its most poignant – remain symptoms of the directness, the presentational immediacy, the impersonality of medieval writing.

Misplaced concreteness: Margery Kempe

Take, for example, three scraps of writing which form a natural group, being by people who knew each other:

Sin is behoveable, but all shall be well, and all shall be well, and all manner of thing shall be well.[7]

Jesu Lord, that madest me
And with thy blessed blood hast bought,
Forgive that I have grieved thee
In word, work and thought.[8]

It befell upon a Friday on Midsummer Even in right hot weather, as this creature was coming from Yorkward bearing a bottle with beer in her hand and her husband a cake in his bosom, he asked his wife this question, 'Margery, if here came a man with a sword and would smite off mine head less than I should commune kindly with you as I have done before, say me truth of your conscience – for ye say ye will not lie – whether would ye suffer mine head to be smit off or else suffer me to meddle with you as I did sometime?'[9]

All three have simplicity: in the first a serenity that includes and transcends fury and pain, in the second mere devotion, in the third rough texture of diction and vivid detail. The first two are to us a little baffling: we expect to find them more personal than they were probably meant to be. The first is from the *Shewings of God's Love* by Julian of Norwich (1343–after 1416). T. S. Eliot used the words in 'Little Gidding' in a delicate balance between their being a quotation and their being an expression of intensely personal religious feeling. But Julian does not think of them as said by herself or any other human being: they are both 'shewings' from God. Their appearance of weight and authenticity has nothing to do with personal conviction or feeling: they stand out in her narrative as given, dense and awaiting explanation.

The second scrap is the first verse of the 'Prayer' of Richard of Caister, a vicar of St Stephen's, also at Norwich, from 1402 to 1420, who when he died was reverenced as a saint. Again, compare it with later prayer-poems, with Hopkins's stormy and introspective 'Thou mastering me / God!',[10] or with George Herbert's poems, published at Herbert's request in the hope that readers might be helped by descriptions of his religious struggles, and one is struck, first by how much any individuality is refined into awe and admission of dependence, compounded with familiarity and a claim on God's attention; and secondly by the realization that Richard's poem is not a record or expression of personal religious feeling but a prayer to be used by anyone who wishes. In fact, the verse was not even written by Richard. He took an earlier poem, rearranged it so that this claim on Jesus as personal creator and redeemer supporting a prayer for forgiveness precedes everything else, and added other verses. It was presumably described as Richard of Caister's prayer as much because he used it as because he made it. Yet in virtue of his telling re-arrangement one might call him the poem's maker, and the verse does have authentic feeling. Nevertheless it is not primarily a personal expression. And if either Julian's or Richard's writings are read only because they express personality or are beautiful, then they are not read for the purpose for which they were designed. Yet feeling, workmanship and delight were not necessarily absent from their making. It is easy for us to feel puzzled and, in one way or another, shut out.

From this bafflement about how to take medieval writing we are a little rescued by the third writer, Margery Kempe, a mayor's daughter of King's Lynn in Norfolk (*c.* 1373–after 1439). Even in this short extract there is present a quite different kind of medieval person, strong-flavoured and stormy: one who comes nearer to us because, although she tries hard (did Richard and Julian even have to try?) to transcend individuality, as is appropriate to the writer and mystic she wants to be, she cannot. She talks of herself in the third person, and by calling herself 'this [God's] creature' claims for herself the same role as anyone who says the first line of Richard of Caister's 'Prayer'. But her individuality, one might say, overwhelms her persona. The concentration of all in this quotation on morality fits what she wants to be (the day of the week, cake and beer turn out not to be gratuitous, for Margery's husband is upset not only because she refuses him his 'kindly' – that is, natural – sexual business but also about her fasting on Fridays). The humour, the natural love of life and its detail, the general background focusing suddenly on the slightly grotesque, though relevant, details of cake and bottle reflect habits of noticing, of building up the world as seen which, while not quite so obviously part of the mystic she wants to be, still could be paralleled in mystical writings and are familiar in the art of her time – the scene would be natural on a misericord. But there is an emotional, an autobiographical concern, even in the pathos of the husband's descending from the high 'commune kindly' to 'meddle' for the same act, which gives us entry to a life felt as we understand feeling.

Margery's *Book*, in fact, gives us exactly what one would want of a historical novel: visits to and conversations with famous or interesting people, including both Richard of Caister and Julian of Norwich; her opinions of them, always shrewd where we can check them, and their opinions of her; a pilgrimage to Jerusalem; a journey with beggars from Danzig to Paris; and concrete detail everywhere, even to an attempt at conversation in Italian ('And then the lady said unto her, "Margerya in poverte?" She, understanding what the lady meant, said again, "Ya, graunt poverte, Madam" ').[11]

Her language, indeed, is just that which Virginia Woolf attributes to the Pastons and (ignoring his irony) to Chaucer. And she resembles closely both Chaucer's principal female pilgrims. Her self-revelation, assumption of being in the right, addiction to pilgrimage, shrewdness, humour and garrulity remind one of her social equivalent, the Wife of Bath: when she was young, she shared the Wife's fondness for profit, social position, conspicuous clothing and sex and, even when she was converted by disasters and visions, only transposed these worldly things to an otherworldly sphere. Her emotional and sensuous piety is just that of the Prioress, and is reflected in her language – which moves easily with a curious memorable force from a description of a pain in her right side, 'so hard and so sharp that she must voiden that was in her stomach as bitter as if it had been gall',[12] to the naïve sublimity of her prayer for relief, 'Ah, Lord, for thy great pain have mercy on my little pain.'[13] Just so the Prioress moves from 'O martyr, souded to [enlisted with and/or united to] virginity' to 'My throte is cut unto my necke-boon.'[14] It would be hard to say whether this ease is more to the praise of Chaucer's observation of a certain kind of person, or to the scope of the language of his day.

She did not intend an autobiography. She wrote in imitation of saints' lives, in particular the *Revelations* of St Bridget of Sweden (d. 1373), which she studied, and sought out St Bridget's serving maid at Rome. She calls it 'a short treatise and a comfortable for sinful wretches',[15] much as one of the copyists of Julian's book describes that as 'full many comfortable words, and greatly stirring to all they that desire to be Christ's lovers'.[16] Many must have treated it as a treatise on contemplation: about 1501, Wynkyn de Worde printed a brief anthology from it which made it just that.

To be that, it should have been focused not on her idiosyncrasy but on God. But she does not really know the difference. In part, this is because of her culture, in part because of her own psyche. The following is a modern diagnosis, for which I am indebted to Dr Anthony Ryle:

> As is so often the case, she revealed a great deal of herself in her opening statement; partly in giving the account of her puerperal breakdown following her first child, which seems to have been psychotic in nature; but more so by revealing her discontent with those who had attempted to help her at this time, and this became recurrent throughout her account.
>
> Prior to her puerperal breakdown, she was already pre-occupied with some secret guilt, and it seems certain, from the evidence later in the story, that this guilt was sexual in nature; thus, she is continually preoccupied with the bad thoughts of others, and even in her sixties, when travelling, was worried that she might be the victim of rape; and, on one occasion, fairly late in life, seems to have had a brief recurrence of a psychotic period lasting a week or two, in which she was deluded and possibly hallucinated about the sexuality of the males surrounding her. Given, therefore, that this preoccupation was probably persistent, whether conscious or unconscious, a great deal of her subsequent behaviour can be seen as some form of defence against this. The defence she has chosen is one which, within the culture, was clearly the most powerful one, namely the assumption of a direct and special link with God. I feel this was a spurious claim, because her main concern, despite the attempts at visionary writing, would seem to be with the view others held of her as a person of particular religious capacity.
>
> Her claims to the special relationship were made mani-fest through conspicuous activities, like dressing in white, weeping copiously and persistently, howling, grovelling on the floor, etc. Those around her, in general, are un-impressed by these various behaviours but, in her own system, their failure to acknowledge her claim was one more proof of its rightness because she could convert their

rejection to a persecution, which she bore for Christ's sake. This system seems to have been, therefore, coherent and largely impenetrable, and she received enough reward from it to maintain her in a reasonable equilibrium but, I imagine, at considerable cost to those around her for most of her life.

I don't think that there is any evidence of a continuing psychotic process at work here. The most satisfactory description would be of a hysterical personality organization; her behaviours served as a constant source of attention and, in her own terms, of confirmation from others around her.

Hysterics are usually highly suggestible. Margery reflects even to exaggeration the quality of her time. This quality is the other reason why she does not see that her frankness and concern with her visions and trials could be taken as egocentricity; for she lives in a world in which our rules for distinguishing subjective from objective do not apply, in which everything, even what is recognized as a dream or delusion, is intensely given, presented, existent in its own right. Among the medieval philosophers, *subjective* does not have our connotation of 'imaginary', nor *objective* of 'existing as it would do if we were not conscious of it': rather, *subjective* means 'existing in itself' and *objective* 'presentational', with no sense of consciousness as a film between the two, or as something projected on to reality. And while mystics like the author of the *Cloud of Unknowing* are, as we shall see, perfectly aware of the phenomena we might ascribe to the unconscious personality, they do not interpret them quite as twentieth-century psychoanalysis would.

The opinions of others on Margery show this. Those who approve of her think of her weeping and other eccentricities as a gift of God. There were many like her; an annotator at the Carthusian monastery of Mount Grace around 1500 remarks, of her falling down at a vision and roaring, that 'Father M. was wont so to doo'[17] – that is, Richard Methley (also of Mount Grace), the translator of the *Mirror of Simple Souls*. Those who doubt or disbelieve her suspect devils – not possession by devils, but delusion – or, sometimes, drunkenness.

Two people suggest something like psychiatric treatment – people of the classes whose function that was, a friar and an anchoress. One of these, a Franciscan friar, diagnoses her as ill, saying that if she could not withstand her fits of sobbing it must be 'a cardiacle or some other sickness'.[18] This is a psychophysical explanation – a superfluity of humours at the heart. Julian of Norwich apparently entered as far as possible into Margery's view of herself, agreeing that tears are a sign of God's visitation, not the Devil's, and advising patience against the language of the world. But she also advised Margery to fulfil whatever God put in her soul 'if it were not against the worship of God and profit of her even – Christian, for, if it were, then it were naught the moving of a good spirit but rather of an evil spirit'.[19] This sounds like a gentle qualification in the terms of Margery's own 'support system'. But what no one in fact does is, as in the modern diagnosis, to treat Margery's consciousness and personality as themselves objects of analysis, apart from her body or the influence of God and other spirits, or to trace her behaviour to subjective roots that are hidden from her.

Margery herself seldom mentions causes of her experiences other than her relation to God. Her second breakdown, for example – twelve days of sexual temptation and visions of men showing her their genitals – she says that God allowed because she doubted whether it was really he who was speaking to her, to show her the difference between his communication and the Devil's. In a way that itself seems significant, she omits all mention of two occurrences that we know of from other records and would naturally suppose to have influenced her. One is that her father died in the year of her final crisis in her sexual relations with her husband – the incident on the road from York which I have quoted – and of her final resolve to dedicate herself to God. Since part of her final arrangement with her husband was that she should pay his debts, probably her father had just died and she had inherited his wealth. But clearly she did not think of any causal link here in her emotions.

The other is that it was her parish priest, William Sawtre, who was the first man burnt for heresy in England under the statute *De Heretico Comburendo*, which was passed hastily to expedite his execution on 2 March 1401. He had been accused of Lollardy on 30 April 1399, abjured publicly at King's Lynn on 25 May, left the town and relapsed. The record of his trial shows him as a forceful, humorous priest, to whom one would guess Margery would have reacted strongly. Throughout her life she was (wrongly) under suspicion of Lollardy, and more than once in danger of burning. But she never mentions Sawtre or his fate. Now her first breakdown was between 1397 and 1401 but most probably in 1400, and the cause of it she says was that she 'had a thing in conscience'[20] for which she had done private penance, but never confessed it: being in danger of death after her first childbearing, she wanted to confess, but her confessor reproved her sharply before she fully said what she meant, so that with fear of his reproof and of damnation she went out of her mind. It may be that, as Dr Ryle suggests, this guilt was sexual. Yet it cannot have been for fornication, for she affirms that she was a virgin except for her husband. And it is curious that she never says what this sin was, though she is free spoken about her sexual difficulties. It seems in the context of her time at least as likely that her sin was listening to William Sawtre; that the abomination of heresy was why her confessor was sharp with her, and why she never mentions it; and that the special relationship with God was her private defence against guilt for a Lollardy she had abandoned.

However that may be, Margery's character finds natural expression in this context of strong emotion, exactly weighed sin, explicit doctrine and contrition, physical penance and immediate special divine causation. There is no writer, moreover, through whom we can better understand how close to the ordinary medieval person might be the unseen world of devils, angels, saints, the Virgin Mary and Jesus in his humanity. She tells, indeed, of plenty of worldly people who said 'Why speak ye so of the mirth that is in Heaven? ye know it not and ye have not be there no more than we';[21] but for her and plenty of others the gap seems to run not, as we expect, between the ordinary world and the unseen but between those together and God in his transcendence. Even that gap she believed herself to have passed on 9 November 1414 in the Apostles' Church at Rome when God the Father took her to wife; but she says 'she was full sore afeared of the Godhead, and she could no skill of the dalliance of the Godhead, for all her love and all her affection was set in the manhood of Christ.'[22] And normally her overflowing emotions attach themselves immediately to figures of contemporary piety – besides Our Lord, to Our Lady, St Mary Magdalene, St Catherine and St Bridget. She projects so straightforwardly that, in a last colloquy with Christ, he restricts himself to telling her what she thinks. Her visions are sensory and she is strangely involved in them. She not only feels Our Lord's toes 'and to her feeling it were as it had

been very flesh and bone',[23] but makes a hot drink for Our Lady
after the Crucifixion.

This in her time is not unusual. She could have learnt much of it
from the popular *Meditationes Vitae Christi*, which tell us not only
to imagine biblical scenes as if we saw them with our own eyes but
actually to involve ourselves in them. They advise:

> Take up, then, the child Jesus in your arms, put Him up on
> an ass, and carefully lead Him along, and if He wishes at
> any time to get off, do you joyfully receive Him in your
> arms, and hold Him lovingly there for a while, at least until
> His mother reaches you, for at times she may be tired and
> walk more slowly.[24]

The step may not be great to Margery's sensations.

Meditation of this kind began with vivid imagination and proceeded to vigorous emotion. It did not include an intellectual
pondering on the scene contemplated: that came in during the
sixteenth century. Louis Martz argues that the difference between
the two kinds is not only parallel to, but actually caused, the difference between medieval religious lyric, vivid and emotional, and
metaphysical poetry with its sinewy intellectual development. The
older kind of meditation was especially associated with the
Franciscans, and had its effect in their sermons and in the lyrics
written or inspired by them. Similar again, and probably associated,
is the feel of the Nativity and Passion plays. Margery knew their
sermons – the Franciscan who diagnosed her state as 'cardiacle'
roused her lamentation with his preaching on the Passion, even
though he thought her response diseased – and, as for plays, the
crisis with her husband on the way back from York happened on the
day after Corpus Christi, when the York plays were performed, so
that probably they were returning with their emotions heightened
from watching them.

Margery at times inclines to a slightly different form of meditation. Hugh of St Victor said that 'God is become everything to you,
and God has made everything for you': one should see the world
transparent to God's meaning, reading it like the letters in a book.
Seeing 'a little manchild sucking' on a poor woman's breast at
Rome, Margery thinks of 'our Lady and her son in time of His
passion'; then Jesus said to her 'This place is holy.'[25] But even this
concentrates on the historic and the visual. More often Margery

concretizes her religious intuition into apparitions and to what the Lollards and the reformers attacked as a religion of works. Christ actually tells her, 'leave thy bidding of many beads',[26] which may mean only prayers, but suggests the rosary. She is convinced of a vocation to wear white, loves pilgrimage, and believes the strangest miracles – as that blood came out of three hosts at Wilsnak in Brandenburg, where she went to see it.

Charles Williams sums up her religion as 'always perhaps foolishly, but certainly sincerely, concerned with her Lord'.[27] But her concern has always to be embodied, whether in busy good works, or in visions, or in weeping, or in ritual acts. She reminds one of C. S. Lewis's comment that 'When Catholicism goes bad it becomes the world old worldwide *religio* of amulets and holy places and priest-craft: Protestantism in its corresponding decay becomes a vague mist of ethical platitudes.'[28] This is the exact contrast between Margery Kempe's book and the next surviving English autobiography – that of the musician and poet Thomas Whythorne (1528–96), who grew up with the Protestant Reformation. He was religious, but his religion is expressed through moral consciousness. He will say 'whosoever doth so fall, it is good for them to call to God for mercy, and to desire him that they have of him the secret and spiritual grace, the which is the forgiveness of their sins and the regeneration or new birth and life',[29] while Margery describes how Christ

> never forsaking His servant in time of need, appeared to His creature which had forsaken Him in likeness of a man, most seemly, most beauteous and most amiable that ever might be seen with man's eye, clad in a mantle of purple silk, sitting upon her beds side, looking upon her with so blessed a cheer that she was strengthened in all her spirits, said to her these words: 'Daughter, why hast thou forsaken me, and I forsook never thee?'[30]

Now whether the supernatural realm exists transcendently or does not exist at all, it is not to be simply identified with the *inner* in the sense of the 'contents of the human mind', nor with the *outer* in the sense of 'the everyday external world', though it may overlap with them. Margery with her visions and Thomas with his moral experiences both tend to make that simple identification. It seems likely that it is this very mistake that drives them, and the parties they represent, apart. For they represent opposite and overemphasized stresses within Christianity and in man's symbolizing faculty. C. S. Lewis points out that the reason for the opposing stresses is that Catholicism is glad and Protestantism reluctant to proclaim the embodying of grace, spirit and immaterial qualities:[31] that is, the various differences tend to be about how literally one should take apparently allegorical language, Catholicism stressing the closeness of the relation between the physical symbol or vehicle and the tenor or thing signified, and Protestantism the danger of mistaking one for the other. We have seen in Wyclif an early example of Protestantism, in his Platonism, his turning to the eternal verities rather than to the authority of the visible church, his stress on the invisible church and on the imperceptibility of the grace of God, his denial of transubstantiation.

The denial of transubstantiation was perhaps the most conspicuous element in the protests and prosecutions of the Lollards; complicated as the various beliefs about it are, it is a clear instance of the general dispute's being about symbolism. All Christians agreed that bread and wine in the Eucharist 'are' the body and blood of Christ and that he is therefore present therein. Catholic doctrine supposed that this means that, while the physical structures and qualities remain, the substance of bread and wine is changed, by a change unlike any other, into the substance of Christ's flesh and blood. This might cover anything from the most mystical awareness to making physical blood (such as Margery Kempe went to see at Wilsnak) simply what is there, as we should always see if our senses were not deceived. What Catholics agreed on was the closeness of relation between what is naturally there and what is supernaturally there. They stressed, as it were, in Christ's words 'This is my body' the literalness of 'is'. Conversely, Protestant beliefs might vary from the strongest assertion that the body and blood are there although you do not touch, taste, smell or see them (as in Wyclif's belief or in Luther's consubstantiation) to the assertion that they are not there (being in the past or in heaven) except as metaphorically spoken of in a historical memorial of the Last Supper or Crucifixion. But all Protestants were agreed that it is in the nature of a sacrament for an outward and visible thing to signify an inward and spiritual grace, for there to be a distinction between tenor and vehicle, a thing signified and what signifies it, this bread and Christ's body. Whatever is true, they protested, transubstantiation is the wrong word to describe it.

In other cases, the thing signified might generate a symbolic act for Catholics which Protestants simply rejected. The image of our life as that of exiles returning to the heavenly Jerusalem is common to Protestant and Catholic; but Catholicism is more likely to think it salutary to connect this with pilgrimages to 'this earthly city Jerusalem',[32] as Margery Kempe does, or to Canterbury, as does Chaucer's Parson. In practice the Catholic stress on the closeness of relation between inner and outer tends to mean that the Catholic will value the outer more highly, seeing it as expressing religious or transcendental values, realities and acts more directly than does the Protestant, who tends to restrict these to the inner. Thus Lollards regarded mystery plays with suspicion because, as one of them said, 'the weeping that falleth to men and women by the sight of such miracles-playing . . . is not principally for their own sins, ne of their good faith within-forth, but more of their sight without-forth'.[33]

Later Protestants extended this suspicion of 'sight without-forth' to destroying images, painted glass and wall paintings. The religion of works (Margery Kempe's religion), mingled with the medieval instinct of display, was, as we shall see in the next chapter, responsible for a great deal in art and architecture: for prayers valued not in relation to the sincerity of the sayer but simply as things done, and so for chantry chapels built for the saying of such prayers and of masses for the good estate of the dead, for the prayers written as formal poems by John Lydgate and painted round the Clopton Chapel at Long Melford, and for the Beauchamp Chapel at Warwick, with their suggestion of being perpetually acted prayer. Langland made his living by saying such prayers, but presents Lady Meed making a shameless confession to a man who assures her

> Woldestow glaze that gable and grave therinne thy name
> Syker shold thy soule be hevene to have.[34]

Syker] sure

The Lollards too denounced such things and, even when their words, as in *Pierce the Ploughman's Creed*, suggest an aesthetic awareness of their beauty, blame the friars for encouraging the luxury of

> Tombes upon tabernacles tyld upon lofte
> Housed in hirnes harde set abouten,

Of armede alabaustre clad for the nones,
Made upon marbel in many maner wise,
Knyghtes in her conisantes clad for the nones,
All it semed seyntes y-sacred upon erthe;
And lovely ladies y-wrought leyen by her sydes
In many gay garmentes that weren gold beten.[35]

tyld] set up   *hirnes*] corners   *conisantes*] badges
beten] embroidered

Again, both sides agreed that we should repent of our sins – but
should that repentance be embodied in particular acts, in acts of
charity, building of churches, going on pilgrimages, buying of relics
or pardons? Is the changed intention enough? As the Reformation
developed from Martin Luther in the 1520s, the central issue
became that of grace, faith and works. All sides agreed that we are
saved only by God's grace. From St Paul to our own time men have
found themselves locked in spiritual impasses from which they know
they have been freed, not by any effort of their own, but by something, 'strength beyond hope and despair',[36] from outside themselves. But how far, being freed, is what you now do your own
responsibility, your own work? Or how far in contrast do your works
depend wholly on how God accepts you, so that you live wholly and
only by faith in him? The Protestant turned inward: what you do
depends on what you are in relation to God; the Catholic turned
outward: what you are is measured by what you do, by each of your
particular acts. The whole dispute – as, for example, it appears in
the books that Sir Thomas More and William Tyndale wrote against
each other in the years 1528–33 – might be reduced to the question
whether good is a word used primarily of actions, so that a good man
is someone who does good works, or primarily of men, so that good
works are the things done by men of charity and faith. There need
have been no dispute: neither More nor Tyndale would have denied
that, as St Paul pointed out, even if I perform the most apparently
good actions, 'though I bestowed all my goods to feed the poor, and
though I gave my body even that I burned, and yet have no love',[37]
there would be no true goodness in it. Both were uncommonly
good, uncommonly delightful men; yet for Tyndale More denied
the inner freedom of the life of the spirit, and for More Tyndale was
irresponsible because the sight of one of them was focused on the
inner and of the other on the outer of human personality.

Allegory of the mind: Thomas Hoccleve

However, as C. S. Lewis again points out, there is a region of the mind where the bifurcation between Protestant preference for inner, Catholic for outer, does not arise: that is, the region where one uses allegory to describe inner in terms of outer. Thus it would be impossible on the basis of his allegory alone to decide whether Langland was Lollard or Catholic in sympathy, although he uses imagery of pardons and pilgrimages and sees in a dream at mass that Christ as

> Piers the Plowman was peynted al blody
> And com in with a cros bifore the comune peple
> And right lik in alle lymes to oure lord Jesu.[38]

For all this may be used sheerly as imagery of the inner world. And in fact, though some theological statements make it plain that he was a reforming Catholic – or indeed neither Catholic nor Protestant but simply medieval Christian, for both chronology and the general feeling of the poem suggest that he is only beginning to feel the kind of strain between inner and outer that Wyclif proclaimed – Langland remained popular with Protestants long after the Reformation.

Not surprisingly, Margery Kempe does not use allegory: everything for her is converted into the literal. One feels the indeterminateness of boundary between the inner and outer worlds, and the presentedness, the givenness, the objectivity of the whole double world much more subtly than in Margery in the allegories which were perhaps the most characteristic literary form of the entire Middle Ages. The two allegories probably most read in the later Middle Ages were the *Romance of the Rose* of Guillaume de Lorris and Jean de Meung, and the *Pilgrimage of the Life of Man* of Guillaume Deguileville, both in French but translated by Chaucer, Lydgate and others; the poets describe themselves as moving through the mental space made by their intentions, values and emotions and by the impact of other people, of society, and as meeting all those things – grace, love, reason, will, imagination, the sins, reward, jealousy, friendship – in the form of elusive figures, heavy with meaning, somewhat as we do in dreams. Commonly, but not necessarily, medieval poets use dreams for their descriptions; but their dreams are aimed directly at describing waking life. The *Romance* describes love in a young man's adventuring to pick a rose, the *Pilgrimage* salvation in the meetings and paths on a journey to a city seen in a mirror in a dream. But allegory enables them to focus not on surfaces but on principles. The poets do not usually seem to be exploring actual experience but rather to be creating ideal patterns of experience. It is not wholly easy, indeed, to make the connection between the actual experience of persons, real or possible, and Langland talking to Reason and Imaginatyf in *Piers Plowman*, Chaucer meeting Cupid and his Queen Alcestis in the *Legend of Good Women* or Gower meeting the court of love in *Confessio Amantis*.

If this region of the mind also seems a little stylized, remote and impersonal, there is again a writer, a contemporary of Margery Kempe and a disciple of Chaucer, Thomas Hoccleve (1368/9–1426), who was familiar with it – he translated some love allegory, and part of Deguilevile – and used its language to talk directly about himself and his own life. This is so unusual, so unprecedented in his time, that some suppose him also to be giving a stylized pattern. But the evidence, both internal and external, points to his telling the truth, so far as one can tell the truth about one's inner life, which to some extent exists only in terms of the conventions of one's age.

The principal reason for thinking that he is telling the truth takes us a long way into his character, and partly accounts for his peculiar self-concern. He was a clerk in the privy seal office at Westminster; and for a time, so he says, his reason left him, returning on All Saints' Day 1416.[39] Now his salary is recorded as, almost invariably, being paid to 'Thome Hoccleve', occasionally with no further specification, normally with the addition 'per proprias manus' ('through his own hands').[40] There is only one variation: on 18 July 1416 his salary for the half-year ending at Easter is paid 'Thome Hoccleve', two parts 'through the hands of' two clerks of the exchequer, and the bulk through his own assistant clerk, John Welde.[41] Such modes of payment are common enough when an official is out of London, as to Henry VIII's knights in the French wars, but Hoccleve's life offers neither reason for nor other example of travel. With this unparalleled payment, moreover, is another thing unparalleled to him, a loan also paid through John Welde. Presumably he was unable to receive his salary in person for some reason which would also explain the loan; possibly he was incapacitated from receiving the small fees for special services by which the clerks supplemented their salaries.

So far as they can, then, the official records support what he tells us, that 'the wild infirmity' cast him out of himself for 'a certain space'.[42] He tells us too an unusual amount of detail about the external circumstances of his life (far more than Chaucer, whom he claims as master and imitates): and this, too, to their limited power the records confirm. Thus he was one of four clerks at the privy seal office, paid £10 a year around 1406–7 (in theory at Michaelmas – the records add Easter – but normally so late as to entail discomfort) rising to £13. 6s. 8d. in 1411–12; and while he had some other small source of income his only real hope of improving his circumstances was by gaining a benefice in the church. Verifiable too are a large number of the names he specifies – of Lord Furnival, the treasurer, whom he begs for arrears of pay in one of his seemingly autobiographical poems, *La Mâle Règle*, and of Somer, the sub-treasurer of whom he also begs, punning and parodying in a roundel to summer. Of the three fellow clerks on whose behalf he begs, one (Hethe) is known, one (Baillay) has a name borne, in that nepotistic time, by three clerks in the office, and one (Offorde) has not been traced; Prentys and Arundel, his two companions who like himself stay up late drinking and often stay in bed till prime (9 a.m.), are also known clerks, though apparently not principal clerks at the office.

The accuracy of all this, with other verifiably probable details, such as his residence at Chester Inn in the Strand, and the friendly atmosphere in the civil service hierarchy, is not surprising, for a large proportion of his poetry was written for topical or practical purposes.[43] He is a topical poet, loving to refer to the clipping of coin, the new broad tippets, the broken soldiers from the French wars, the burial of Richard II's bones by Henry V at Westminster; and he addresses himself to a number of patrons, claiming Henry V when Prince of Wales and Humphrey, Duke of Gloucester, as especially gracious to him, and loving too to refer to details of their careers.

The sheer quantity of verifiable detail gives one confidence, though no actual proof, of his interest in recording accurately the circumstances of his life. It fits very well that Hoccleve was the first Englishman to be so fascinated by individuality as to cause to be made a portrait of an admired friend – Chaucer. As all Hoccleve's personal information, so his personal acquaintance with Chaucer has been doubted; but he worked within yards of Chaucer's home in Westminster, so that his explicit statement has something for and nothing against it:

> [my] fader Chaucer fain wold han me taght
> But I was dull and lerned lite or naght.[44]

People doubtless had previously wanted to preserve some memorial of a loved or revered person. And, by the time Hoccleve was born, sculptures had been made in England which look like portraits, although we cannot for the most part attach names to them, nor do more than guess at the motives that created them. Only royal persons – Richard II certainly with his wife Anne of Bohemia, and his grandparents Edward III and Philippa probably – seem as yet to have had effigies or memorials that are also portraits; and those seem a little stylized or idealized. Hoccleve, going beyond these precedents, tells us that he wants by Chaucer's 'lyknesse' to remind other men of his 'persone', much as images in church 'Maken folk thenke on God and on His seyntes'. The word 'persone', coupled with the portrait itself, suggests that he wants not only the resemblance in words or paint of rank, function, achievement or approximation to ideal beauty, but the lively, the essential singularity of a man's face

> That thei that have of him lest thought and minde,
> By this peinture may ageyn him fynde.[45]

In the book in which he put Chaucer's portrait, in 1412 – *The Regement of Princes* – Hoccleve also put a picture of himself presenting the book to Prince Henry, soon to be Henry V. Hal's pudding-basin hairstyle, long nose, proud pale face and firmly closed mouth fit the official portrait of him, and it is a fair guess that the figure of Hoccleve is a portrait too. Gervase Mathew speaks of Hoccleve's 'thick black hair and highly coloured face, the long nose and bitterly drooping lips';[46] but of course any interpretation is subjective. I could persuade myself rather of a slight uncertainty, an anxiety to please, a meticulous neatness combined with originality and wry humour. Such is the character that emerges from his poems, and it is this that is really the strongest argument for the truth of his descriptions of his inner life; for it is consistent with itself, with a clerkly zeal for accuracy, and with the kind of breakdown he seems to have had.

In 1406, in *La Mâle Règle*, he described his sins against Health, to whom he addresses the poem:

> . . . twenty wyntir past continuelly,
> Excesse at borde hath leyd his knyf with me . . .
> I dar not telle how that the fresshe repeir
> Of Venus' femel lusty children deere . . .
> At Paul's Head me maden ofte appeere . . .

Paul's Head was a tavern famous long before and after, situated south of St Paul's and half a mile from Chester Inn. There he bought the girls sweet wine and thick wafers in return for kisses, which contented him 'bettre than I wolde han be with the deede', since when men spoke of that 'For shame I wexe as red as is the gleede' (glowing coal). Drinking devours your money and makes you 'speke of folk amis'; but he had an advantage here – his 'manly cowardyse' made him afraid of arguments. He was 'for "A verray gentil man" y-holde' in the taverns at Westminster Gate for his extravagance; and in summer, when he should have returned

> Hoom to the Prive Seel, so wowed me
> Heete and Unlust and Superfluitee
> To walke unto the Brigge and take a boot,
> That nat durst I contrarie hem all three.

With the boatmen who 'my riot knewen . . . was I itugged to and fro',

> For Riot paieth largely everemo;
> He styntith nevere til his purs he bare.

They called him 'maistir', which made him feel 'y maad a man for evere'.

But he is contrite, asks Health for grace, and prays him to give Lord Furnival a token or two to pay the £10 owing him since Michaelmas.[47] Is this what is thought 'bitter'? The humour which will not allow that even his sins were serious, only unhealthy and inconvenient to himself, suggests a quite different temperament. That, and his slightly ambiguous station in life as an impecunious but clubbable London clerk of literary leanings (another of his poems urges Somer, now chancellor of the exchequer, to provide a May Day dinner for the Court of Good Company, the Temple dining club they both belonged to), put one in mind of the nineteenth century – Mr Guppy and others of Dickens's clerks, but above all of Charles Lamb.

He was like Lamb in another way: they both had mental breakdowns. Maybe the humour of both was partly accommodation to their temperaments: Hoccleve's three personal poems are so much his best as to suggest that he was inspired by personal depression. If it be accepted that he has an autobiographical concern, it seems significant too that both he and Margery Kempe, novel in their age for this, were also mentally disturbed. One thing new in their age, in particular, they have in common – the fear of burning for heresy 'unto ashen drye',[48] as Hoccleve says of John Badby, burnt in 1410 for denying transubstantiation. Badby was led astray by Thought: *thought* is a loaded word for Hoccleve, meaning 'anxiety' and 'worry' as well as 'thinking'.

> Be war of Thoght, for it is perillous;
>   He the streight wey to discomfort men ledeth;
> His violence is ful outrageous;
>   Unwise is he that besy Thoght ne dredeth.[49]

It must have been an edgy generation.

He does not describe his breakdown itself, since 'the substaunce of my memorye / Wente to playe',[50] but he does describe the state he was in somewhat later, and the symptoms people expect to see in him still:

> Men saide I loked as a wilde steer,
> And so my look aboute I gan to throwe
> Myn hede too hye another said I beer.
> 'Full buckish is his brain, well may I trowe';
> And saide the thirde, 'and apt is in the rowe
> To sitte of hem that a resounless rede
> Can geve – no sadnesse is in his hede.'
>
> Chaunged had I my pas, som saiden eke:
> For here and there forth stirte I as a ro,
> Non abode, non arrest, but all brain-seke.
> Another spake, and of me saide also,
> My feete weren ay waving to and fro
> Whan that I stonde sholde and with men talk,
> And that myn eyen soughten every halk.[51]

This, of course, is merely the kind of thing people say about a man they suspect of going a little mad; it does not follow that they are remembering how Hoccleve had in fact behaved during his troubles. But the list is sensible enough and suggests, as does Hoccleve's whole description, a substantial tradition of intelligent clinical observation, and medical approach to mental illness. It may be contrasted with the lengthier, more confused and apparently second-hand list in Bartholomaeus' *De Proprietatibus Rerum*:

> These ben the signes of frenesye: discoloured urine duringe the fevere, with woodnes and contynual wakinge, mevynge and castinge aboute the iyen, ragynge, strecchinge, and castinge of hondes, mevynge and waggynge of hede, gris baitinge and knockinge togedres of teeth. Alwey he wole arise of his bedde; now he singeth, now he laugheth, now he wepith, and bitith gladliche and rendith his wardeyne and his leche; selde he is stille, but he crieth moche. This hath most perilous sekeness, but he knowith not that he is seke.[52]

I give Dr Ryle's description of the apparent sequence of Hoccleve's troubles, both as confirming the plausibility and coherence of the account in the poem, and as providing a contrasting modern language. He suggests that Hoccleve suffered

> . . . from a bi-polar manic-depressive illness, having experienced a minor depressive episode in 1406 (*Mâle Règle*) and a worse and more prolonged one starting in 1411 (*Regement*) terminating in an attack of mania or hypomania which cleared in 1416 (*Complaint and Dialogue with a Friend*), after which time he was but mildly depressed.
>
> This diagnosis is based upon the very clear history he gives of a change in his normal state of relatively abrupt onset, which he experienced as an illness. The depressive phases are characterized by insomnia, depression, self-castigation, anxious ruminations, and an obsessive concern, possibly delusory, at the prospect of poverty. All these symptoms are typical of a manic-depressive illness. He gives (in *Complaint and Dialogue*) a rather sparse account of a manic episode, and probably had little recall of it, but his

report of his friend's account would support the presumption that it was indeed a manic, or hypomanic, attack.

To have suffered a first attack in the fourth decade of his life and a second more severe one in the fifth is a common sequence with this condition, and, though his mental health may have remained satisfactory, he would have been at an increased risk of a further episode as he grew older.

I think Hoccleve was right to protest that his attack should be regarded as an illness; this condition runs in families, and though more common in those of certain temperaments, notably those who are conscientious but sociable people, which I think would describe Hoccleve, there is relatively little evidence to suggest that the lifestyle or habits of an individual play a significant part in provoking further attacks.

Hoccleve's meticulous and helpful temperament is apparent in the last work of his we have, a collection of forms and examples of the documents used in his office, composed about the time that he was pensioned off in 1423–4. He seems to have died in March or April 1426.

His insistence on regarding his condition as an illness, although considerably nearer twentieth-century habits of thought than Margery Kempe's ideas, is still of his age. He is not laying stress on a world of mental and emotional causation, as a psychologist would, nor primarily thinking of the possibility of cure through mastering the causes. He does indeed agree to follow his friend's advice in the *Complaint* not to work too hard but insists

> . . . that nevere studie in book
> Was cause why my mynde me forsook
> But it was causid of my long seeknesse
> And othir wyse not in sooth fastnesse.[53]

What this previous sickness may have been he does not say: it might be the trials of a writer's life listed in the *Regement* – the concentration which does not allow them to 'Talken and syng and make game and play' as 'artificers' can while they work, the stooping which causes backache and stomachache, and the eyestrain[54] – or the depression that Dr Ryle would imply, or the sinfulness that Penelope Doob has argued for. It scarcely matters; for the sickness which was the immediate cause is quite distinct from the madness, and the important thing about the madness was that it was 'the stroke of God'. Nor, though it was a chastising, was it in itself something to be ashamed of, like homicide, extortion or any sin that 'proceden of frailtie of man hymselfe – he brewyth alle tho'.[55] God took Hoccleve's wit from him 'when that he se that I it mysdyspente'.[56] Yet even that is not stressed, and one may fairly infer from the opening of the whole meditation on madness that, like the fall of the leaf at Michaelmas, it was primarily a warning of the mutability of the world and the universality of death. Hoccleve leaves the matter a devout mystery. His illness is set in a single world where all sickness, physical or other, depends on the will of God; where none should presume to judge another man's sanity, since

> . . . no wight knoweth, be it he or she
> Whom, how ne whan God woll him visite:[57]

and where one's primary response should be repentance and open gratitude when God withdraws his stroke.

If we take it – as I think we must – that Hoccleve's inner debate and his apparent autobiographies concern a real inner life, it is curious to consider how these develop out of medieval conventions that are not really adapted to them. For Hoccleve, though a humourist, is not an ironist on Chaucer's scale: it is with his obsessive meticulousness that he cites Geoffrey de Vinsauf's architectural advice on the need for decorum and a prior plan.[58] In fact he uses such a variety of genres as to tend to confirm the idea of a quite different, autobiographical drive behind them. *La Mâle Règle* is a begging letter which parodies the penitential lyric, the *Prologue to the Regement*, and the *Complaint and Dialogue* are both frames for books with a strong flavour of the genre of 'Consolation', and into these he incorporates other elements. Most important is that incorporation of the poet's self into the story that Chaucer partly learnt from Dante, partly from other sources, and turned to comic use, for the humour of making the creator of the Canterbury Pilgrims the only one among them unable to create his own story, for the advantage to both poet and reader of having an eye in as well as over the story, and as a gesture of humility. But for Chaucer, as for Langland too, the needs of the poem rather than the poet's own character are the cause of the person in the poem: for Hoccleve it seems – and from *La Mâle Règle* to *Complaint* increasingly so – that the poem is being led off to manifest the character. Again, he perhaps takes, as John Burrow has suggested, from Criseyde's paired monologues the rather more internalized conversations with himself which he introduces with two pathetic personal situations, the first peering into the mirror in his chamber:

> To loke how that me of my chere thoughte,
> If any other were it than it oughte;
> For fain wolde I, if it had not be right,
> Amended it to my cunning and might.

the second:

> As that I ones fro Westminster cam,
> Vexed full grevously with thoughtful hete,
> Thus thoughte I, 'A grete fole I am
> This paviment adayes thus to bete,
> And in and out laboure faste and swete
> Wondring and hevinesse to purchace,
> Sithen I stonde out of all favour and grace.'

> And then thoughte I on that other side:
> 'If that I not be seen amonge the prees,
> Men deme woll that I myn hede hide
> And am worse than I am, it is no lees.'
> O lord, so my spirit was resteless . . .[59]

He seems to take refuge from his troubles in continual move-ment, physical and spiritual; and so far from the reader's feeling that he is illustrating conventional personae, one is inclined rather to feel that he takes refuge, after such painful and surely personally reminiscent details as the mirror, in a convention like the 'wofull man' consoled by Reason whom he took from Isidore of Seville.[60]

But the important point is that he has learnt from all these: and particularly and significantly, as one would expect in a man of his age, from Augustine's description in the *Confessions* of his own 'unwar youth' and from the penitential tradition in general. 'His psychological insight,' observes Eva Thornley, 'which imparts a realistically human pettiness and pathos to his portrait, stems never-theless from the penitential tradition, with its introspective analysis, and distinction between action, or word, and intention.'[61]

The outcome is a language which, even more than Chaucer's,

gives the lie to Virginia Woolf's assertion that medieval English is too stiff for psychological analysis. But the medieval style of innocent presentedness, the confessional style, is still there. Hoccleve sees what happens to him, not from one of the many centres of men's consciousness, relativistically, but in the one world ordered teleologically under the will of God.

Twentieth-century writers tend either to the objective, causal, scientific description of the mind, even to interesting themselves in describing outer behaviour to the exclusion of mind; or to the intensely subjective, in representing the inner stream of consciousness. But Hoccleve is innocent of these extremities: although he is describing his own painful isolation, his style is public. He has been isolated, cut off from contact with the mass of men, but not cut off from ordinary language in the solipsistic prison on which twentieth-century writers lay stress. He describes himself as if he were observing such a man as modern behaviourists assert all men to be, a man whose inner life and sensations are confined to silent mental acts, and who is best spoken of in terms of his public behaviour. Yet not only is he remote from any sense of mental causation such as behaviourists resort to; he is not even interested in the 'cardiacles' and other psychophysical causes of Margery Kempe's friar. Nor at the other extreme does he or any other medieval writer resort to the streams of fragmented images by which Virginia Woolf and other modern writers try to convey the sensation of subjectivity. But he has a method to convey just this, the method of most medieval writers: that is, an allegory so lightly stressed and all-pervading that we notice only its most obvious uses and are apt to mistake for frigid and impersonal what is in fact warm and breathing. We have already seen (in addition to the two obvious examples of literary convention, the letter addressed to Health and that written by Cupid) a number of pieces of allegory which only the use of capital letters makes obvious. There are the wooing by Heat, Unlust and Superfluity; Riot, created out of 'my riot' three lines earlier; Excess with his knife at board; and above all Hoccleve's enemies, resorting Sickness and Thought. C. S. Lewis with some reason compares Hoccleve's power to Aeschylus' in some lines in which Thought

> . . . that fretyng adversarie
> Myn herte made to him tributarie
> In sowkyng of the fresschest of my blod.[62]

Whenever this pervasive, heavily or lightly stressed allegory is noticed, one finds that it is prepared for by, or merges into, a style in which all nouns denoting abstractions or mental experiences are liable to have what I would call 'substantial quality'. Thus 'my riot' above already passes into 'Riot', and in the first verse of the *Regement* the final line, 'Thought me bereft of sleep with force and myght',[63] which is clear personification allegory, is prepared for by the weighty nouns of the first lines:

> Musyng upon the restles bisynesse
> Which that this troubly world hath ay on honde.[64]

Again, the lines of the *Complaint* quoted above, about Hoccleve's thoughts on his way from Westminster, continue:

> O lord, so my spirit was restelees;
> I soughte reste and I not it fond,
> But ay was trouble redy at myn hond.[65]

The movement of 'spirit' develops from – is still partly the same thing as – the movement beating along the pavement, making substantial an echo of the unclean spirit of the Gospels which 'walketh through dry places seeking rest'. Then the repetition 'restelees . . . reste', with the continued sense of spatial movement 'soughte . . . fond', gives weight and substance to 'reste'. And when that is over 'trouble' is given first a slight suggestion of personality by 'redy', then of physicality by 'at myn hond'. Spirit, rest and trouble, though not outright allegories, seem to do more work in the sentence, to be more solid than if they were mere abstractions. They suggest a world in which a phrase like Hoccleve's 'substance of my memory' means an enduring substance, thoughts are as *thingish* as things, and things easily merge – as according to the Aristotelian doctrine of intelligible species they should merge – with the world of thought. Hoccleve gives us precisely the latter sensation when he says that when the leaves yellowed and fell at Michaelmas 'that change sank into mine hearte root'.[66]

Significantly, too, Hoccleve uses the distinction quoted before from the Lollard sermon against miracle plays, and common at the time, between 'withinforth' and 'withoutforth' – not as the Lollard did to contrast inner and outer but to bring them together. His friends, he says, would not believe he was whole, although

Day by day they sy me by hem gon
In hete and cold, and neither still nor loude
Know they me do suspectly – a derke cloude
Her sight obscured within and withoute.[67]

A reader's perception of 'substantial quality' is obviously highly subjective. But it would be congruous with this single world that we have described among the philosophers and others that such a quality should exist, that one aspect of the frailer distinction between inner and outer should be the closeness of thoughts to things and of things to thoughts. And I think experience shows that there is no better rule for enjoying the barer diction not only of Hoccleve but of Chaucer and indeed of most writers up till the mid-seventeenth century than to be sensitive to the weight they put on abstractions.

These habits of expression have not vanished. The curious weighty though bare Chaucerian diction is liable to reappear when anyone tries to describe, to restore, a sense of a single universe of matter and spirit combined. Wordsworth, possessed by such a sense of the world, writes in such a way; and it is very striking how in him as in Chaucer and other medievals the stylistic trait with regard to spirit – the substantial, thingish response to abstractions – goes with a shared stylistic trait with regard to matter: that in Wordsworth's poetry, as Virginia Woolf says of Chaucer's, common things are so arranged 'that they affect us as poetry affects us, and are yet bright, sober, precise as we see them out of doors'.[68]

It happens that Wordsworth and Hoccleve wrote surprisingly similar poems – Wordsworth's 'Resolution and Independence' or 'The Leechgatherer' and Hoccleve's *Prologue* to the *Regement of Princes* which illustrate the similarity in describing mental experience along with a certain difference. In each poem, the poet tells us that after a

. . . stormy nyght was gon
And day gan at my window in to prye,
I roos me up, for boote fonde I non
In myn unresty bed lenger to lye[69]   (Hoccleve)

and walked into the fields, brooding on his uncertain fate, on his own troubles and on the world's. There

> A poor old hore man cam walkyng by me[70]   (Hoccleve)
>
> The oldest man he seemed that ever wore grey hairs.[71]
>
> (Wordsworth)

A conversation follows, marred by the poet's absentmindedness, but ending in his receiving comfort from the old man's fortitude.

The poems have the same seven-line stanza, rhyming ababbcc (rhyme royal), except that Wordsworth lengthens the last line of each stanza by two syllables. So, although Hoccleve's poem was not printed till after Wordsworth's death, the coincidences seem great enough to suggest that Wordsworth had seen one of the manuscripts, possibly that in his own college of St John's, Cambridge, attracted perhaps by reading in Warton's *History of English Poetry* about the portrait of Chaucer, and moved by the theme he puts in his poem of 'Mighty poets in their misery dead'.[72] If so, Hoccleve's poem would have given form to an incident that certainly happened to Wordsworth.

However this may be, what concerns us here is, first, that both poets when they speak of their inner state use a kind of allegory. But, secondly, Wordsworth's is not like 'Thought, that fretting adversary . . . sucking of the freshest of my blood.' Hoccleve describes immediate and articulate consciousness allegorically. If Wordsworth's allegory works at that level of the mind, it seems conventional and imposed:

> . . . the fear that kills;
> And hope that is unwilling to be fed . . .[73]

Where it is powerful, it concerns anxiety not further verbalizable:

> And fears and fancies thick upon me came;
> Dim sadness – and blind thoughts, I knew not, nor
>   could name.[74]

To quote other poems by each, Hoccleve uses the same technique with the same substantial quality for the content of his immediate and articulate consciousness – 'I soughte reste and I not it fond'[75] – that Wordsworth uses rather for dim upwellings from the unnamable limits of his mind:

> Blank misgivings of a creature
> Moving about in worlds unrealised . . .[76]

One can extend the comparison further than Wordsworth. Personification of parts of the psyche remains common today, in the writings of Freud and other psychoanalysts, and in the accounts of themselves given by some people under stress; but it tends to be used of the mysterious and hardly describable hinterland of the mind.

Just as the level of personal inner experience where Hoccleve and other medieval allegorists find it natural to use allegory is both nearer to the surface and more definite than the level where Wordsworth and the moderns do so, so with the outer and with the moral and metaphysical framework of the world. Wordsworth's grey old man carries a great weight of symbolism. He is like, says Wordsworth, a huge stone so strangely placed that it seems intelligence must have brought it there, a stone 'endued with sense: / Like a seabeast crawled forth'. He is like a still cloud, or

> Like one whom I had met with in a dream,
> Or like a man from some far region sent . . .[77]

He is, all these images suggest, a boundary figure between consciousness and the other side of things, and the consolation he gives is not only moral. It is also assurance, to someone troubled by hyperconsciousness and by a sense of division from the world, assurance of repose and of something rooted in the dark. Wordsworth inherited generations of the attempt to distinguish subjective and objective in the modern sense. He is trying to reverse the attempt, struggling to assimilate the two, to realize a single world, by an inspired, surprising symbolism. He explores the depths of the inner world for what is furthest and most mysterious, tries to catch the shadows that lurk there, and waits on the outer world for some message, looking into the limits of each to see if there is something that underlies both. Both within and without he looks for and sometimes finds this mysterious substance as something coming from behind experience, which appears only in symbols.

Hoccleve, with all his mental troubles and need for comfort, is not in need of a cure for alienation. The consolation the old man gives him is entirely made up of articulated moral truths, derived from experience, which are part of the revealed explicit structure of the world. And, for Hoccleve, this is enough.

Hoccleve's old man could not be called symbolic in any way: he is the bearer and example of moral truths. Of course, there are figures much more, and more mysteriously, laden with meaning in medieval literature. One might instance Chaucer's haunting and disconcerting old man in the *Pardoner's Tale*, very different from Hoccleve's, though the meeting with him is curiously like that with both Hoccleve's and Wordsworth's. He has been thought by scholars to be the immortal Wandering Jew, the allegorical Old Man of Sin spoken of by St Paul, or Death himself. It is likely enough that Chaucer meant such – perhaps all these – overtones to be picked up; but none of the words that suggest them goes beyond the limits of a naturalistic conversation between a quirky old man and a drunken youth. These ambiguities one might well feel to be like the reality and mystery of Wordsworth's solitary old man. But it is still true that all the significances one feels inclined to suggest for the Pardoner's old man touch more on public references in the structure of a shared world, are more definite, more able to come to the full light of consciousness, than is the case with Wordsworth's.

For all medieval writers as well as for Hoccleve, I think depth and surfaces, inner and outer, are not widely separate. They have no need to search far for a single world. Immediate experience is weighty and substantial and joins inner and outer. However much they may seem to confine their descriptions to the surface of experience, they do not normally feel shallow. Indeed, because they appear to feel the world as seamless, even the lesser writers like Hoccleve, much more Langland or Chaucer, have for us the healing power that Wordsworth found in the Leechgatherer himself – which is one reason why the Romantics, Wordsworth, Coleridge and the rest found them fascinating.

One aspect of this is that most medieval writers, seeming to feel at home in the world, seem also to find it easy to laugh, and especially to pass abruptly from laughter to solemnity and awe. The great defect of Wordsworth in 'The Leechgatherer' is that, trying to keep up the strange awe and melancholy of the meeting with the old man *qua* symbol, he makes his conversation with the actual old man pompous and bathetic. The absentmindedness into which he falls in the gap between symbol and reality is very justly parodied by Lewis Carroll in the White Knight's song about the 'aged aged man'. Wordsworth, forgetting that he has already asked the old man about his occupation, says:

> – Perplexed, and longing to be comforted,
> My question eagerly did I renew,
> 'How is it that you live, and what is it you do?[78]

and the White Knight consequently sings in parody:

> So, having no reply to give
>   To what the old man said,
> I cried 'Come, tell me how you live!'
> And thumped him on the head.[79]

But Hoccleve incorporates something that sounds Carrollian into his ordinary narrative with no feeling of bathos:

> He sterte up unto me, and seyde, 'Sleepes thou, man?
> Awake!' and gan me shake wonder faste,
> And with a sigh I answered atte laste
> 'A, who is ther?' 'I', quoth this olde grey
> 'Am heer' . . .[80]

This sort of transition is a characteristically medieval habit. Langland in his most tremendous passage still portrays Satan giving orders to resist Christ's conquest of hell:

> Ac arise up, Ragamoffyn, and areche me alle the barres
> That Belial thy beelsire beet with thy dame
> And I shall lette this lord and His liht stoppe[81]

Ac] And   *beelsire*] grandfather

The mystery plays are full of this holy laughter, and indecorous mirth is part of the essence of Chaucer's irony. But indeed it was part of the stuff of common life, in such ceremonies as the election of a boy bishop in the Christmas season, or in the presence of a Fool as a common member of a great household. It is striking that Robert Bolt in his normally faithful *A Man for All Seasons* cannot afford to give us the sheer zany farcicalness of Sir Thomas More's wit. In this as in much else, More was a medieval man more than a humanist: it was going out of fashion in the decade of his death, when boy bishops were suppressed by law. Religious seriousness and classicist ideals of decorum killed it: these are qualities we must suppress in ourselves if we are to appreciate the sublimity of medieval literature undiminished by its grotesquery.

There were no doubt many causes for this wild humour, but I think the central cause was that no one thought it either natural or admirable for a man to feel himself isolated in the universe: hence a certain unnecessary dignity, a false pride, was not usually admired.

Chesterton points out that the Overreacher – the tragic hero of
Marlowe's time and later, embodied in such figures as Tamburlaine
– is a figure of farce in the morally identical Herod of the mystery
plays,[82] the memory of whom lingered in Hamlet's advice to the
players not to 'out-Herod Herod'.[83]

If this is so, then I think medieval humour may be linked with
another and apparently very different medieval characteristic: the
lengthy dullness which is the typical vice of their poets – and which
is again something that, to a less degree, Wordsworth shared with
them. Even more than Wordsworth, they seem to take the
interestingness of statements of fact and value for granted. And
unlike Wordsworth most of them take for granted man's place in
the world and his relation to it. They did not find it necessary to
exhibit the struggle of which Wordsworth's ally Coleridge speaks,
the struggle of consciousness to absorb an objective world whose
resistance enables it to realize its own existence. For the objective
world, in their understanding of it, naturally presents itself to their
consciousness, as we have seen in looking at their philosophers.

Hoccleve is certainly typically medieval in his meticulous didacticism. One can find it attractive as a trait of his odd character, but in
his own century it was thought absolutely excellent: of his *Regement
of Princes* forty-five manuscripts survive, only six fewer than of
Gower's *Confessio Amantis*. For us – although his style has
commonly an admirable carefulness which when he has a good
subject, as in his three passages on the death of Chaucer, can achieve
great heights – he is much at his most readable when he struggles
with the expression of his own character. And in this struggle he is
untypical. Presumably because of his mental disorder, he is
unusually absorbed by his private mental world; and to an unusual
degree, therefore, the union of inner and outer that he nevertheless
retains appears in him in the mental world at the expense of its
appearance in the outer, physical world.

The universe of symbol: Thomas Usk

In turning, so to speak, from the outerness of the inner world, from
the allegorical embodiment of the mind, to the innerness of the
outer world, we must leave Hoccleve, but we can still find help in a
comparison with Wordsworth. C. S. Lewis observes:

Nature has that in her which compels us to invent giants:
and only giants will do. Gawain was in the north-west
corner of England when 'etins aneleden him', giants came
blowing after him on the high fells. Can it be an accident
that Wordsworth was in the same places when he heard
'low breathings coming after him'?[84]

Some scholars would disagree so far as to remove the physical aspect,
the sound of breathing, and translate *aneleden* simply as 'pursued'.
But even if this were right, giants would still be creatures of the high
fells, brought into being like other creatures of myth, partly from
the response to nature of mythopoeic people. Wordsworth's experience was created partly in the same way. But he carefully stresses
the interplay of the subjective and the outer worlds, explaining that
he heard pursuit partly because he felt out of place in the still night
and guilty at stealing from another boy's snare. The *Gawain* poet
simply presents the happening in the outer world. It does not follow
that he necessarily believed in giants. Chaucer in another vein makes
his Wife of Bath explain that although in King Arthur's day the
landscapes appropriate were full of fairies –

> The elf queene, with hir joly compaignye
> Daunced ful ofte in many a grene mede[85]

– 'now kan no man se none elves mo' because the friars have driven
them away and displaced them as seducers. This does not suggest
that Chaucer believed in the supernatural of folklore. But both he
and the *Gawain* poet find it natural to include wholly in the outer
world what Wordsworth must explain as a balance of inner and
outer.
   If fairies and giants were fully and literally believed in, they would
be in a measure detached from the physical world that gave them
birth. And if one expected to find elves in green meadows and giants
on high fells, then the elfish quality would no longer be a quality of
the meadow itself nor the titanic a quality of the actual fells. Elves
and giants would resemble the visions that owed their existence to
the projected inner feelings of Margery Kempe. But there is a widely
diffused medieval sense of the world somewhat like Margery's
response to the poor woman's house at Rome – 'This place is holy'
– which holds inner and outer in balance. It is felt in a remark by an
earlier admirer of Chaucer than Hoccleve, Thomas Usk, that 'kindly

[natural] heaven, when merry weather is aloft, appeareth in man's eye of colour in blue, steadfastness in peace betokening within and without.'[86]

I take him to mean that the blue of the sky means — one might almost say is, or participates in — fine weather outwardly, and that is a kind of steadfastness in peace; and inwardly and spiritually the natural thing itself means the steadfastness in peace which God bestows. Perhaps he implies further that the steadfastness in peace of heaven natural means the steadfastness in peace of heaven supernatural: and all this not by merely personal, subjective interpretation, but by nature. Usk's phrases imply that here, as in the allegory of the mind, is a balance of inner and outer. But what he means by 'within and without' differs from what the Lollard preacher we quoted earlier meant, and from what in general we have meant in dealing with allegory. Usk's 'within' is not part of the life of the individual's mind and soul, but is the spiritual meaning of an object concretely existing 'without', in the natural universe, not a metaphor, nor a play made by a poet, nor an image designed to express an artist's meaning. The sky for Usk is what the Romantics were to call, in contrast to allegory, a symbol: 'a thing being wholly itself is laden with universal meaning'.[87] Coleridge, following the romantic quest to revive a single world, has a comment very like C. S. Lewis's observation that allegory exists in a region of the mind where the bifurcation into Catholic and Protestant has not occurred. But Coleridge's version is that there are two powers of the mind: one the reason, which tends toward the abstract, the visionary, the universal, the all, and corrupts into mere abstract theorizing and doctrinaire revolutionary politics; the other religion, 'the concentration of All in Each', which brings universal truths to life as particular individuals and duties, and corrupts into superstition, with its amulets and pilgrimages, friars and pardoners. Reason and religion acting together, motivated by wisdom and love, perceive the symbolic world.[88]

It is certainly to such a life and such a world that Usk portrays himself as having been shown the way by love. Whether he really was a wise and loving person is for the reader of his two autobiographical documents to decide. Readers differ as they differ about Margery Kempe, Hoccleve, or any living person.

What is most tempting is to describe him as a romantic in the sense of a man sustaining his values in an ideal world though they have been shattered in practice. His two surviving documents deal with his life in London in ways that differ much as do the pictures of Florence by Villani and Dante with which we began Chapter 2 – one positive and political, the other symbolic and personal, both claiming to embody the truth.

In the first document, a deposition of 1384, Usk describes how as clerk to John Northampton, Mayor of London, he joined in a plot 'in John Willingham's tavern in the Bow'[89] to keep Northampton's party permanently in power, exciting dissension between the small people and the great, and removing all the senior officers of the city. For Northampton's party said that 'thilke persons that held the contrary of his meaning were enemies to all good meaning'.[90] Northampton himself, when he lost the next election, declared to the people at Goldsmiths' Hall, 'Sirs, thus be ye shape for to be overrun and that I nel nought suffer: let us rather all be dead at once than suffer such a villainy'.[91] The open violence that followed 'is in point to trouble all the realm, and the city hath stand in great doubt and yet doth'.[92] For all of this Usk, confessing and repenting that he 'was a full helper and promoter', asks 'grace and mercy of my liege lord the King, and afterward of the mayor, and of all the worthy aldermen, and of all the good commons of the town, as he that will nevermore trespass against the town . . .'[93]

After this confession, he was taken under the patronage of the king's party and of the mayor, Sir Nicholas Brembre, and for this, when King Richard's enemies, the Lords Appellant, took power in 1388 and Brembre was executed on trumped-up charges (for example, that he had designed to restore to London its mythical name of New Troy), Usk also suffered a lingering and painful death, protesting to the last the truth of his accusations against Northampton.

Deserted by both parties, he wrote *The Testament of Love*, which tells how Love came to him in prison, examined and counselled him, and assured him that everyone whom she sets to serve is successful in their service. He answered her by telling how, eight years before, at the end of October 'when barns ben full of goods as is the nut on every halk', he went walking to 'see the winding of the earth . . . by woods that large streets were in, by small paths that swine and hogs hadden made',[94] and took refuge on a ship from feral pigs. The walk is naturalistic enough – one might think that he had actually taken such a walk and only later seemed to approach its meaning – but the ship was Travail, its crew Sight, Lust and Thought, and its master Will, driven through storm to an island where Love had come to Usk. She showed him in a blue mussel shell a Margaret, that is a pearl, like the pearl of great price in the Gospels, the jewel 'that (all other left) men should buy, if they should therefor sell all their substance'.[95] But he has ever since been hindered from achieving the pearl, his heart's desire, by enemies, by lack of wealth, and by his own unworthiness.

At this point in the book, it seems plain that the pearl, Margaret, is his lady, and that the *Testament* is to be an allegory of love like the *Romance of the Rose*. And, indeed, not only here but through most of the book at one level it is a treatise on courtly love. By that notion of love, in a society where the natural destiny of a woman was to be a wife, and of a wife to be her husband's servant, all the counter-balancing possibilities were fulfilled: the male lover was the servant, devoted in a religious adoration that inspires all good qualities in him, through all hardships, to a woman who may be indifferent to him, and whom he may perhaps never possess in marriage or otherwise. In theory at least the knight had two counterbalancing values, war and this love. Love tells Usk that the badge she gives her retinue (as every lord in our period gave a badge to his household) is 'meekness in countenance, with a manly heart in deeds and in long continuance'.[96] She honours those who are 'lions in the field and lambs in chamber; eagles of assault and maidens in hall; foxes in counsel, still in their deeds; and their protection is granted, ready to ben a bridge, and their banner is areared, like wolves in the field'.[97] One is reminded of Chaucer's Troilus; and indeed Love tells Usk to read 'the book of Troilus', written a year or so earlier, and says that better than Chaucer, or his equal, 'in school of my rules could I never find'.[98]

But now Usk goes on to describe to Love how it has come about that his enemies are defaming him, and in so doing he tells, albeit more personally, the political story told in his deposition. His confusions and troubles of conscience are now those typical of many people who, drawn in youth 'to certain conjurations and other great matters of ruling of citizens',[99] have found that the policies that seemed to promise profit to friends and to the community were 'of tyranny purposed'.[100] His nineteenth-century editor, Skeat, in full Victorian confidence that Northampton's party was the party of progress, says that Usk 'is too full of excuses, and too plausible; in a word too selfish'.[101] But indeed in his struggles he sounds not unlike

Wordsworth, Blake and Coleridge in their disappointment with the revolution in France and in their conflict of loyalties when Britain declared war on it. Abused for giving evidence against his master, his defence is that peace 'was in point to be broken and annulled', especially in the city of London, to which he has 'more kindly love than to any other in earth, as every kindly creature hath full appetite to that place of his kindly engendrure'.[102] This may be that patriotism which is 'the last refuge of a scoundrel':[103] yet 'kindly' – that is, natural – makes a prime value for Usk, even to the words of his book, which is in English rather than Latin or French because, he says, men should show their fantasies in the language 'kindly to their mouths'.[104]

At this point the whole allegory of the opening of the *Testament* appears like a frame for Usk's political apologia, the narrative of the voyage only his political life in the mirror of allegory, and Margaret perhaps the peace of his native place. This would have been a familiar enough use of allegory. Allegorical pageantry was then, and was to remain until the mid-seventeenth century, a common way of expounding or proclaiming political and social ideas. Langland, when he presents the ideal of a kingdom in a coronation at which 'an angel of heaven'[105] stoops to advise the king, may probably recently have seen, close to Cornhill where he describes himself as living, the golden angel that appeared in a pageant before Richard II's coronation. This was only a grand example of a pageantry frequent in the streets of London, surviving today in the Lord Mayor's Show.

But political allegory is not the whole truth about Usk's *Testament* either. His theme widens out, drawing in a large reading (Boethius' *Consolation* and Chaucer's translation of it; Chaucer's *Troilus and Criseyde* and *Legend of Good Women*; Higden's *Polychronicon*; *Piers Plowman*; Aristotle, Augustine, a treatise of Anselm *On the Concord of Foreknowledge, Predestination and the Grace of God with the Will* and the Bible) to interpret his painful and perplexing life in the context of the whole world.

The world is not only described in allegory but is itself, apart from all description, deeply symbolic. The meaning of the blue of heaven as steadfastness in peace is not allegorical for Usk but symbolic, that is naturally inherent: it goes out to meet and create other meanings, to interpret the blue of the allegorical mussel shell which contained Margaret. But blue is also Mary's colour; so real pearls and their formation in mussels radiate out in meaning again to suggest the

incarnation of Christ, who also is every man's pearl, in the body of
Mary. Whereas Margery Kempe brings meaning in to specific and
concrete images and things (in Coleridge's sense, religion) and
Whythorne and Hoccleve (reason and allegory respectively, in
Coleridge's terms) both move from concrete happenings and images
towards inner meanings, emotions, sensations and abstractions,
Usk's meaning extends from thing to thing in the total universe,
though it ends in the three centres of Christian thought: God, his
incarnation and his sacramental presence in the mass.

But Usk does not abandon his starting-points in the specific and
concrete. At the end of his book he explains his symbolism as
meticulously as befits a mayor's clerk. Margaret, he says, is a woman,
and 'betokeneth grace, learning or wisdom of God, or else holy
Church';[106] and he justifies this betokening by two analogies. First,
Old Testament events, being wholly themselves, are figures of New
Testament events: 'How was it that sightful manna in desert to
children of Israel was spiritual meat? Bodily also it was, for men's
bodies it nourisheth; and yet, never-the-later, Christ it signified.'
Secondly, bread is made the flesh of Christ. The two analogies are
connected, for the portrayal of the manna that fed the Israelites in
the desert as being like the host in the mass is common in church
windows and elsewhere. This echoing and re-echoing is particularly
welcome to Usk; but he is careful further to echo Christ's words on
the bread from heaven, saying that ' "It is the spirit that giveth life;
the flesh, of nothing it profiteth." Flesh is fleshly understanding;
flesh without grace and love naught is worth. "The letter slayeth;
the spirit giveth lively understanding." '[107]

Usk's personal and slightly dizzying delight in correspondences is
typically medieval, drawing on familiar responses. And here we
return to the quotation from Bartholomaeus' encyclopedia with
which we began this chapter: through knowledge of the physical
world men can understand the spiritual meanings hidden in the
Bible. The normal interpretation of the Bible proposed a number of
meanings: common is a list of four as described by Aquinas and
Dante. If you read in the Psalms 'When Israel came out of
Egypt . . .' you understand *literally* the original historical event,
the Exodus. But the text has a second level, by which you read a
moral allegory, the escape from sin to a new life. Moreoever, these
are both related to a third meaning (the Exodus by foreshadowing,
the escape from sin as effected by), the resurrection from death of

Jesus: *the historical allegory*. And consequent on these three is the fourth, the *anagogic* meaning achieved by what Bartholomaeus calls the 'contemplation unmaterial of heaven': when you read Exodus on this level you understand the passing over of the soul from this life to heaven. Evidently this is an interpretation not only of the Bible but of history and its relation to eternity.

Hugh of St Victor said, in a thought we have already looked at, that God has two books; and our reading of the Bible has its counterpart in the way in which we read God's other book, the world. You might, developing such thoughts, write your own book after this pattern of multiple meanings in the Bible. Usk did so; according to the letter to Can Grande said to be by Dante himself, and in any case medieval, Dante did so in the *Divine Comedy*; in some sense Langland did so as he revealed the successive inner meanings of *Piers Plowman*; Chaucer makes his Parson direct our eyes, as well as the pilgrims', to the anagogic meaning of the journey to Canterbury:

> To shewe you the wey, in this viage,
> Of thilke parfit glorious pilgrymage
> That highte Jerusalem celestial.[108]

Usk ends his final paragraph by seeming to assure us that the meanings work in both directions: we do not simply read this and understand that, but all the objects in the web of meaning illuminate each other: 'Charity is love; and love is charity'.[109] Early in the *Testament*, Love says that the knot between Usk and Margaret is fastened by consent of two hearts; idiots 'ween forsooth, that such accord may not be, but the rose of maidenhead be plucked. Do way, do way; they know nothing of this.'[110] This evidently makes little sense except of sexual love; and Usk needs the devotion of courtly love to illuminate the love of God and even political devotion, which, in return, illuminate courtly love itself.

Margaret, then, is to be treated as a real woman at the first level of reading: we need not suppose that she was historically real beyond Usk's story, though it is quite possible that she was. Chaucer in his *Legend of Good Women* connects the pearl with the daisy which resembles it, and makes both the emblem of the good queen Alcestis, whom he calls 'myn owen hertes reste'.[111] It might be that the same high and distant woman, full of mercy and grace, was in the mind of Usk as of Chaucer: it has been conjectured that she was Richard II's queen, Anne of Bohemia.

This is tenuous argument, but certainly, fictional or not, in Usk's book there is a woman who is the object of courtly devotion. We shall see more of this love in its relation to society in Chapter 5; here what concerns us is the ideal, the ideal that Usk makes the model for many other things. 'All things', he says, 'to workings of mankind evenly accordeth, as in turning of this word *love* into *truth* or else *righteousness*.'[112] He is talking of disinterested devotion, which as love, honour or integrity is always its own reward. He wants us to recognize that everything anyone values is valued only because of love; and love cannot be willed, only given in response to the beloved. Here, he argues, is the answer to many problems, showing how it is that we are good not by our own effort but only by the grace of God, and how, too, whatever evil seems to happen to us, we have all good if we love. In love of any form, whether it be expressed in politics, church discipline or the mystical way to God, no one can approach his heart's desire through riches, dignity, power or renown. The only way is by devoting will in one sense, the kind of will that appears in emotions to the will that appears in purpose, and purpose must be inspired by the beloved. So 'all the thoughts, busy doings and pleasance in thy might and in thy words that thou canst devise ben but right little in quitting of thy debt. Had she not been, such things had not been studied.'[113] Thus, like Augustine and Bradwardine, Usk concludes that

> . . . thy ginning and ending is but grace alone. . . . Love have I none, but through grace of this Margaret pearl. It is no manner doubt, that Will will not love but for it is loving, as Will will not rightfully but for it is rightful itself. . . . And although this loving will come in mine heart by freeness of arbitrement [choice] . . . yet owe [ought] I not therefore as much allow my freewill, as grace of that Margaret to me lent . . .[114]

Thus Usk fulfils the intention he announces at the beginning of this book: to justify (like Milton) God's ways to man by writing a treatise that actually is 'of love, and the prime causes of stirring in that doing, with passions and diseases for wanting of desire'.[115] He can do this because for him as for Bartholomaeus Anglicus the universe is symbolic: because (much more straightforwardly than for Milton) the means to bring man to know and love his creator 'is the consideration of things made by the creator, where through by thilk things that ben made understanding here to our wits, are the unseen privities of God made to us sightful and knowing, in our contemplation and understanding'.[116]

For Usk 'every creature crieth, ''God us made'' ',[117] and conversely 'everything, a this half God [is] made buxom [responsive] to man's contemplation, understanding in heaven, and in earth, and in hell.'[118] Moreover, man understands the whole universe because he participates profoundly in it, summing up in himself every way of existing.

> Hath not man being with stones, soul of waxing with trees and herbs? Hath he not soul of feeling, with beasts, fishes and fowls? And he hath soul of reason and understanding with angels; so that in him is knit all manner of livings by a reasonable proportion. Also man is made of all the four elements. All university is reckoned in him alone; he hath, under God, principality above all things. Now is his soul here, now a thousand mile hence; now far, now nigh; now high, now low; as far in a moment as in maintenance of ten winter; and all this is in man's governance and disposition. Then sheweth it that men ben like unto gods, and children of most height.[119]

As usually with Usk, most of this is medieval commonplace. As we have already felt with Hoccleve, so with Usk one feels that, in Owen Barfield's words, 'In his relation to his environment, the man of the Middle Ages was rather less like an island, rather more like an embryo, than we are.'[120]

One must not take this too far. Most kinds of attitude to the world seem represented in most ages. And one can find men who feel lost and alienated in the world in the fourteenth century as in any other. Ockham's philosophy gave them a vehicle – as we have seen, it may have tempted Chaucer – and even in the Bible the Book of Ecclesiastes offered them imagery and sentiment. Thus we find the meditative poet of the Vernon manuscript singing:

> Dieth mon, and beestes die,
>   And all is oon occasion;
> And all o deth bos bothe drie
>   And han oon incarnacion;
> Save that men beth more slye

All is o comparison.
Who wot yf monnes soule stie
    And beestes soules sinketh down?
Who knoweth beestes' intencioun
    On her creatour how they crie
Save only God that knoweth her soun?
    For this world fareth as a fantasy.[121]

oon occasion] one happening   *o death . . . drie*] must endure
the same death   *slye*] clever   *stie*] rise up

But men whose attitudes seem untypical of their age tell one a great
deal about their age by the limitations within which they write, and
by the assumptions through which their attitudes are expressed.
This poet, with all his doubt about the meaning of life, does not
suggest that the gap runs between man and the world, between
intelligible spirit or self and unintelligible object or matter: he
thinks of an unintelligible but still seamless world with a gap
between itself and its creator. Neither does he doubt the existence of
man's soul, nor conversely does he suppose that man's soul is a
substance needing nothing but itself in order to exist, dynamic and
self-justifying, as many later philosophers have thought. Of the
existence of the creator, on whom man's soul like all the world
depends, he raises no doubt. In all these convictions and assumptions, he represents his age.

Symbol and sight

If indeed most human attitudes occur in most ages, and if it is
illuminating to consider the means by which the people less
characteristic of an age express themselves, it is also illuminating to
consider what is the special quality that makes people natural to an
age. The three people we have so far principally looked at, though
very diverse, were not eccentric in their opinions. Usk transforms the
world of practical and immediate experience into a maze of noble
meaning; Margery Kempe concretizes meaning into a world of
fleshly understanding. Hoccleve, much more tentative than either,
and relatively less concerned with religion, goes with Kempe rather
than Usk in his interest in himself; and, while this may be connected
with their personal troubles, we saw in Chapter 1 that others of their
generation, such as Audelay and James I of Scotland, share this turn

of interest. But Hoccleve too unfolds his experience into substantial patterns, as if mental experience were visible or tangible – a habit shared by all three which gives a peculiar expression to each of their temperaments. The hysteric Margery Kempe is encouraged by this habit to believe in her projections; the depressive Hoccleve, to treat the issues and aspects by his conscious mind as allegorical substances and persons; the romantic Usk, disappointed by his secular loyalties, to discover a meaning to which he can devote himself, clear in the architecture of the world. All three share a sense of the meaning of the world inherent in something like visible surfaces: as Owen Barfield again puts it, they live

> . . . as if the observers were themselves *in* the picture. Compared with us, they felt themselves and the objects around them and the words that expressed those objects, immersed together in something like a clear lake of – what shall we say? – of 'meaning' if you choose. It seems the most adequate word.[122]

The metaphors 'visible surface' and '*in* the picture' are a great deal more than descriptions of the way in which medieval thought and poetry strike modern sensibilities. It was a widely diffused medieval opinion that abstract thought naturally embodies itself best in visual images; and it was a perfectly conscious medieval practice that embodied such mental images in stone and paint. Their philosophers were the heirs of Aristotle, for whom 'the soul never thinks without a picture',[123] 'the thinking faculty thinks of its forms in mental pictures':[124] 'no one could ever learn or understand anything, if he had not the faculty of perception; even when he thinks speculatively he must have some mental picture with which to think'.[125] This sort of theory lies behind the stress on visual images we noted from the handbooks on meditation that probably influenced Margery Kempe. Reginald Pecock in his *Repressor of Overmuch Blaming of the Clergy* (*c.* 1449) argues that such visual mental images need support from the outer world: men who 'haunt daily contemplation', he says, know how hard it is for a man 'to wrestle withinforth in his own imaginations without leading withoutforth had by beholding upon images'.[126]

Frances Yates in her book on *The Art of Memory* has argued that there may have been a close connection between the imaginary buildings, adorned with images arranged in order, which were

recommended from the classical period onward to help in remembering complex arguments and structures of thought, and the visible
and physical Gothic cathedral. Abbot Suger of St Denis, one of the
creators of Gothic architecture, more mystically observed in the
twelfth century in his Neoplatonic praise of the works of art at St
Denis that meditation on the beauty of its jewels transfers 'that which
is material to that which is immaterial', to meditation on the sacred
virtues so that 'it seems to me that I see myself dwelling as it were, in
some strange region of the universe which neither exists entirely in
the slime of the earth nor entirely in the purity of heaven'.[127] The
thirteenth-century biographer of St Hugh quoted in Chapter 1
speaks less metaphysically, but similarly.

Literature fits naturally into this unity of visual and intelligible:
one thinks again of Virginia Woolf's praise of Chaucer's 'bright,
sober and precise' showing of things, echoing, though I do not know
if she knew it, *Caxton's Book of Courtesy* praising Chaucer's
language because it

> . . . seemeth unto man's hearing
> Not only the word but verily the thing.[128]

More specifically, Chaucer's set pieces, like the House of Fame or the
temples in the *Knight's Tale*, resemble the intelligibly visual buildings conjured up by the art of memory. As we have observed before,
qualities that the greatest writers of an age reveal to us, once noticed,
illuminate lesser writers. Stephen Hawes's *Pastime of Pleasure*
becomes a most enjoyable book when one has acquired the knack of
using it to see pictures. And one is not surprised to discover that its
noble sequence in which childhood gives place to manhood,
manhood to love, love to age, age to death, death to fame, fame to
time, and time to eternity was paralleled, even to small details like
the brace of greyhounds that follow manhood, in what 'Master
Thomas More in his youth devised in his father's house in London, a
goodly hanging of fine painted cloth, with nine pageants, and verses
over every of those pageants: which verses expressed and declared,
what the images in those pageants represented: and also in those
pageants were painted the things that the verses over them did (in
effect) declare.'[129]

The people of this period created in their arts, verbal and visual,
the unity of intelligible and visual that they found in nature. And
even the coarsest minds could respond to something in the result,

even if not exactly to what the artists intended. The author of the *Tale of Beryn*, continuing Chaucer's *Canterbury Tales* to the arrival of the pilgrims in Canterbury Cathedral, delightfully observes:

> The Knyghte wente with his compeers toward the holy
>   shryne,
> To do that they were com for, and aftir for to dyne;
> The Pardoner and the Miller, and othir lewde sotes,
> Sought hem selfen in the chirch, right as lewde gotis;
> Pyrid fast, and pourid, highe oppon the glase,
> Countirfeting gentilmen, the armys for to blase,
> Diskyveryng fast the peyntour, and for the story
>   mourned,
> And a red it also right as wolde rammys hornyd.[130]

> *Pyrid*] Peered   *the armys for to blase*] to interpret the heraldry
> *Peyntour*] painting   *a*] they

Dream, self-examination and discovery

The symbolic world sometimes seems like an enchanted dream, with the connotation natural to us of an escape from reality. The Franciscan John Marignolli, having about 1349 journeyed to Ceylon, incorporated all that he recorded of it in a history of mankind since the Fall, commenting that 'from Seyllan to Paradise, according to what the natives say after the tradition of their fathers, is a distance of forty Italian miles; so that, 'tis said, the sound of the waters falling from the fountain of Paradise is heard there'.[131] Almost as dreamlike is Sir John Mandeville's combination of physical and ethical reasons in his apology that of Paradise 'ne can I speak properly. For I was not there. It is far beyond, and that forthinketh me; and also I was not worthy.'[132]

But the note of contrition in Mandeville's remark warns us of something else, of the psychological fact that, although dreams may begin as self-indulgent romance, the result of the mind's wandering unchecked down paths of habit and wish-fulfilment, it is also in dreams that the mind lies most open to alien truth. Mandeville's whole book is strange in just this way: it is a fiction, the dream of a man who shows no evidence of travelling beyond western Europe, extracting from earlier travel books the most grotesque, wonderful and romantic tales, and so delusive a fiction that it was taken seriously long after Colombus's time. It portrays the enchanted geography, the union of sense and significance, that medieval men (other, no doubt, than hardheaded merchants like the Polos) delighted to believe in. But equally it is the reaction of an intelligent man to the great opening of the world that came and endured with the Mongol Empire, in the later thirteenth and earlier fourteenth century, when there was a Catholic archbishop and several bishops even in China. Mandeville is in his way as open to other cultures as Montaigne in his essay on the cannibals; except that Montaigne, being a sixteenth-century man, made knowledge of the relative validity of other cultures feed his own scepticism, while Mandeville, being a fourteenth-century man, found it confirmation of his faith that God is everywhere to be recognized, and a wonderful proof of Christ's saying 'Other sheep I have, which are not of this fold'.[133] The good heathen is accepted by God: that, along with the wonderfulness of the world, seems to be one of Mandeville's messages in his book. It is counterbalanced by a rebuke: the good heathen is accepted by God rather than the Christian who, with the advantage of revelation given him, is lukewarm enough to let the land of the revelation remain in the hands of unbelievers. In both ways, his enchanted book aims at strange and even shocking truth.

Mandeville's book was widely read, notably by Chaucer and the *Pearl* poet, to whose special wisdom, at once tolerant and acutely penitential, it perhaps contributes. They draw on him, it seems, for their own visions of paradise, quite deliberately using the dreamlike quality of the enchanted world as material for poems overtly in the form of dreams, with the characteristic dangers of real dreams. It is dangerous to dream of paradise, because you may forget the bitter realities of the world and – much more dangerous – because you may discover the truth about yourself. In *The Parliament of Fowls* Chaucer, with characteristic self-awareness, describes the making of dreams:

> The wery huntere, slepynge in his bed,
> To wode ayeyn his minde goth anon . . .
> The syke met he drynketh of the tonne;
> The lovere met he hath his lady wonne.[134]

The syke met] The sick man dreams   *tonne*] barrel

And then in the garden that he enters, whose green wall reminds one of the mossy green walls about Mandeville's paradise, he describes the psychological discoveries within, in this case about the various views of love, with characteristic irony and openendedness. All through his work from the *Book of the Duchess* to the *Nun's Priest's Tale* he returns to the problems of dreams, and those very qualities about them that so powerfully and naturally appeal to him: openendedness, ambiguity, self-consciousness, symbolic picture, irony and truth. What, for example, is the meaning when Criseyde dreams that an eagle takes the heart from her breast? It is caused by hearing a bird sing outside her bedroom – 'Paraunter [Perhaps] in his briddes wise [bird's way] a lay / Of love'[135] – but it signifies, perhaps, Troilus' future conquest of her, or Diomede's; or perhaps (though medieval dream lore would suggest that it is predictive) it simply reveals her wishes and her gentle, 'sliding'[136] character. Over medieval dream love Chaucer overtly worries, and especially over the contrast between *phantasma*, delusive dream, and true dream, *visio*.

The transition from romantic wish-fulfilment and self-justification (*phantasma*) to truth (*visio*) is implicitly but evidently the structure of the dream in *Pearl*. This it is worthwhile to compare with the *Testament of Love*. Both have the form of a dream in which a man crossed by fate is examined by a woman: an apparently real woman, called a Pearl, whose reality is surrounded by echo on echo of further meanings, meanings brought out by the examination, through which the narrator learns a little how human love illuminates the freedom of divine grace. Both were written about the same time, and although all arguments as to which influenced the other (for example, that since Usk imitates so many books he must be imitating this one too, or that Usk gives much more the tentative impression of a man thinking his way through, so *Pearl* must build on him) are weak, some connection is probable enough. But, though both writers unveil the symbolic world, a bright intricacy of depth on depth of meaning, Usk seems to do little more. In form, he copies Boethius' account in his *Consolation of Philosophy* of his examination by Philosophy, and though he once brings this situation to startling life, when Love 'all at once started into my heart: "here will I onbide", quoth she "for ever" ',[137] and although his thought, at the end, on love and grace is wise and just, the result is a revelation of something totally enclosing, enchanting but static. It resembles, indeed, the illusionism beloved by Gothic architects and artists, the rooms like those imaginary ones of the art of memory in which one seems to be enclosed by one man's mind although they intend to show the symbolic truth of the world, as in the painted room at Longthorpe Tower, or the tapestry of the Lady with the Unicorn at the Musée de Cluny. Usk misses in particular the real shock to the reader of Boethius' *Consolation*, the moment in the last paragraph when the whole process of reading the book, and with it the world, is turned inside out. Boethius encourages the reader, step by step and patiently, to contemplate the world and through it God; to grant that he will understand the world better and be more free the nearer he approaches to 'thilk divine thought that is yset and put in the tower . . . of the simplicity of God',[138] because there in eternity the past, present and future of the world are seen at once in the present: then suddenly he turns God's vision of the world quite round on the reader – calling on him to act in the awareness that 'ye worken and don . . . before the eyen of the judge that seeth and deemeth all things'.[139]

Something like that surprise seems the essence of *Pearl*. The narrator is continually surprised, at first by happiness beyond belief at seeing Pearl, then by bitter disappointment that he cannot stay with her. These things probably do not surprise the reader; but the reader may well be surprised, first by the way in which the courtly love language of the beginning lures him into expecting a love story and then presents him, not with a woman or a goddess of love, but with a child who died at less than two years; secondly, by the way in which the same courtly love language, asking him at the first line of the poem to share the narrator's love for a 'Pearl, plesaunte to princes paye' (a joy for a king's treasury),[140] merges like Usk's into the identification of that pearl with the single jewel in Jesus' parable for which one would sell all that one has, and finally returns in the last line to make oneself the object of love, the thing totally dear to Christ:

> He gef uus to be his homly hyne
> Ande precios perles unto his paye.[141]

homly hyne] household servants

There is nothing else, I think, in medieval English literature quite so close to Boethius' ending as this. But the twin effects, of finding that your book or your dream is quite other and more truth-telling than the entertainment you had promised yourself, and of finding the principal character being looked at through eyes you never thought would judge him, are common. If the enclosed effect of the *Testament* is like Gothic illusionism, then it may not be too fanciful to liken this sudden awareness of being laid open to the gaze and awareness of someone else to the surprise effect loved by architects of the years just before Chaucer was born, of finding yourself open to light or space where you did not expect it. Thus you come from the aggressive Norman nave of Ely into the light of the octagon (1322–42); realize at Gloucester that the east window is wider than the choir it lights (1337–57); or find yourself disoriented by the sections omitted between the vaulting at St Augustine's, Bristol (1298–1310), and the staring openings in the inverted arches of Wells (1338–40). This is perhaps an extreme, initial variation on what became a general possibility in Perpendicular architecture, with its huge expanses of windows – of finding yourself at the centre of a lantern that lights inwards, when you thought you were reading stories painted on glass.

Fanciful or not, this last seems to me a fair description of the effect of the *Canterbury Tales*, particularly in the hilarious but disturbing moments when the Host finds Chaucer himself wanting as a story-teller – 'Thy drasty rhyming is not worth a turd'[142] – or when we find ourselves wholly unable to say who has been made a fool of by the end of the *Pardoner's Tale*, or when the Knight reminds both Host and Pardoner that they are only playing a game. Chaucer never says so explicitly, but surely we are at times meant to wonder among the pilgrims, 'Is that one like me?' It is only himself he condemns, humorously through the Host, seriously in his *Retraction*; but perhaps the author of the *Tale of Beryn* bears witness to our analogy's having some truth to fifteenth-century feeling when he says that the lewd sots of the company 'sought themselves' in the stained-glass windows.[143]

Not surprisingly, the nearest effect to *Pearl*'s is found in the same author's *Gawain and the Green Knight*: there not only are we first encouraged to believe in Gawain's being the perfect knight by the symbolic description of the pentangle on his shield, and in his story's being a chivalrous entertainment about a knight retaining a perilous and perfect balance through elaborate seductions, and then shaken suddenly out of the belief; but at the moment of shaking we are made to look, not through his eyes, as the poet's powers of empathy and drama have heretofore made us do, but through his tempter's:

> How that doghty, dredless, dervely ther stondes
> Armed, ful awless; in hert hit him lykes.[144]

dervely] boldly

Langland has the effect of offering us a faery May morning romance at the beginning of *Piers Plowman* and then giving us a prophecy, a demand and a spiritual pilgrimage, and his long quest among the creatures of his mind gives something of the self-consciousness I am speaking of. The most formal effect is Gower's: having offered us in *Confessio Amantis*, like Chaucer in the *Canterbury Tales*, a world of instances to measure ourselves by, and built up the character of his narrator Amans through his elaborate interrogation by Venus' chaplain, he surprises Amans and the reader alike by Venus' revelation of his sole weakness in love, a discovery that every reader must be allowed to make for himself.

Gower's pattern suggests something that must be behind many of these effects – the confessional, enjoined since 1215 to be used by the laity at least once a year. With the elaborate questionings recommended in priests' handbooks, it must have done much to shape, even in large measure to create, the self-consciousness of the time. It is explicitly important in *Gawain and the Green Knight* and in the *Parson's Tale*, and may well contribute to the inquisitions of *Pearl* and the rest. Augustine's *Confessions*, too, offered a powerful influence in making self-examination before God the paradigm of self-consciousness.

But indeed this awareness of self before God runs in the very nature of Christianity, and especially in the Christianity of the late Middle Ages, with its constant evocation of the pleading of the suffering Christ.

> In the vaile of restless mind
>   I sought in mountein and in mede
> Trusting a trew love for to find
>   Upon an hill then took I hede;
> A voise I herd – and nere I yede –
>   In great dolour complaining tho:

'See, dere soule, my sides blede,
   Quia amore langueo.'[145]

Quia amore langueo] For I am sick of love

Walter Hilton recommends in his *Ladder of Perfection* a thought experiment that Hume repeated in the eighteenth century. Look, he says, within yourself, suppressing all images and imaginations of bodily things, and I will tell you what you will find: you will find nothing. Hume deduced from the experiment that there is no substantial self, Hilton only that we are darkened within by the roots of sin. But Hilton does not expect, if the roots of sin were dried up, to find the self: he says we should find Jesus. Julian of Norwich saw her 'soul so large as it were an endless ward, and also as it were a blissful kingdom; and by the conditions I saw therein I understood that is a worshipful city. In middes of that city sits our lord Jesus . . . .'[146]
   In this poet and the mystics, self-consciousness ceases to be only self-awareness before God: at its centre, it is awareness of God. The sense is very striking that before you reach this centre you wander in yourself as in an empty space. Langland does the same, searching through allegories and dreams spread out in mental space, like those of Hoccleve, representing the forces of one mind. Everywhere he searches for Piers Plowman who is, within and without, the capacity for Christ in everyman. The exploration of the outer universe, in which

   . . . oure joy and oure juele, Jesu Crist of hevene,
   In a povere mannes apparaille pursueth us evere[147]

is matched by exploration into an inner and equally Christ-haunted universe. Here, in visions quite unlike the promised faery dream, Langland finds true what Walter Hilton says in exegesis of the Song of Solomon: 'I sleep and my heart waketh. . . . The more I sleep from outward things, the more wakeful I am in knowing of Jesu and of inward things. I may not wake to Jesu, but if I sleep to the world.'[148] It is in everyday life that we defend ourselves by fantasy against the reality that faces us in other modes of consciousness. Beyond all images and allegories, Langland finds one reality that is neither fantasy, projection, image nor allegory: Christ.

Above inner and outer: The Cloud of Unknowing

G. K. Chesterton averred that 'by one light only, / We look from Alfred's eyes',[149] by the light of a shared Christianity. If, as these last quotations suggest, the one reality at the heart of medieval self-awareness and symbol is Christ, this must be true, and not only of Alfred: many scholars would affirm it of the whole Middle Ages. We have, however, found it possible to translate what Margery Kempe and Thomas Hoccleve say about their mental troubles into the clinical language of our time and culture without recourse to religion; the task is more difficult with the less disturbed mentality of Usk, but to a large degree we understand without translation the language of all three. But the act of translation sets one wondering whether our experiences and theirs, clearly affected as they are by the languages that describe them, could have a common language to express both equally well. We find the nearest thing to this, I think, in the work of another mystic, *The Cloud of Unknowing*. It is perhaps the one medieval book that you might read nearly all through with no awareness of period whatever, only of a thunder-clap of demand expressed in terms that are upsettingly close. Only towards the end is there a parable about the Devil's one nostril opening into his brain, where nothing is to be seen but hell fire, which together with some grotesque pictures of the physical antics of false mystics reminds one of Breughel and Hieronymus Bosch.

We know little about the author, except the force with which he affects us: only that he was probably a priest from the North-East Midlands, who between about 1350 and 1395 wrote books and letters of advice for people anxious to be contemplatives. This hiddenness, like his sitting loose to period, is as it should be. He was not concerned to remember himself, much less that he should be remembered. He distinguishes between two kinds of humility, the kind that is to know oneself as one really is, and the kind that is awareness of God through love of him, and recommends the former only as a means to the latter. In contemplation, if you are to be aware of your own wretchedness, be aware of it only as the one un-analysed word 'sin'. 'Mean [by] sin, a lump . . . none other thing but thyself.'[150] Reduce that awareness of your own existence to a sorrow that it remains between you and 'a naked intent unto God'.[151] The awakening and development of this intent in his reader is all he cares for.

He was undoubtedly much read in the generations that im-mediately followed him. Hilton wrote his *Ladder of Perfection* probably partly to modify the dismay with which the uncomprom-isingness of the *Cloud* may strike its readers; and the omnivorous

Usk has a phrase lamenting the 'cloud of uncunning that stoppeth the light of my Margaret pearl',[152] which suggests he knew the book. At any rate, like Usk, the author of the *Cloud* proclaims a single treasure for which he gives all his substance. 'What weary wretched soul and sleeping in sloth is that which is not wakened', he asks in a phrase that T. S. Eliot took from him, 'with the draught of this love and the voice of this cleping?'[153]

Once again, as with Julian and the rest, we recognize the particular medieval simplicity and, so to speak, personal objectivity. Yet, apart from the 'substantial quality' of his nouns and the imagery of two passages already noted, the principal sign of his coming from the context we have so far discussed is that he is more careful than a modern writer would need to be to guard his readers against the dangers of misplaced concreteness and misunderstood sensory allegory. He warns us not to think that, because we have to speak 'in bodily words',[154] there is any bodily sense in which heaven is *up*, or indeed is like any of the descriptions of visionaries who, having read

> . . . that men should lift up their hearts unto God, as fast they stare in the stars as they would be above the moon, and hearken when they shall hear any angels sing out of heaven. These men willen sometime with the curiosity of their imagination pierce the planets, and make an hole in the firmament to look in thereat . . .[155]

He probably has in mind Richard Rolle and his proliferating followers when he speaks of angels' song, but what he says would apply to many medieval people – to the more literal side even of Dante, for example, and certainly to Margery Kempe. Visions of saints, such as she was to be proud of, he thinks are only shown to people not spiritual enough to do without physical appearances. He follows a different kind of meditation from Margery's Franciscan, emotive kind, or Usk's symbolism. Theirs in their various forms are what he may have been the first in English to call the affirmative way; his is the negative. Affirmative mystics stress that everything is like God, everything may be a symbol; negative mystics that God is like nothing. The statements are compatible: as Aquinas points out, we praise a statue for being like a man, but not a man for being like a statue.[156] But the difference of stress is everything.

The author of the *Cloud* would have followers of this way attend to nothing on this side of God: to nothing, therefore, in Usk's phrase that is 'buxom to man's contemplation',[157] only God of whose dalliance Margery Kempe 'could no skill' and who, says the *Cloud*, 'may well be loved, but not thought. By love may he be gotten and holden: but by thought neither.'[158]

What the author of the *Cloud* would attend to is not in this apparent world at all. Hence, perhaps, his relative freedom from his age. And here where most of the writers we have looked at – except the Lollard preacher against miracle plays, and Tyndale – tend by nature to close the gap between inner and outer, he distinguishes sharply between *outer* and *inner* and has a third term, *above*. Your attention, he says, may be directed like a marksman's to his target, in three directions: first, towards the bodily world, in which case you may be said to be 'below' and 'outside' yourself; secondly, towards the spiritual world, towards yourself or the souls of others, towards ethics or emotions, in which case you are 'within' yourself.[159] What you fix your attention on will always come between you and that in union with which you are 'above' yourself: God, known as different from yourself and from all, in that 'He is thy being [and the being of all] and thou not His.'[160]

Imagination (which, he points out in an almost Freudian way, is, waking and sleeping, uncontrollably active unless restrained by the light of grace in the reason) confuses the realms, making us conceive the spiritual in bodily, the bodily in spiritual terms. By the former he presumably means the taking of words like 'up' literally, and perhaps the visions of a Rolle or a Kempe. By the latter he may mean the complementary errors of ambitious ascetics, who, having strained their hearts 'up' or their eyes 'in' in a physical way, have consequent unnatural physical sensations, warmth, light, sweet taste and smell, which they suppose to be spiritual gifts. He speaks too of what looks like a confusion of *inner* and *above*, of those who think that the sudden impulse of grace in the soul, springing up like fire to its true place in God, is an activity of the mind: they too, he says, manufacture a false experience, neither spiritual nor bodily. One wonders what he would have made of Abbot Suger's praise of his church as making him seem to be in a realm neither wholly of earth nor wholly of heaven; but presumably he would have condemned it.

It is not, however, the case that he disapproves of all symbols. As regards visions in physical form, and sacraments, he tells us indeed that we should strip off their husk to eat the kernel. But there is a vast difference between the withering away of the whole symbolic context, which we saw in a Protestant like Thomas Whythorne, and this writer's transcending a context on which he still draws. We are not, he says explicitly, to do 'as those heretics do', anticipators of extreme Protestantism, 'the which be well likened to wode [mad] men having this custom, that ever when they have drunken of a fair cup, cast it to the wall and break it. . . . For men will kiss the cup, for wine is therein.'[161]

As regards his own style, his book might be described as an experiment in using symbols to transcend themselves. He would have nothing, least of all his book, come between you and God. The element of symbol, therefore, is fined down to something totally metaphorical, which points utterly beyond itself, and is sparingly used, because all its meaning lies beyond it, and can only be grasped by attentive concentration, not, as with Usk, by development: intensively, not extensively. Such is his style when the question at the heart of his book – what this point of attention may be – arises:

> But now thou askest me and sayest: 'How shall I think on Himself and what is He?' and to this I cannot answer thee but thus: 'I wot never.' For thou hast brought me with thy question into that same darkness, and into that same cloud of unknowing that I would thou were in thyself. . . . Fonde [try] for to pierce that darkness above thee, and smite upon that thick cloud of unknowing with a sharp dart of longing love; and go not thence for thing that befalleth.[162]

Yet he would not have you choose this as if it were necessarily the only or the best way for you to God. It follows from this central belief in the incomprehensibility of God that one could never define a single way to him. The *Cloud* says indeed that to centre all one's attention on God is the best way that Christ commended in Mary, choosing the one thing needful like the merchant seeking pearls. But when a young man enquires of the *Cloud*'s author whether he should become a hermit, he characteristically replies in the *Epistle of Discretion of Stirrings* that this decision must be made by the individual according to his bent; for

> . . . silence, it is not God, ne speaking, it is not God; fasting, it is not God, ne eating, it is not God; onelyness it

is not God, ne company, it is not God; ne yet any of all the
other two such contraries. He is hid betwixt them, and may
not be found by any work of thy soul, but all only by love of
thine heart.[163]

The 'betwixt' is subtle: evidently no abstract compromise is meant,
but a true transcendent (like, perhaps, T. S. Eliot's use of 'between'
in 'heard, half-heard in the stillness / Between two waves of the
sea'[164]).

In urging attention to the transcendent, he does not despise the
created world. An act of contemplation, he says, benefits all mankind, not only the contemplative himself. He implicitly recognizes
the contemplative's function of counselling, and says indeed that contemplatives find themselves 'suddenly and graciously changed',[165]
so that in conversation they are at home with everybody, even sinners,
though without sinning themselves; they understand people's
needs, speak straightforwardly and hold themselves physically
upright: people feel themselves 'holpen by grace unto God in their
presence'.[166]

Despite his discouragement of introspection, moreover, his
practical knowledge of psychology is excellent, and here his style
shifts to something like Hoccleve's, the common substantial near-
allegory. Thus he recommends 'two ghostly devices that be helpful'
in dealing with obsessive temptations, distractions and remembered
though repented sins: first 'to try to look as it were over their
shoulders, seeking another thing: the which thing is God', and,
secondly, 'when thou feelest that thou mayest in no wise put them
down, cower thou down under them as a caitiff and a coward overcome in battle, and think that it is but a folly to strive any longer
with them, and therefore thou yieldest thee to God in the hands of
thine enemies'.[167]

Often the degree to which he is reporting a personal experience
and a personal relation is made overwhelmingly clear, as when he
says that, in order to make your love more spiritual, you should hide
it from God as if you were a child playing with its father, or strays
near heresy in suggesting that you should purge your love towards
God of anything bodily because God, though omniscient, knows
the spiritual more than the bodily.

Of experience of God he says only that God will 'sometimes
peradventure send out a beam of ghostly light, piercing this cloud of

unknowing that is betwixt thee and him: and show thee some of his privity';[168] he says nothing further, because this act is God's alone, and 'of that work that falleth to only God, dare I not take upon me to speak with my blabbering fleshly tongue.'[169]

The unthinkable and indescribable of which the *Cloud* speaks is not abstract, nor a confusion of abstract and concrete, but personal and transcendent; not static or passive, but active; not the good, but God: as the author says in his *Deonise* (Dionysius') *Hid Divinity* 'in itself and to itself evermore free: within all creatures, not enclosed: without all creatures, not shut out: above all creatures, not borne up: beneath all creatures, not put down: behind all creatures, not put back: before all creatures, not driven forth' – and yet 'to man's understanding . . . overlaid with unnumerable sensible bodies and understandable substances, with many a marvellous fantastic image'.[170]

Usk's pearl and Usk's Margaret might in contrast be criticized for offering beautiful and concrete allegories without persuading us that their ultimate meaning ('grace, learning, or wisdom of God, or else holy church') is more than a bare moral abstraction, a kernel less rich than the husk. The basic trouble is perhaps the image of courtly love itself. The beloved is so royal, needing to do so little to engage her lover's devotion that she provides a fatally static image for grace. She is indeed herself, in some sense, near-abstraction as the ideal of a lover, and may all too easily make a symbol for abstract moral ideal, for the idea of the 'good' or for Aristotle's God, superior to action, who moves the world as being loved. The author of the *Cloud* is more radically Christian:

> Let that thing do with thee and lead thee whereso it list. Let it be the worker, and thou but the sufferer . . . be thou but the tree, and let it be the wright: be thou but the house and let it be the husbandman dwelling therein. . . . It sufficeth enough unto thee, that thou feelest thee stirred likingly, with a thing thou wottest never what, else that in this stirring thou hast no special thought of anything under God; and that thine intent be nakedly directed unto God.[171]

His aim – to see himself and the whole world only as they have their cause and being in God – is implicit in much of the medieval self-consciousness we have described in Margery Kempe, Thomas Hoccleve and Thomas Usk, which, I think, illuminates the personal impersonal quality of Chaucer, Langland and the other poets. But no one achieves this aim so explicitly as he, or so purges metaphor to do it. His own purgation by his awareness of God's awareness of him resembles, but only as opposites resemble, Margery Kempe's projection of her own emotions on to God. At the beginning of his book he expresses the self-consciousness of his age in its purest form in a prayer which, characteristically of that self-consciousness, is taken from the liturgy. Cranmer, as very often, made the tradition of the centuries immediately before him available for succeeding generations when he made it, in the Prayer Book of 1549, the introduction to Holy Communion:

> God unto whom all hearts ben open and unto whom all will speaketh, and unto whom no privy thing is hid, I beseech thee so for to cleanse the intent of mine heart with the unspeakable gift of thy grace, that I may parfitly love thee and worthily praise thee. Amen.[172]

Notes

1 John Trevisa, translating Bartholomaeus Anglicus, *On the Properties of Things*, eds M. C. Seymour *et al.* (Oxford, 1975), *Prohemium*, p. 41; Romans 1:20.
2 *General Prologue*, l. 333.
3 Virginia Woolf, 'The Pastons and Chaucer', in *The Common Reader* (London, 1925).
4 *Franklin's Tale*, ll. 865–93.
5 *Troilus and Criseyde*, Bk 2, ll. 757–8, 794; see J. A. Burrow, *English Verse 1300–1500* (London, 1977).
6 Kittredge, I think, but am not sure.
7 *A Book of Showings to the Anchoress Julian of Norwich*, ed. E. Colledge and J. Walsh (Toronto, 1978), p. 405.
8 In *Medieval English Lyrics*, ed. R. T. Davies (London, 1963), p. 146.
9 *The Book of Margery Kempe*, ed. S. B. Meech and H. E. Allen, EETS (Oxford, 1940), ch. 11, p. 23.
10 G. M. Hopkins, *The Wreck of the Deutschland*, ll. 1–2.
11 *The Book of Margery Kempe*, ch. 38, p. 93.
12 Ibid., ch. 56, p. 137.
13 Ibid.
14 *Prioress's Tale*, ll. 579, 649.
15 *The Book of Margery Kempe*, opening words, p. 1.

16 Julian, *A Book of Showings*, p. 201.
17 *The Book of Margery Kempe*, p. 174.
18 Ibid., p. 151.
19 Ibid., p. 42.
20 Ibid., p. 6.
21 Ibid., p. 11.
22 Ibid., p. 86.
23 Ibid., p. 208.
24 *Meditations on the Life of Christ, attributed to St Bonadventure*, trans. Sister M. Emmanuel (St Louis, 1934), p. 69; quoted in L. Martz, *The Poetry of Meditation*, rev. edn (New Haven and London, 1902), p. 74.
25 *The Book of Margery Kempe*, p. 94.
26 Ibid., p. 17.
27 Charles Williams, *The Descent of the Dove*, new edn (London, 1950), p. 144.
28 C. S. Lewis, *The Allegory of Love* (Oxford, 1936), p. 323.
29 *The Autobiography of Thomas Whythorne*, ed. James M. Osborn (Oxford, 1961), p. 113.
30 *The Book of Margery Kempe*, p. 8.
31 C. S. Lewis, op. cit., p. 323.
32 *The Book of Margery Kempe*, p. 67.
33 *A Tretise of Miraclis Pleyinge*, in *English Wycliffite Writings*, ed. Anne Hudson (Cambridge, 1978), p. 102.
34 *Piers Plowman*, B text, ed. A. V. C. Schmidt (London, 1978), Passus III, ll. 49-50.
35 *Pierce the Ploughman's Creed*, ed. W. W. Skeat (Oxford, 1906), ll. 181-8.
36 T. S. Eliot, *Ash Wednesday*, III.
37 1 Corinthians 13:3 (Tyndale's translation).
38 *Piers Plowman*, B text, ed. Schmidt, Passus XIX, ll. 6-8.
39 *Thomas Hoccleve's Complaint*, ll. 55-6; in *Hoccleve's Works*, ed. F. J. Furnival, EETS (London, 1892; reissued with additions by J. Mitchell and A. I. Doyle, 1970).
40 Ibid., vol. 1, pp. li-lxx.
41 Ibid., vol. 1, pp. lxi-lxii; cf. M. C. Seymour, *Review of English Studies*, N.S., 20 (1967), p. 482.
42 *Complaint*, ll. 40-2.
43 T. F. Tout, *Chapters in the Administrative History of Mediaeval England*, vol. 5 (Manchester, 1930), pp. 70-110.
44 *Regement of Princes*, ll. 2078-9.
45 Ibid., ll. 4997-8.
46 G. Mathew, *The Court of Richard II* (London, 1968), p. 203.
47 *La Mâle Règle de T. Hoccleve, passim.*
48 *Regement of Princes*, l. 287.
49 Ibid., ll. 267-70.

50 *Complaint*, ll. 50–1.
51 Ibid., ll. 120–33; text from J. A. Burrow, *English Verse 1300–1500* (London, 1977).
52 *On the Properties of Things*, Bk 7, ch. 5; vol. 1, p. 349.
53 *Complaint*, ll. 424–7.
54 *Regement*, ll. 1009–22.
55 *Dialogue with a Friend*, ll. 79, 71–2; cf. P. Doob, *Nebuchadnezzar's Children* (New Haven and London, 1979), pp. 229–30.
56 *Complaint*, l. 401.
57 Ibid., ll. 103–4.
58 *Dialogue*, ll. 639–44; cf. Chapter 1, pp. 20–3, above.
59 *Complaint*, ll. 158–61, 183–94; text from Burrow, op. cit.
60 *Complaint*, l. 310; see A. G. Rigg, *Speculum*, 45 (1970), pp. 564–74.
61 E. Thornley, *Neuphilologische Mitteilungen*, 68 (1967), pp. 295–321.
62 *Regement*, ll. 88–90.
63 Ibid., l. 7.
64 Ibid., ll. 1–2.
65 *Complaint*, ll. 194–6.
66 Ibid., l. 7.
67 Ibid., ll. 290–3.
68 Woolf, op. cit.
69 *Regement*, ll. 113–16.
70 Ibid., l. 122.
71 'Resolution and Independence', stanza 8.
72 Ibid., stanza 7.
73 Ibid.
74 Ibid., stanza 4.
75 *Complaint*, l. 194.
76 'Ode on Intimations of Immortality', stanza 9.
77 'Resolution and Independence', stanza 16.
78 Ibid., stanza 17.
79 Lewis Carroll, *Alice Through the Looking Glass*, 'The White Knight's Song'.
80 *Regement*, ll. 131–5.
81 *Piers Plowman*, C text, ed. D. Pearsall (London, 1978), Passus XX, ll. 281–3.
82 G. K. Chesterton, 'The humour of King Herod', in *The Uses of Diversity* (London, 1920).
83 *Hamlet*, ed. E. Hubler, Signet edn (New York, 1963), III. ii. 14.
84 C. S. Lewis, 'On stories', in *Essays Presented to Charles Williams* by Dorothy Sayers and others (Oxford, 1947), p. 95.
85 *Wife of Bath's Tale*, ll. 860–1.
86 Thomas Usk, *The Testament of Love*, Bk 2, ch. 12; in *Chaucerian and Other Pieces*, ed. W. W. Skeat (Oxford, 1897), p. 92.
87 Charles Williams, *Witchcraft* (London, 1941), p. 78.
88 Coleridge, *The Statesman's Manual* (London, 1816), appendix C.

89 *The Appeal of Thomas Usk*, in *A Book of London English 1384–1425*, ed. R. W. Chambers and M. Daunt (Oxford, 1931), pp. 18–31, l. 7.
90 Ibid., ll. 65–6.
91 Ibid., ll. 185–7.
92 Ibid., ll. 224–6.
93 Ibid., ll. 228–30.
94 Usk, *Testament*, Bk 1, ch. 3, p. 15.
95 Ibid., Bk 1, ch. 3, p. 17.
96 Ibid., Bk 1, ch. 5, p. 24.
97 Ibid.
98 Ibid., Bk 3, ch. 4, p. 123.
99 Ibid., Bk 1, ch. 6, p. 26.
100 Ibid., Bk 1, ch. 6, p. 27.
101 Ibid., p. xxv.
102 Ibid., Bk 1, ch. 6, pp. 27, 28.
103 Boswell's *Life of Johnson*, 7 April 1775.
104 *Testament*, Bk 1, Prol., p. 2.
105 *Piers Plowman*, B text, ed. Schmidt, Prol., l. 128.
106 *Testament*, Bk 3, ch. 9, p. 145.
107 Ibid.
108 *Parson's Tale*, Prol., ll. 49–51.
109 *Testament*, Bk 3, ch. 9, p. 145.
110 Ibid., Bk 1, ch. 9, p. 40.
111 *Legend of Good Women*, F version, l. 519.
112 *Testament*, Bk 3, ch. 8, p. 139.
113 Ibid., Bk 3, ch. 7, p. 136.
114 Ibid., III, Bk 3, chs 7 and 8, pp. 136–8.
115 Ibid., Bk 1, Prol., p. 3.
116 Ibid., Bk 1, Prol., p. 2.
117 Ibid., Bk 2, ch. 13, p. 96.
118 Ibid., Bk 1, ch. 9, p. 39.
119 Ibid.
120 Owen Barfield, *Saving the Appearances* (London, 1957), p. 78.
121 Vernon MS., *English Verse 1300–1500*, ed. J. A. Burrow (London, 1977), pp. 250–6.
122 Barfield, op. cit., p. 95.
123 Aristotle, *De Anima*, 431a, 17; cf. translation with Aquinas' commentary, K. Foster (trans.), *De Anima* (London, 1951), p. 442.
124 *De Anima*, 431b, 2; cf. Foster (trans.), op. cit., p. 443.
125 *De Anima*, 432a, 9; cf. Foster (trans.), op. cit., p. 454. These translations are from W. S. Hett's Loeb translation (1935), quoted by Frances Yates, *The Art of Memory* (Harmondsworth, 1969), p. 47.
126 Reginald Pecock, *Repressor of Overmuch Blaming of the Clergy*, ed. C. Babington, Rolls Series (London, 1860), pp. 114 ff.
127 *Abbot Suger on the Abbey Church of St Denis*, ed. E. Panofsky, 2nd edn (Princeton, NJ, 1979), pp. 62–5.

128 *Caxton's Book of Cartesye*, ed. F. J. Furnivall, EETS (1868); in D. S. Brewer (ed.), *Chaucer: The Critical Heritage* (London, 1978).
129 *Pageant Verses*, in St Thomas More, *The History of King Richard III*, etc., ed. R. S. Sylvester (Yale, 1976), p. 114.
130 *The Tale of Beryn*, ed. F. J. Furnivall, EETS (1909); in H. S. Bennett, *England from Chaucer to Caxton* (London, 1928), pp. 219–21.
131 *Cathay and the Way Thither*, ed. H. Yule and H. Cordier, new edn (London, 1914), vol. 3, p. 220.
132 *Mandeville's Travels*, ed. M. C. Seymour (Oxford, 1967), ch. 33, p. 220.
133 Ibid., ch. 32, p. 214.
134 *The Parliament of Fowls*, ll. 99–105.
135 *Troilus and Criseyde*, Bk 2, ll. 921–2.
136 Ibid., Bk 5, l. 825.
137 *Testament*, Bk 3, ch. 7, p. 137.
138 Chaucer's *Boece*, Bk 4, prosa 6, 46–8.
139 Ibid., final words.
140 *Pearl*, ed. A. C. Cawley and J. J. Anderson (London, 1976), l. 1.
141 Ibid., final lines.
142 *Sir Thopas*, l. 930.
143 *The Tale of Beryn*; in Bennet, op. cit., pp. 219–21.
144 *Sir Gawain and the Green Knight*, ll. 2334–5; ed. with *Pearl*.
145 *Oxford Book of Medieval English Verse*, ed. C. and K. Sisam (Oxford, 1970), pp. 357–61.
146 Julian, *A Book of Showings*, p. 639.
147 *Piers Plowman*, B text, ed. Schmidt, Passus XI, ll. 184–5.
148 Walter Hilton, *The Scale of Perfection*, ed. E. Underhill (London, 1923), Bk 2, ch. 40.
149 G. K. Chesterton, *The Ballad of the White Horse*, Dedication, stanza 9.
150 *The Cloud of Unknowing*, ed. P. Hodgson, EETS (Oxford, 1944), ch. 36, p. 73.
151 Ibid., ch. 3, p. 17.
152 *Testament*, Prol., pp. 3 ff.; cf. Bk 3, ch. 9, p. 144.
153 *Cloud*, ch. 2, p. 14, and (with 'drawing' for 'draught' and 'calling' for 'cleping') T. S. Eliot, 'Little Gidding', V.
154 *Cloud*, ch. 61, p. 114.
155 Ibid., ch. 57, p. 105.
156 Aquinas, *Summa Theologica*, Ia, Iae, iv, 3, ad 4; in *Theological Texts*, ed. T. Gilby (Oxford, 1955), p. 8.
157 *Testament*, Bk 1, ch. 9, p. 39.
158 *Cloud*, ch. 6, p. 26.
159 Ibid., ch. 67, pp. 119–20.
160 *The Book of Privy Counselling* (published with *Cloud*), p. 136.
161 *Cloud*, ch. 58, pp. 107–8.
162 Ibid., ch. 6, pp. 25–6.

163 *A Pistle of Discrecioun of Stirings*, in *Deonise Hid Divinite*, ed.
     P. Hodgson, EETS (Oxford, 1955), p. 71.
164 'Little Gidding', V.
165 *Cloud*, ch. 54, p. 100.
166 Ibid.
167 Ibid., ch. 32, p. 66.
168 Ibid., p. 62.
169 Ibid.
170 *Deonise Hid Divinite*, p. 6.
171 *Cloud*, ch. 34, p. 70.
172 *Cloud*, Prol., p. 1.

Select bibliography

Two enterprising explorations of medieval consciousness are Carolly
Erickson, *The Medieval Vision* (New York, 1976), and Owen Barfield,
Saving the Appearances (London, 1957), which is the stimulus of this
chapter, though without accepting Barfield's metaphysics it is hard to know
how far his remarks can be taken beyond simple description. C. S. Lewis's
The Discarded Image (Cambridge, 1964) and *The Allegory of Love* (Oxford,
1936) clearly owe much to Mr Barfield's stimulus. I have tried to develop the
thesis further in M. Glasscoe (ed.), *The Medieval Mystical Tradition in
England* (Exeter, 1980), which has weightier essays also. An important
byway into medieval minds is Basil Clarke's *Mental Disorder in Earlier
Britain* (Cardiff, 1975).

4 Art and architecture in the late Middle Ages

NICOLA COLDSTREAM

Change and destruction: the church and the churches; unified vision; artists and their organization

The two centuries from the accession of Edward III to the death of Henry VIII saw immense changes in the visual arts. Our period opens in a world accustomed to the pointed arches and rib vaults of Gothic churches, and the flat, elegantly swaying figures of tapestries and manuscript paintings. It ends among artists and patrons struggling to understand the implications of the revival of classical antiquity in the Italian Renaissance. The years between had witnessed an increase of interest, common to the whole of Europe and not only Italy, in the naturalistic representation of human beings, animal and plant life, and the setting of scenes in realistic interior space. The two-dimensional design of the fourteenth-century manuscript page was forced to give way to the three-dimensional setting of Holbein's royal group portrait for the Palace of Whitehall.

This was a radical change, not accomplished without struggle, with phases of intense activity and periods of calm. Radical changes are seldom predictable to those taking part in them, even in our world of global communication and instant commentary; English artists of the fifteenth century did not know that their entire artistic outlook was shortly to be transformed by the twin impacts of the Renaissance, which altered their style, and the Reformation, which altered the subject matter of their pictures. With hindsight it is tempting to select only those works of art that seem significant for the later centuries, but this is to forget that contemporaries saw great significance in works that did not affect the future at all. Greater understanding of late medieval art comes from forgetting both that there was a future and that we know what that future held.

The changes of which I have spoken took place against a background that altered more slowly, and before looking at the artistic developments in detail we should consider some themes common to the period as a whole. The first is destruction. Any discussion of medieval art is based on incomplete material, for immense quantities have simply disappeared. Henry VIII is not the sole culprit, although his policies were almost entirely responsible for the destruction of thousands of precious metal objects belonging to churches, which makes any attempt to assess the role of the so-called minor arts in England almost impossible. Puritans and other iconoclasts have smashed sculptures, crucifixes and other church fittings. Painted miniatures have been cut out of manuscripts for collectors or as gifts. On the secular side, time and man's desire to replace outworn buildings have between them nearly obliterated the picture. This has created an unfortunate imbalance, giving the impression that the laity had no visual arts for their own secular enjoyment. Such survivals as there are, together with written descriptions, show us that this is not a true picture, but the fact remains that, despite the efforts of iconoclasts and others, most surviving medieval art is the art of the Christian church.

The dominant role of the church as patron and recipient of lay patronage is the most important of our general themes. Even here there was gradual change, and lay patronage of the church was more characteristic of the early part of the period than of the later, when the laity were equally interested in their own material surroundings. Lay endowment of the church was founded both in the traditional interdependence of church and laity, and in a more personal need to safeguard the fortunes of the soul after death. The church was there to preach salvation, the church building to represent the kingdom of God on earth, a reminder of the life to come. In the early Middle Ages kings and great landowners had founded monasteries as their burial churches, ensuring that the monks would say masses perpetually for their souls. By the fourteenth century the impetus of the monastic movement had passed, but men still feared for their souls. Leading families built smaller burial churches, to be served by colleges of secular priests rather than monks, and, although the king and higher nobility were still the main patrons, different types of patron were now beginning to appear. The late thirteenth century saw the emergence of the landed gentry, and signs of interest in patronage among merchants. Their tastes reflected those of their social superiors on a humbler scale. The gentry refitted the chancels of their parish churches, with tombs, and seats for the clergy, and many people, especially in towns, endowed altars, providing for a chantry priest to say masses for the souls of their families.

The higher clergy, the bishops, were not only apt to come from landed families but were landed aristocrats in their own right, administering the vast lands now owned by the church. They themselves could be generous donors: John Grandisson of Exeter was an active patron of both architecture and the minor arts; Hotham of Ely is said to have paid for repairs to the choir of his cathedral, damaged by the fall of the central tower in 1322; and William of Wykeham, Bishop of Winchester, not only rebuilt the nave of his cathedral, among several other large projects, but provided finance in his will, should the work be unfinished at his death.

However generous they might be as individuals, bishops connived at parting humbler people from their money. There were various ways in which this could be done. A major church with a shrine could use the offerings of pilgrims to finance grand programmes of rebuilding. Indulgences (remission of punishment for sins) would be granted by the bishop in return for moneys paid towards the new buildings. Archbishop Thoresby of York was among many who resorted to threats: when the choir of York Minster was to be replaced in 1361, Thoresby demanded contributions from every parish in the province of York, with the threat of excommunication from the church to those who did not comply. There was also persuasion: the promise of earthly glory followed by heavenly joy in return for a suitable contribution is nicely caught in *Pierce the Ploughman's Creed*:

> And myghtestou amenden vs. with money of thyn owne,
> Thou chuldest chely bifore Crist. in compas of gold
> In the wide windowe westwarde. wel nighe in the
>   myddell,
> And seynt Frauncies him self. schall folden the in his
>   cope,
> And present the to the trynitie. and praie for thy synnes.[1]

Thus a patron could be depicted in a stained-glass window he had given, with saints praying for his salvation before the entire congregation.

Belief in the power of intercession with God was vested in the saints and above all in the Virgin Mary, who were often shown in wall paintings or windows, or as statues. The image was imbued with the holiness of its subject, and prayers directed to it would be, as it were, passed on. Some images were believed to have miraculous curative powers, and many miracle stories are concerned with images that come to life to save innocent victims from death or worse. Important as the salvation of men's souls was, however, it was only part of the central activity of the church, and it was towards the central activity that church art and, more particularly, church architecture were directed.

The main function of the church was to commemorate death, in the mass, the sacrifice of Christ on the cross, his death and resurrection for our salvation. The importance accorded to his death was justified by the importance of what it represented: the beginning of eternal life. The commemoration of this greatest death was reflected in that of many lesser deaths, those of the saints, martyrs, bishops, nobility and anyone buried in or near the church building. Every church, however small, was dedicated to a saint, whose relic was in the altar. The altar was, therefore, a kind of tomb; round it stood reliquary boxes with relics of other saints, shrines that were in themselves representative tombs; and near them stood the tombs and memorials of those who were buried in the church. The nearer the altar, the holier the spot, and great laymen were placed in magnificent tombs as near to the altar as they were allowed. Their bones were guarded by the living priests and the dead saints, who, by prayer and intercession, eased the soul in its passage through purgatory to the eternal life.

The architecture of the church building, however humble, reflected this. By tradition the chancel, in which the main mass was celebrated, was the responsibility of the clergy, and the nave, where the congregation stood, was that of the laity. The chancel was usually more elaborately decorated, because it was the holiest part of the church and because, following from that, more money was spent on it. Many church buildings were halted for several years after the chancel was built, as, once the altar and priest were adequately protected, a makeshift shelter could house the congregation until such time as there was money enough to continue the building. In the course of our period, however, changes in the type of patron altered this state of affairs, and many parish churches built in the fifteenth century have naves as glorious as their choirs, since patrons looked to their own needs as well as those of the clergy.

It is difficult to describe a typical church building, because there was no such thing. Most churches were of more than one build; that is, they were an accretion of parts added or replaced at different times, with varying degrees of lavishness. Their status and function were reflected in their layout, monastery churches having special provision with an enclosed choir for the monks, important pilgrimage churches having elaborate extensions for the main shrines. Canterbury Cathedral, the goal of Chaucer's pilgrims, was a very grand building indeed. Like many English cathedrals it was also a monastery, and after the martyrdom of Thomas à Becket in 1170 it increased its income by exploiting the shrine of its saint.

Canterbury Cathedral is built on different levels, with the shrine behind the altar at the highest point. The twelfth-century cathedral had had a raised choir, and although this was not the usual English custom its theatrical possibilities were not lost on the monks when they came to rebuild the choir after its destruction by fire in 1174. The tall base of the shrine was set into a mosaic floor, surrounded by the dark marble columns of its chapel, and irradiated by the colour streaming from the stained-glass windows telling the story of the life and miracles of St Thomas. It dominated the pilgrims as they climbed the long flight of steps from the nave. The base had niches in its sides, in which the pilgrims could insert a diseased limb in the hope that proximity to the saint's bones would give a miraculous cure. The jewelled metal reliquary containing the bones was hidden under a canopy which could be raised. As an archbishop murdered at the behest of a king, Becket was always a possible focus of discontent, and this was so well understood by Henry VIII that his agents were particularly instructed to obliterate all traces of the shrine; but while it existed it was lavishly endowed with gold, silver and jewels, including a ruby presented by Louis VII of France shortly after Becket's murder. When Erasmus visited the shrine in the early sixteenth century, the prior of Canterbury himself pointed out each jewel to the pilgrims, and gave its value. A description in Stow's *Annals* of 1538 reads:

jewels of gold set with stone, wrought upon gold wier, then again with jewells, gold as brooches, images, angels, rings, 10 or 12 together, cramped with gold into the ground of gold, the spoils of which filled two chests such as six or eight men could but convey out of the church.[2]

The Trinity Chapel behind the high altar, in which the shrine stood, is surrounded by a processional way, with several chapels opening off it, once containing shrines of lesser saints and lesser relics of the great saint. Beyond the Trinity Chapel stands the round Corona, in which was kept the relic of Becket's scalp. The liturgical choir was screened off between the Trinity Chapel and the nave, so that the monks could sing their services undisturbed. Several steps below the level of the choir the great nave, rebuilt in the late fourteenth century, provided space for the laity, while the transepts, the cross-arms under the central tower, allowed extra chapels and burial places. The north side was the site of the martyrdom, an essential stop on the tour of the shrines.

Canterbury is one of many different centres of pilgrimage; its popularity and international fame had enabled the monks to refine the business of managing pilgrims to a profitable and dramatic art. It was first and foremost a pilgrimage church; no great layman was buried near the shrine until the death of the Black Prince in 1376, and no single family was associated with Canterbury. For churches with strong family associations we have to look beyond cathedrals to monasteries. The choirs of Bristol and Tewkesbury were rebuilt in the early fourteenth century as mausolea for the Berkeley and Despenser families. The Berkeleys at Bristol have a burial chapel, but they are also entombed round the side walls of the choir, while the Despensers at Tewkesbury occupy a series of elaborate tombs round the high altar.

These families were following established tradition. A newer idea was the family burial church served not by monks but by priests, as at the Yorkist mausoleum of Fotheringhay, Northamptonshire, established in the early fifteenth century in the parish church, which was rebuilt on a grand scale. Others, especially the clergy, who were not officially founders of dynasties, did not build churches but put chapels into existing buildings. They could either be highly decorated little boxes right inside the building, like Wykeham's chantry at Winchester, or chapels attached to the east end, like

Alcock's chapel at Ely. Family chapels – for example, the Poulett Chapel at Hinton St George, Somerset – were added to parish churches.

Parish church interiors are more difficult than almost anything else to reconstruct for the twentieth-century imagination, because changes in religious attitudes as well as time have wrought destruction. Their architecture was usually simpler than that of the larger buildings, and extremely varied. Although some splendid parish churches were built in the fifteenth century to give us the great Perpendicular monuments that survive today, many more exist, like cathedrals, as a series of additions over centuries, which makes them more interesting to visit but less easy to reconstruct at any one period of their history. A parish church might have traces of round-arched Norman work in the nave, a thirteenth-century chancel, and aisles added to the nave in the fourteenth or fifteenth century – all evidence of someone's desire to endow new altars, probably as chantries, at different times. Some churches are cross-shaped, with transepts, others are not. Inside, the work of Victorian restorers is ever-present, with open spaces cluttered with rows of pews, heavy screens and choir stalls. Pews were not part of the medieval furnishings, but during the late Middle Ages the fashion grew for screening off different parts of the building to make chapels, and the chancel was always divided from the nave by the rood screen, on which stood a carved representation of the Crucifixion, with Mary and St John, associated as by the *Pearl* poet (ll. 383–4):

> Bot Crystes mercy and Mary and Jon,
> Thise arn the grounde of all my blysse.[3]

Although many screens survive all over the country, rood screens were the victims of iconoclasm, as was much of the other decoration. The austere look that most medieval churches have today is entirely misleading. Each one achieved some kind of decoration according to its wealth, and none is really complete without it. Walls were painted with representations of the saints or the Last Judgement, still surviving in some places, for example St Thomas, Salisbury. Stained-glass windows showed the lives of Christ and the saints. Carved stone heads supported wooden roof beams; there were sculptured tomb niches, carved wooden bench ends, misericords in the choir seats; alabaster altarpieces and small statuettes stood on the altars. Every church, however small, represented the kingdom of God upon earth; if the wild monsters of the woods, the 'green men' with faces surrounded by foliage, also crept into the sculpture, they were part of God's creation and had a place there. It all contributed to the late medieval ideal of decoration: overall surface unity.

The unified vision of late medieval art is our next general theme, one we find working on several levels. One aspect lay in the nature of what the artist was required to do: medieval artists differed from modern ones in that they worked to the wishes of the patron and were not free to act as inspiration led them. We shall see this, for example, in the arrangements for the fifteenth-century Beauchamp Chapel of Warwick. In the Middle Ages no distinction was made between art and craft. The artist was a craftsman and vice versa; just as a decorated chair was a work of art, so was an ivory relief of the Crucifixion a piece of craftsmanship. Few records of critical praise survive, but they invariably comment on the fine workmanship, as if they see beauty through workmanship. Pictures, whether painted or carved, were designed to an established iconography – that is, the subject matter of each scene was arranged in a way traditional over several centuries. Extra symbolic figures might be put in or left out, but the scene remained the same. English artists did tend to be wilful (a twelfth-century commentator wrote of English miracle stories, 'English mists beget vapourish imaginings'[4]): an example of this wilfulness is the emergence in the fourteenth century of the scene of St Anne teaching the infant Virgin to read – a charming little domestic picture invented here and uncommon elsewhere.

Iconographic unity was matched by unity of visual outlook. All the arts were interdependent and complementary, and the most rewarding approach to them is to take all of them, including architecture, together, and see how motifs were shared and exchanged between them. Just as the same iconography appeared in stained glass, a carved relief, and on the back of the officiating priest when he wore his embroidered cope in feast-day processions, so did the same motifs appear in metalwork, architecture, paintings and sculpture. Chaucer's parish clerk in the *Miller's Tale* had the design of St Paul's rose window on his shoes. Niches and pinnacles appeared on everything from a tiny ivory carving to the façade of Exeter Cathedral (Plates 4 and 6). In many buildings the architecture, paint, glass and sculpture should not be separated.

In architecture itself unity was sought for another reason. In the middle of the thirteenth century the French king had built a chapel, the Sainte-Chapelle, in his palace in Paris, especially for the relics of the Passion which he had recently acquired. It was designed to resemble a metal reliquary in stone, and was both a symptom of the importance attached to holy relics at the time and a cause of change in ideas about how a building should look. From that time onward architects throughout northern Europe became preoccupied with the two themes expressed in the Sainte-Chapelle: the creation of a unified interior space, and the overall decoration of surfaces. A unified space enclosed the relics in an enlarged version of the reliquary box itself. It is not surprising that the little arches, pinnacles and statuettes of gilt reliquaries should have their exact counterparts on buildings that are themselves intended to be understood in the same role (Plate 3).

This development is of vital importance for our period, as it affected buildings of every size and kind. It leads us to the last of the general themes I shall discuss in this section – namely, the artists themselves and their organization. If architects of different countries were thinking in the same way about buildings, so were painters and sculptors about their craft. Ideas moved about Europe with remarkable speed, carried by travelling artists, patrons, and any small object that was portable. Although the art of each region has unmistakable characteristics, there was considerable mutual influence. In England especially ideas were taken from abroad and transformed into an English idiom, and the opening of our period coincides with the moment when the English idiom was in its turn becoming highly prized abroad. English embroidery was known as *opus anglicanum*, and vast quantities were exported as wall hangings or liturgical vestments: copes of *opus anglicanum* survive at Pienza in Italy and in the south of France. At the same time English architectural ideas were beginning to penetrate the continent, where they helped to change the logical clarity of French Gothic into the twisting fantasies beloved of late medieval architects. The English idiom, in both the figured arts and architecture, was linear and decorative. In architecture they loved surface decoration, and the creation of patterns on vaulted ceilings (Plate 4); in manuscripts the flat page was a challenge to their genius for creating an exact balance between surface pattern and narrative picture (Plate 7). It gave way only in the fifteenth century, when an influx of continental painters coincided with the new ideas from Flanders of realistic representation of narrative scenes.

Artists were mostly professional laymen, based in the big cities, but liable to be summoned anywhere for a specific project. As the artist normally supplied his own materials, he had to be within reach of good trading centres; stained glass, for example, was imported from the continent. They had a system of guilds and workshops, and any large undertaking was a collective endeavour. If an illuminated manuscript was to be made, the text was written in the vellum pages by the scribes, who handed it to the painters for illustration, the layout of the page having been decided in advance. Some pages would have full-page miniatures, others decorated letters and marginal illustrations (Plate 5). The master of the shop designed the pictures and decided on the colours to be used, writing the instructions on the picture or in the margin. The master and his assistants then painted the book, gold being put on first over a prepared ground, then the colours, with highlighting done last. Up to six or eight painters, each with his own style, may have worked on the same book, and, to complicate matters further, more than one painter may have worked on the same picture.

In the same way a building project was a collective enterprise. Stonemasons travelled a good deal, as can be seen by the numerous examples of general and specific influence of one building on another, not only within England, but between England and other countries of Europe. Large building works drew masons from all over the country, and the movements of some can be traced through documents. The organization and process of a new building depended on its size and on the patron; the royal works, for instance, were organized on a permanent basis, while a cathedral would employ a small staff for running repairs, calling together a large team, with master architects, only for a big undertaking.

In the building of a cathedral or large church, the master mason was the architect and engineer. He devised the plans, designed templates ('forme pieces') for the mouldings of piers, arches and vaults, and supervised the building as it rose. Although the design of each bay may be read as an individual unit – and there are instances of the elevation's being changed as the building rose – on the whole the building was planned in its entirety before the work started. The plan and elevation were normally set out on mathematical systems of proportion according to traditional number sequences, which made the process of laying out a complicated building much easier in an age of primitive measuring instruments. Favourite proportions can be observed: the lower storey of a church, for example, is often related to the upper storey in the ratio of 1 to the square root of 2, as at Long Melford in Suffolk. This ratio, based on the side of a square and its diagonal, is particularly easy to obtain without complicated measuring instruments, but it must have been used as much for the visual result as for the structural expediency that gave rise to it. The foundations were laid out as a whole, and the building put up a few bays at a time, which were vaulted as they went along. There was thus practical advantage in the aesthetic self-sufficiency of the bays: should lack of funds halt the building, at least part of it could be used. The stone was shipped from the quarry in rough blocks and cut into its final shape on the site. Decorative sculpture, such as pier capitals, was usually carved before it was put in place. A system of scaffolding and rope pulleys was used to haul the stones up, and before the scaffolding was taken down the vaults were painted and the upper windows glazed.

The building of a small parish church was a simpler operation, and the king's architectural undertakings vastly more complex. The king's office of works was responsible for all his buildings, be they permanent houses, castles and churches, or ephemeral pavilions and jousting grounds. Leading masons were appointed masters of the king's works north and south of the Trent, and, together with the master carpenter, they designed and supervised all the royal buildings. They often worked for other people at the same time: William Ramsey worked at Lichfield and St Paul's while he was master of the king's works, and William Wynford left the king's works at Windsor to become Wykeham's master mason at Winchester, but he still went on working for the king. Their skills and fashionable designs were much prized.

The administrative aspects of the king's works were handled by the clerk or surveyor. Huge sums of money were involved, at least £51,000 being spent at Windsor alone between 1350 and 1377. Wykeham administered the royal building works before becoming Bishop of Winchester, and Chaucer performed the role of surveyor between 1389 and 1391. Some have fanced an ironic echo of the lists for which he was responsible for the jousts at Smithfield in 1390 in his description of the theatre in the *Knight's Tale*:

For in the lond ther was no crafty man

That geometrie or ars metrike kan,
Ne portreyour, ne kervere of ymages,
That Theseus ne yaf him mete and wages,
The theatre for to maken and devyse.[5]

kan] knew   *yaf*] gave

Prominent among the stonemasons were the 'ymagiers', the figure-sculptors and tomb-makers. The similarity of detail in much medieval art is partly explained by the fact that one craftsman could make many different kinds of object. Henry Yevele and Stephen Lote, mason contractors to the king, made the tomb of Richard II and Anne of Bohemia in the 1390s, designing motifs very similar to those used in both monumental architecture and the minor arts.

The independence of artists, particularly the masons, should be stressed. They were not so closely involved in the world of the household described in Chapter 5. Tied as they were by their obligations to tradition and to their patron's taste, they were also free to seek work where they could, and to inspect the work of others. Although royal masons received fur robes and gloves at Christmas, they were not so much part of the royal household that they could not work elsewhere. A competent mason had many sidelines – such as properties in the city, or acting as a contractor to supply building materials – which brought him great wealth. Henry Yevele did this to great personal gain. The extent of the artist's freedom to come and go is reflected in the art of the period: while instantly recognizable as English, it is constantly alive to influences from elsewhere.

1330–1350: unity and illusionism; Perpendicular and Decorated

We have discussed some aspects of the general background to late medieval art. The rest of this chapter is devoted to the changes over the whole period, dealt with in seven subdivisions that roughly match the sequence outlined in Chapter 1. We shall see how, against the general background, the styles of all the visual arts changed over two centuries, and how they affected one another. The idea of unity is ever-present, as we shall see in the works with which the period opens.

Two buildings, in contrasting styles and with very different patrons, pursued this theme in the 1330s: the choir of Gloucester (Plate 3) and the Lady Chapel of Ely. When the choir of St Peter's

Abbey, Gloucester (now the cathedral), was altered to receive the mortal remains of the murdered King Edward II, the job was done by royal masons from London, and we can assume that the main patron was Edward III. Royal works tended to lead the fashion, and Gloucester was no exception. It was refaced in the style now called Perpendicular: the heavy Norman piers and arches of the central vessel were cut back and cased from floor to roof in a series of thin rectangular stone panels, built as an openwork screen across walls, glass or empty air, transforming the choir into a box of stone netting. The tomb of Edward II stands on the north side, surmounted by a delicate canopy of slender pinnacles, airy arches and miniature flying buttresses, enclosing the beautiful alabaster effigy of the king.

The choir is a complete, self-sufficient chapel, visually exclusive of the rest of the church, its decorative aspect turned in on itself. It is, in fact, a descendant of the Sainte-Chapelle in Paris, and, although it is doubtful whether anyone seriously believed in the sanctity of Edward II, it is significant that his burial chapel was modelled on a building with all the connotations of royalty and relics. We can go further than this: although one or two buildings in London may have experimented with the style of Gloucester before the 1330s, the only building before Gloucester with a complete covering of openwork panelling like this is the reliquary chapel of St Thibault in Burgundy, and it seems that the style selected for Gloucester was a deliberate choice.

The effect of Gloucester is of flat, thin walls, with very little substance, enhanced by the huge east window, which has the same tracery as the walls. The king's tomb and the net pattern of the vault are the only parts not severely restricted to the horizontal and vertical discipline of the walls; they are not in the Perpendicular style, but in the slightly older style now called Decorated, which was the fashionable style of the day. The Lady Chapel at Ely, contemporary with Gloucester, is in this style, which was well named. The style relies for its effect on bulk and illusionism, applying to the structural bones layers of decorative sculpture, bulbous leaves, twining figures, pinnacles, small gables, frilly tracery, and the ubiquitous ogee arch, formed of two reversed S-curves. Its appearance is the very opposite of Gloucester's.

At Ely the upper walls are dominated by huge windows, once filled with glass that was probably painted with scenes and symbols

1 (above) Carved head, Bishop's house, Ely (c. 1330). Photo: N. Coldstream.

2 (right) Alabaster relief of the Trinity, from an altarpiece (15th century). Victoria and Albert Museum.

3 Gloucester Cathedral choir (1337–73). Photo: National Monuments
Record.

4   Westminster Abbey, Henry VII's Chapel (1502–9). Photo: National
Monuments Record.

5   *St Omer Psalter*, BL Yates Thompson MS 14, fo. 7, the *Beatus* page
(*c*. 1330). Reproduced by permission of the British Library.

6   *The Beaufort Hours*, BL Royal MS 2 A.xviii, fo. 23^v, Annunciation
(before 1415). Reproduced by permission of the British Library.

7 *The Carmelite Missal*, BL Add. MS 29704, fo. 93, Presentation
(1390s). Reproduced by permission of the British Library.

8 Wooden chest front with scenes from *The Pardoner's Tale* (*c*. 1400).
Photo: Museum of London.

9 Screen with two Orders of the Angels, Barton Turf church, Norfolk (*c*. 1450). Photo: B. T. Batsford Ltd.

10 Cadaver on a tomb, Feniton, Devon (1400–50). Photo: F. H. Crossley, © Canon M. H. Ridgway. Reproduced by permission of the Courtauld Institute of Art.

11 Bronze effigy of
Richard, Earl of Warwick,
St Mary's church,
Warwick (1449–50).
Photo: University of
Warwick.

Tho: Wiatt Knight.

12 Portrait drawing of
Sir Thomas Wyatt
(1503–42) by Hans
Holbein. Reproduced by
gracious permission of
Her Majesty The Queen.

related to the chapel's patron saint, the Virgin Mary. Between the windows and along the walls beneath is continuous canopy-work in stone, with ogee arches which nod forwards, and shafts which seem to vanish behind the ogees to reappear higher up. The walls are concealed by layers of shifting planes. Figures of saints once stood beneath the canopies by the windows, a series of relief sculptures runs along the walls beneath the windows, while the small figure of a priest stands on the apex of every arched niche. These sculptures were once painted in bright colours against a gilded background, after the manner of an illuminated manuscript. Nowadays, stripped of its paint and stained glass, the Lady Chapel is suffused in abundant greenish light; in the mid-fourteenth century the monks would have been surrounded by deep colour from the windows and walls. The shafts, arches and sculptures would have shifted and glinted continuously in the flickering candlelight, and on all sides mysterious stone figures would have silently witnessed the ritual of the mass. The whole room conveyed that sense of being part of the mystical household of Christ which was consummated daily, not so much in the infrequent act of receiving bread and wine as through the eye, in the spectacle of the elevation of host and chalice. This is caught in the culminating lines of *Pearl*, dedicating it to Christ:

> That in the forme of bred and wyn
> The preste uus schewes uch a daye
> He gef uus to be his homly hyne
> Ande precios perles unto his pay.[6]

The vision of *Pearl* is set before the gardens of Paradise, with the New Jerusalem visible beyond them, and the hosts following the wounded lamb. That such a vision was meant to be embodied in churches can be found as early as *c*. 1100 in Theophilus' treatise *On the Various Arts*. Contemporary with Ely is the vault of Tewkesbury Abbey (Gloucestershire), whose sculptures depict a paradise garden, and it can also be found in manuscript illuminations.

Ely shows English Decorated at its maturity, at a time of considerable experiment all over the country. At Wells, Bristol and Ely polygonal groundplans were tried with success. The great central octagon at Ely created new effects of light, as did the bridge-like vaults in the aisles of St Augustine's, Bristol. Light strikes from unexpected angles, and creates uncertain depths and limits. Windows were being filled with flowing patterns of tracery, and within the churches tombs of the benefactors were being adorned with ogee arches and cresting of foliage sculpture. The rectilinear stone trellis of Gloucester was not entirely a reaction to this billowing exuberance. Beneath the most luxurious essays in the Decorated style lay the symmetry and restraint necessary to any building that must remain standing, and the self-absorbed quality of Gloucester is fundamentally like that of Ely: however different in superficial appearance, this is the essence of the Decorated style at its most successful. The two styles emerged from artistic developments fostered by royal patronage at the end of the thirteenth century, when both the ogee curve and the rectilinear panel appeared as decorative motifs on a number of objects made for the king, such as the coronation chair, and contemporary tombs.

The busy artistic world of London in the early fourteenth century was also the source of important developments in painting, which influenced the work of the manuscript painters known as the East Anglian school, who were reaching their apogee in the 1320s after nearly thirty years of activity. Many of the books are connected to monasteries or families in Norfolk and Suffolk, and these counties have altar screens made by the same workshop. Influenced from both Italy and France, the painters show interest in three-dimensional solidity; modelling in light and shade invades the swaying, graceful figures. The East Anglian manuscripts are characterized by the rich profusion of marginal decorations to their pages, in which birds, animals, humans and grotesques join a continuous dance among frames and foliage tendrils. This interest in marginalia was just beginning to weaken by the 1320s, and the magnificent manuscript that in a sense opens our period is restrained in this respect.

The St Omer Psalter (Plate 5) is one of a series of fine psalters for private use surviving from the work of the East Anglian school. It was begun around 1330 for the St Omer family of Norfolk. It was not finished until the fifteenth century, but its early style is represented on several pages, with decorated borders and historiated initials (capital letters at the beginning of an important part of the text, containing a small picture usually related to the text that follows). The initial to Psalm 1 shows as is usual the Tree of Jesse, with the ancestors of Christ enclosed in medallions made of a twining vine-scroll. The picture is set against a chequered blue and pink background in the top corner of a page framed in gold, with further vine-scroll medallions in the frame. Little branches of grouped leaves stretch out to the edge of the page, and upon each one is an animal or bird, delicately drawn from life, and tiny scenes of men engaged in felling trees, wrestling and escaping from a unicorn. The medallions themselves contain scenes from the book of Genesis, from the Creation of Man to the Drunkenness of Noah. Everything is on a minute scale: the page itself is no bigger than a modern book, and, although the composition is well balanced and does not seem crowded, every space is filled. The figures are tall, with black hair, pointed shoes, a slightly swaying stance, and shaded folds to their draperies. The attempt to set the figures in some definable space reflects Italian influence, although this is done without the use of buildings, for unlike the Italians the English artists of this period were not interested in the use of architectural recession to define interior space. The illustrations of the St Omer Psalter are all linear grace and movement, with a mixture of seriousness and anecdote, artificial pattern and attention to details from life, which is typical of the time.

A similar attitude to pictorial subject matter can be seen in the Painted Chamber of Longthorpe Tower near Peterborough. It belonged to Robert de Thorpe, steward of the Abbey of Peterborough, and the paintings date from around 1330. The colouring is in warm reds and yellows; there was some gold, but there is no sign of blue or green. The subjects range from symbolic depictions of the Seven Ages of Man and the Wheel of the Five Senses, to representations of saints and kings, with a border of beautifully realized fenland birds. Anticipating the morbid preoccupations of the fifteenth century, the story of the Three Living and the Three Dead is also shown: three kings meet three skeletons which turn out to be their own, a lesson in the futility of earthly power, as we must all come to dust in the end. Longthorpe is a unique survival of early fourteenth-century house decoration; that there were many such painted rooms is suggested by Chaucer's lines in the *Book of the Duchess* (1369), describing the chamber in which he dreams that he awoke:

And alle the walles with colours fyne
Were peynted, bothe text and glose,
Of al the Romaunce of the Rose.[7]

It would, however, be unwise to draw general conclusions from

Longthorpe, though it is worth remarking that the Thorpes had risen rapidly from lowly social status, and, although Robert was the second successive member of the family to become steward of the abbey, they were not finally released from villein status until 1324. Along with surviving tombs in parish churches, Longthorpe is evidence that the lesser subjects of the king could now afford to live and die among the painting and sculpture hitherto accessible only to the highest in the land.

Village life was portrayed by the artists of the Luttrell Psalter, made around 1340 when the East Anglian school had passed its zenith. In this book the marginal grotesques are too monstrous to delight the eye. But the margins are also filled with small scenes of home life, agriculture, sport and travel, an illustrated guide to daily life in the fourteenth century. These little scenes, and the grotesques, the creeping hominids and the satyrical 'babewyns', are part of the decorative repertory of all the arts of the time. The self-contained decoration of Gloucester and Ely is the architectural equivalent to the feast of detail on a page of an East Anglian manuscript, which can be interpreted as the paradise garden referred to earlier. A world in miniature envelops the spectator and shuts him away from the world outside; but in architecture the instinct towards clarity was stronger, and Gloucester, in many ways the perfect child of its time, gave new ideas to the new generation.

1350–1380: court taste and ceremony under Edward III; advance of Perpendicular; brief incursions of realism

The middle years of the reign of Edward III saw much pageantry and ceremonial, with grand new buildings at Windsor Castle expressing Edward's idea of kingship. One of the greatest losses from the Middle Ages is of domestic buildings, especially the many royal palaces: we know something from documents of their contents in terms of paintings and tapestries, but, although we can reconstruct the religious ceremonial of Edward's court, his domestic surroundings have gone. Windsor was to be the centre of the court and chivalry, with the new military patron, St George, and the headquarters of the new chivalric Order of the Garter, St George's Chapel. The individual heraldic badge began to appear on personal dress, plate and decorations; later it was to be used on a building or stained glass paid for by the person concerned. What had begun in a small way in the reign of Henry III was to become a dominant theme in architectural decoration two centuries later.

One of Edward's main undertakings was to finish the royal chapel of St Stephen in the Palace of Westminster. Founded in 1292, it was finally decorated in the 1350s. The chapel was destroyed by fire in 1834, and only its crypt survives in the Houses of Parliament. It was another direct descendant of the Sainte-Chapelle in Paris, a richer, finer version of the Lady Chapel at Ely, and as an example of a building in which all the arts contributed to the final effect it could scarcely be bettered. Of the entire scheme there survive a few pieces of miniature stone battlements, glass and fresco, and a strong effort of the imagination is needed to envisage it as it was. From the fragments and surviving drawings, we know that it exploited all the tricks of illusionism and minute detail that had delighted previous generations. The decoration and glazing were under the direction of Hugh of St Albans and William of Walsingham, but all the men who worked on St Stephen's were essential to the effect it was designed to create. The stonework was the frame for the clothing of decoration. It glittered and gleamed with gilt gesso, glass inlay, paint, stained glass and sculpture. It was furnished with silver-gilt statuettes, reliquaries and at least one panel painting. It was itself a jewelled reliquary writ large.

The wall paintings of St Stephen's are remarkable. They were executed in an oil medium, using the most expensive reds, and lapis lazuli for blues. The surviving fragments show figures in architectural settings, and although the figures have the weightless, twisted English pose there were real attempts to set them in credible space. The painted architecture recedes and they kneel on tiled floors. The illusionism of earlier years was not lost, but further exploited: the settings of the painted royal figures on the altar wall combined real with fictive architecture, and the entrance wall had painted figures in niches, done in monochrome grisaille technique to imitate stone, a technique inaugurated by Giotto in Italy and taken over by the French, whence it came to England. The receding architecture and some of the figures show Italian influence; the iconography, especially the portrayal of living royalty adoring the altar, is probably French, and these mixed influences abounded in English painting for many years to come.

English painters in general did not at once pursue the experiments in spatial representation and other adventurous Italian ideas.

They enjoyed and excelled in two-dimensional linear decoration, and were gifted storytellers. English work is characterized by bustling anecdotal narrative, and exaggeration of both grace and villainy: ruffians are especially ruffianly. A series of books was made for members of the Bohun family around 1370, ranging from private devotional psalters to a copy of *Lancelot du Lac*. They are representative of the kinds of books that were being made, still with emphasis on service books: missals containing the mass, psalters, Bibles, and books of hours with offices of the Virgin to be said after the main services, or privately. Illustration of these books followed a standard scheme, with some full-page miniatures, such as a Crucifixion scene before the consecration prayer of the mass, Bible pictures before the psalms, and decorated letters at the beginning of each psalm or hour. The Bohun manuscripts have elaborate architectural settings for every scene: the initials are overhung by toppling canopies of spiky pinnacles, which are not, as we shall see, entirely fantastic creations. One of the psalters also shows how far an English artist was reluctant to explore depth in his pictures: it contains historiated initials with scenes from the life of Christ set in charming flower-studded landscapes. The tooled gold background abruptly cuts off the promise of an airy green field.

The pinnacles of the Bohun manuscripts are motifs borrowed directly from architecture, and they were used in all forms of art, and on stonework of every scale. The poet says of Sir Bercilak's castle in *Gawain and the Green Knight* (*c.* 1360–1400):

> So mony pynakle payntet was powdred ayquere
> Among the castel carneles, clambred so thik
> That pared out of papure purely hit semed.[8]

The slender, vertical elegance reflected royal tastes. The Neville screen in Durham Cathedral was made in London in 1372 and shipped north in boxes to stand between the high altar and the shrine of St Cuthbert. Both sides consist of tiers of housings for statues, with octagonal tabernacles and pyramidal gables, pinnacles set diagonally and small ogee arches. The screen displays all the interest in polygonal shapes which was so marked a characteristic of the Decorated style. Inasmuch as the screen is a wall of light-catching facets, a more rectilinear version of ideas prevalent at the beginning of the century, it is a reminder that artists explored themes familiar to their predecessors, and it demonstrates one of the paradoxes of metropolitan taste in the fourteenth century: although always in the vanguard of ideas and an arbiter of fashion, at a deeper level the art of the court played variations on long-tried themes.

On a larger scale the ideas of Gloucester were gradually taking effect. The new choir of York Minster, founded in 1361, was the first Perpendicular building in the North, and caused the immediate abandonment of the Decorated style, which had flourished in that area until that moment. Unlike that at Gloucester, the choir was not fenced in, but the panelled effect was used in the upper storeys. Parish churches were also being built anew on the wealth of shipping or wool merchants. St Mary Redcliffe at Bristol was one of the first to show the influence of Gloucester. Built on the wealth of Bristol trade, it is one of the largest parish churches in the country. Its nave was rebuilt around 1375, and the panelled motifs were put in the windows and on the walls between the windows and the arcade, so that the whole upper wall was decorated with blank panels. There is strong vertical emphasis, with all extraneous detail subordinate to it; for instance, the pier capitals have been reduced almost to nothing. The vault complements the walls, with a simple rectilinear pattern of ribs.

The two biggest ecclesiastical undertakings at the time in the South were the naves of Canterbury and Winchester cathedrals, each of interest for several reasons. Canterbury makes a serious attempt to apply the unified concept of architecture to a building with aisles. The architect tried to solve the problem of fusing the separate spaces of nave and aisles by enormously raising the height of the aisles. They are the main source of light for the nave, whose upper storeys are crowded into a small space under the vault, and the effect is to make the whole area seem like one space.

At Winchester there was a technical problem, solved so brilliantly by the architect Wynford that it was unsuspected until the great antiquary Robert Willis examined the building in the nineteenth century. Wynford, like any competent mason, was capable of building anything from a castle to a jousting pavilion. When he came from Windsor after 1366, he was asked to take into account a substantial quantity of enormously thick masonry from the Norman nave, which had not been removed. Needing arches through to the aisles, he could not put a screen of tracery in front of the piers, as at Gloucester, so he covered the Norman elevation with panels of tracery and thin, vertical mouldings, reducing the capitals to the minimum and bringing the main vaulting shafts uninterrupted to the floor. The thickness thus concealed is apparent only in the clerestory, where the deep Norman window openings could not be reduced to a single plane. The nave has a rectilinear vault pattern, and the effect of the whole is of an enormous long, closed box.

The see of Winchester was occupied until 1404 (though with a period of royal disfavour) by one of the greatest patrons of the age, William of Wykeham. It was one of the richest in the land. As we have seen, Wykeham ensured that money was available for his architectural ventures, and, being a trained administrator of humble parentage, he made wise use of it. His other great works were Winchester College and New College, Oxford. Wynford's name appears on the hall books of New College, and the work there resembles other buildings of his, so to him (under Wykeham's patronage) is given credit for this, the first collegiate building erected to a plan. It was built round a quadrangle, with the hall and chapel placed end to end along one side. The T-shaped plan of the chapel and antechapel may derive from the unfinished earlier chapel of Merton College; but what was accident at Merton was designed at New College, and it set the pattern for college chapels for years to come. Into the antechapel Wynford put all the airy lightness denied him at Winchester: tall, slender piers, with shafts and hollows, support shallow arches, and the window tracery is regular, rectilinear and a little dull; but the architecture here and in the chapel itself was designed as a neutral setting for an overwhelming display of stained glass and a massive altar screen of figures in niches. The life of the building depended on its decoration, and much of it has been destroyed.

The niche defined as sacred the area it enclosed, and the canopied niche containing a figure was the leitmotif of the time (Plates 4, 6 and 9); it seems natural that some of the most evocative lines about architecture written around 1400 should be:

> In a tabernacle of a toure,
> As I stode musing on the mone,
> A crowned quene, most of honoure,
> Apered in ghostly sight . . .[9]

Canopied niches were applied to screens, tombs and facades, and elaborate canopies were used as settings for figures in stained-glass windows. The stone altar screen at Christchurch, Hampshire (*c.* 1360), is a series of canopied niches built against the wall, in which reside the remains of a Tree of Jesse, and in the middle an Adoration of the Magi. This is carved in a soft style with clinging drapery and no individuality in the faces – a style also seen in the decaying figures of kings on the west front of Exeter Cathedral.

In the later fourteenth century there was work for every craftsman who could find a patron; as the gentry ordered tombs and small sculptured reliefs for their personal devotions, the output of work-shops in London and the provinces increased enormously. Effigies in stone and alabaster, monumental brasses, alabaster reliefs and statuettes abounded, and much alabaster work was exported to the continent. But it must be said that the quality of the alabaster work was variable, ranging from beautiful and delicately carved effigies to crudely executed biblical scenes in relief, and many of the pieces are of interest other than aesthetic.

The slight interest in realism shown at St Stephen's Chapel made only a brief impact on the outside world, but it was manifest in several ways. The wooden statues of the Annunciation at Wells show the Virgin in the conventional drapery and swaying pose, but the angel is dressed in the fashionable clothes of a contemporary woman. On a few of the alabaster reliefs with biblical scenes there are hints of the direct influence of the mystery plays. These panels are rarely more than 2 feet high, and much activity was crowded into them. This was similar to the treatment of sculptured roof bosses, and may reflect only the artist's *horror vacui*; but the Betrayal of Christ seems sometimes to have been depicted as it was acted on stage, and the demons' headdress used for wicked people is a direct borrowing from stage practice.

Royal interest in realism was not confined to the wall paintings of St Stephen's Chapel. In 1376 Queen Philippa employed Jean de Liège to make her white marble funeral effigy, an effigy that is clearly taken from the life. It is in fact a portrait in the sense that we would understand the term today. 'Portraits' had certainly existed earlier as both statues and effigies, but they did not convey real character or likeness; they were idealized representations intended to show such specific qualities as holiness or kingliness or wisdom. Such indeed is the gilt copper effigy of Edward III, which is an idealized portrayal of a wise old king, in marked contrast to the plain and homely features of his queen.

Jean de Liège was influenced by experiments in realistic portraiture being made at the French court. This was a new idea in monumental painting and sculpture, but it came of a long tradition in small architectural sculptures such as head-stops on doorways and corbel roof supports (Plate 1). There since the thirteenth century sculptors had carved lively portrayals of their friends and enemies, but it was not until the late fourteenth century that tentative moves were made to show people as they really were on a monumental scale. The realism of Philippa's tomb was not imitated at once: her son the Black Prince was shown with a moderate likeness imbued with the essence of his greatness, in his case soldierliness. Some people preferred drama to realism: Edward, Lord Despenser, is represented on the roof of his little chantry chapel between two piers of Tewkesbury choir, kneeling in prayer towards the high altar.

The gentry chose between a monumental brass or an effigy upon a sarcophagus. They continued to found chantry chapels, or to rebuild existing church choirs as their mortuary chapels. Thomas, Earl of Warwick, who began the chancel of St Mary's, Warwick, in the 1360s, is buried in the middle of the choir before the high altar. He and his wife are stiffly carved in alabaster. On the sides of the sarcophagus stand little figures, weepers, representing the mourners – usually, as here, members of the family. These little alabaster figures are dressed in the height of fashion and are not noticeably grief-stricken. Monumental brasses were similar in style to three-dimensional tombs, and there is clear evidence that a group of tomb-makers was emerging in London, men who were prepared to supply tombs or effigies in stone, alabaster or bronze. The figure on a brass is shown beneath a canopy very similar to those on tombs, or in the contemporary Bohun manuscripts. A dog or lion was placed beneath the feet as on a marble tomb, but on a brass the engraver could decorate the figure and its setting with minute detail. The Dallingridge brass at Fletching, Sussex (*c.* 1380), has ogee gables similar to those on the chantry chapel built by William of Wykeham in the nave of Winchester Cathedral shortly before his death, where the upper gables and canopies for statues are tall ogees with the canopies bent back to show the vaulting within.

1380–1400: International Gothic; Richard II and royalty; domestic comfort and Perpendicular light

The Bohun manuscripts may have been made in London, which

continued as an important centre of artistic production. The missal (mass book) made for Abbot Nicholas Lytlington of Westminster in 1383-4 is perhaps related to the Bohun manuscripts. It has historiated initials, with a full-page Crucifixion scene set in a broad frame containing small pictures of scenes from the Passion of Christ. Against a tooled gold ground, the Crucifixion is depicted according to Italian iconography, with the two robbers sharing the scene, the Virgin fainting with grief, and skulls scattered at the foot of the cross to denote Calvary. The foreshortened back view of the soldier Stephaton offering the sponge is a brave attempt to master an Italianate pose. The bright black eyes and shading of the draperies resemble the Bohun manner, but the style here is drier, with hard outlines. The eyelids and nose seem almost etched into the face, and lurking at the edge of the picture is a figure in the tradition of English caricature.

The reign of Richard II had already begun, and in 1382 he celebrated his marriage to Anne of Bohemia. She brought with her a large retinue, among whom may have been at least one painter, for another book belonging to Westminster is close in style to contemporary Bohemian painting. This, the *Liber Regalis*, contains the order for the coronation of a king and queen, and has a full-page miniature of a king enthroned, being crowned by two prelates and witnessed by two noblemen. The style is soft and shaded, with black outline used for the edges of the faces. The figures have huge hands with long, curving fingers; their black eyes stare in all directions from their well-modelled faces, and the distinctive straight, jutting nose can also be found in the slightly earlier wall paintings at Karlstein, near Prague in Bohemia. The late fourteenth-century retable in Norwich Cathedral is another work in the style of Bohemia. The subject matter, scenes of the Passion of Christ, is thoroughly to the taste of English artists, with plenty of opportunity for storytelling and exaggerated characterization; this approach can be found in contemporary alabaster work, but here the figures are all pushed to the foreground, recession cut off by the tooled gold background; the figures are slender and expressive, with long hands and great emphasis on the modelling of the heads. This style owes nothing to the alabasters, and is much closer to the style of the Bohemian painters.

These painters gave England her first taste of the International Gothic, the intriguing style that dominated the main artistic centres of Europe from *c.* 1380 to *c.* 1430. It embodied a manner of rich and sinuous grace of figure and fine colouring, combined with a growing interest and delight in exploring the natural world. The most exciting works of this time are *Les Très Riches Heures* of the Duc de Berry, painted by the Limbourg brothers, and the sculptures of Claus Sluter at Dijon. While England never achieved anything of that quality, her painters and sculptors took some interest in it. The style became 'International' for various reasons. Charles IV of Bohemia was brought up in France, married a French princess and wanted to model his court on that of Paris. Richard II married a Bohemian princess and, after her death, a French one. The French royal family had long been active patrons, and now, with the courts of Burgundy and Berry as great as that of Paris, large numbers of Franco-Flemish artists could enjoy the conditions necessary for their work: money in the hands of educated, interested patrons. There was a great movement of craftsmen between Italy, France, Germany, Bohemia and England, dominated by the Flemish and the Dutch. More closely than ever, the courts of Europe shared artistic tastes and attitudes: not only did they emulate each other, but they employed the same artists.

Much of the surviving English painting of the 1380s is in the English–Italian style of previous decades, of poor quality and lacking any real talent. Inspiration arrived in the 1390s, in the work of one of the painters of the Carmelite Missal. This book was made for the London house of the Carmelite order; the illustrations are mostly in the form of historiated initials, painted by three different hands, of which two are readily explained by current English styles. The third, however, introduces carefully modelled figures, with properly foreshortened faces, and shows interest in exploring spatial depth. The scene of the Presentation of Christ (Plate 7) depicts a chapel with its side cut away to show the interior, a floor decorated with a receding pattern of tiles, and figures grouped round an altar set in definable space. The general disposition of this picture is similar to contemporary scenes of the Annunciation and Presentation painted by Melchior Broederlam on the wings of the great triptych at the Chartreuse de Champmol in Dijon. The Carmelite artist seems to have been a Dutchman who knew these pictures or others like them.

The Dutch artist was probably working in London, which, with Westminster, was a lively artistic centre in the reign of Richard II.

Richard's preoccupation with the sanctity of kingship led him to devote himself to the cult of the sainted king, Edward the Confessor, in contrast with the cult of St George assiduously fostered by Edward III and, later, Henry V. Richard paid for the completion of the abbey nave and, when that was under way, turned his attention to a building close by: the Great Hall in the Palace of Westminster. Richard, like Henry III before him, fully appreciated the value of the outward signs of kingship. His sacred lineage could be seen in the abbey; he needed a royal hall in which his court could complement his sovereignty. Westminster Hall had originally been built by William Rufus in the 1090s, and had recently required extra buttressing. Inside, the double row of stone piers needed to support the roof used up valuable space. In the 1390s the king's master mason, Henry Yevele, acted as adviser for the removal of the piers and other alterations, and Hugh Herland, carpenter, designed and made the roof. The Norman side walls were largely retained; new, bigger windows with Perpendicular tracery were put in, and a wide screen facade with niches for statues was added to the north entrance. Further statues of kings flanked the dais at the south end of the hall. Some of these survive – huge figures with orbs and sceptres carved in the round, and great crowns on their heads, royal predecessors to Richard, a visual reminder of his ancestry. They seem to have influenced many of the figures of kings that became a prominent feature of fifteenth-century screen work. The north and south ends of the hall were lit by large Perpendicular windows, and the king, when seated upon the dais, was intended to be seen in a halo of coloured light, although he was deposed before it was finished and probably never used it.

Richard's heraldic badge, the white hart, was carved on the string course beneath the windows. This was one of the first uses of a badge on architecture, and it was to have far-reaching effects. Richard's badge was used again on the crossing piers of York Minster when they were strengthened during his reign, and from this time on the badge was used on tombs and buildings as it had hitherto decorated smaller objects.

The glory of Westminster Hall is Hugh Herland's wooden roof, riding tier upon tier from its low supporting walls. It is the earliest surviving hammerbeam roof in the country. In this type of roof the main arch braces stand on hammerbeams projecting from the wall, supported by braces corbelled into the wall itself. Wide spans can be roofed by this method, and the relatively narrow arch braces, supported in a series of steps, can clear a lofty height. Westminster Hall was transformed from an aisled building to a single space, and in this sense it is a link between the single cell of Gloucester choir and the rectangular box of King's College Chapel, Cambridge. At Westminster the gaps between the roof beams were filled with openwork panelling, and the hammerbeams each support a wooden angel bearing a shield of arms, a foretaste of the great East Anglian 'angel roofs' half a century hence. Herland's roof grew from a long tradition of ingenious carpentry; there was a long series of wooden vaults, of which the most famous are the fourteenth-century vaults of York Minster, and much of the intricate work was carried out by the king's master carpenters.

Richard's adored Queen Anne died in 1394, and he immediately commissioned their joint tomb, to complete the circle of royal tombs round the shrine of Edward the Confessor in Westminster Abbey. The gilt copper effigy of Richard hints at portraiture, albeit in the highly refined court style, with slender, pointed features and minutely engraved surface decoration. The short beard, high cheekbones, thin nose with flared nostrils and short wavy hair reappear in the other two known portraits of Richard, the iconic, enthroned regal figure in Westminster Abbey, and (beardless) the Wilton Diptych.

This beautiful and mysterious diptych was probably made around 1395, by an artist who may have been Parisian, but who knew London work. On the left-hand panel Richard kneels in a landscape, with his patron saints John the Baptist, King Edmund and Edward the Confessor standing behind him. They are presenting him to the Virgin and Child, who are on the right-hand panel, surrounded by eleven angels. The grass at their feet is strewn with flowers, and the backgrounds are in punched gold diaper. Round the king's neck is the French heraldic necklace of broom cods with the white hart pendant. This emblem was later added to the angels, appearing to symbolize Richard's two courts, that of earth and that of heaven. The problems connected with this picture involve dating, attribution and interpretation, and there is not enough space to discuss them adequately here. Monumental portraits were, as we have seen, being made in England under French influence, and in France, too, is found the idea of a lay figure being presented to the Virgin by his patron saint. The soft sway and draperies of the right-hand panel seem to be French in feeling, although the modelling of the faces on the left side owes much to Sienese painting, and the diptych is painted on gesso in the Italian manner. The 'Sienese' face style, the slender hands and the dusting of decoration on the draperies of the left-hand figure are very close in style to Richard's copper effigy, while the staring black eyes and peculiarly foreshortened faces of the angels bear some resemblance to the work of the Dutch artist in the Carmelite Missal. The artist of the Wilton Diptych had intimate knowledge of recent London work. The colouring of the right-hand leaf is in shades of blue with pinkish flesh tones, while the king and saints have browner skins, with red, brown and cream draperies. The draperies of the kneeling angel are governed by the form of the body beneath, and this combination of exquisite colour and realistic modelling can be seen in the other important picture of this time.

This is the miniature known as the Beaufort Hours Annunciation (Plate 6), a single leaf bound into a later book. It shows the Annunciation with two donors, taking place inside an open Gothic room, as in the Presentation scene of the Carmelite Missal. Space is handled with the adroitness of the Dutch artist – who may in fact have been the painter – but the pinkish flesh tones and soft modelling are nearer to the diptych than the missal. The figures are infused with qualities lacking in the iconic art of Richard's court: drama, emotion and movement. On the Virgin's prie-dieu is written 'Omnia levia sunt amanti; siquis amat, non laborat: da daer' ('All things go smoothly for those who love; he who loves does not work; da daer'), which reappears in manuscripts associated with Herman Scheerre (of whom more later). It is a curiously ambiguous little motto, reminding one of the exactly contemporary 'Amor vincit omnia' ('Love conquers all') on Chaucer's Prioress's brooch,[10] and perhaps reflecting the newly expressed interest in non-religious aspects of life. On the frame of the miniature is the distinctive border motif of an acanthus scroll wrapped round a rod, which also reappears in many of Herman Scheerre's works, and perhaps early in his career he worked on the manuscript of which the Beaufort Annunciation was once a part.

Another manuscript of the late fourteenth century, the sketch-book now in the Pepysian Library at Cambridge, has one page of birds painted in a naturalistic style akin to that of Herman's contemporary, John Siferwas. Their vivid, accurate characterization recalls Chaucer's *Parliament of Fowls*. It seems from the surviving works of visual art that they may have been responding to interests in the world alone, distinct from God, which had been long established in literature, in love lyric, beast fable and romance. However, few illustrated secular manuscripts survive from the late fourteenth century, and none at all from the court; but this may be accidental, as other objects with known royal connections illustrate familiar stories. Tristan and Isolde figure on a cup belonging to Edward III, and the Black Prince owned a tapestry illustrating the story of Saladin. Thomas, Duke of Gloucester, could look upon the tapestried legends of Charlemagne and Godfrey de Bouillon adorning his walls. Away from the king's court, a poem on Godfrey de Bouillon and the siege of Jerusalem is one of a collection of French poems apparently belonging to Henry Despenser (*c.* 1400), but its illustration is confined to border decorations. The *Canterbury Tales* likewise attracted few illustrations. The manuscript of *Pearl* has four miniatures featuring the narrator, and a copy of Richard Rolle's poems is illustrated by a perhaps idealized picture of the author; but there was no iconographical tradition for these books, and, although the *Canterbury Tales* should have appealed to the narrative abilities of the painters, such illustrations as do exist were executed with little bravura. Woodcarvers were much more confident: there are robust illustrations of the *Pardoner's Tale* on a wooden chest (Plate 8), and splendid versions of the Arthurian stories survive on misericords at Lincoln and Chester.

From the late fourteenth century, men's minds turned to comfort and privacy as well as to fortification. The designer of Bodiam Castle, Sussex, begun in 1386, attended to all these needs. The weakening of royal power in the 1370s and 1380s led to a revival of the independent military power of the nobility, and the lord maintained two separate households, working and military. At Bodiam, as in many other castles in northern Europe, there are two complete sets of living quarters, one for the working and one for the military household. The lord controlled the gatehouse and the water supply, and the soldiery had direct access neither to the lord nor to the gate. The width of the moat allowed large windows in the living room, and the family had its own private apartments in addition to the hall and solar, ensuring an easier existence than that afforded by the keep-gatehouse of earlier days. The state rooms built for John of Gaunt at Kenilworth Castle in the 1390s had oriel windows and fireplaces with beautiful tracery and mouldings, carefully protected by stern defensive towers. Brick was now becoming popular: the gate-house of Thornton Abbey, Lincolnshire, was built in brick with stone dressings around 1380. At first sight it is a forbidding structure, defensive and authoritarian; closer inspection reveals that the front of the building once had an imposing array of sculptured figures in niches, and inside the gatehouse are some charming rooms for receiving guests, with large fireplaces and an oriel window.

Delicate mouldings are also found in contemporary parish churches, where the desire for unified interiors was producing build-ings with slender piers and clear, wide spaces. The quiet, repetitive tracery panels of the Perpendicular style, with the depressed four-centred arch used for windows and arcades, slowed the rhythms and gave an atmosphere of calm. The tendency towards uncluttered spaces may have been encouraged by the example of the friars' churches, which stood in many large towns. With their particular emphasis on preaching, the mendicant orders needed uninterrupted space, and were followed in this by such parish churches as St Nicholas, King's Lynn, in Norfolk. The windows were filled with stained glass. The parish churches and Minster at York possess a large quantity of late medieval glass, the style of which was intro-duced by John Thornton of Coventry, who glazed the great east window of the Minster in 1405–8. The huge window has twenty-seven rectangular panels below the tracery head, filled with scenes from the books of Genesis and Exodus, and of the Apocalypse, with figures of kings and churchmen in the lowest register. The tracery head contains half-length figures. Thornton's work shows how styles spread far and wide: his style seems to depend on that of Thomas Glazier of Oxford, who made the glass for New College Chapel in 1380–6, and the great Jesse window of Winchester College around 1393. The figures here and at York have firmly modelled faces, rather dry, frizzy hair and softly falling drapery. Happily for posterity, Thomas drew a picture of himself in the Jesse window. It cannot be called a portrait in the sense of depicting a likeness; rather, Thomas was illustrating a man, and identifying it as himself the glazier by the inscription, 'Thomas operator istius vitri'. This is in the tradition of the scribes and illuminators of manuscripts, who over several centuries had shown themselves in their pages in like manner. It is far removed from the attempts to convey likeness, perhaps character, and certainly kingliness, in the portraits of Richard II.

*1400–1430:   decline   of   grandeur;   thriving   of   smaller   arts;
emblematic iconography*

The first half of the fifteenth century is not a happy period in
English art. Owing to the stagnant economy, most people had less
money to spend, although some individuals were extremely
wealthy. Burials were more rarely accompanied by all the splendour
of a funeral effigy; a brass would suffice, and, for those families for
whom a brass had hitherto sufficed, a considerably cheaper one was
now ordered. As for the main source of patronage, the crown,
although Henry IV and Henry V were noted book lovers, they were
not active patrons of the visual arts, their interests being dissipated
in fighting their enemies. The less able soldiers among English kings
have usually shown the greatest appreciation of the arts. Henry V's
brothers – John, Duke of Bedford, and Humphrey, Duke of
Gloucester – did employ artists to some extent, and their patronage
helped to relieve the desert created by the long minority of Henry VI.
A few individuals who had materially benefited from the French wars
or landed inheritance could build on a grandiose scale, as at
Tattershall, Lincolnshire in the 1430s; but these were isolated
endeavours, and most of the visual arts revived only around 1440, and
proceeded with gathering momentum into the sixteenth century. The
small-scale arts – manuscript paintings, alabasters and brasses – are
exceptions.

By chance, two manuscript-painters of the early fifteenth century,
each the master of a large workshop, have left their names on record.
Johannes Siferwas worked in the years round 1400 and Herman
Scheerre slightly after that date. Both of these men in their different
styles exploited the new interest in depth, in the handling of space
and of the human figure, which had been manifest in the work of
the Dutch artist of the Carmelite Missal. Siferwas, a Dominican
friar, wrote his name in the missal made for Sherborne Abbey
between 1396 and 1407. Many of the later pictures in this enormous
book were painted by assistants, but Siferwas seems to have painted
the Crucifixion picture that was placed before the canon of the mass.
He adopted the Italianate scheme of the Lytlington Missal, but the
composition is much more crowded, with at the same time more
attempts at recession in the rising landscape. The frame of the
miniature is shaded to suggest wood. Shading is also applied to the
figures, hair, faces and draperies being carefully modelled in light

and dark, with curious, distinctive, heavy white eyelids over large black eyes. The Gospel lectionary given to Salisbury Cathedral by John Lord Lovell before 1408 is also signed by Siferwas. It contains a portrait of Lord Lovell receiving the book from the scribe, and displays in miniatures no bigger than a hand the meticulous delicacy of the true miniaturist.

Other artists painted in the Siferwas style, and the more eclectic of them managed to combine it with that of the other identifiable painter, Herman Scheerre. He has been tentatively traced in London wills of 1407, and he may have come from Cologne. If the 'Herman lymnour' of the documents is indeed the Herman who painted the books, he was also a Carmelite friar, and Dr Rickert has associated his style with the Carmelite books, including the great missal. His style resembles the Dutch artist's. It is soft and rather dreamy: the colours are muted, the figures have no hard edges, and they seem spiritually withdrawn. Modelling is achieved by careful shading and highlights, hair is pale gold and slightly wispy, and nowhere is the exaggeration or hint of the grotesque that informs the work even of Siferwas.

The psalter and hours made for John, Duke of Bedford, around 1416 shows Herman's mature style. The Annunciation miniature at the beginning is closely based on the Beaufort Hours, whose possible connections with the Dutch artist and with Herman we have seen. The decoration of the Bedford Psalter is in the form of initials illustrated with narratives, many of which include highly individual portrait heads, executed with great skill. Herman's hand can be detected in only a few of these, but one of his characteristics was to give individual personalities to biblical figures as well as to contemporaries.

Herman seems to have been the master of a large shop, but even in one shop there were mixtures of styles. English painting was at the mercy of influences from Flanders, Holland, Italy and France, combined in any way that appealed to a particular painter. Many illuminated manuscripts were produced, some of real distinction. The narrative-historiated initial was the main decorative device, with much emphasis on borders, which became steadily more florid, with thicker-painted foliage and fewer hairline sprays. One manuscript with both framed miniatures and historiated initials is the Hours of Elizabeth the Queen. It seems to be contemporary with the Bedford Hours, and is painted by several hands, of which the main one may be that of 'Johannes' (not Siferwas) who had earlier painted a copy of Marco Polo's *Li Livres de Graunt Caam*, notable for its perfectly recognizable picture of Venice. His figures have large heads with eyes that are deeply shaded yet manage to bulge at the same time. He was interested in exploring spatial depth and suggested this with carefully placed diagonals and a single source of light within the picture. His compositions remained crowded, his figures types rather than individuals.

The habit of depicting people in contemporary dress instead of the somewhat indeterminate draperies that have a late classical origin had been growing for some time. In manuscripts members of the peasantry had been shown wearing a form of kilt since the twelfth century, and funeral effigies had always portrayed the subject in the clothes of the day; but in fifteenth-century religious art all over Europe, all persons except the figures of Christ, the Virgin and the Apostles could be shown in rich contemporary costume. The Corpus Christi manuscript of *Troilus and Criseyde* has a full-page miniature of Chaucer addressing a crowd in an elaborate wooded landscape, which recedes upwards to a city. The sky is tooled gold and there is little individualization in the faces; but everyone is dressed in fine contemporary costume. In 1411 Hoccleve had painted for his *Regement of Princes*, explicitly to preserve Chaucer's memory, a picture of the poet. Although it was done eleven years after Chaucer's death, and may be related to the earlier clumsy and unindividual picture in the Ellesmere *Canterbury Tales*, it is certainly like a living portrait, dressed again in contemporary costume, but now very soberly. The attempts at landscape painting and portraiture show the direct influence of the painters and sculptors in the entourages of the royal dukes of France, and are common to manifestations of the International Gothic.

John, Duke of Bedford, and Humphrey, Duke of Gloucester, commissioned many books. The Duke of Bedford had been regent in France, and patronized both French and English illuminators. Bedford died in 1435, Gloucester in 1447, and their deaths coincided with the loss of France and the beginning of the troubles that were to become the Wars of the Roses. Perhaps coincidentally, manuscript painting suffered; there seems to have been a marked absence of obvious patrons, and in contrast to the other arts manuscript painting went into a decline from about the 1430s. Until then, along with alabasters and brasses, it had held the field.

The great could still afford funeral effigies, and a series of fine alabasters represents such people as William of Wykeham (*c.* 1400) and Henry IV and Queen Joan (*c.* 1410–20). In these figures and in those of monks praying at the feet of the prelate, there are signs of characterization and individual portraiture which show the influence of Burgundian sculpture. The Nottingham and York alabasters are more crudely handled than the London works, and the effigies tend to be finer than the relief panels. In the reliefs, hands, feet and heads were exaggerated, and caricature was well marked in any figure representing an ordinary mortal. By contrast, divine figures tend towards a rather vapid grace. The reliefs were painted in gold and bright colours, and later scenes were set beneath a battlemented canopy which may have been adapted from the canopy over a mobile stage, although battlement cresting had been a decorative device in all the arts since the thirteenth-century. Alabaster reliefs were exported in large numbers to France, where they can still be found in many Breton churches, and in the middle of the century an English pilgrim to Compostela presented the church with an alabaster altarpiece showing scenes of the life of St James. Few of the reliefs can claim admiration, but their robust cheerfulness, even in scenes of tragedy, gives them undoubted charm.

The subject matter now included themes that were emblematic rather than purely narrative (Plates 2 and 9). The fifteenth century saw a move towards didactic, emblematic presentation which reflected a change in religious attitudes. The Te Deum, the Five Joys of Mary, the Ten Commandments and the Seven Sacraments appeared for the first time, and depictions of the suffering Christ with the Five Wounds or the Instruments of the Passion became popular. The combination of the use of the eyes with articulation and numbering to help contemplation is natural to the emblem. Many manuscripts survive in which verse prayers accompany pictures of each of the Instruments, evidently to help devotion. Poems patterned on the Joys or the Wounds were also introduced at this time. These tend to be merely conventional, but Lydgate makes powerful use of the Wounds:

> The five rooses portrayed in the sheeld
> Splayed in the baneer at Jerusalem.[11]

A curious variation of the Instruments picture, known today as Christ of the Trades, in which implements of trade replace those of the Passion, has no exact parallel in literature, although the power-ful imagination of the omnipresence of Christ in his suffering appears in other forms throughout our period, as in John Grimeston's

> Gold and all this werdis win
> Is nought but Christes rode.[12]

werdis win] world's joy   *rode*] cross

Chaucer's Pardoner's more grotesque imagination – that, in swear-ing, men 'Christes blessed body all torente'[13] – is found also in a painting at Broughton (Buckinghamshire) in which richly dressed men hold Christ's dismembered parts. Traditional stories were not forgotten, either by painters or by writers: the lives of Christ and the Virgin, and saints both local and of universal importance, were the most usual stories, but the interest lies in the new emblematic themes.

Memorial brasses became popular in the early fifteenth century, and their compositions reflect the arrangement of three-dimensional effigies, for which brasses were a cheaper substitute. In the Drury brass at Rougham, Suffolk (*c.* 1405), the knight lies armed, his hands in an attitude of prayer, his feet resting on a lion with a handsome plumed tail. His wife, in contemporary dress, rests her head on two superimposed pillows – a motif taken directly from sculptured tombs – and a lapdog gazes up at her from her feet. On some brasses, as on some tombs, husband and wife hold hands. The Drury brass is very lightly engraved with the detailing of the dress, but this was perhaps a matter of choice and expense. The brass of Thomas, Earl of Warwick (d. 1401), and his countess is engraved over most of its surface. The disposition of the earl and his wife is similar to that of the Drury brass, even to the iconographic type of the lapdog, but the earl's feet rest on the bear which was the family emblem. It is an interesting reflection on the times that, while Thomas's parents lie beneath a sarcophagus and effigies, and his son, Richard, was to have one of the most handsome of chantry chapels, he himself is commemorated only by a brass.

Monumental stone sculpture was not altogether neglected, although subsequent destruction has created an unnatural dearth. The fashion had developed for rows of figures in niches, and in many places they have been smashed. Towards 1411 Prior Chillenden of Canterbury, following the new fashion for elaborate screens, built the cathedral choir screen, an elaborate compilation of niches for statues. The canopies have the complicated star vaults that were used in many chantry chapels, being an ideal decoration for a small roof span. The canopy pinnacles are tall, set against openwork panels. The incidental foliage decoration is square and static. The style of this screen is moving towards the encrusted stiffness of later Perpendicular work. As elsewhere, many of the statues have been destroyed, but six figures of kings remain. They have the heavy crowns, orbs and sceptres of the kings at Westminster Hall, but these figures are invested with considerable individuality, and the slight turn of head and hand gives them both depth and life.

1430–1470: obsession with death; incursions of Flemish realism

Much of the artistic expression of the fifteenth century was concerned with the fortunes of the soul after death. From the greatest in the land to lesser persons and parish guilds, in architecture, sculpture and paint, comes the obsession with death and decay that peculiarly distinguishes the fifteenth century. This was the great period of foundations of colleges of chantry priests to pray for the souls of individual families, such as the York family at Fotheringhay. There could be a charitable motive: Ewelme (Oxfordshire) was founded in 1432 by William de la Pole, Earl of Suffolk, with church, almshouses and school. From the middle of the century come three interesting chantries put up for individuals: Henry V; Humphrey, Duke of Gloucester; and Richard Beauchamp, Earl of Warwick.

The chapels are very different from one another, both in form and in feeling. Henry V's chantry is a bridge, built eastwards over the ambulatory of Westminster Abbey, above Henry's tomb, which lies as near as possible to St Edward's; the Beauchamp Chapel is a small, intensely decorated building lying between the chancel and the south transept of St Mary's, Warwick; Humphrey, Duke of Gloucester's chantry is an arch between two piers of the presbytery of St Albans, to the south of the shrine. The Henry V and Beauchamp chantries are dedicated to the Annunciation; the Virgin was regarded as the greatest of all intercessors, but the Virgin Annunciate had special connotations of humility, and this dedication was appropriate to the chantry altar of a great man. The chantry of Henry V is covered in sculptured figures, mostly in relief –

all a hymn of praise to the earthly achievements of the dead man. The figures of the patron saints of France and England are prominently shown, and scenes in relief depict a martial king on horseback, and two moments in the coronation service, with nobles paying homage exactly as written in the *Liber Regalis*.

The contemporary chantry of Henry's brother Humphrey shows a different aspect of the mortal man. The duke had literary and humanist interests, and his patronage of letters in England and Italy had fostered a close friendship with Abbot Whetehamstede of St Albans; Gloucester was buried there at his death in 1447. The great arch over his burial vault is decorated with pierced tracery panels, with pinnacles, housings for statues and deep ogee arches. Among the remaining decoration, Gloucester's heraldic badge appears many times, as had the swan and antelope on the chantry of Henry V; but Gloucester's badges are accompanied by representations of a cup full of flowers. This unusual motif has been explained as a *memento mori*, a reference to the Gardens of Adonis, where quick-growing flowers were put into a pot to flourish, fade and die. This survived from classical times through the writings of St Jerome, and appears in fifteenth-century Italian painting. Gloucester may have heard of it through his scholarly friends. Its presence tells us something of the man, its meaning something of the age.

From what we know of Richard, Earl of Warwick, we would expect his chantry chapel to emphasize his triumphs and achievements in the same way as the chantry of Henry V. He was seen by his contemporaries as the embodiment of chivalric courtesy, and his deeds of chivalry were later collected by one of his chaplains, John Rous. But, according to Rous, 'our Lady told a recluse at All Hallows, Northgate, York, that thorowe the Reame of England was no persone lorde ne other like to hym in habilite of grace and true feithfulnesse',[14] and this is the spirit manifest in his chapel. Figures of the earl and his family in the glass of the east window kneel in adoration before Christ and the Nine Orders of the Angels carved on the window mullions. (The Nine Orders of Angels appear on glass at St Neot's, Cornwall, at New College, Oxford, and on the screens of Barton Turf, Norfolk (Plate 9) and Southwold, Suffolk, reflecting the late medieval fascination with hierarchies and symbolic figures.) In the glass of the side windows, angels sing words on scrolls from hymns sung in honour of the Virgin on her great feast days. The Annunciation was shown on the reredos, the Virgin appearing again in the roof boss over the earl's tomb. The eyes of the brass effigy are directed towards hers, his hands are raised in prayer, and this small, brightly painted building with its gilded and enamelled tomb is redolent not of the statesman and politician but of the pious and faithful man, desirous to save his soul. The effigy, in a suit of armour, reflects Warwick's soldierliness, but all the other figures in the chapel present a vision not of earth but of heaven, not unlike the Van Eyck 'Adoration of the Lamb' altarpiece in Ghent.

The effigy itself shows deliberate realism (Plate 11). The forehead is lined, and the delicate, veined hands seem almost to move. The back of the effigy is as fully decorated as the front, and it is clothed in a suit of armour so fashionable that it imitates a Milanese suit made after the earl's death. Although the Warwickshire Malory who followed Beauchamp to Calais in 1436 is not now thought the most likely author of the *Morte Darthur*, the spirit of the chapel is very like that of Lancelot's death, seen as he was by a hermit heaved up to heaven by 'more angels than ever I saw men in one day', and of his funeral when his corpse was laid in the choir at Joyous Gard, his face 'naked, that all folks might behold him, and Sir Ector lamented: "Ah, Lancelot, thou were head of all Christian knights" '.[15]

Most of the artists came from London. The glazier, John Prudde of Westminster, was closely supervised by the executors who stipulated 'glass from beyond the seas', with as little white, green or black glass as possible. The surviving glass shows that Prudde obeyed the injunction, and he produced work of great delicacy and richness. The men who worked on the tomb are recorded, the most important of whom seems to have been Bartholomew Lambespringe, 'Dutchman and Goldsmith of London', who was responsible for gilding the effigy, weepers and angels on the tomb. The style of the weepers, their withdrawn sadness and heavy folds of drapery, is close to the funerary art of Claus Sluter in Burgundy. The same heavy, graceful folds are in the draperies of the window figures, and they may all be by the same unnamed artist. The executors – Thomas Huggeford, who had been on Warwick's council, Nicholas Rodye, Warwick's steward, and William Brakeswell, Dean of St Mary's Church – kept tight control over the iconographical programme and supplied the images to which the sculptors were to work.

The tranquil radiance of such works as the Beauchamp Chapel does not prepare us for other, more shocking sights. The idea that all men, however magnificent in life, must in death become 'food for worms' was expressed in tombs and paintings. The story of the Three Living and the Three Dead became enormously popular in the fifteenth century, as did the *danse macabre*, the Dance of Death, which drags all men in its train. It was painted in the cloister of St Paul's in the 1430s, inspired by the verses of John Lydgate, who had seen it in the Cemetery of the Innocents in Paris; but it was also painted in North Italy, and all Europe was in the grip of this obsession. Great Last Judgement paintings were placed on the chancel arch or west wall of many parish churches, usually painted by a local man, but none the less effective for that. In the later fifteenth century several of Lydgate's poems were illustrated in churches and secular buildings, but in the Clopton Chantry of Long Melford, Suffolk, verses from two of his poems were painted, without pictures, round the cornice. They express, through Lydgate's words, the personal penitence of John Clopton. The more nauseating physical aspects of death were brooded upon with a relish that modern man reserves for major disasters rather than personal bereavement; but hardship and physical pain were men's daily companions, with regular epidemics of lethal and horrifying plague. Nevertheless, earlier centuries had suffered equally, and the morbidity of fifteenth-century man was far more pronounced.

This morbid attitude gave rise to some notable tombs (Plate 10). The alabaster effigy of Alice, Duchess of Suffolk, made in the 1470s for the chancel at Ewelme, is a fine piece, a tranquil portrait of an elderly lady in plain but good widow's clothes. Beneath, and behind an iron grille, lies the *memento mori*, a representation of the grisly, decaying corpse of the grand lady above. A particularly horrifying shrouded skeleton adorns the tomb of Sir John Golafre in Fyfield, Berkshire, and the corpse was frequently shown being devoured by worms. On one or two brasses, such as that of Richard Notfeld in Margate, Kent, a mere skeleton was substituted for the effigy.

The preoccupation with death among churchgoers was affecting the church building itself. Vast new building undertakings were now going forward, often with chantries in mind. The fifteenth century saw the transformation or rebuilding of hundreds of parish churches, especially in East Anglia, the Midlands, the Cotswolds and Somerset, where the wool and cloth trades had generated enormous wealth, which guilds and individuals alike were willing to see turned into architecture. In some places the town and parish guilds reclothed an existing interior: St Mary's, Calne, in Wiltshire, was given a Perpendicular exterior of battlements and broad windows round an earlier nave. Many, however, were completely rebuilt: the beautiful, leisurely Perpendicular churches of East Anglia, now in tiny villages that were once very much bigger, were built at this time. The plan is simple, having a nave with aisles, a square south porch and a western tower. There are no transepts. The windows are wide and high, sometimes with two to each bay in the clerestory. In these churches the proportions, of height to width, of lower storey to upper, are very important, since they give the architecture of the building its character; this is well illustrated at Long Melford, where the easy repetition is saved from monotony by the different windows for aisle and clerestory, and by the relation of the two storeys. Porches were broad and boxlike, with a battlemented parapet and diagonal corner buttresses. The great square towers were equally distinctive, their pinnacled parapets concealing flat roofs.

Within the church building elaborate essays in carpentry were changing the general appearance. Individual chantry chapels and aisles were now being enclosed by screens, and rood screens were becoming more complex in design (Plate 9). In East Anglia they were often painted with saints and angels below, and had an elaborate trellis of tracery above. Attleborough, Norfolk, has no tracery, but the parapet has a series of shields and the coving is a ribbed star vault. West country rood screens were magnificent, stretching across the whole church, with Perpendicular traceried 'windows', and parapets carved with minutely detailed stylized foliage, supported on a coving of decorative vaulting. They, too, were brightly painted and gilded. The carpenters' greatest efforts were preserved for the ceiling: English parish churches are rarely vaulted in stone, and from the middle of the fifteenth century there developed the great angel roofs, hammerbeam roofs with an angel attached to the end of each hammer. Wooden ceilings without beams were painted or patterned with ribs.

A quantity of excellent stained glass has survived from the fifteenth century. Oxford, where several colleges were being built, was an important centre, as were Norwich and York, which still have the largest collections of stained glass in their parish churches, and where prosperous guilds were willing to give generously. Each, as a large centre attracting workmen, influenced a wide area. Glass-painters were generally interested in displaying figures under architectural canopies, without background or perspective. In York, workshop traditions went back to John Thornton and the east window of the Minster, but the minute, hard detail of the early fifteenth century was softened and broadened later on – for instance, at All Saints, North Street, in the 1440s. Draperies fall gently; heads are carefully modelled. A new influence had crept in, that of Flemish realism, in which solid, volumetric figures were set in definable space. This Flemish style was beginning to disturb the two-dimensional linear delicacy at which English painters excelled. It pervaded English manuscript painting in the late fifteenth century, and is shown most clearly in the wall paintings of Eton College Chapel (1480s), which depict the miracles of the Virgin in grisaille. Of the two painters, Gilbert and William Baker, one shows interest in the Flemish style of setting solid figures in space, while the other paints in a flatter style that suggests he was unable to accept the full meaning of Flemish realism (cover illustration).

1470–1510: Edward IV's revival of crown patronage; experiment in architectural decoration; Henry VI's symbols of piety and legitimacy

Renewed Flemish influence probably came in the train of Edward IV (1461–83), who had been exiled in Bruges. With his reign, crown patronage revived. Henry VI had founded Eton and King's College, Cambridge, as acts of personal piety, but they were a long time in the building. Edward IV was not much better than Henry at finishing off works he had started, but in trying to manage the nobility by emulating the Burgundian Order of the Golden Fleece he refounded St George's Chapel at Windsor, home of Edward III's Order of the Garter. It was completed under the Tudors, but in essence it belongs to the earlier phase: light, subtly moulded and without sculpture, the building is in strong contrast to what was to come. The depth and delicate richness of the mouldings make this building a sumptuous setting for Garter ceremonies.

Edward IV also added an impressive Great Hall to Eltham Palace, Surrey; private houses had continued to become less martial, and even Tattershall Castle, built by the Lord Treasurer Cromwell in the 1430s, had large traceried windows and a fine series of state rooms included in its otherwise military plan. Country houses, such as Ockwells Manor, Berkshire (*c.* 1450), were not castles at all.

Ockwells is timber-framed, filled with brick. The timber frame acts as support for a huge display of window: all along the upper wall the frame becomes upright window mullions, and a large six-light oriel opens beside the high table. Walls composed of windows in this manner were built around 1475 in the Prior's House at Much Wenlock in Shropshire, and became typical of early Tudor domestic architecture.

Like Ockwells, Eltham has large windows, with a fine transomed oriel to light the dais. The plain stonework is surmounted by a hammerbeam roof with a new feature: the vertical hammer posts are continued down below the level of the hammerbeams to make pendants. Pendants, apparently invented by carpenters, were to have an intriguing effect in stone vaulting. The late fifteenth century saw the final acceptance of a new kind of vault: the fan vault (Plate 4). This type of vaulting, a series of upended cones covered in Perpendicular tracery, had been used in 1366 to roof the cloister at Gloucester, but its relatively untested properties were not trusted for large spans for almost another hundred years. Around 1500 the use of fan vaults over the main span became fashionable, with a beautiful example in the eastern extension of Peterborough Abbey, while Bath Abbey was built with fan vaults by William Vertue of Oxford.

The conoid fans were, however, used in a different way at the Divinity Schools in Oxford (vaulted around 1475). They were divided by strong transverse arches, which cut through the centres of the cones; pendants drop from the centres next to the arches. This idea was modified a little later at St Frideswide's (now Oxford Cathedral), where the pendants were made as if to hang from the transverse arch itself. In both buildings, the result is pure illusionism, for the pendants are not structural at all. The pendants at the Divinity Schools were carved as tabernacles with figures seated therein, and this building is equally important for its sculpture and for the soft light catching facets of its mouldings. Here, as in the latest figures on the west front of Exeter Cathedral and the choir screen in York Minster, is represented a late fifteenth-century revival in architectural sculpture.

The architect of the roof of Oxford Cathedral is not known, but in the city at that time there were several families of masons; in addition to the Vertues, the families of Orchard and Janyns worked equally for Oxford and the court, and with John Wastell were to be responsible for the greatest late Perpendicular buildings. The early Tudors properly revived the court school, in both architecture and sculpture. Henry VII was a man of his time, and expressed this in slightly surprising acts of grandiose personal piety. He also wished to emphasize the legitimacy of his line. How better to combine these aspirations than to found a chapel to his Lancastrian ancestor, Henry VI, and to finish the building of that ancestor's own act of piety, the chapel of King's College, Cambridge?

The memorial chapel to both kings was originally intended to be at Windsor, but towards 1500 Henry VII decided instead to put it in the place of the thirteenth-century Lady Chapel of Westminster Abbey. In the event, the body of Henry VI lay at Windsor, and the new chapel became the mausoleum of Henry and Elizabeth of York (Plate 4). This is a building that seems to exploit all virtuosity of vaulting and architectural sculpture, and to deny the existence of a plain wall. Although its elements are entirely English, it should be seen in the context of contemporary memorial chapels in northern Europe, such as that of Margaret of Austria at Brou, in which extravagant visual effects were likewise sought and achieved; and although its style is unmistakably English the thought behind it is continental.

The Henry VII Chapel has aisles, a ring of eastern chapels and great octagonal buttresses, which become turrets at roof level. Its faceted windows catch the light, turning the exterior into a sparkling, shifting curtain of glass and delicate stonework. Inside, the chapel becomes steadily more ornate as the eye travels upwards, with the faceted eastern chapels, sculptured figures under canopies beneath the upper windows, and great cusped arches leading into the vault. The vault itself is a piece of sheer illusionism: it is highly ornate, with long pendants as the centre of fan cones. The fan tracery is so deeply and crisply cut that it seems to be detached from any ceiling; and, where the cones meet, a neat little pendant fills the space. The roof appears to be floating on air, but it is held together by the transverse arches, which run above and through the fan cones, thus taking the design of Oxford Cathedral roof a stage further. The architect of this extravaganza may have been Robert Janyns the younger, who worked at Windsor, where similar vault construction can be found; he was also employed on Henry VII's tower at Windsor, which had the same faceted windows as the Henry VII Chapel.

The chapel was structurally complete by 1509, and Henry's will provided for the decoration. In addition to the obligatory series of heraldic devices, the walls are covered in sculptured figures of prophets and saints. They are weighty figures, with abundant heavy draperies, turning the pages of books in their hands, or glaring downwards from beneath overpowering hats. The realism is Flemish, and the faces, built up of solid, simple volumes, will be found again in the work of Holbein.

By contrast, King's College Chapel in Cambridge seems restrained. Its apparent simplicity is deceptive but undeniably restful. In his 'will' of 1448–9 Henry VI had stipulated that the college be built 'in large forme, clene and substancial, settyngye a parte superfluite of too gret curious werkes of entaille and besy moldyng'.[16] In 1485 five bays had been roofed and the rest hardly begun, and there matters stayed until 1507, when Henry VII began to take an active interest. John Wastell was employed as architect, a man whose work displays the new love of the decorated, textured surfaces that are a feature of his Bell Harry Tower at Canterbury Cathedral, the Oxford Divinity Schools and Henry VII's chapel at Westminster – all light-catching facets and decorative sculpture. Although the interior of King's seems very unified, the later phase can be distinguished at once from the earlier phase in the choir. The chapel seems to be a single cell, an enormously enlarged version of the choir of Gloucester, with the leisured, restrained fan vaults unifying the whole space. Closer inspection reveals side chapels, walled off in the choir, screened in the antechapel, and the cones of the fan vaults are cut by the heavy, four-centred transverse arches normally associated with pendant vaults. These divide the chapel into bays, preventing the eye from rushing too rapidly along the huge, flat, uniform windows and absolutely rectilinear divisions made by the transoms and string-courses. Whereas the choir, according to the wishes of Henry VI, has little sculptural enrichment, the antechapel, built by the Tudors with Tudor money and attitudes, is covered in heraldic devices. The panelling under the windows of the antechapel is stiffly encrusted with royal arms and badges, crowns, portcullises and Tudor roses, and on the outside Wastell placed more badges and heraldic beasts. Such is the force of the architecture, however, that the sculpture remains subordinate to the strong piers and huge windows, which imperceptibly merge with the vault.

1510–1550: Italian Renaissance and Flemish realism; Henry VIII and his courtiers; the Reformation and the break in religious art

King's College Chapel has miraculously preserved much of its stained glass, and with it we move into a changing world. Artists in England had remained oblivious to the European Renaissance until the early sixteenth century, and when its influence came it was not as the discovery of English artists but was brought by foreigners. The revival of classical forms in Italy came naturally to that country, which had never forgotten or ignored its classical past; but the northerners, whose classical heritage had always been at second hand, brought in by the Romans, had had to discover it and re-discover it several times during the Middle Ages. In the early sixteenth century, the style that Henry VIII called Antick (Antique) was never more than superficial; it was not absorbed sufficiently to become the essence of a style, but it was manifest in all the arts, and may be approached by way of stained glass.

Humphrey, Duke of Gloucester, had been interested in literary humanism, but the fifteenth-century Florentine pictorial style did not find its way into his books, nor into any other fifteenth-century English works. When the new pictorial style arrived, it came through the work of Dutch and German glass-painters, who worked in the naturalistic style we have seen evolving in northern Europe throughout the fifteenth century, with the classical overlay acquired on their journeys to Italy. We saw an example of Flemish realism in the Eton wall paintings: people were set firmly in believable space, but their forms and the other motifs were quite unclassical. This style reappeared in the windows of Fairford Church, Gloucestershire, between 1495 and 1505. The twenty-eight windows have a single theme: the Apostle's Creed, treated with biblical scenes and emblematic subjects. Thoroughly medieval in subject matter, some of the scenes show traditionally rendered figures and scenes under heavy Perpendicular canopies. Others, however, do not: some of the scenes are spread across the windows without regard to the vertical divisions. The canopies were abandoned, and the figures set in architectural interiors or landscapes, with space suggested by flocks of birds or little receding clouds. The human figures, in weighty Flemish costumes, are softened, the drapery folds shaded by stippling, and the strong primary colours are invaded by pinks, greens and purples, showing a change of taste from that of the

Beauchamp executors (p. 209). The style is Gothic with as yet no
classical references.

Much of the work of the so-called Flemish glass-painters, the
Southwark group, is probably lost to us. In 1515–17 the Fleming,
Barnard Flower, king's glazier, was responsible for the four early
windows in King's College Chapel. The subject is entirely
traditional: the lives of the Virgin and Christ, presented with their
Old Testament antitypes. Flower's figures are still hieratic, dressed
in heavy draperies and standing under canopies, but their gestures
are more vigorous, and new elements are introduced into the scenes,
such as Roman lettering, shell ornament, swags and lion masks –
all signs of superficial knowledge of classical ornament. These
characteristics are even more pronounced in the windows made from
1526, where the curious imposition of classical motifs on an
essentially medieval figure style and subject matter is typical of the
Renaissance as experienced in northern Europe.

The only existing object to be unequivocally influenced by Italian
work is the base of the tomb of Henry VII in Westminster Abbey.
Commissioned first from Guido Mazzoni of Modena, the tomb was
finally given to a Florentine, Pietro Torrigiano, a fellow pupil of
Michelangelo in the studio of Ghirlandhaio. He was in England
from 1511 to 1520, working for others besides Henry VIII, who was
paying for his father's tomb. Louis XII of France had employed an
Italian tomb-maker for his own father's tomb in 1504, and Henry's
choice of sculptor may have been prompted by the desire to emulate
the French court. The tomb has a moulded base, pilasters and
cornice, with plump Italian putti supporting the royal arms on the
end. The effigies, though portraits, are still more idealized than
they would have been in Italy, with no hint of the classical.
Torrigiano's tomb of Lady Margaret Beaufort in Westminster Abbey
(1511) similarly combines a Renaissance tomb chest with a Gothic
effigy.

Torrigiano spent some time in Flanders, and adapted himself to
northern tastes. Other Tuscans worked in England in the 1520s and
1530s, as did the French and the Dutch. Both Henry VIII and
Wolsey were active patrons, largely for reasons of display. In his role
as a European Renaissance prince, Henry desired a court more
splendid than that of his rival in France; but his interest was not
profound, and the purely propagandist nature of it is perhaps
reflected in the effect of his patronage upon Hans Holbein, whose

strongly characterized early style of portraiture became much more iconic during his years in Henry's service.

Wolsey's Hampton Court was England's main architectural centre in the 1520s. Some Italians were employed there: Giovanni Maiano made the terracotta roundels with the heads of Roman emperors, similar to the terracottas with putti at Sutton Place (Surrey), and similar also to the window frames at Layer Marney (Essex), both built by courtiers, colleagues of Wolsey. The nearest stylistic parallel to these terracottas is in the early sixteenth-century châteaux of France, and despite the Italian workers much of the Renaissance influence on England was filtered through French taste. Artists who had worked at Fontainebleau came to Nonsuch, Surrey (destroyed), in the late 1530s, and were at Longleat, Wiltshire, in the 1560s, and the middle years of the sixteenth century were dominated by French ideas.

The magnificent wooden choir screen of King's College Chapel, made in 1533–8, completes the royal patronage of four reigns. It is articulated in the new idiom: classical arches are supported on pilaster strips, and these are decorated with urns and floral and grotesque ornament, which is French rather than Italian; and the same influence is felt in the De La Warr Chantry at Boxgrove, Sussex, of 1532. Here the decoration combines Gothic with Renaissance, pendant vaults with classical foliage, urns and putti supporting heraldic devices; but the Renaissance decoration is the French type, and the Gothic is the swirling curvilinear Flamboyant of late medieval France.

The influence of the court school of François I is felt on tombs as well as buildings. East Anglia has several of these – some terracotta tombs at Layer Marney and Wymondham, and the series of tombs in the Howard family mausoleum at Framlingham, Suffolk. These, which were made over a long period from around 1520 to the 1560s, have the fluted pillars, shell niches, strapwork and frieze of griffins and acanthus that can be found at Blois and other châteaux belonging to the French court. As always the new style is only superficially grafted upon the old: one fragment of an early tomb has an egg-and-dart motif with a Gothic leaf instead of the dart, and the style of the figure sculpture is that of a shop working in the English tradition of the late fifteenth century.

Circumstances under Henry VIII were leading to an unmilitary society: the world of the courtier was replacing that of the soldier.

When Edward Stafford, Duke of Buckingham, was beheaded in 1521, his castle at Thornbury, Gloucestershire, was unfinished. Buckingham kept there a standing garrison of 200 men; begun in 1511, it reflected the mood of the earlier period. It was one of the last great houses to be planned for the needs of two households, with the garrison quartered separately from the working household.

The castle was grandly envisaged. The base court, in which the garrison lived, was entered by the great gate, and an elaborate towered entrance, with towers and bastions with gunloops along the outer walls, led to the inner court, in which were domestic offices, the old hall of the original building and the state rooms. Somewhere beside this court was to be the collegiate church founded by Buckingham for the salvation of his soul. The gatehouse was joined to the lord's rooms, which faced away from the hall, and had a separate entrance to the chapel. Facing south over a garden court, the state rooms were very different from the severe towered fronts; a succession of rooms for entertaining looked upon the garden through large oriel windows of foiled plan. The plans of the window are not unlike those of Henry VII's chapel at Westminster, and the arrangement of the state apartments is similar to those of the king's houses at Windsor and Richmond.

Thornbury, like Hampton Court, had elaborately patterned and moulded brick chimneys, in plan as complicated as the windows of the state rooms. Hampton Court was built entirely of brick, which had become ever more popular since the late fourteenth century. Brick was quick to use and cheaper than stone, and it was not long before bricks were being cut and moulded to produce relief patterns. The great gatehouse of St Osyth's Abbey, Essex, was built in the early years of the sixteenth century of brick and flint, with flushwork panels of tracery and battlements decorated with a chequered pattern. The use of brick in royal dwellings such as Hampton Court (taken over at the fall of Wolsey in 1529) and Richmond helped to create a fashion for it, just as the new arrangements of their rooms were reflected in the lesser houses. The formal succession of state rooms was a new idea, together with the long gallery, which was developed simultaneously in France and England. Buckingham built a long gallery at Bletchingley in Surrey, and another example, following closely upon the long galleries at Whitehall and Hampton Court, survives at The Vyne, Hampshire (*c.* 1530).

Henry VIII scarcely moved out of South-East England, and his power was based there; the greater houses of early Tudor courtiers are to be found in that region. The Vyne, an unfortified house, was built by Lord Sandys, who moved in the same circles as Weston and Marney, and the long gallery bears Sandys's crest and arms, and the rebus of his wife Margery Bray. Among them are depicted many times the crown and arms of Henry VIII. The Tudor courtier displayed, along with his own badges, those of the ruling dynasty. Nowhere can this be better seen today than at Ightham Mote, Kent, which as we shall see at length in Chapter 5 was rebuilt and redecorated by Sir Richard Clement in the early 1520s. Ightham Mote was the house of a newly emerged courtier; it reflects the passing of the old order and the donning of the new. Like The Vyne, the chapel has glass painted by the Southwark school, but whereas the programme at The Vyne survives sufficiently to show portraits of Henry and Katharine beneath scenes from the story of the Passion and saints, amid fantastic architectural settings, Ightham Mote has suffered; but it is perhaps significant that the two figures whose pictures survive under Renaissance arched niches should be the time-honoured medieval intercessors, the Virgin and St John.

Henry VIII was a powerful patron, but he had little interest in the abilities of those he employed. The principal kind of wall decoration in his palaces was not wall painting but tapestry, and the greatest painter at Henry's court, Hans Holbein (1497–1543), was only dimly appreciated by the monarch. In England Holbein is famous for his portraits, but, had events turned out differently on the continent, he could have been a great religious painter. Born in Augsburg, he came to England in 1528 at the age of 30, a fully mature artist. He was escaping the troubles of the Reformation in Basle and came furnished with letters from his friend Erasmus to Sir Thomas More and his circle of English humanists, and it was from them that he received his first commissions. Holbein was already a practised and skilful painter of portraits; this art was more fully developed on the continent than in England, where, as we have seen, there was only very moderate interest in portraiture before 1500, and little of that was painted from life. The portrait of Sir Thomas More shows Holbein's first English style: he was interested in portraying the character of the sitter through the dignity of his office, and this is shown in the pose as well as in the face. In three-quarter pose, he seems a solid figure, but the background is cut off by a curtain, and Holbein was always less interested in bulk than in simple planes and linear grace. The severe yet lively line and rich colour show the artist's unique ability to combine richness with austerity. The same firm yet sensitive line can be seen in the portrait studies in chalk of More's family, which are almost all that survives of the group portait Holbein painted for More's house in Chelsea.

Holbein went back to Basle, but returned to England in 1532 to find his former patrons dead or fallen from grace. A different artistic climate also prevailed. The Henrician Reformation was launched, and for the religious communities life was soon to be at an end. The dissolution of the monasteries had been inconceivable until it happened; monasteries had launched building programmes to the last (as the gatehouse of St Osyth's testifies), unaware that their lives were ending. There was no demand for altarpieces, and the English had not yet developed a taste for classical mythology; but they were moderately interested in allegorical subjects and were becoming enthusiastic about portraiture. In those days the artist painted what his patron wanted, or he starved. Holbein was employed by German Merchants of the Steelyard to paint portraits and allegorical pictures, and then he was noticed by the king; from about 1536 he was the 'servant of the king's majesty'. Holbein had painted two courtiers, Thomas Cromwell and Robert Cheseman, in 1533, but the picture of Jane Seymour of 1536 marks the beginning of his employment by the king. The more mundane decoration of pavilions, banners and requirements for masques was mostly carried out by the serjeant-painter to the court, but Holbein himself designed jewellery, robes and decoration for weapons, and Henry ordered him to go to paint portraits of various ladies during his search for a wife in the late 1530s.

From now on Holbein's style became flatter, with more linearity and surface decoration, and less individual character of the sitter. It may be that his first English style came as too great a shock to a country accustomed to the delicate two-dimensional decoration of an illuminated manuscript, and the exploration of personality was also something to which they were unused. But a similar tendency can be seen in the court portraits of France and northern Italy, and it must to some extent have reflected the general taste of the time. Holbein made his preliminary studies from life (Plate 12), but there were few sittings. He composed the final oil painting from the preparatory chalk drawings. The series of drawings at Windsor Castle are the contents of his studio at the time of his death from the plague in 1543; and from these and his finished portraits studio assistants and imitators made many copies. Holbein's later style was very influential. England, not ready for what he had to offer in the 1520s, was prepared to accept the Holbein of the 1530s.

In 1537 he painted a commemorative group for the Privy Chamber of Whitehall, consisting of Henry VII and Elizabeth of York, with Henry VIII and Jane Seymour. The two kings are depicted in life size. The inscription glorifies the house of Tudor, and the figure of Henry VIII was said to be so imposing that it struck awe into every visitor. The cartoon of this figure survives, a pose with straddled legs, vastly padded robes and the curiously inscrutable facial expression; it set the type for ceremonial portraits and was often copied. The bust was used again in a small portrait of Henry similar to that of François I by Clouet. Both portraits are iconic, bombastic and empty.

Holbein also painted miniatures, which began to assume importance in the reign of Henry VIII, although their greatest flowering was yet to come. Illustrators of devotional manuscripts were without work, and they began to paint tiny portraits on vellum laid on card, after the manner established by Clouet at the French court. Luke Horenbout, a Fleming who, judging by his salary, was more highly prized at court than Holbein, made an early portrait miniature of Henry. Holbein applied consummate technical skill to his own miniatures. Most houses, with large windows and walls hung with tapestry, had scant room for large paintings, and small, skilled miniatures, painted with the quintessence of technical refinement, were more popular. Yet, for all the move away from traditional themes, the English were not the leaders of change. Henry himself, for all his pretensions to being a Renaissance prince, had gone to the Field of the Cloth of Gold with all the pageantry that Wolsey could devise to suit a medieval knight setting forth to engage the enemy; and Holbein's last monumental work, commissioned by the Barber–Surgeons to celebrate their new royal charter in a reasonably enduring form, showed Henry on a huge scale seated behind the group of tiny barber–surgeons. To find the exploration of character and realism in Holbein's latest work, one must study his preparatory drawings. Pictures intended to be on view were still symbolic and iconic.

Domestic architecture, portraiture and tombs: with these lay the future of artists in England. The break with Rome and the dissolution of the monasteries had cut off the country's immediate past, just as Protestantism had affected other countries of Europe; in Italy and France artistic style and subject matter continued to evolve. Court circles in England encouraged some developments, but in the provinces established styles lingered well on into the seventeenth century. English artists were deprived of a living by political and artistic developments. The invention of printing in the late fifteenth century, with books illustrated by woodcuts, contributed to the death of the illuminated manuscript; and the interest in three-dimensional realism and linear perspective that accompanied the classical revival was not to the taste of those whose excellence lay in the surface pattern of a manuscript page. Sculptors had, as we have seen, been producing much the same kind of figures for years; no sculptor of talent emerged after Torrigiano, nor was there scope for such a man for much of the sixteenth century.

By the end of our period the steady stream of foreign artists had become a flood, and they were to dominate English art until the eighteenth century. Men, however, inevitably die and need tombs; and while they lived they had their portraits painted and built themselves magnificent houses on the proceeds of church lands, and indeed on the sites of the monasteries, given to his courtiers by a greedy monarch with an eye for the church's wealth. Some of what has been discussed in the foregoing pages was destroyed by the Puritans in the seventeenth century; some has been destroyed by time; some has survived; but the vast majority of shrines, statues, reliefs, ivories, jewellery and manuscripts that are either mutilated or gone for ever were destroyed by Henry VIII and Thomas Cromwell, either for their mineral value or because their survival would encourage the church to hope. Wriothesley built his new gatehouse in the exact middle of the nave of Titchfield Abbey, facing into the cloister garth. To such arrogant insensitivity do we owe the destruction of medieval art, for contemporaries and for us.

Notes

1 *Pierce the Ploughman's Creed*, ed. W. W. Skeat, EETS (London, 1867), ll. 123–7.
2 Stowe, *Annals* (London, 1631), p. 576.
3 *Pearl*, ed. A. C. Cawley and J. J. Anderson (London, 1976), ll. 383–4.
4 Letter from Pierre de Celle to Nicholas of St Alban's, in Migne, *Patrologia Latina*, vol. 202, p. 614.

5 *Knight's Tale*, I (A), ll. 1897–1901.
6 *Pearl*, ed. Cawley and Anderson, ll. 1209–12.
7 *Book of the Duchess*, ll. 332–4.
8 *Gawain and the Green Knight*, edited with *Pearl*, ll. 800–3.
9 '*Quia amore langueo*', in *Mediaeval English Lyrics*, ed. R. T. Davies (London, 1963), pp. 148 ff., ll. 1–4.
10 *Prologue* to the *Canterbury Tales*, I (A), l. 162.
11 John Lydgate, 'Transient as a rose', in *Mediaeval English Lyrics*, ed. Davies, pp. 191 ff., ll. 59–60.
12 Ascribed to John Grimeston, 'Crucified to the world', in *Mediaeval English Lyrics*, ed. Davies, p. 130, ll. 1–2.
13 *Pardoner's Tale*, VI (C), l. 709.
14 *Pageant of the Birth, Life and Death of Richard Beauchamp Earl of Warwick*, ed. Viscount Dillon and W. H. St John Hope (London, 1914), pl. 47, pp. 93–4.
15 Malory, *Morte Darthur*, in *Works of Sir Thomas Malory*, ed. E. Vinaver, 2nd edn (Oxford, 1967), vol. 3, p. 1259.
16 Henry VI's 'Will', quoted in John Harvey, *The Mediaeval Architect* (London, 1972), p. 255.

Select bibliography

The whole period is dealt with in the following volumes of the Pelican History of Art, the standard works of reference, containing full bibliographies:

Rickert, M. *Painting in Britain: The Middle Ages*, 2nd edn, Harmondsworth, 1965.
Stone, L. *Sculpture in Britain: The Middle Ages*, 2nd edn, Harmondsworth, 1972.
Webb, G. *Architecture in Britain: The Middle Ages*, 2nd edn, Harmondsworth, 1965.

The best short account of medieval architecture will be found in:

Kidson, P., Murray, P., and Thompson, P. *A History of English Architecture*, Harmondsworth, 1965.

The most valuable study of late medieval art and architecture, still not superseded, is:

Evans, J. *English Art 1307–1461*, Oxford History of English Art, vol. 5, Oxford, 1949.

See also:

Holbein and the Court of Henry VIII, Catalogue of the Queen's Gallery exhibition (1978–9), London, 1978.
Knowles, Dom D. *Bare Ruined Choirs*, Cambridge, 1976. (An account of the dissolution of the monasteries.)
Platt, C. *The English Medieval Town*, London, 1976.
Wood, M. *The English Medieval House*, London, 1965.

See also the section on 'Iconography' in the bibliography to Chapter 1.

5 The age of the household: politics, society and the arts c. 1350–c. 1550

DAVID STARKEY

The enacting clause of the *Black Book* (Edward IV's main household ordinance) begins with a splendid flourish, which hails the king's household as 'the new house of houses principal of England in time of peace'.[1] As if this were not enough, the preamble had already traced the ancestry of Edward's household from the house of God, through the households of Solomon, King Lud, Cassivellaunus and Hardicanute, to the better-documented establishments of Henry I and Edward III. All this may seem grandiloquent for a text that deals mainly with humdrum matters of wages and rations. But such a judgement would be anachronistic. In the later Middle Ages household and family were (to an extent inconceivable today) the central institution of society. The household was the main unit of economic activity: the household of the farmer worked the land; the household of the artisan supplied manufactured goods; and the household of the noble was the centre of conspicuous consumption. The family and family relationships were the chief channels through which wealth was transmitted. The household was the foundation of political alignment. As far as the arts are concerned, the greater household provided both the patronage that financed them and the setting that shaped them; it even conditioned the language in which literature expressed itself. Moreover, the dominance of the household, and above all the chief household – the royal court – increased greatly in our period, as its obvious rivals – the church and the urban community – underwent decline or collapse.

Household and social class

Our chapter on intellectual history opens with a passage written some years before our period begins. That – bearing in mind the continuity of late medieval thought – is legitimate. Conversely, I shall begin with a work that was not drafted till thirteen years after our period ends. This anachronism is also justified; and for two reasons. The first is particular: the late Middle Ages (as we have already seen) were unused to introspection or self-description; the later sixteenth century, on the other hand, was much more adept at the practice. The second reason is more general: understanding of historical change comes only retrospectively and selectively. Or, in Hegel's more flowery language, 'The owl of Minerva spreads its wings only with the falling of dusk.'[2] So Sir Thomas Smith's *De Republica Anglorum* (*Of the English Commonwealth*) provides as good a starting-point as any for a discussion of the England of the last Plantagenets and the first Tudors.

For Smith there were two main ways of analysing the state, or (as he puts it) of making 'division of the parts and persons of the commonwealth'.[3] To begin with, following his own eyes as well as Greek political theory, he made the household the basic social and political unit: 'the commonwealth . . . consisteth of a multitude of houses and families, which make streets and villages; and the multitude of the streets and villages make towns; and the multitude of towns the realm.'[4] But this 'division' was not enough. In addition, the male heads of household belonged to various social groups or classes:

> We in England divided our men commonly into four sorts:
> gentlemen, citizens and yeomen, artificers and labourers.
> Of gentlemen the first and chief are the king, the prince,
> dukes, marquises, earls, viscounts, barons, and these are
> called . . . the nobility . . .; next to these be knights,
> esquires and simple gentlemen.[5]

This classification, which was peculiar to England, is crucial. In France, as in most of western Europe, the rank of nobility was inherited by all the male children of a noble. The French nobility was thus a 'nobility of blood' and numbered thousands. In England, on the other hand, the fourteenth and fifteenth centuries had seen the development of a very different concept of nobility or peerage. Nobility was also inherited, but it was inherited by only one descendant at a time – usually the eldest son. This meant that the English nobility was not so much a social class (like the French) as a tiny status group (numbering only fifty to a hundred) at the head of the much larger class of gentlemen. The gentry as a whole was essentially the class of greater landowners. In addition, the practice of certain learned professions like the law conferred the title of gentleman. But above all gentility was a question of lifestyle and hence of the wealth that supported it. Or, in Smith's own words, 'who can live idly and without manual labour, and will bear the port, charge and countenance of a gentleman . . . shall be taken for a gentleman'.[6] So, as this circular definition shows, entry into the gentry was casual in the extreme: 'gentlemen . . . be made good cheap in England'.[7] In contrast, entry into the French nobility was jealously regulated. The basic reason for the difference is straightforward. In France the status of noble conferred enormous privileges, judicial and financial (including exemption from personal taxation); in England, on the other hand, gentility (or even nobility) gave great social prestige but few concrete privileges. Indeed, Smith could claim with a measure of truth that 'the gentleman is more charged [than the rest], which he beareth the gladlier and dareth not gainsay for to save and keep his honour and reputation'.[8] Chaucer's Franklin is such a gentleman, significantly a great 'householder' in his hospitality, and often 'knight of the shire' (member of parliament), yet anxious to claim 'gentilesse' to a degree that elicits the scorn of the Host – himself not a 'gentleman' but a leading 'citizen'.[9]

In Smith's time the number of gentry had increased disproportionately; in the years 1350–1550, they were a much smaller social group – almost certainly no more than 1 per cent of the population. (That would mean with a population of 2,500,000 that there were about 2000 gentry families. This figure fits well with the assertion of the Croyland Chronicler that, thanks to the excellence of his memory, Edward IV was able to recall the 'names and estates' of everyone that mattered in the kingdom, even 'if they held the rank only of a private gentleman'.[10]) The remainder of the population was made up of Smith's other three categories: the 'citizens' were the merchants and more substantial industrial producers in the towns; the 'yeomen' were the larger non-gentle cultivators of the land; the 'artificers and labourers' (the great bulk of the population) were the tillers of the soil or lesser industrial workers.

Smith, of course, was writing after the great upheaval of the Reformation. To readjust his picture to the realities of the later Middle Ages, we have to rebuild what the 1530s partly demolished – the great fabric of the medieval church. Strenuously the church had fought to maintain itself as a separate entity in a world dominated by the family, and in a measure its struggle had been successful. The church had a separate consciousness of itself as a member of an international corporation; it had a distinct and separate system of law and legal administration; the clergy were distinguished from the laity by visible signs – by both their special dress and the tonsure; and there was above all the rule of clerical celibacy. But the reality did not fully accommodate itself to these clear-cut distinctions: in particular, it was the church's vast landed wealth that dragged it back into the world; that, and the very human difficulty of maintaining the rules of celibacy and abstinence from ordinary social pleasures like gambling or extravagant dress. The result was that the household of a bishop could look very much like the household of any other great peer; a monastery could seem like a corporate gentle or even noble household, while, thanks to the figure of the clerical housekeeper/mistress, the household of the parish priest could merge almost undistinguishably into that of the typical peasant. But however overlaid it might have been by the things of the world, the clerical consciousness always remained a reservoir of difference and possible dissent.

So late medieval society consisted of two stepped pyramids, one clerical, one lay. Each level of either pyramid had a particular social experience, to which there probably corresponded a particular variety of literature and literary experience. At this distance in time the degree of correlation must remain uncertain.

The best that we can do is to suggest that to the nobility and gentry there corresponded a courtly literature (ultimately derived from French), whose main concerns were the two chivalric interests of love and personal combat; this included both the Chaucerian literature centred on London and the royal court, and one stream of alliterative poetry (like that of the *Gawain* poet) probably associated with the households of the nobility or gentry of the North and West.

The church, and especially the lesser clergy, were probably responsible for the other stream of alliterative poetry – the critical and mystical kind whose greatest figure is Langland. From the church came also, of course, a great body of devotional and mystical literature, and sermons which might include sharp social criticism. ✗

Church and citizen co-operated in the mystery and miracle plays. Outside all these classes among country labourers there existed ballads and songs of which only fragments remain.

These distinctions are not, of course, hard and fast: men like Chaucer and Usk would read and listen to anything or everything. Nor were the people whose tastes were responsible for the existence of a particular sort of literature necessarily those who composed it. Most devotional literature was written by the clergy (though there were exceptions like the work of Sir John Clanvowe or Henry of Grosmont); much of its audience, however, was lay. Similarly, courtly literature was composed less by the upper classes themselves (with exceptions like Gower and, once again, Clanvowe) than by members of the clerisy – that is, the professional literate class: royal servants like Chaucer in the customs and Hoccleve in the privy seal office, or monks like Lydgate. Some drama – moralities, for example, like *The Castle of Perseverance* and *Everyman* – was performed and possibly composed by professional players. These might normally be attached to some great household, like the Players of the King's Interludes maintained by Henry VII, but when not needed they would travel, performing before other households or (charging admission fees to the audience) before all comers.

Finally, there is evidence of a good deal of shared taste among all classes. Courtly literature was popular among citizens, not unknown in monastic libraries, and probably percolated among the labourers in ballad form: there survives, for example, a ballad version of *Gawain and the Green Knight*. As for religious drama, both Richard II and (probably) Margery Kempe travelled a long way to watch the mystery cycle at York. That drama in particular must have formed a binding element throughout the community, though it may have been little understood where it was not supported by reading or good preaching. The extreme limit of the shared experience of the whole late medieval community is perhaps represented in the 'old man about sixty' at Cartmel in Lancashire who was told in 1644 about redemption through the cross of Christ. ' "Oh sir", said he, "I think I heard of that man you speak of once in a play at Kendall, called Corpus Christ's play, where there was a man on a tree, and blood ran down . . ." '[11]

Household and family

English society was created by the interaction between Smith's pattern of social classification and the household. Smith defines the household (*Domus seu familia*) as 'the man, the woman, their children, their servants bond and free, their cattle, their household stuff, and all other things which are reckoned in their possession.'[12]

There are two distinct elements here: the biological family, on the one hand, and its social and economic extensions (i.e. goods and servants), on the other. The former was universal; the latter varied with social class. I shall discuss each in turn.

At the heart of every household – from the peasant's to the great noble's – was the same basic unit: the family. Moreover, the actual family unit of noble and peasant seems (remarkably enough) to have been very much alike. Even more remarkably, this common late medieval family seems not to have been greatly dissimilar to the modern Western family. Historical demographers (basing themselves on the painstaking statistical techniques of 'family reconstitution') show that the late medieval English family was a nuclear one: in other words, it consisted (as Smith wrote) of a husband and wife, and their dependent offspring. It was relatively rare for other blood relatives to live under the same roof, and very rare indeed for two married couples (however closely related) to share the same home. The extended family, in short, scarcely existed.

For the ordinary people a family of four or five – that is, the married couple and two or three children – was probably fairly typical. Enormous families – like that of Thomas Howard, the second Duke of Norfolk (1443–1524), who had ten children by his first wife and no less than thirteen by his second – were, in the main, the prerogative of the upper classes. The basic reason for this difference lay in a combination of economic and social factors. In the absence of contraception, the fertility of any marriage is governed by the gap between the age of marriage of the wife and the time of her menopause or death, whichever comes the sooner. The latter points were fixed at about the same age for all social groups: the menopause came at roughly 40, but death often came hideously early with the average expectation of life standing at only 35 or 40. Moreover, the rates of infant and child mortality seem to have been broadly similar for all classes, with some 30–40 per cent of all children dying before the age of 15. The crucial variable in determining family size was thus the age of marriage.

And this is where the economic differences between the upper and the lower classes had their effect. Because the practice of living with in-laws was so rare, a couple who wished to marry had to be able to set up house independently. This meant, of course, that they had to have a sufficient income. Among the upper classes, such an income was usually supplied by parents and parents-in-law. As we shall see, the future married couple were formally endowed by a marriage settlement, which might in turn be further supplemented according to need. And even if parents found the cost of setting up independent households for their children too heavy, others (especially the king) might help out. This external endowment meant that the gentry and nobility could marry comparatively young: women at 17 or 18, men at 22 or 23. This early age of marriage gave the wife (if she lived that long) at least eighteen child-bearing years, which more or less inevitably led to big families.

But financial independence came less easily to the poorer members of society. They obtained self-sufficiency either through their own efforts or through inheritance after their parents' death. In either case, a longish wait was generally involved. Consequently marriage came later: farmers would marry at 25–30, their women-folk some two years earlier. Now if a woman does not marry until she is 24 or so this greatly reduces her child-bearing years – hence, above all, the generally much smaller size of families lower down the social scale. Moreover, periods of economic stringency (whether caused by bad harvests or plague or whatever), by making self-sufficiency harder to attain than ever, held back the age of marriage still further and reduced the number of children per family even more. The age of marriage, therefore, which was itself a product of economic pressures, provided an effective regulator of family size and hence of the overall size of the population.

But the similarities of the late medieval to the modern family must not be pushed too far. Alike though the two are in structure, in terms of attitudes they are very different. In most families in most periods two distinct elements are involved: the prudential and the affectionate. The balance of these obviously varies between different families in the same age, but certain broad developments in time can also be traced. Very simply, the modern family is emotional rather than prudential; the late medieval family prudential rather than emotional. That is not to say that the age had no idea of love. Obviously, as the huge volume of its love poetry shows, it did.

But the idea of love was by no means necessarily connected with the idea of marriage. Marriage served other purposes.

At the highest political levels, the first function of marriage was to cement alliance: the Earl of Warwick's astonishing reconciliation with the house of Lancaster was symbolized by the marriage of his daughter to Edward, Prince of Wales; while the much better-founded agreement between Henry VII and the principal Yorkist faction was ratified by his marrying Elizabeth, eldest daughter of Edward IV. Something of this idea of alliance penetrated well down the social scale, but on the way down it was overtaken in importance by the chief objective of late medieval marriage: gain. Money figured so largely because of the economic realities of the times. Now we assume that wealth will be earned; the late Middle Ages, on the other hand, assumed that it would be inherited. And the vehicle of inheritance was the family, whose central institution was marriage. The marriage game had three distinct phases: the choice of partner; the marriage itself; the dissolution of the marriage and remarriage. Each involved property.

The choice of partner (normally made by family and friends rather than by the individual in question) was a delicate exercise which could last for years. For example, the negotiations for Elizabeth Paston's marriage began in 1449 and ended (at least five proposed partners later) in 1459. The young girl was well endowed, so her family could bargain hard. First on the list was Stephen Scrope, the son of Sir Stephen. He was a distinctly mixed prospect. On the one hand, he was heir to considerable property; on the other, he was nearly 50, a widower, and as well had 'suffered from a sickness that kept [me] a thirteen or fourteen years ensuing, whereby I am disfigured in my person and shall be whilst I live'.[13] But these personal drawbacks counted for little compared with the possible complications produced by the child of his first marriage: would she inherit, or would his putative children by Elizabeth? This made Elizabeth's cousin, Elizabeth Clere, have doubts – as she wrote to Elizabeth's brother, John Paston:

> Meseemeth he were good for my cousin your sister, unless you might get her a better. . . . Cousin, it is told me there is a goodly man in your Inn [the Inner Temple] of which the father died late, and if you think that he were better for her than Scrope, it would be laboured; and give Scrope a

goodly answer that he be not put off till you be sure of a better.[14]

Luckily for Elizabeth, the Scrope match fell through, but others were soon lined up: there was 'Knyvet the heir', who was 'for to marry; both his wife and child be dead, as it was told here';[15] Knyvet was followed by Sir William Oldhall, then by John Clopton. The next initiative came from outside the family: Lord Grey of Hastings offered one of his wards, on condition that Elizabeth's fortune went to him as sponsor. Unsurprisingly, the ward rejected these terms. At this point Elizabeth's other brother William lost patience, remarking: 'At the reverence of God, draw to some conclusion; it is time.'[16] Finally, however, she was married to Robert Poynings, an influential Kentish gentleman who had been one of the leaders of Cade's rebellion. Soon after her marriage she wrote to her mother, with artless ambiguity:

> As for my master, my best beloved that you call, and I must needs call him now, for I find no other cause, and as I trust to Jesu, none shall; for he is full kind to me, and is as busy as he can to make me sure of my jointure.[17]

In other words, affection (developing after marriage rather than before it) was not excluded by such marriages, but their foundation in property (the 'jointure') was always near the surface.

These two recurring themes – affection and property – were of course expressed in the actual marriage itself. Affection was a predominant element in the Christian theology of marriage, which also preached the 'marriage debt' of sexual intercourse mutually owed. These two were combined in the promises of the wedding service, such as the wife's to be 'bonney and buxom [cheerful, responsive and obedient] at bed and at board'.[18] Property came to its own in the preceding marriage contract or settlement. This recorded a double transaction: the future bride brought with her a dowry (usually in cash); in return, the future groom or his family were required to provide for her maintenance both during the marriage and after it. (Women tended to outlive their husbands then as now.) This was done by the 'jointure', to which Elizabeth Paston's letter refers. Jointure was a joint tenancy of lands: that is, the husband was required to set aside lands (often a third or more of his estate) that would be held jointly by husband and wife during the husband's life and solely by the widow for the period of time that she survived her spouse. Only after the detail of these arrangements was as fast as the law could make it was the actual ceremony of marriage contemplated.

Jointure brings us to remarriage. Provision for widowhood on the scale just outlined created some exceedingly wealthy widows. In 1527, for example, the Dowager Countess of Oxford's income was assessed at £940 a year, which was exactly the same as that enjoyed by the then Earl of Oxford himself. The dowager Marchioness of Dorset was only a little worse off, with £924 a year, while the Dowager Lady Hastings and Hungerford could muster a fortune of £1333. 6s. 8d. a year. (The translation of fifteenth- and sixteenth-century money into modern values is an almost impossible exercise. First, because the speed of late twentieth-century inflation tends to make any estimate out of date before it is printed. Second – and more fundamentally – because the same commodities have different relative values at different periods of time. Clothing, for example, was disproportionately expensive by modern standards: as late as the seventeenth century, as Pepys shows, a secondhand velvet cloak cost as much as a domestic servant's wages for a year. However – providing these problems are borne in mind – the multiplication of late medieval prices by at least 100 will give a not too misleading idea of comparative value.) Incomes like these were as exceptional as the rank of the ladies in question, but most widows of gentlemen and substantial citizens were well-off. That made them highly desirable commodities. Often the breath was scarcely out of the husband's body before fresh suitors were offering themselves to the widow. An outstanding case is Elizabeth Stonor, who was married successively – virtually *ex officio* – to three gentlemen of Henry VIII's privy chamber. Her first husband was Sir William Compton, who died in 1528. In just over a year she had married her second husband, Walter Walsh; he in turn died in 1538, and within two years she had married Sir Philip Hoby. With each marriage, of course, the property vested in her became still greater. Probably the most sought-after widows, however, were those of London merchants. Here again the privy chamber scored highly: Sir Richard Long picked the plum by marrying Margaret Kitson, widow of the immensely rich Sir Thomas Kitson, the builder of Hengrave Hall; Anthony Knyvet repudiated his first wife to secure the wealthy Avicia Gibson, widow of 'Nicholas Gibson, grocer, one of the sheriffs, 1539';[19] while Sir William Tyler invoked the aid of Henry VIII himself to secure the widow of his choice. We learn of the incident from Sir Thomas More who was acting as intermediary between the king and Wolsey. On 17 September 1523 he informed the cardinal that Henry had commanded him

> to write unto your Grace that whereas it hath pleased our Lord to call to his mercy Mr Myrfyn, late Alderman of London, his Grace very greatly desireth for the special favour which he beareth toward Sir William Tyler, that the same Sir William should have the widow of the said late Alderman in marriage.[20]

Wolsey was to make the necessary arrangements. More's language is free from every trace of disapproval; indeed, with surely unnecessary unction, he goes on to speak of Henry's intentions in this matter as 'his virtuous and honourable appetites'.[21]

Lower down the social scale second marriages might allow more freedom of choice – as for the Wife of Bath, who, having made her fortune with three 'rich and old' husbands, ends with a handsome clerk half her age 'Which that I took for love, and no richesse.'[22]

With marriage and remarriage so determined by property, relations within the family itself were also naturally seen largely in terms of property. The wife – with a few reservations – was the property of her husband, while the children were the nearly absolute property of their parents. The children of the poor were so many pairs of hands, to be set to work as soon as possible to help maintain the family; the children of the rich were bargaining counters with a readily cashable market value. In the mid-fifteenth century, for example, John Wyndham of Felbrigg in Norfolk, a widower, wished to marry the widow of Sir John Heveningham. This Sir John had left large debts, £200 of which were still unpaid. And the responsibility for this sum, of course, fell on his widow. But the widow's misfortune was the widower's advantage. Wyndham offered to pay her debts in return for her marrying him. The money would be raised by the sale of the marriage of his young son by his first wife. That would fetch £400, which would leave at least £200 over after paying off the lady's creditors.

Indeed, it is possible to take this line of argument further. I suspect that the age's characteristic respect for the old owed little to sentiment and much to recognition of their control of property.

Certainly, when the old passed on part of their wealth to the young while they were still alive, they were too shrewd to rely, Lear-like, on filial affection to guard their interests. Instead they resorted to the protection of the law. In 1386, for example, Christine (widow of Thomas Compton, who had died eight years previously) made an agreement with her eldest son Edmund. She leased him for the term of her life her manor and manor house of Compton Wynyates, reserving one room for her own use. In return, Edmund was to hold her in food, drink, clothing and shoes. Twenty-eight years later, Edmund's widow Agnes made a nearly identical contract with her own son William.

In short, money was not so much the root of all evil as the root of most relationships. There were exceptions, of course. For example, John Paston the younger's courtship of Margery Brews began as the usual hardheaded commercial negotiation, yet quickly transmuted itself into a passionate love affair. The obstacles to be overcome were not, however, great. Margery's dowry was not as large as the Pastons wanted, but her mother was enthusiastic about the match, and John's shrewd diplomacy was equal to coping with his family's doubts. This type of match, in which love chose a partner that prudence could not fault (or at least not fault much), must have been fairly common – if only because the children of the upper classes were naturally thrown very much together. But far rarer are those cases where love actually defied property. One is well known: the long-resisted but eventually successful love match between Margaret Paston and Richard Calle, her brother's steward. Few lovers, however, seem to have been equipped with such courage and persistence – and certainly not enough to break the general rule of arranged marriages.

On the other hand, as we have already briefly mentioned, arranged marriages did not exclude affection or even passion. But the passion developed after the bond was made. John of Gaunt's marriage to Blanche, daughter of Henry of Grosmont, was arranged by Edward III, probably to gain part of the Lancaster estates for the royal family, while the two were still children. But when after ten years of marriage she died, Chaucer wrote his consolation for John in the *Book of the Duchess*, assuming that the affection of the two, of the man in black for 'goode faire White',[23] had all the depth and delight of a love affair. Anne of Bohemia's effigy shows that she was not beautiful, and her marriage to Richard II was purely political;

yet Richard's frenzy of grief at her death led him to tear down their palace of Sheen, and played a part in the events that led to his deposition. For his second wife, the Princess Isabella of France, aged 7 when he married her and 11 when he died, Richard naturally seems never to have developed more than a considerate affection.

It is impossible to tell which of Richard's marriages was the more typical. But Langland makes scorchingly clear how unpleasant was the emotional life of many of the upper class:

> Ho so lyveth in lawe, and in love doth wel
> As these wedded men that this worlde susteynen? . . .
> Ac fewe folke now folweth this, for thei geveth here
>   children
> For covetise of catel and connynge chapmen;
> Of kyn ne of kynreden acounteth men bote lytel.
> Thogh she be loveliche to loken on, and lofsom abedde,
> A mayde wel ymanered, of good men yspronge,
> Bote she have eny other good, have here wol no riche.
> Ac let here be unlovely, unlofsom abedde,
> A bastard, a bond on, a begeneldes douhter,
> That no curtesye can, bot let here be knowe
> For riche other wel y-rented, thogh she revely for elde
> There nys squier ne knyght in contreye aboute,
> That he ne wol bowe to that bonde, to beden here an
>   hosebonde,
> And wedden here for here welthe, and wisshen on the
>   morwe
> That his wyf were wex or a walet ful of nobles.
> In jelosye, joyles, and jangelynge abedde
> Thei lyve here lif unlovely, til deth hem departe.
> Many payre sithen the pestilence-time han plighte
>   treuthe to lovye,
> Ac they lyen lelly, here nother lovethe othere.
> The fruyt that thei bryngen forth aren many foule
>   wordes,
> Thei han no children bote cheste, and choppes hem
>   bitwene. . . .
> Forthi ich counseile alle Crystene, coveyte nevere be
>   wedded
> For covetise of catel in no kynne wyse;

Bote maydenes and maydenes marieth yow togederes;
And wydewers and wydewes wedden ayther othere,
And loke that love be more the cause than lond other
      nobles.[24]

Ac] But   *covetise of catel*] covetousness of property   *chapmen*]
bargainers   *riche*] rich man   *bond on*] serf   *begeneldes*]
beggar's   *can*] knows   *other*] or   *revely for elde*] be wrinkled
with age   *wex*] wax   *sithen*] since   *lelly*] truly   *cheste*]
quarrelling   *chops*] knocks   *Forthi*] Therefore   *kynne wyse*]
manner of method   *other nobles*] or money

Langland's attack is closely paralleled in sermons. Hoccleve, again,
who prides himself on having married for love, in spite of all the
ensuing poverty, talks of the strife and heaviness of those that marry
'for muk and good', and attacks the rich for their childhood
betrothals, and the 'lordes marriages' made by couples who have
never seen each other.[25]

One escape from this intolerable life was by way of ritualized
fantasy. The rituals (like most others) were based in perceived social
reality. We see this in the pastoral poetry and May Day celebrations
of Henry VIII's reign. Whereas the upper class had their emotions
fettered by the constraints of property and convention, they saw (or
thought they saw) the lower orders enjoying the freedom they were
denied. Or, as Sir Anthony Denny put it in attempting to comfort
Henry after his disastrous marriage to Anne of Cleves, 'the state of
princes . . . [was] in matters of marriage, far of worse sort than the
condition of poor men. For princes take as is brought them by others
and poor men be commonly at their own device and liberty.'[26]

This perhaps exaggerated contrast provided the emotional steam
behind the pastoral convention which, long present in French court
poetry, and echoed in *The Flower and the Leaf* and Chaucer's
Legend of Good Women, became a dominant literary theme after
Alexander Barclay adopted it from the classics and Italy around
1514. The same contrast led to an idealization of the sexual prowess
of the lower orders (comparable to the white man's attitude to the
black in our own time). Thus temporary release for the great could
come from ritual identification with the common people. On May
Day, then, Henry VIII and his gentlemen-in-waiting dressed up as
woodmen (in velvet, silks and taffetas) and rode off into the green-
wood to bring their true loves boughs of may blossom:

Ye that in love find luck and sweet abundance,
And live in lust of joyful jollity.
Arise for shame, do way your sluggardy:
Arise, I say, do May some observance.[27]

The last line of this song reminds one (and was possibly meant to) of Chaucer's Arcite 'risen . . . to doon his observaunce to May'.[28] But earlier celebrations had had a slightly different flavour. Neither in Chaucer nor as late as Malory's maying of Guenevere in the *Morte Darthur* is there any suggestion that love or maying involved imitating the lower classes. Malory's regret is nostalgia for 'King Arthur's days' when people could 'love seven years without licorous love' while now men 'cannot love sevennight but they must have all their desires'.[29] St Valentine's Day in Chaucer's *Parliament of Fowls* only distinguishes the classes on the ground that eagles, doves and gentlefolk will be truer in unsuccessful love than ducks, cuckoos and churls.

But with Chaucer and Malory we are in a world of more exquisitely ritualized fantasy: the world of love talking, presumed to be the main occupation of courts in the conversations of Sir Bercilak's wife with Sir Gawain in *Gawain and the Green Knight*, and portrayed in the garden where the narrator of the *Romance of the Rose* spends his time carolling with Mirth, Gladness, Courtesy, Beauty, Richesse, Largesse, Franchise, Idleness and Youth in the presence of the god of love – before he falls in love. In this world, contracts about property are out of place. The cult of the daisy mentioned in Chapter 3, on the other hand, finds its place here, and the division of court lovers into servants of the Flower and of the Leaf which is first mentioned around 1385 by Chaucer in the *Legend of Good Women*, and still apparent around 1435 in the poems of Charles d'Orléans and after 1450 in *The Flower and the Leaf* itself. It is the realm of courtly love, derived above all from the courts and literature of France, and in this realm, if a man does fall seriously in love, marriage, though not excluded, is not central.

This dream too had a basis in reality. Very often men must have found love outside marriage: that is, with a mistress. Her role, indeed, was formalized to a considerable extent. As in ancient Athens, there were two types of sexual relationship for men: the institutionalized (with the wife) and the passionate (with the mistress). In both societies, marriage was about property and procreation, while the mistress supplied emotional and intellectual companionship and imaginative sex. The division of function between wife and mistress meant that the two could coexist fairly happily. Langland, like other moralists, might fulminate against bastardy and bed-games except in wedlock; but a wife's tolerance was often extended even to her husband's bastard children. Lady Anne Grey, who directed in her will (1 October 1557) that her tomb be embellished with 'a memorial of the stock that I came of',[30] was enormously proud; nevertheless she left tokens of friendly regard to the three bastard daughters of her husband, Sir Richard Clement. Many bastards were highly regarded figures at court, and Chaucer's miller's wife in the *Reeve's Tale* prides herself on being the daughter of the (naturally celibate) parson.

Here, then, is a major paradox. Both the real world and the courtly literature of the fourteenth and fifteenth centuries present clear pictures of sexual relationships. But the two pictures are different: in reality, as in Langland's satire, licit relationships centred on money; in courtly literature, on love. This is as true in England as in France, in Latin literature as in the vernacular. The Latin poet of the Arundel manuscript (which is written in a hand of the later fourteenth century) writes ecstatically of his love:

> Herself hath given back my life to me,
> Herself hath yielded far
> More than had ever hoped my misery.
> And when she recklessly
> Gave herself wholly unto Love and me,
> Beauty in heaven afar
> Laughed from her joyous star.[31]

And Chaucer himself only sounds a variation on the theme:

> Upon my trouthe I sey you feithfully
> That ye ben of my lyf and deeth the quene;
> For with my deeth the trouthe shal be sene.
>   Your yen two wol slee me sodenly;
>   I may the beautee of hem not sustene,
>   So woundeth it thourghout my herte kene.[32]

yen] eyes

Characteristically, Chaucer undercuts his own poem with the

succeeding 'Sin I fro Love escaped am so fat . . .',[33] but this does not alter the fact that between literature and life there was a gulf.

As we have seen in French courtly literature, which provided the norm throughout western Europe, the two worlds seem to have met in the person of the mistress: romantic love was directed not to the wife but to the more alluring figure of the paramour. But English literature introduces a variation. The French pattern often remains and may reflect court practice, but in many English romances the goal of love becomes marriage. *Sir Degrevaunt* and Melydor live married for thirty years and have seven children, *Sir Torrent of Portyngale* finally marries Desonel, *Sir Eglamour* Christabelle, and so on. Chaucer is, as always, magnificently comprehensive. His references to his own marriage, which may or may not be serious, imply a total absence of romantic love. The lovers in the *Knight's Tale*, on the other hand, intend to marry Emily. But, again, scholarship has not decided whether Troilus and Criseyde are to be thought of as married or not: certainly no public ritual was performed between them. The *Franklin's Tale* demonstrates a difficulty in addition to that of the economic basis of marriage. For the convention in literature, and perhaps in life, was that the woman was the dominant partner in love (hence, of course, the word 'mistress'), while the marriage contract made the husband master. The tale aims at reconciling these opposites, for the knight Arviragus is 'Servant in love and lord in mariage',[34] but this seems to be meant as an ideal paradox.

One masterpiece of this tradition of courtly love ending in marriage – *The Kingis Quair* – may be about a real love. It presents itself as being written by James I of Scotland about the marriage he made while a prisoner in England. But it is deliberately reminiscent of the loves of Palamon and Arcite in the *Knight's Tale*; and it may be that James wrote it rather about the courtship that should by literary convention have happened than about the actual marriage arrangement.

However that may be, for the most part the late Middle Ages display a striking coexistence of contradictories: of wife and mistress; of the reality of love and the family and their literary expression. One important aspect of this coexistence is the almost total absence of radical social satire from the courtly tradition. As we have seen, Langland and the preachers comment on the nobility from outside with vigour and humorous intelligence. Chaucer, socially an odd fringe figure, a merchant's son and a civil servant with the entrée to the court, introduces oblique reflections with a wry and gentle irony. Hoccleve follows him. Authors from the gentry like Gower and Sir John Clanvowe write satire based on moral universals without much concern for particular social practice; but there is little evidence that the propertied classes were at all generally aware of the conflict between what they did and what they imagined.

After Hoccleve, little social satire seems to have been written on the gentry, even from outside, for three generations. But in the sixteenth century there is a change, and for the first time we see members of the ruling class reflecting in acute discomfort on the gap between their own social theory and practice. Many elements – educational, religious, philosophical – were involved in this change: all these will be discussed later. For the moment we need concern ourselves only with the consequences in relation to moral and, in particular, family relationships: above all, with marriage. The most complete and developed instance of this revised attitude is Wyatt's *Third Satire*, addressed to Sir Francis Bryan. It has a double theme: the moral degeneracy of the times, and the courtier as the extreme example of that decay. For the present, we shall deal only with the first of these themes; the second will feature largely later on. The ostensible purpose of the poem is to teach Bryan how to make money; the method recommended is to exploit human relationships. First, batten on the old:

> Sometime also rich age beginneth to dote:
> See thou when there thy gain may be the more,
>   Stay him by the arm whereso he walk or go,
>   Be near alway, and if he cough too sore,
> When he hath spit, tread out and please him so.
>   A diligent knave that picks his master's purse
>   May please him so, that he withouten mo
> Executor is . . .
>
> *mo*] more

Second, marry a rich widow:

> The widow may for all thy charge deburse:
> A rivelled skin, a stinking breath, what then?
> A toothless mouth shall do thy lips no harm,

The gold is good, and though she curse or ban,
Yet where thee list thou mayst lie good and warm:
    Let the old mule bite upon the bridle
    Whilst there do lie a sweeter in thine arm.

Third, prostitute any woman entrusted to your charge:

    Thy niece, thy cousin, thy sister or thy daughter,
    If she be fair, if handsome be her middle,
If thy better hath her love besought her,
    Advance his cause, and he shall help thy need.

But in all let money, money alone, rule:

But 'ware, I say, so gold thee help and speed,
    That in this case thou be not so unwise
    As Pandar was in such like deed.
For he, the fool, of conscience was so nice
    That he no gain would have for all his pain.[35]

In this passage we see the interpenetration of two streams: the ideas and even the language ('rivelled') of Langland become part of the courtly tradition itself. Even Chaucer, one of the original founts of that tradition, is transformed. His amiable Pandarus from *Troilus and Criseyde*, the gentlest of criticisms on the folly of helping a friend in a shaky love affair, gives place to Wyatt's thoroughgoing pimp.

Wyatt composed his *Third Satire* about 1538. Hence Marx could not have been wider off the mark when he wrote in 1848 that it was 'the bourgeoisie [that] has torn away from the family its sentimental veil, and has reduced the family relation to a mere money relation'.[36] On the contrary, it was the gentry family of the late Middle Ages that displayed the 'mere money relationship' in its full perfection; the 'sentimental veil' itself was a later development associated with the 'bourgeois revolution' that Marx condemned.

The great household

As we have already seen, there was a considerable difference in size between the families of rich and poor. But family size was not the only or, indeed, the most important difference between their households. This distinction lay elsewhere: in the employment by the wealthy of large numbers of domestic servants who lived in their masters' houses. And the higher a man's social status, the more servants he was expected to employ. Indeed, the *Black Book* of Edward IV envisaged a clear hierarchy of households: an esquire would have 10 servants, a knight 16, a knight banneret 24, a baron 40, a viscount 80, an earl 140, a marquis 200, a duke 240 and the king himself nearly 500. Beneath this great range of size, however, were fundamental similarities. Every upper-class household fulfilled basically the same functions and was organized in basically the same way.

The household performed three main tasks: it supervised the estate administration on which the master's wealth depended; it provided him with the daily necessities of food and drink on the one hand and body service on the other; and it maintained his social position. Its size and splendour in time of peace testified to his wealth; its size and power in time of war or civil disturbance gave him the means of self-defence or (if he so wished) of aggression.

The actual institutional organization of the household was closely related to the geography of the typical medieval house. (This survives in nearly its full perfection at Haddon Hall in Derbyshire.) The central apartment was the hall, which was essentially a communal dining room. At one end was a raised platform or dais, on which the master and his family ate. The servants, on the other hand, took their meals in the body of the hall. At the opposite end to the dais were the screens. Over the screens was the minstrels' gallery; behind the screens was a passage, with hatches leading into, first, the kitchens and, second, the buttery, from which wine and beer were served. On one side of the dais was usually an oriel window; on the other, a doorway to a staircase that led to the first floor. On this floor was the master's chamber, where he slept, ate many of his meals, received visitors and stored his valuables. There was thus a clear division of function between the various areas. The actual line of division came at the foot of the dais: on one side – the dais and chamber – was the master's side of the household; on the other – the body of the hall and the service quarters – was the servants' side. This division corresponds closely to the 'upstairs' and 'downstairs' of the eighteenth- or nineteenth-century household and, like that distinction, was the basis of the departmental structure of the household. The body servants of the chamber formed one department, while the menials of the hall and kitchens

– headed by the accountants and managers of the household –
formed the other. In the royal household the two departments were
known, respectively, as the chamber and the household (proper).
The former was directed by the lord chamberlain, the latter by the
lord steward.

In the fourteenth century, the line between public and private
became more sharply marked as the lord, save on very rare occasions,
ceased to eat on the dais in the hall and instead took nearly all his
meals in the privacy of his chamber. Langland characteristically
interprets this change as being due to meanness:

> Elenge is the halle, ech day in the wike,
> Ther the lord ne the lady liketh noght to sitte.
> Now hath ech riche a rule – to eten by hymselve
> In a pryvee parlour for povere mennes sake,
> Or in a chambre with a chymenee, and leve the chief
>   halle
> That was maad for meles, men to eten inne,
> And al to spare to spille that spende shal another.[37]

Elyng]Miserable   *for povere mennes sake*] because of the
poor   *to spare to spille*] to avoid destroying

It is at least as likely, however, that the aim was simply the same
desire for greater privacy that (as we saw in Chapter 4) was a
dominant element in the building of contemporary castles like
Bodiam and Kenilworth. In any case, it had no impact on the
organization of the household until the very end of the fifteenth
century.

The great household as we have just sketched it was, as well as
being the linchpin of society, the chief element in politics. It was
also the focus and principal patron of the arts. There were
exceptions, of course, as even a brief glance at the complex and
debatable history of the alliterative revival shows. The author of the
earliest datable poem of this revival, *Winner and Waster* of 1352–3,
clearly saw his poetry as belonging of right, to the great household.
Unfortunately, or so he says, it was no longer appreciated.

> Whylom were lordes in londe that loved in thaire hertis
> To here makers of myrthes, that matirs couthe fynde.[38]

Now, on the other hand, beardless jesters who can jangle like a jay are preferred. The poet, of course, exaggerates (or, rather, is half-right). What happens in fact is that the alliterative tradition divides. Many of the poems of the alliterative revival (the courtlier kind, like *Gawain and the Green Knight*) suggest a household origin; a few, on the other hand, have stepped outside that world. *Piers Plowman* in particular seems to owe more to two cultures that lay outside the frame of the household than to the great household itself: the world of the peasant, and the closely associated world of the lesser clergy. Its fusion of the three worlds is part of its eccentric greatness.

Outside the great individual households were the products of the corporate patronage of the community – urban or rural. This patronage was exercised above all through the multitude of guilds, largely unions of tradesmen and workers devoted to organizing their occupations and social relations, but all having some religious dedication. Such patronage was responsible for the cycles of mystery plays and for the rebuilding of many a church. But even here caution is necessary. Lavenham Church in Suffolk is one of the most famous wool churches, and as such is generally seen as an outstanding example of communal patronage. However, a glance at its decoration tells a rather different story. Everything depends on the use of badges, which (as we shall see) were the master symbol of the household. The spandrels of the arch of the porch are carved with the boar badges of the De Veres, Earls of Oxford; the roof timbers of the south aisle are covered in stars or mullets (another De Vere badge) and Tudor roses; while the plinth of the tower is ornamented with shallow panels, each set with a badge: the De Vere mullet, the merchant mark of Thomas Spring, the leading clothier of the township, and (most interesting of all) a Tudor rose superimposed on the De Vere mullet. Lavenham Church is not, therefore, simply a manifestation of the pride and wealth of one of the new centres of the cloth industry; the pride and wealth were there, but they were articulated by one man: John De Vere, thirteenth Earl of Oxford. He was both lord of Lavenham and a principal supporter and beneficiary of the new regime of Henry Tudor. The rebuilding of the church, which began soon after Bosworth, was carried out at his instigation and under his patronage; while the use of his household badges and the king's turned the whole structure into a complex symbol. Pride in the community was fused with family pride, and both in turn were fused with pride in a particular, household attachment to the new dynasty.

Furthermore, even when the guild was sole patron, the influence of the household was not thereby eliminated; for the guild itself, like the monastery, was organized as a corporate great household. Its social life (like the household's) revolved round the guild's hall; in the guild's chamber, on the other hand, the guild masters (so called since they were the heads of both their own particular households and the corporate household of the guild) transacted private and, above all, financial business. Thus it is that even today the chief financial officer of the City of London has a title redolent of the medieval court: he is called the chamberlain.

Almost everywhere in the arts, therefore, we find the household. Those arts – like some aspects of music or dancing or recitation – that it was seemly for a gentleman to practise found their expression as incidents in the daily life of the great household. So the *Black Book* of Edward IV reminded the esquires of the household (that is, the gentlemen-in-waiting) that it was a long-established custom that they should 'winter and summer, in afternoons and in evenings, . . . draw to lords' chambers within the court, there to keep honest company after their cunning, in talking of chronicles of kings and of other policies, or in piping, or harping, singing, [etc.]'.[39] The purpose of all this is stated with almost brutal directness: it was 'to help occupy the court and accompany strangers, till the time require of departing'[40] to bed.

This frank utilitarianism applied even more strongly to the great bulk of the arts, whose practice was unfitting to the highly born. Their executants were menials and, like most other menials, were generally members of a household. Naturally, the royal household had the fullest complement of such servants. In particular, its musical establishment was impressive. Under Edward IV it fell into two sections, religious and secular. First, there were staff of the chapel royal: twenty-six chaplains and gentlemen-clerks, and eight children with their master. Their function was to supply the musical accompaniment to the religious life of the household. This changed with the church's calendar, which in turn was profoundly coloured by the changing seasons of the year. In particular, the beginning of the festive season of winter was marked on 1 November when 'Memorandum that the king hath a song before him in his hall or chamber upon All Hallows day . . . by some of these clerks and children of chapel in remembrance of Christmas'.[41] The administration of the household used this moment of religious festivity as a chronological signpost: after the song was over the king was to inform the steward and treasurer of the household where he intended to keep Christmas.

The secular establishment of the court included the minstrels, whose main task was to make the ceremonial noises that accompanied each stage of the court day, 'whereof some use trumpets, some shawms, and small pipes'.[42] Finally, there was the wait 'that nightly, from Michaelmas till Shere Thursday, pipeth the watch within this court four times, and in the summer nights three times'.[43] Here, then, we have art at its most functional: the wait was a human clock; melodious, but practical.

Under Henry VIII, who was himself an enthusiastic and competent musician, the musical staff of the royal household increased in number and improved in quality. In addition, a handful of highly favoured musicians were recruited for the king's private delectation. The earliest of these was a Venetian, Dionysius Memo, who was one of the tiny circle of intimates that accompanied the king when he sought refuge from the plague in Windsor in 1517. This intimacy foreshadowed the natural development of Memo's position: appointment to a formal post of body service within the privy chamber itself. Memo never in fact made the full transition, but his successors Mark Smeaton and Philip Van Wilder did. Smeaton's promising career was cut short in 1536, when he was executed as one of Anne Boleyn's paramours, but Van Wilder's success was uninterrupted. Hence he displays to the full the characteristic combination of performing artist and body servant. On the one hand, he enjoyed a reputation for the highest virtuosity: when he died, some anonymous poet was moved to write an elegy later included in *Tottel's Miscellany*, which ends:

> The string is broke, the lute is dispossessed;
> The hand is cold, the body in the ground,
> The lowering lute lamenteth now therefore
> Philips her friend that can her touch no more.[44]

In his other aspect, however, this distinguished performer was little more than Henry VIII's musical odd-job man: he tutored the royal children in the lute; acted as director of the court conservatoire of young musicians; looked after Henry VIII's personal collection of musical instruments; and replaced the king's broken lute strings.

Even the less obviously domestic arts were, whenever possible, fitted into the structure of the household. Very few men apart from the king were such regular builders as to have a clerk of the works on their regular household payroll. But when buildings were actually in progress, the leading craftsmen would often be treated as temporary members of the household: even as late as 1611, at Kyre Park in Worcestershire, the 'chief mason' was given boots, slippers, a coat, 'cognizance hat-band, feather, and cognizance of silver'.[45]

Again, therefore, Marx's formulation of the course of cultural change seems to be lacking. The bourgeoisie, he tells us, 'has stripped of its halo every occupation hitherto honoured and looked up to with reverent awe. It has converted . . . the poet [and] the man of science into its paid wage-labourers.'[46] In fact, the exact opposite would seem to be the case: it was the household culture of feudalism that treated the artist as a menial, and the market society of the nineteenth century that honoured him as a demigod. Moreover, the contrast in attitudes appears nearly as strongly in the sixteenth century itself. This is well shown by the use of the word 'architect'. In the aristocratic, household society of England the term, with all that it suggests about the independent rank and dignity of the practitioner of the art, had scarcely become current by the end of the sixteenth century. On the other hand, the little Alsatian town of Sélestat (one of the centres of the humanist Renaissance) boasted an officially appointed town architect at least fifty years earlier. His name was Stephen Ziegler, and his practice was profitable enough for him to build, in 1538–45, a handsome town house. The decoration of its great oriel window, which is in the latest Grotesque style, is organized round fourteen medallion portraits of the great architects of classical antiquity. The house is thus both pattern-book and boast: in the one aspect, it showed a possible customer what Ziegler could do; in the other, it established the splendidly long and distinguished genealogy of his profession. The basic explanation for the difference between England and Sélestat is not far to seek. The architect was a relatively new social animal, who had to be fitted into an existing pattern of social classification. In aristocratic societies (along with other artists) he was naturally labelled as a servant, and therefore took the status of one. In self-governing towns, on the other hand, he stood as a professional among professionals and was respected accordingly. England eventually caught up with the new attitude towards artists, but it followed its own route.

The household thus provided both the setting within which the arts functioned, and the bulk of the regularly salaried posts available to artists. In so doing it determined the social status of artistic activity itself. Important though this is, however, it does not give us the full measure of the artistic significance of the household. The great households (in the virtual absence of any factories, apart from the royal dockyards at the very end of our period) were by far the largest single economic units; while domestic service itself was by far the largest single category of non-agricultural employment. And this it was to remain until the beginning of the twentieth century. Indeed, it is possible to argue that the disappearance of the servant is the crucial point of difference between the last fifty years and all our previous social history. Service conditioned everything: from individual psychology to the whole range of public and social behaviour.

For example, the modern concept of privacy – probably the foundation stone of twentieth-century attitudes – is possible only in a servantless world. Before, dressing and undressing, even relieving oneself, were not solitary activities but rather social, for a crucial part was played in them by personal attendants. And the higher the master's rank the more intimate that attendance tended to be. The toilet routine of an ordinary member of the upper classes is described in John Russell's *Book of Nurture* of about 1452: the 'chamberlain' or bedchamber servant was to

> See the privy-house for easement be fair, soot, and clean;
> And that the boards thereupon be covered with cloth
>   fair and green;
> And the hole himself, look there no board be seen;
> Thereon a fair cushion, the ordure no man to teen.
> Look there be blanket, cotton, or linen to wipe the
>   nether end,
> And ever he clepith, wait ready and entende,
> Basin and ewer, and on your shoulder a towel.[47]

soot] sweet   *teen*] annoy   *clepith*] calls   *entende*] prompt(?)

This passage would suggest that the master relieved himself alone, only calling in the 'chamberlain' when he wished to wash his hands. But the royal etiquette was different. For example, in 1528 Thomas Heneage, one of Henry VIII's leading personal attendants, wrote to

Wolsey to apologize for not having come to see him, but (he explained) 'there is none here but Master Norris and I to give attendance upon the King's Highness when he goeth to make water in his bedchamber'.[48] The king, that is, was waited on even at the actual moment of evacuation, and this continued to be the case for at least another 150 years. Naturally, a society where all this was taken for granted had a very different attitude from our own towards what was permissible. It is this – not mere coarseness – that accounts for such conversations as the following between Henry VIII and Thomas Heneage, whose intimate services we have already noticed. The conversation, which is recorded with due solemnity in the State Papers, took place early in 1540, when the king was reeling under the shock of his disappointment in his new wife, Anne of Cleves. Henry (as Heneage reports)

> said plainly that he mistrusted her to be no maid, by reason of the looseness of her breasts, and other tokens. And furthermore, that he could have none appetite with her to do as a man should do with his wife, for such displeasant airs as he felt with her.[49]

It is against this tradition that Chaucer, Skelton or Rabelais must be read, not against later social conventions which would make their bawdry what Alexander Pope called it, 'beastly'.

But the effects of service on language went far beyond a mere extension of the bounds of decency; indeed, it permeated the whole world of speech. Service had its own language or vocabulary, characteristic features of which appear in the following passage. The passage, taken from chapter 55 of the Eltham Ordinances, details the high standards Wolsey expected of the king's body servants: the latter were

> diligently [to] attend upon [the king's] person in his said Privy Chamber in doing humble, reverent, secret and lowly service about all such things as his pleasure shall be to depute and put them to do; not pressing his Grace nor advancing themselves either in further service than his grace will . . . assign them unto.[50]

Such, then, were the virtues of a servant, of which the prime was 'diligent attendance'. The opposed vice was irregularity, and it was from a charge of this that Ralph Sadler sought to excuse himself in (probably) 1539: he was, he wrote to his patron Thomas Cromwell, appalled that the king

> seemeth to impute unto me a great default for non-attendance. . . . If there be any such fault in me I trust his Highness is of such benignity as upon my reconciliation and amendment his Majesty will forgive me, which once remitted I shall beware our Lord willing how to offend his Majesty in that behalf or any other.[51]

The language of service, therefore, was both flexible and rich. But what really mattered was the social role of service itself. Since the service of one man to another was the dominant social relationship, the vocabulary of service tended to be used by analogy to describe virtually every other relationship too − be it religious, amorous or political. St Ignatius Loyola enjoined himself (as Wolsey ordered the servants of Henry VIII's privy chamber) 'to labour and not to ask for any reward'; to this day the name of the act of worship is 'service' and the Pope's proudest title 'servant of the servants of God'; and the metaphor recurs again and again in the church's prayers, as in the magnificent paradox 'Cui servire regnare est' ('to serve whom is to be a king'), which Cranmer translated with characteristic economy as 'whose service is perfect freedom'.[52]

If possible, the language of love was even more soaked in the vocabulary of service than the language of religion. A man's love was his 'mistress', whose authority he protested he would 'serve and suffer patiently'[53] − we have already seen Chaucer's Franklin's paradoxical reconciliation of this service with the husband's sovereignty. The title of one lover's poem prays 'his service to be accepted and his defaults pardoned', and the text itself

> . . . That ye vouchsafe in all
> Mine humble service. And if that me misfall
> By negligence, or else for lack of wit
> That of your mercy you do pardon it.[54]

The anonymous poet might simply be versifying Ralph Sadler's letter quoted above.

But it is with politics that the interpenetration of language becomes most complete. In (probably) 1539 Sir William Parr wrote to Cromwell to beg that his nephew William might be appointed to the king's privy chamber; in return he promised Cromwell the young man's loyalty and clientage. The request, that is, was for a post of domestic service; the *quid pro quo* was to be political attachment. But the language Sir William used for these two (in our eyes very different) ideas was the same: the vocabulary of service. Young Parr's desire was 'to have some stay in the court whereby he might during the pleasure of the King's Majesty bestow his service about his Grace'; his consequent loyalty to the minister would result in his 'binding himself during his life to your lordship next to the King's highness, with his poor heart and service'.[55] In this case, the fusion of language also represented a fusion of realities: in a society that knew little of ideological commitment, the basis of political attachment was (as we shall see) most usually the bond of service, or was quickly assimilated to that bond.

This pattern of linguistic borrowing had major literary repercussions. It was the common basis of the languages of love and of politics in the vocabulary of service that gave the elaborate love games between Elizabeth I and her courtiers such political power and effect; it was the same common basis of the languages of politics and religion that makes the fallen Wolsey's speech to Sir William Kingston so poignant: 'If I had served God as diligently as I have done the King, he would not have given me over in my gray hairs.'[56]

So far, this section has discussed two things: first, the effect of the household on the status of art and the artist; and, second, its effect on the means of expression. We must now turn to its impact on the world of thought and ideas to which the artist had to respond.

The dominant ideals in the secular literature of the Middle Ages were (naturally enough) based on the aspirations of the dominant group in medieval society: the aristocracy. The aristocratic model of behaviour centred on the virtue of magnanimity. Magnanimity – in its literary formulation at least – had its origins in the description in Aristotle's *Ethics* of *megalopsychia*: that is, highmindedness or proper pride. This is an attribute peculiar to the superior soul; indeed, it is essentially such a soul's recognition of its own merit. From this recognition flows a whole pattern of behaviour. Its essence is a kind of self-containment or detachment: the highminded man is jealous of his honour, but the only judgement of honour he values is that of other similar souls. And even their recognition brings not elated gratitude, but only a quiet sense of getting one's due. Again, the highminded man will desire wealth and office – but only for the honour that they bring. And even about the latter, as we have seen, he is restrained. He willingly confers benefits, but loathes to receive them. He insists on his dignity with his equals, but with his inferiors is all graciousness. He will strive for nothing petty, and is open in his likes and dislikes. He will not gossip or upbraid people, save when he wishes deliberately to insult someone. He prefers his possessions to be beautiful and useless 'rather than that they should be profitable and meant for use, because this goes to show that he is sufficient to himself'.[57] He is deliberate and unhurried in movements and speech. Aristotle's ideal (which was itself no more than a systematization of existing aristocratic attitudes) underwent two major modifications. The first came from the Romans. Their translation of *megalopsychia* was *magnanimitas*. Now *psyche* meant only soul or mind, but *animus* meant both soul and courage. So to the idea of greatness of mind was added the idea of great physical courage. Secondly, Christianity infused the already expanded notion with its own complex conception of virtue. And this conception – which gave so much importance to love and humility – did much to soften the sternness of the Graeco-Roman model.

So the final idea of magnanimity was both rich and various. Different authors at different periods stress different elements: the early knightly romances concentrate on brute physical courage to the exclusion of almost everything else; in contrast, in Chaucer's *Franklin's Tale*, 'gentilesse' (which is his equivalent for 'magnanimity') means the suppression of anything mean or selfish. However, all the variations are variations on a type – a type, moreover, that was not simply an intellectual abstraction but also a social fact.

The point is this. The nobleman was automatically the head of a great household. His virtue of magnanimity was thus – by definition – the virtue of the head of a great household. And inevitably the institution shaped the qualities associated with it. This becomes clear if we take the two outstanding aspects of magnanimity. These were the contrasting attitudes of condescension to inferiors and cool self-sufficiency *vis-à-vis* equals. The former is the essential quality of the master of many servants; while the latter was a function of the very real material autonomy of the great household and the landed estates of which it was the centre. From many points of view such estates were little kingdoms and their heads were little kings, whose dealings with their fellow petty monarchs were almost as elaborately regulated as the diplomatic intercourse of genuine sovereigns.

So the household undoubtedly helped to form a dominant literary theme of the later Middle Ages, but it did so only in rather a general way. However, magnanimity did not stand alone. With it was associated another Aristotelian quality – 'magnificence' – whose links with the great household are much more direct. Magnificence, as the *Ethics* defines it, is the employment of great private wealth in the public interest: 'The magnificent man reveals his character in spending not upon himself but on public objects; his gifts are a sort of dedication.'[58] He will endow religion; construct public buildings; and turn great moments in his private life – like weddings and funerals – into public spectacles. Magnificence, in short, is the outward material face of magnanimity. It could express itself in many different contexts, but its supreme and chosen vehicle was the household. The size of a nobleman's house, the splendour of its furnishings and the number and costly dress of his servants did two things: on the one hand, they advertised his wealth; and on the other, they provided the material foundations of his power. Public power lay in the command of men, and the household was the institution through which that command was bought.

The connection between magnificence and the household was well understood by contemporaries – above all, by the administrative machine of the royal household. This was staffed by relatively large numbers of educated clerks and officials. These men were proud of their posts and jealously guarded their departmental traditions: that is to say, they did not merely administer the household; they also thought about what they were doing. This self-reflection produced the *Black Book* of Edward IV, which takes the two main divisions of the royal household – the lord chamberlain's department and the lord steward's department – and moralizes them. Both are given a characteristic virtue: the lord chamberlain's department is the 'Household of Magnificence'; the lord steward's department is the 'Household of Providence'. Each virtue is explained and elaborated in a Latin text that derives (again) from Aristotle's *Ethics*; each is also illustrated by a pen-and-ink sketch. Magnificence is shown by a drawing of the king dining in state: a canopy and the royal arms hang over his head, while great covered cups stand on the table. For providence, on the other hand, there is a picture of the officers of the counting house in session. These men, who were the key administrators of the household below stairs, appear with all the essential tools of bureaucracy: books, rolls, pen and ink, and counters and coins. Over their heads are scrolls with the names of the cardinal qualities of their profession: 'reason', 'circumspection', 'discretion', 'intelligence', and so on.

So to the quality of magnificence has been added another, coequal virtue: providence. Normally we would think of the two as contrasting if not contradictory. And indeed a certain tension between them does appear in both the *Black Book* and its Aristotelian source. Providence (Aristotle's *phronesis* or prudence) rests on a perpetual calculation and reasonableness; magnificence, on the other hand, requires a willing suspension of calculation. As Aristotle insists, the magnificent man

> will spend gladly and generously, for there is something petty about exact book-keeping; he will be more deeply interested in embodying his conception in its most beautiful and appropriate form than to ask himself how much it will cost and the cheapest rate at which it can be done.[59]

But this conflict is more apparent than real. If we look more carefully at the *Black Book* we see that the two qualities (like the two departments of the royal household that they represent) are interdependent. It was the task of providence to amass the resources to sustain magnificence; at the same time, magnificence itself was penetrated by calculation: by a careful reckoning of what could be afforded on the one hand, and by a subtle assessment of the ends to which lavishness was directed on the other.

Nor, in fact, was this combination of ideals impossible to realize. Edward IV – the commissioner of the *Black Book* – in his later years at any rate managed a successful linkage of economy with magnificence. The supreme embodiment of prudential ostentation, however, was not Edward but his son-in-law, Henry VII. Simultaneously, he made Burgundians wonder at the splendour of his court and Venetians marvel at the endless hours he devoted to book-keeping.

Of course the *Black Book* circulated only within the royal household. But its general theme of the relationship between magnificence and providence was almost a literary commonplace. At the very beginning of our period there stands the 'refrete' (i.e. debate)

of *Winner and Waster* of 1352, and at the end John Skelton's interlude (or verse play) *Magnificence* of 1516. The earlier poem opens
with the opposing armies of Wynnere (i.e. providence) and Wastour
(i.e. lavishness or liberty) drawn up ready for battle. However, King
Edward III (who certainly stands for magnificence) intervenes and
commands the two to submit their dispute to his arbitration. Each
presents his case. The last part of the king's final judgement is lost,
but enough survives to suggest a resolution that would follow the
position taken for granted in the *Black Book*. The king would have
said (we can guess) that magnificence needs both Wynnere and
Wastour: it is characterized essentially by lavishness, but lavishness
in turn must be disciplined and regulated by providence so that
expenditure does not exceed income. In short, lavishness is the end,
providence the indispensable means. With Skelton there is no need
to guess. His play (in which, as in *Winner and Waster*, the characters
are personalized qualities) begins with Magnificence enjoying regal
state. This he is able to do because Measure (i.e. providence) is his
prime minister or 'chief ruler'.[60] The action then shows how
Magnificence's fortunes collapse after he has been persuaded to
drive Measure from office and give Liberty – the latter's rival – his
head. At last, humiliated by poverty and deprivation, Magnificence
learns his lesson. He is restored to his state and again takes Measure
as his chief councillor. This done, Redress and Sad Circumspection
lecture the chastened prince on the proper relationship between
Liberty and Measure:

REDRESS.
For of nobleness the chief point is to be liberal,
So that your largesse be not too prodigal.
SAD CIRC.
   Liberty to a lord belongeth of right,
   But wilful waywardness must walk out of the way;
Measure of your lusts must have the oversight,
   And not all the niggard or the chinchard to play;
   Let never niggardship your nobleness affray;
In your rewardes use such moderation
That nothing be given without consideration.[61]

The household thus bred – and professional littérateurs rein-
forced – an all-pervading attitude that combined profuseness with
shrewdness. This attitude in turn formed the taste of the chief group

of consumers of works of art: the heads of great households and their upper servants. One of the clearest examples of the spirit in operation is George Cavendish's *Life and Death of Cardinal Wolsey*. The *Life* was written in 1556–8 and is usually thought of as a biography. It is so, however, only in a very particular sense. Essentially, the book is a household-eye-view of Wolsey. Cavendish had been Wolsey's gentleman usher, and he both paints and judges Wolsey as the master of a great household:

> Now have I showed you the order of his house, and what officers and servants he had . . . attending daily upon him. . . . And whensoever we shall see any more such subjects within this realm that shall maintain any such estate and household, I am content he be advanced above him in honour and estimation.[62]

It is this precisely stated standpoint that makes Cavendish's comments so valuable. Most revealing of all are his attempts to convey the unbelievable wealth of the cardinal. He rarely (as a twentieth-century writer would be tempted to do) resorts to a wash of high-sounding adjectives; instead he measures and quantifies, producing as it were an inventory of splendour:

> Then came in a new banquet before the King's majesty . . . wherein I suppose was served two hundred dishes. . . . My Lord Cardinal rode out of Calais with such a number of black velvet coats as hath not been seen with an ambassador . . . many great and massy chains of gold were worn there. . . . Thus passed he forth with three gentlemen in a rank, which occupied the length of three quarters of a mile or more.[63]

Cavendish is a particularly sustained example of this mode of judgement, but he is unusual only in that. Sir Anthony Browne, as a gentleman of the privy chamber, held an analogous if rather superior position in the royal household to Cavendish's in Wolsey's. In 1527 he was sent as ambassador to the court of François I. While he was there he took part in a masque. This he found singularly un-impressive, as the following (unfortunately mutilated) report to Henry VIII makes clear:

There was done no notable . . . nor no great excess in charges; we can assure yo[ur Grace it is] our opinion that the King spent not in this feast . . . one hundred crowns above his ordinary, for as for [the] masking habits, they were but coarse . . . except it were those of the Cardinal of Lorra[ine and] his brethren, the best was but white satin.[64]

So Browne also employs Cavendish's touchstone of quantity and cost, but this time it is used to condemn for deficiency rather than to praise for excess. And his standard of value is all the more important as Browne was one of the outstanding early sixteenth-century patrons: his buildings at Battle and Cowdray were on the largest scale, while his painted and gilded alabaster tomb in Battle Church is an exceptionally lavish example of French Renaissance taste.

Much of this is characteristic of all our period. Malory measures Guenevere's love for Lancelot by the touchingly direct 'It hath cost my lady the Queen twenty thousand pounds the seeking of you.'[65] The magnificence of Richard II's household, reflected even in his cookery book; the praise given by Chandos Herald to Richard's father the Black Prince, that he 'knew the doctrine of largesse';[66] and the splendour in *Gawain and the Green Knight* of the households of both the king and a remote provincial knight like Sir Bercilak de Haut Desert: these need no amplification.

Where the customer, be it Richard II or Sir Anthony Browne, led, the theorist and practitioner followed. In the visual arts we see only the results – in particular, the relentlessly sumptuous ornamentation of early Tudor architecture. But in literature the whole process – from abstraction to realization – is visible.

Medieval literary theory was essentially rhetorical theory. This traced its roots to the orators of antiquity (and to Cicero in particular), but it had been given its characteristic shape by the rhetoricians of the twelfth century. Their advice on style was set out under two contrasting headings: 'abbreviation' and 'amplification'. But in fact abbreviation had only a formal interest for them; amplification was their true goal, and to this was all their ingenious armoury of language devoted. Moreover, for once practitioners followed the theorists. Medieval verse especially valued not succinctness and precision but rather elaboration and elegant variation. Example was piled on example, adjective on high-sounding adjective, until the ostensible subject came near to disappearing under the rich ivy-growth of ornamentation. Probably the outstanding example of this tendency is John Lydgate, the fifteenth-century poet-monk who wrote some 145,000 lines (twice as much as Shakespeare, three times as much as Chaucer). For him, prolixity was a felicity of style, deliberately to be cultivated:

> For a story which is nat pleynli told,
> But constreynyd undir woordes fewe
> For lak of trouthe, wher thei be newe or old,
> Men bi report kan nat the mater shewe;
> These ookis grete be nat doun ihewe
> First at a stroke, but bi long processe;
> Nor longe stories a woord may nat expresse.[67]

> *pleynli*] fully   *ookis*] oaks   *doun ihewe*] cut down

In addition, his vocabulary has a self-conscious latinate floweriness that proved too much even for some of the Tudors. Skelton sensed this, and neatly contrasted Chaucer, whose 'termes were not dark / But pleasant, easy, and plain', with Lydgate, with whom 'some men find a faute / And say he writeth too haut'.[68]

It is, of course, dangerous to identify too simply stylistic and socio-moral qualities, but here there does seem to be a close connection. The fondness for amplification corresponds precisely to the lavishness that was the hallmark of magnificence or nobility. Moreover, as adjectives and figures of speech come cheap in comparison with gold plate (or even with well-carved stone), considerations of prudence put far less of a brake on the tendency to extravagance in literature than they did in most other areas of artistic activity. Prudence, in fact, expressed itself not so much in the style of late medieval literature as in its content. It is this that accounts for two of the outstanding features of fifteenth-century writing: its heavy moralizing and its didacticism. Moral examples abound, as do 'how to do it' books: on cooking, carving, good manners and politics – to name but a few.

In literary terms, therefore, the essential problem with household culture was its onesidedness. To hazard an enormous (though useful) generalization, some element of tension seems to be essential to high artistic achievement: be it between inner and outer, or simplicity and elaboration, or individual expression and publicly acknowledged rules. The late medieval household, on the other hand, knew little of these uncertainties: in an age of political pageantry, display and reality merged into each other with disconcerting ease; similarly (as we have seen at length) the eternal debate between decoration and plainness was nicely subverted by the *Black Book*'s reconciliation of magnificence and providence. At a more fundamental level still, the problem lay in the near-absence of alternative social institutions. English towns were relatively weak, while by the fifteenth century the English church had become very largely absorbed in the surrounding secular culture. In the original areas of the Renaissance – Italy and Flanders – tension was reintroduced mainly through the towns; in England, however, the change came from the mutations of the household itself.

*   *   *

Late medieval England, therefore, revolved around the household – either in the simple sense of family, or in the extended sense of family together with servants. Nor was there any fundamental change in this pattern in our period; indeed, the household domination of English society stretches far beyond the years 1350–1550 in both directions: back to the Anglo-Saxons, and forward to the industrial revolution. But the late Middle Ages did see important changes of emphasis within the overall continuity. These innovations were twofold: the first group consisted of changes in the relationship between the wealthier and the poorer households; the second, of changes in the relationships between the wealthier households themselves. The first (economic change) had relatively little direct impact on literature; whereas the second (political change) had far-reaching consequences. These we shall now discuss.

The household and politics

The structure of politics The history of late medieval politics depends essentially on the interaction between the structure of politics on the one hand, and the actual personality of the various sovereigns on the other. The latter is well enough known, but the former is deceptive. English political structure consisted of two elements, which can be called the formal and the informal. The formal is the set of institutions and conventions that make up the substance of constitutional history. There was a hereditary monarchy, equipped with far-reaching special powers (the prerogative) to enable it to conduct the everyday government of the country. But though very strong, the monarchy was not absolute. It could neither tax its subjects nor change the law without consent. And that consent could be given only by parliament. The law was enforced by a judiciary chosen very much as it is today – from the leading practising lawyers. In addition, there was a small, though fairly efficient, central civil service. This consisted of the exchequer, which controlled finance; and a complex secretariat, which was made up of the offices of the keepers of the three seals: the lord chancellor, the lord privy seal and the secretary. There was, however, no local bureaucracy and no standing army. Instead, the localities were administered by royal commissioners. These were groups of amateur, largely unpaid gentlemen, to whom the king assigned particular tasks. The most important were the commissioners of the peace (usually known as the justices of the peace) who handled the maintenance of law and order as well as the enforcement of an increasing amount of social legislation. In addition, there were special commissions (with frequently overlapping personnel) to assess and collect taxes, maintain waterways, and so on. The military needs of the country were dealt with similarly. In an emergency – invasion, rebellion or foreign war – the king sent out commissions of array to selected peers and gentlemen who were directed to raise such men as they could from their own and their dependants' resources. Almost invariably, the commissioners (of whatever sort) were drawn from the area to which the commission was directed.

Here, then, is a paradox. In comparison with most of continental Europe, late medieval England was an unusually unified country, and its monarchy was unusually strong. Its boundaries were roughly the same as the England of today, and within them there was (more or less) one language, one system of secular law, and a remarkable absence of internal customs barriers. On the other hand, the king of England had nothing to compare with the increasingly elaborate local bureaucracies that his brother kings of France and Aragon-Castile were establishing from the mid-fifteenth century onwards. In part, such bureaucracies were unnecessary in the English situation; in part, their tasks were dealt with in a different way – by the informal machinery of government. And it is to this that we must now turn.

From what has been said, it is clear that the formal machine of government had a dangerous and too often ignored weakness: there was little that bound together the central, professionalized administration around the king and the amateur, fragmented government of the localities. It was here that the informal structure of government came into its own. It centred round one institution: the household. It was the royal household that kept the king in touch with the localities; it was the household of the local gentleman that gave substance to the formal powers conferred on him by royal commission. The way in which the latter worked is straightforward. The gentleman's household servants provided him with the physical force to arrest a suspect or overawe a riot; while his private legal counsel and household administrators would help him cope with the paperwork of his job. The functioning of the royal household was more complicated. It depended on two things. As the court, the royal household was the fountain-head of patronage and favour. It was the place to which everyone who wanted anything of significance had to go for part of the time at least. In one sense, therefore, it acted centripetally, pulling men to the centre. But it also acted centrifugally, sending its own personnel to the localities. This was because, with a small number of exceptions, the leading servants of the household-above-stairs were not full-time. They spent only a part of the year at court; the rest of the time, they lived on their own estates, like any other gentleman. But of course their double life turned them into natural intermediaries: their neighbours used them to press suits at court; the king tapped them for information about local events. Indeed, the *Black Book* actually recommended that the esquires of the household should 'be of sundry shires, by whom it may be known the disposition of the countries [i.e. counties]'.[69]

But the role of the household went further still. The household was not merely the core of the informal system of government; it was also the foundation of the formal administration. All the departments of state – from the exchequer or chancery down – had originally been part of the royal household, or (more precisely) of the upper household or chamber. Moreover, even after the establishment of these departments of state, the king still conducted much administration himself. And – like any other householder – he turned to the expert servants of his household to help him. The household thus frequently found itself duplicating the work of the

financial or secretarial departments and even on occasion substituting itself for them entirely. Always, in fact, it was a reservoir of
administrative initiative and reform. The case is seen at its most
extreme in the army: the army of England was essentially the royal
household on a war footing, with the accounts department of the
household-below-stairs acting as the commissariat.

The household and politics: bastard feudalism   So both the formal
and informal systems of government rested on the public, political
activity of the private institution of the household. This public
activity was nothing peculiar to the late Middle Ages; indeed, it was
a dominant characteristic of English administration until the
creation of bureaucratized local government in the nineteenth
century. Nevertheless, between about 1350 and 1550 the operations
of the household took on a highly specific form known (con-
veniently if misleadingly) as bastard feudalism. Bastard feudalism is
characterized by two closely linked elements: the badge and the
retainer.

Badges were a branch of heraldry. They were thus used by the
greater members of the ruling class, which was by definition the
armigerous class. But the badge was something of a heraldic
curiosity. Unlike coat armour or the crest, which were borne
exclusively by their possessor, the badge was used as freely by the
lord's dependants as by the lord himself. In other words, it was a
form of labelling by which any object, animate or inanimate, could
be marked out as the lord's own. Of necessity, therefore, badges had
to be simple emblems – easy to recognize, easy to remember, easy
to reproduce. These requirements had one important consequence.
They limited, rather sharply, the number of symbols that were
suitable for use as badges. A few familiar objects – some natural,
like animals, birds or flowers; some man-made, like a lock or
manacle – were used time and time again. This meant that there
was considerable and often confusing similarity between the badges
of different families: for example, several houses bore some form of
knot as their device; while the outcome of one of the decisive battles
of the Wars of the Roses depended on a confusion between the
badge of York (the sun in splendour) and the badge of De Vere (the
star or, more properly, the mullet). The reasons for the adoption of a
particular badge were diverse. Some seem to have been chosen
arbitrarily; some were taken from the charges of the bearer's coat

armour; some – like Henry VII's badge of a hawthorn bush and crown – commemorated a specific incident; and some were rebuses or visual puns. To this latter category belonged the bray or hemp press of Sir Reginald Bray and the boar (in Latin *verres*) of the De Veres.

This formal description contains one key point. Whereas most heraldic symbols represented an individual and were peculiar to him, the badge represented a relationship between individuals: between a superior and his subordinates. Now late medieval society was composed precisely of such relationships; it was a network of interwoven hierarchies of patrons and clients, masters and men. From this fundamental relationship derived most others: social, political, artistic. Consequently the badge – as the prime symbol of the dependence of man on man – was able to represent the whole range of derived relationships too. Already in 1388 Thomas Usk could talk of the meekness characteristic of a lover as the 'cognizance of livery' derived to him by Love as one of her retinue.[70] The badge had become, and was to remain, the dominant expression of the years 1350–1550.

But to begin at the beginning. Everything depended on the badge as a symbol of clientage. The personal following of a great man – or, what comes to the same thing, the wearers of his badge – centred firmly on his household. All the servants of the household were sworn to their master's service, and all wore his livery, of which the principal feature was the badge. The only real variation between the different categories of servants was the way in which the badge was worn. The lesser men would wear it on their caps, on their sleeves or on their breasts. Sometimes it would be pinned on; sometimes embroidered. Knights, in contrast, wore their master's badges hung at their necks on the livery chains that John of Gaunt was among the first to introduce into England. But, wherever it was worn, the badge was the distinguishing mark of the household. Indeed, badge and household were so closely associated that in *Henry VI Part 2* Shakespeare writes of a 'household badge' rather than a 'lord's badge'.

In certain circumstances, however, the household could undergo an adventitious expansion. Persons with only the loosest ties of service or none at all could be sworn as the lord's men and given his badge. This was usually done with some formality, by means of a document known as an indenture of retainer. Indenture in this sense was a contract between the lord and another man (who was ordinarily a gentleman) whereby the latter agreed to serve the former in peace and war along with his own household following. On the lord's request the retainer and his servants would turn out 'defensibly arrayed', with horse, armour and weapons; in return the lord offered his 'maintenance'. Maintenance could mean one of two things: either that the lord would lend protection and good offices; or (more perniciously and probably more usually) that he would pervert the course of law and justice in the retainer's interests.

These retainers, together with the lord's household servants proper (or at least such as were fit to bear arms), formed the bastard feudal band. Some of these – like the followings of Lord Hastings or the Duke of Buckingham in the mid-fifteenth century – were both large and well organized. Buckingham's band, for example, had its own headquarters separate from the duke's ordinary residence; there was also a system of couriers to put non-resident retainers on the alert.

This expanded and militarized household was used to advance the lord's interests by fair means and foul. At meetings of the council or parliament, the peers would compete with each other in the size and lavish equipment of their followings. In part this was mere self-display, but the retainers also served the practical purpose of protecting their master and intimidating his opponents. However, it was probably at local level that retainers were most important. With them the lord could turn his regional primacy into a cruel tyranny: he could pack juries, manipulate the processes of county adminis-tration, or even resort to outright violence.

In terms of behaviour there was probably little to choose between the household servant proper and the retainer, but the two classes were sharply distinguished by contemporary legislation. The former were of unquestioned legitimacy, while the latter from the Ordinance of 1390 were subject (on paper at least) to increasingly stringent regulation and were banned altogether in 1504. The distinction was shrewd. The thing that made bastard feudal bands so dangerous was their size. Now, big though fifteenth-century households were, not even the wealthiest peer could have afforded to pay and feed his whole bastard feudal band as ordinary members of his household. The attractiveness – and therefore the danger – of the indentured retainer was his relative cheapness to his lord. Nothing but his expenses for his periods of actual service had to be paid; otherwise, as we have seen, his recompense was not cash but protection. Thus the law intervened only where it was needed: to limit the number of indentured retainers; control on the size of the household could be safely left to economics. However, given the weakness of fifteenth-century law enforcement, the appropriateness of the legislation was largely academic; not till the Tudors did it start to matter.

The household, then, was the core of bastard feudalism, but its essential flavour was given by the armed bands that were largely made up of indentured retainers. These bands – and their inevitable concomitant of badge giving – grew rapidly in the later fourteenth century. Three things contributed largely to this development: the first was the exclusion of the levying of private war from the Treasons Act of 1352; the second was the renewal of large-scale foreign war under Edward III; while the third was the collapse of firm royal control during that king's senility and the ensuing minority of his grandson Richard II. The result was that by 1390 badge wearing had become a major feature of society. In that year (as we have seen) there were the first attempts to regulate it by law; at the same time, contemporary writers were showing an ever-increasing interest in it. This interest took two forms: on the one hand, there was a vigorous condemnation of the excesses of armed retainers; on the other, badges were used as the principal source of imagery in political verse. When, for example, the author of *Mum and the Sothsegger* wished to show his disapproval of Richard II's savage revenge on the lords appellant in 1397, his ostensible theme was borrowed from Pliny. The nature of the hart, he insists, was

> . . . coltis not to greve,
> Ne to hurle with haras ne hors well ytamed,
> Ne to stryve with swan though it sholle werre,
> Ne to bayten on the bere ne bynde him nother.[71]

The particular reference of this apparently innocent discourse on natural history is given by the badges of the principal actors in the drama of 1397. The hart was Richard himself; while the hart's three victims – the horse, the swan and the bear – were the king's enemies, the earls of Arundel, Gloucester and Warwick.

The new phenomenon of badge wearing – new at least in extent and systematization – presented the monarchy with a major challenge. The smooth running of the kingdom depended largely on the king's handling of the magnates. Retaining, however, gave the peers greatly increased power, which made them generally less amenable to royal control. It was, for example, difficult to take a firm line with an Earl of Gloucester who could muster a retinue of three bannerets, twenty knights, seventy-seven esquires, 200 horse archers and 200 foot archers. But, of course, for the king's subjects this political problem mattered less than the social results of bastard feudalism: the occasional violence of the retainer and the frequent perversion of the legal process by the lord. This is the England of the Pastons and their long war to keep Caister Castle against the aggrandizement of the Duke of Suffolk. It may contribute also to Malory's picture of England before Arthur's crowning 'in great jeopardy . . . for every lord that was mighty of men made him strong, and many weened to have been king',[72] and therefore to Malory's whole feeling for Arthur and his Round Table as the return of chivalric order to an anarchic country.

Described in these terms, bastard feudalism seems to merit most of the contumely that has been heaped upon it. But there is another side to the picture. Even its military aspect had a clear utility. The king had no other forces to call on for foreign war; nor was there anything else to crush domestic rebellion. Bastard feudalism, then, was ambivalent, and it was in the ambivalence that the problem lay: retainers and maintenance were often a nuisance, but the household structures of which they were a part were essential to the running of the kingdom. In other words, effective royal control of late medieval England depended not on the rooting out of bastard feudalism but on its proper management. This could be achieved in different ways. One can be called presidential. Edward III and Henry V made little attempt to limit even the military aspect of retaining. Nor did they build up great followings of their own. Instead, from the bastard feudal bands of the great lords they forged coalition armies that they led to repeated victories against the French. In other words, their power was that of a *primus inter pares*, whose primacy, moreover, was guaranteed only by success in battle. But this method of management was relatively rare. It needed a king who had both high military talent and an unfair share of good luck. More usual – if less glorious – was the approach adopted by Richard II in the second half of his reign.

Richard (as we have seen already) had to cope with the problem of retaining in a particularly acute form. Since he was no great soldier, the tactics of Edward III were unavailable to him. Instead he was faced with a more limited choice. Either he could seek to limit retaining, or he could exploit it for his own benefit. Richard in fact tried both policies in turn: the first briefly and insincerely, the second with sustained and deliberate effort.

The first step in this second policy of exploitation was taken with his loudly proclaimed adoption of the badge of the white hart at the Smithfield tournament of October 1390. Thereafter he used it in two principal ways. He built up a large band of retainers, who bore 'harts on high on their breasts';[73] he also (as we saw in Chapter 4) made the emblem a conspicuous feature of the works of art he commissioned: the Wilton Diptych, Westminster Hall, the king's tomb, and so on. So used, the badge had a clear role as propaganda. In the matter of retaining Richard was only imitating his greater nobles, but his employment of the badge in the fine arts seems to have been more or less original. This sustained and general use of the white hart was the key to Richard's royal policy: he was determined to be master, not so much because he was king, but rather because he had made himself the biggest bastard feudal lord of all. This policy eventually failed, but the important thing is the precedent it set. Richard's combination of a vigorous exploitation of the social structures of bastard feudalism with an equally vigorous propaganda campaign based on his bastard feudal badge provided the model that most major aspirants to political power sought to follow over the next 150 years.

After the usurpation of 1399 the initative both in politics and in the arts passed from the king to the great lords. Henry IV had inherited the great Lancastrian bastard feudal following from his father, John of Gaunt, but he was too poor to build much; Henry V was too busy fighting; Henry VI was a minor till 1437 and thereafter was more interested in the salvation of his soul than in the management of his kingdom. (His major building venture – the east end of King's College Chapel, Cambridge – is strikingly free from bastard feudal ornament.) The result was that the great bastard feudal monuments of the first half of the fifteenth century were erected not by the crown but by the leaders of the two factions that competed for power under the feeble Henry VI. The Duke of Suffolk built the great arcaded south aisle of the chancel of Wingfield Church, Suffolk, while the Duke of York began the construction of the enormous collegiate church of Fotheringhay in Northamptonshire.

Both buildings were situated in the heart of the family lands, and both were dominated by their respective family badges: the ape-clog, and the falcon and fetterlock.

With the successful usurpation of Edward IV there was at last a king who was capable of taking up the inheritance of Richard II. But he did so only gradually and tentatively. Initially his finances were weak and his personal following was minute. These two problems came near to solution only by 1475. Consequently his bastard feudal policy remained a sketch. This is particularly true of its artistic side: the rebuilding of St George's, Windsor – dominated by Edward IV's badge of the sunburst – had got no further than the chancel at his death. But a similar incompleteness (admittedly fully justified by circumstances) also marred his politics. After his exile and restoration to the throne in 1469–71 Edward devoted much effort to building up a great bastard feudal following. This centred (like Richard II's) on the knights of the body in the royal household, but (unlike Richard's) it was essentially based in the Home Counties. So far as it went it was successful. Throughout the South-East (even in traditionally rebellious Kent) the heads of the leading county families – the Brownes, the Guildfords, the Hautes, the Norrises – all threw in their lot with Edward. However, this well-tried policy was applied only to the area round London. In remoter districts Edward took greater risks. His actions were still part of a bastard feudal policy, but this time royal control was exercised at one remove. The king deliberately consolidated the power of certain great peers – who were either members of the royal family or officers of the royal household – and made them regional Gauleiters. These magnates commanded followings comparable to the king's own. While Edward was alive, he could hold the balance, but after his death the very political structure he had created made the factional strife of 1483–5 more or less inevitable.

The great beneficiary of the strife was Henry VII. Richard III had carried out a sweeping simplification of the political map of England. One by one the great regional peers established by Edward IV were executed or exiled, till only Stanley enjoyed a precarious survival. At the same time Richard's own excesses drove the power-ful gentry retinue that Edward had built up into Henry's hands. The battle of Bosworth gave the new pattern its final shape. Richard was defeated and killed, while the only great magnate family that he had endowed – the Howards – were put at the new king's mercy.

Henry thus came to the throne with three enormous advantages:
first, his obvious rivals – the great regional magnates – had been
virtually eliminated; second, the crown lands had been vastly
increased by Richard's attainder of his opponents; and third, a
ready-made bastard feudal following (which had taken a decade to
assemble) had fallen into his hands. Nor, unlike most usurpers, was
he forced to dissipate these advantages. What had damned his
predecessors had been the support of a single great magnate: with
Henry IV it was Northumberland; with Edward IV, Warwick; with
Richard III, Buckingham. In each case, the magnate (having put
another man on the throne) was insatiable for reward; nothing could
satisify him, and the whole aspect of politics was distorted until the
boil was lanced by his unsuccessful rebellion. But Henry VII had
received the wholehearted support of only one of the greater
peerage, the Earl of Oxford, and he had been a penniless exile on
the eve of Bosworth. For him honours and the restoration of his
estates were reward enough: there was no need to pillage the royal
lands for his benefit as well.

Building on these secure foundations, Henry VII and his son
Henry VIII took Richard II's abortive bastard feudal policy to full
maturity. Having increased the number of their gentlemen retainers
to levels undreamed of by Richard II or Edward IV, they jealously
guarded their supremacy against noble encroachment. Peers with
overlarge followings were ruthlessly humiliated, especially by Henry
VII, while Henry VIII showed himself to be particularly sensitive to
the poaching of his followers. Sir William Bulmer, a king's knight,
had transferred his service to the Duke of Buckingham. He was
unwise enough to reappear at court, where his presence provoked
one of the famous Tudor rages. As the chronicler Hall reports it,
Bulmer knelt trembling while the king thundered

> that he would none of his servants should hang on another
> man's sleeve, and that he was as well able to maintain him
> as the duke of Buckingham, and that what might be
> thought by his departing, and what might be supposed by
> the duke's retaining, he would not then declare.[74]

But the bluster must not blind us to the importance of Henry's
words. These – as his use of such key terms as 'maintain' and
'retain' shows – amounted to a clear recognition that his power as
king rested in large measure on his power as bastard feudal lord.

A challenge to the latter had to be resisted as a threat to the former.

The propaganda role of the royal badges was pursued with a similar singlemindedness. Indeed, the early Tudor court and the palaces built or rebuilt to house it were monomaniac in their decoration. The ceilings, hangings and upholstery, the table furnishings and bookbindings, the window glass and the very royal robes were covered in endlessly repeated badges: to name only the most important, the Tudor rose, the Beaufort portcullis, and the red rose of Lancaster, together with emblems of Henry VIII's first wife, Katharine of Aragon – the arrows of Aragon, the castle of Castile and the pomegranate of Granada. This was, of course, a recognizable extension (albeit taken to almost absurd lengths) of Richard II's use of the white hart. But there was also a more novel development. As we have seen, knightly retainers wore their master's livery in the form of great gold collars or chains. These collars formed an ordinary part of the dress of their wearers; accordingly from the early fifteenth century they appear on tomb brasses and effigies. There is, however, no evidence that retainers used their masters' badges more generally. This changed under the Tudors. From 1485 it became increasingly fashionable for the king's servants (who formed an ever-growing proportion of the leading gentry families) to decorate their houses and chantry chapels with a mixture of their own badges and the ruling dynasty's. Fine examples of these mixed badges are to be found in the carving of Lavenham Church (which has already been described) and in the painted parlour ceiling of the Vernon mansion of Haddon Hall in Derbyshire. But sometimes loyalty went further: the retainer's own badges were suppressed and the royal emblems appeared alone. The outstanding surviving house of this type is Ightham Mote in Kent. Its main structure is the work of the fourteenth- and fifteenth-century owners of the house. However, in 1521 Sir Richard Clement, a former courtier, bought the manor and began an ambitious programme of rebuilding. He reglazed the windows of the hall, put a handsome gabled facade on the private apartments, and constructed an entirely new chapel. In all these various works the decorative scheme is the same. The hall windows have five stained-glass lights: in the centre are the royal arms, with to the left the pomegranate of Spain and the Tudor rose, and to the right the rose of Lancaster and the Beaufort portcullis; the bargeboards of the gabled front are carved with roses and pomegranates;

while the wooden barrel-vault of the chapel is painted with an endless succession of roses, pomegranates and portcullises, together with two further Spanish emblems: the castle of Castile and the arrows of Aragon. In short, glazing, woodcarving and painting meet in unison: all are dominated by the badges of Henry VIII and Katharine of Aragon. Clement had turned his house into a hymn of gratitude to the dynasty that had made him.

So far, early Tudor bastard feudal policy appears as a variant – albeit an inventive one – of Richard II's. But in one important respect its ancestry is different. Richard II had combined his innovative attitude towards the informal machinery of government with a remarkably conservative approach to the formal administration of the kingdom. It was left to Edward IV to bastard-feudalize the inner workings of government; and where he and his brother led, after some hesitation the Tudors followed. The principal area affected was finance. Before the Yorkists the revenues from the royal lands had been small. Edward IV, however, initiated a deliberate (if rather patchy) policy of increasing both the extent of his estates and the income from them. The result of this policy was to make the crown dependent for a significant part of its revenue on the same resource – land – as any member of the upper class. Moreover, the methods Edward employed in pursuit of this policy were the same as those of any great feudal landlord. He took much of the work into his own hands; what was left he delegated to trusted servants of his household. The treasurer of the chamber (who was, in effect, keeper of the king's privy purse) was put in charge of the receipt and disbursement of funds at the centre; while oversight of the collection of revenue in the localities was given to various lesser servants of the chamber who acted as auditors and surveyors of the royal estates. This system was continued by Richard III; Henry VII first rejected it and then within a few years restored and perfected it. For the Yorkist period, quantification – the soul of financial history – is impossible, since the main chamber accounts are missing, but by 1500 some certainty is possible. In that year, virtually the whole revenue of the crown was being handled by the treasurer of the chamber, and of this at least a third came from land. Nor were the advantages of the greatly increased royal estates simply financial. The king, like any other bastard feudal landlord, used his lands to cement his territorial influence. Indeed, Edward IV's activities in this area were seen by the Croyland chronicler (a shrewd and well-informed observer) as a mainstay of the political stability of the last years of the reign:

> as he had taken care to distribute the most trustworthy of his servants throughout all parts of the kingdom, as keepers of castles, manors, forests, and parks, no attempt whatever could be made in any part of the kingdom by any person, however shrewd he might be, but what he was immediately charged with the same thing to his face.[75]

With the early Tudors, therefore, the household or bastard feudal influence on government reached its apogee. Not merely was it a question of politics (especially local politics) or propaganda, but of the very *arcana imperii*. The exchequer, the most ancient and complex part of the bureaucracy, was effectively displaced by the chamber of the royal household and its auxiliaries. This triumph of the household was reflected in a part, and a very important part, of contemporary literature.

Perhaps the best illustration of the trend is Edward Hall's great chronicle, *The Union of the Two Noble and Illustre Families of York and Lancaster*, which was published posthumously in 1548. The chronicle is really a panegyric of Henry VIII. And, just as Cavendish wrote a household-eye-view of Wolsey, so Hall gives a household-eye-view of his hero and king. The origins of Henry's regime are explained in household terms: the political troubles of the fifteenth century appear as a struggle between the household followings of York and Lancaster; Henry VII, by his marriage to Elizabeth of York, unites the two warring factions; consequently his son, Henry VIII, the issue of the united houses, rules as unchallenged king. The events of Henry's own reign are weighed against the same set of values. As each household is embodied in its head for the time being, so the whole narrative of English history centres on the king: when he spends the summer hunting, Hall laconically notes that 'nothing happened worthy to be written of'.[76] Second only to the king himself in the chronicler's eyes came the ordinary entertainments of the royal household – the joust and the masque. These were covered with an elaborate symbolism that allegorized them beyond themselves. The joust became an act of war, while the masque became a political pageant. Hall's language shows a full acceptance of the trans-mutation. When in 1515 Henry introduced a couple of his favourites to the joust, the chronicler's words soar above the petty event:

the King delighting to set forth young gentlemen, called
Nicholas Carew and Francis Bryan, and caused divers other
young men to be on the counter part, and lent to them
horse and harness [i.e. armour] to encourage all youth to
seek deeds of arms.[77]

With this indiscriminate use of language, the distinction between
ritual and reality disappears and the one fuses with the other. But
(even more than in the joust) it is in Hall's descriptions of masques
and pageants that his household bias becomes most clear. The
account of a revel on Shrove Tuesday 1510 is typical: the king with
the Earl of Essex 'came in apparelled after Turkey fashion, in long
robes of baudkin, powdered with gold, hats on their heads of
crimson velvet, with great rolls of gold, girded with two swords,
called scimitars, hanging by great baldrics of gold'; while two of the
ladies had 'their faces, necks, arms and hands covered with fine
pleasance black: some call it Lombardine, which is marvellous thin,
so that the same ladies seemed to be negresses or black Moors'.[78]
Now Cavendish and Sir Anthony Browne had, as we have seen, a
tendency to produce effect by itemizing, but in Hall's chronicle
itemizing becomes a true inventory. And just how true can be
shown, thanks to the survival of the accounts of Richard Gibson,
who organized the royal revels in this period. For the Shrove Tuesday festivities he notes among his purchases: 11 yards of 'Cologne
baudkin' (heavily patterned cloth of gold) for two Turkish robes
worn by the king and Essex; 1½ yards of 'crimson velvet of Genoa'
for their Turkish caps, together with rolls of gold to trim them; and
finally two Turkey knives (Hall's scimitars), which cost 13*s*. 4*d*.
each. Gibson's itemization of the Moorish ladies' costume parallels
Hall's description even more precisely: seven pieces of black
lombardine were bought to cover their 'heads, necks, faces and
arms'.[79] In short, the resemblance between Hall's and Gibson's
descriptions is too close to be accidental. The chronicler must have
used the revels accounts, or some closely related document, as one of
his sources. But we can go further. Apart from More's *History of
Richard III* and (probably) some printed broadsides of speeches from
the scaffold, the revels accounts were Hall's chief written source –
and they were the only one that a modern scholar would call primary
material. Here, then, we have the literary apotheosis of the household: the itemized accounts of the festivities of the royal court

become the backbone of the most important contemporary history of early sixteenth-century England.

The household and politics: household and court But there is another side to the picture. Hall was no backwoodsman – he was educated at Cambridge and the inns of court, and served long as a member of parliament; he did not, however, belong to the inner circle of the court and politics. And there, at the very heart of the household system, developed ideas and ethics that were profoundly opposed to their matrix.

Essentially this was a consequence of the nature of the early Tudor court itself. By origin, of course, the court was no more than the greatest of the great households: the 'house of houses principal of England', as the *Black Book* had called it. But (as so often) this quantitative difference led to a qualitative one too. As we have seen, two things accounted for the pre-eminence of the royal household under the first two Tudors: the first was the disappearance of rival noble households; and the second was the great size of the Tudors' own bastard feudal following. These two factors further led to a remarkable centralization of politics, which had no immediate precedent save for the last years of Richard II's reign. Fifteenth-century politics were struggles between great regional lords, whose power depended on their local strength. Politics under Henry VIII, on the other hand, were court politics: the strength of the participants depended not on their bastard feudal followings but on their place in the royal favour.

This political centralization created a new cultural atmosphere. Fifteenth-century culture was as regionalized as fifteenth-century politics, and like politics it centred on the great noble household. Typical of their time were figures that we have discussed already, such as the poets who clustered round Humphrey, Duke of Gloucester, and the Earl of Warwick's chaplain, John Rous. Rous was, as we have seen, a chaplain in the Beauchamp Chantry at Warwick, and in the early 1480s produced a series of exquisite rolls glorifying the successive holders of the earldom of Warwick – Beauchamp, Neville and Plantagenet. Elements of this survived under the Tudors. For example, the poet Alexander Barclay, who for much of this life was a monk at Ely, had a special relationship with the Duke of Norfolk, the great peer who dominated the surrounding countryside. He dedicated two of his works to the duke: his life of *St George* and his translation of Sallust's *Bellum Jugurthinum* (*c.* 1520). The latter, Barclay tells us, was composed at Norfolk's 'commandment' and was addressed to him as the 'most worthy and convenient' of the 'noblemen of this region'. The author's purpose (the Preface continues) was the general 'pleasure and profit of all the gentlemen of this region, but namely [i.e. especially] of your highness and of the noblemen of your progeny and affinity'.[80] However, Barclay represented what was for the moment a tradition in decline. Just as Barclay's master the Duke of Norfolk knew that he became a political cipher the moment he left court to go and sulk at Framlingham, so too did every other gentleman of ambition. In the country one was nothing, at court one might be everything. To court, therefore, the gentry went. But there the head of a household found himself shorn of his household: his multitude of attendants was cut down to a handful, and even leading courtiers like Sir John Russell and Sir Anthony Browne – both gentlemen of the privy chamber and owners of vast mansions – might find themselves forced to share a bedchamber in the palace. Nor was that all. The court not only stripped the leading members of the political nation of the protective cocoon of their own households; it also brought them – as individuals – face to face with each other in a lively and often viciously competitive society. Behaviour, manners and dress were nicely observed; rumours started and reputations made and lost. The world of the Tudor court, in short, reproduced the crucial features of the Italian city, which historians of the Renaissance now see as the cradle of the great cultural changes of the fourteenth and fifteenth centuries. Like the city, the court was extravagant, individualistic and competitive: an ideal soil for novelty.

In part, this novelty was deliberately introduced by the king and his advisers to suit their own ends. Renaissance motifs – especially in the visual arts – were imported as a matter of fashion and prestige, while the English Reformation began as a mere political reformation: a final stage in the long struggle between crown and papacy for control of the English church. Neither of these changes – important though they were – presented fundamental challenges to household society. What did, however, was the reaction to the Renaissance and Reformation with the inner court circle. This reaction is typified by Sir Thomas Wyatt, who was the outstanding English poet of the first half of the sixteenth century.

Wyatt was born into the Tudor following. His father, Sir Henry, was a lifelong servant of the dynasty: clerk of the jewels to Henry VII, he continued in office under Henry VIII and eventually became treasurer of the chamber and privy councillor. Thomas, his eldest son, may well have gone to Cambridge; certainly, his knowledge of both classical and modern literature was unusually good. With such a background and education the young Thomas inevitably came to politics very early: he was clerk of the jewels and an esquire of the body before he was 20; at 22 he had distinguished himself on embassy in France. Soon after began his involvement with Anne Boleyn: at her coronation in 1533 he was chief ewerer; at her fall in 1536 he came within a hair's breadth of the axe too. Thereafter he was abroad on embassy – in France, Spain, Germany and the Low Countries – almost continuously until his early death in 1541.

Wyatt's life, though dramatic, was in no way unusual. Every major aspect of it could be paralleled in the biographies of a dozen or more of his contemporaries at the court of Henry VIII. Moreover, much of his poetry is equally conventional. It is better constructed than most and more modish in metre, but its substance and purpose remain solidly traditional. In short, it is an elegant but impersonal addition to the great body of verse that catered for the ever-changing yet ever-similar demands of the court year: the great feasts of winter, the lovers' rites of spring and the long hunting season of the summer progress. But there is another and much more original side to Wyatt. In some of his poems the anonymity of the maker is torn aside and a passionate self-awareness bursts through. 'I', 'I', is repeated: insistent, urgent, infinitely individual. It appears most startlingly when Wyatt takes a conventional theme and bends it to his own purpose. One such convention was the 'lament'. This was a poem written in a time of real or imagined trouble and often heightened with a Latin refrain. An unusually neatly turned specimen is William Dunbar's *Lament for the Makers*, which was written in about 1508. The poet, himself sick, sees death sweeping all away, including the greatest of his fellow poets:

> I that in heill wes, and gladnes,
> Am trublit now with gret seiknes,
> And feblit with infermite.
> *Timor mortis conturbat me.*

> The stait of man dois change and vary,
> Now sound, now seik, now blith, now sary,

Now dansand mery, now like to dee,
Timor mortis conturbat me.

He [death] has done petuously devour
The noble Chaucer, of makaris flour,
The Monk of Bury and Gower all thre.
Timor mortis conturbat me.[81]

Timor mortis conturbat me] The fear of death distresses me
sary] sorry

When Wyatt, himself a prisoner in the Tower, witnessed the
execution of his friends of the Boleyn circle in May 1536 he too
turned to the lament. But the tone is quite different from Dunbar's:

These bloody days have broken my heart:
    My lust, my youth did them depart,
    And blind desire of estate.
    Who hastes to climb seeks to revert:
    Of truth, *circa regna tonat*.

The bell tower showed me such sight
    That in my head sticks day and night;
    There did I learn out of a grate,
    For all favour, glory or might,
    That yet *circa regna tonat*.[82]

circa regna tonat] lightning strikes about the throne of kings

The contrast is clear: Dunbar looks outward and sees the universality
of his state; Wyatt looks inward, and sees his only refuge in his own
conscience.

Circa regna tonat is an occasional piece. That is, it is a response to
a particular, identifiable event. As such, it is characteristic of the
best of Wyatt's verse. Here is a clue to his unique quality. Wyatt is a
poet of conflict – above all, of conflicting values. Normally, such
values are held simultaneously, their contradiction suspended. Only
in specific incidents does their irreconcilability become manifest.
And such incidents are the essential triggers to Wyatt's verse.

Most early sixteenth-century Englishmen remained happily free
from Wyatt's anguish. But the conflict he experienced was none the
less real, even though the majority refused to perceive it. Early
sixteenth-century England was in some respects like modern Africa

or India. It was a society undergoing cultural colonization. Everything fashionable was Italian or French (that is to say, secondhand
Italian): dress, building, ornament, painting, ideas, literature, food.
At the same time (again like the modern Third World) there was a
vehement nationalism, a proud consciousness of being English. In
Wyatt's case the intensity of the conflict is suggested by a comparison
between his portrait and his *Second Satire*. The portrait shows the
complete Italianate Englishman, a fine-featured profile in a cameo-
like roundel; in the *Satire*, on the other hand, nationalism (even
parochialism) is rampant. The poet (he says) is not in France to be a
gourmet; in Spain to be a slave; or in Flanders to be a drunkard and a
glutton, but (thank God) 'I am here in Kent and Christendom'.[83]

However – as the splendid combination of 'Kent and Christendom' shows – the parochialism is only superficial. Kent may be a
little place, just as the conscience of man is a little thing; but for
Wyatt both were associated with a set of universal values. And these
values were firmly rooted in Wyatt's humanism. The literary
Renaissance, as it affected Wyatt, had four principal elements. The
first was stylistic. Petrarch and his followers had invented new
metres and new verse forms. These Wyatt was the first to adapt into
English. He worked essentially through the medium of translation,
and translation – at least when it is well done – inevitably
produces a heightened sensitivity about language. The second was
the revival of stoic moral philosophy, with its stress on internal self-
judgement, rather than the praise or blame of others. Wyatt was
soaked in this tradition: he translated Plutarch's *Quiet of Mind* and
recommended Seneca and Epictetus to his son. The third element
formed an intellectual link between the first two. This was the re-
discovery in the early fifteenth century of Cicero's main works on
rhetorical theory. These were concerned essentially with the
emotional effects of language: that is, in practice, with the connection between words and action, between inner and outer.
Finally, there was the revival of the satirical tradition whose greatest
exponents in antiquity had been Horace and Juvenal. As we have
already seen, there was something of a native English equivalent to
this tradition in the works of (above all) Langland, but in the
fifteenth century it seems to have fallen into desuetude. However,
during Wyatt's boyhood Skelton and Barclay had done something
to revive satire's realism and concern with the conflict between real
and ideal.

From this quadruple source – stylistic innovation, stoic philosophy, rhetorical theory and satire – Wyatt forged an intensely felt doctrine of authenticity or, as he called it, honesty. In his second letter to his son he defines it by contrast: honesty is not merely seeming to be honest; it is the quality in action: 'Seek not, I pray thee my son, that honesty which appeareth and is not in deed . . .; if you will seem honest, be honest, or else seem as you are.'[84] This doctrine Wyatt applied with devastating effect to three areas: human relationships, religion and politics. From the first came much of Wyatt's lyric verse, with its stress on men's and women's doubleness: double-dealing and double-talking; from the second came Wyatt's quasi-Protestantism, and his partial admiration for Luther; while the third produced his remarkable *Third Satire*. The general theme of this poem – the degeneracy of the human condition – has already been discussed; here, however, we have to deal with Wyatt's treatment of the courtier as an extreme example of the general decay. In this aspect, the satire gives Wyatt's characteristically sturdy answer to conventional Renaissance political theory.

The theory in its early sixteenth-century form was largely the work of one man, Baldassare Castiglione, whose great work, *The Courtier*, had finally been printed in 1528. Castiglione (like his predecessors) drew heavily on the political thinkers of the ancient world, and on Cicero in particular. Cicero himself had based his teachings firmly on Aristotle. The latter – following the dominant republican tendencies of the Greek city state – saw political activity as the essential attribute of the citizen. But Cicero gave the idea a new twist by the emphasis he placed on rhetoric. In his scheme all the arts and all learning are handmaidens to rhetoric since – in a free society – rhetoric (or persuasion) is the key to politics itself. Revived by the Renaissance, the Ciceronic theory became the foundation of civic humanism. This was an educational programme which, through the proper teaching of rhetoric, sought to equip men to be better citizens of their states. Obviously, in both origins and practice, the programme was fundamentally republican. That had suited very well in the Italian city states of the fourteenth and fifteenth centuries, but in the sixteenth century it was becoming increasingly awkward. Italy itself was more and more dominated by princes and courts, while the Renaissance was also spreading to the great European monarchies beyond the Alps. Castiglione's stroke of genius was to adapt civic humanism to the world of the court. His technique was simple: for the citizen persuading his fellow citizens to virtue, he substituted a favoured courtier leading his prince to a similar goal. The means employed were to be the same also: rhetoric or honest speaking. So on this reading the central passage in *The Courtier* is the following:

> the end of the perfect courtier . . . is, by means of the accomplishments attributed to him by these gentlemen, so to win for himself the mind and favour of the prince he serves that he can and always will tell him the truth about all he needs to know, without fear or risk of displeasing him.[85]

In other words, free speech is the end and justification of the courtier.

At first sight this seems to fit well with Wyatt's obsession with honesty. But his experience of the Tudor court had taught him otherwise. He expressed his disenchantment with Castiglione (whom he had certainly read) in his *Third Satire*. As ever, an actual event was the stimulus of the poem: in this case the tottering political state of Sir Francis Bryan, a leading royal favourite and gentleman of the privy chamber. Bryan had an interestingly complex personality. On the one hand he was a flamboyant rake (affectionately known by Henry VIII as his 'Vicar of Hell'); on the other, he had a European reputation for daring to speak plainly and honestly even to his king. What Wyatt does in the *Satire* is to stand Castiglione on his head. Bryan, he explains, is bad enough in everyway to be a successful courtier save one – he is honest, and that will undo him:

> Nay then farewell, And if You care for shame
>   Content thee then with honest poverty,
>   With free tongue what thee mislikes to blame,
> And for thy truth sometime adversity,
>   And therewithal this gift I shall thee give:
>   In this world now little prosperity,
> And coin to keep as water in a sieve.[86]

So the defining characteristic of Castiglione's ideal courtier is used to predict (correctly) the downfall of the real Tudor politician.

The household: the end of a monopoly

Something of Wyatt's importance is now clear. The point is best made by contrast. In one of its aspects the Renaissance could be used simply to reinforce the existing culture. Such is self-evidently the case with what can be called the vulgar Renaissance. In architecture this led simply to the addition of a new and half-understood category of ornament (called the 'Antique' or 'Antick') to the already bulky repertory of Tudor Perpendicular decoration; similarly in literature Ciceronian rhetoric could serve merely to augment an already over-rich descriptive vocabulary. In both cases the result was the same: the structure remained constant, only the surface changed. This is even true of Castiglione, for all his learning and sophistication. As far as content is concerned (as we have seen) he put humanist philosophy unreservedly at the service of monarchy. In terms of form his achievement is more conservative still. *The Courtier* is couched as a series of evening conversations in the palace at Urbino. These soirées are really household pastimes or court games: in other words, the great speechmakers of the *Courtier* – Ottaviano Fregoso or Pietro Bembo – are the collateral descendants of Edward IV's esquires of the household, who had been required (it may be remembered) to tell stories to amuse the court 'till the time require of departing' to bed. Castiglione, in fact, has turned political theory into salon entertainment. Like his successors – the fashionable *philosophes* of the eighteenth century – he could not altogether suppress the pungency of his material, but he did his best. But Wyatt, with his instinctive radicalism, would have none of this. His insistence on honesty, on a correspondence between words and action, cuts the ground from under Castiglione's smooth reconciliation of republican theory and monarchical setting.

   In Wyatt, however, the criticism of court politics never turns into criticism of the king himself – even though the drift is clear enough. Some later writers were more explicit. Bluntest of all was John Ponet, a Protestant bishop who fled to the continent when Mary came to the throne. In 1556 he wrote an astonishing exposé of Tudor politics called *A Short Treatise of Politic Power*. Its epigraph, taken from Psalm 118, speaks for itself: 'It is better to trust in the Lord, than to trust in princes.' Under Elizabeth I only a few Catholic exiles went as far as Ponet. But Castiglione's reconciliation of humanist political theory and the court was not completely restored.

Instead, a significant number of the more intelligent and sensitive of the ruling class (Fulke Greville and Sir Walter Ralegh, for example) found themselves sharing Wyatt's awareness of their potential contradiction. However, this awareness, like Wyatt's own, was highly sensitive to immediate political circumstances. So a skilful sovereign like Elizabeth could prevent the contradiction from emerging too clearly; but with clumsy monarchs like James I and Charles I the tension became obvious.

Though Wyatt was incomparably the most important poet at Henry VIII's court, he was not alone. Indeed, he was surrounded by something of a circle of court poets. Of its remaining members the Earl of Surrey is the best known, and George Blage probably the most interesting – not poetically but politically. He (by his membership of both) links the Wyatt circle – the most advanced proponents of the literary Renaissance in England – with the Denny circle, who were the vanguard of English Protestantism. The latter were even closer to the centre of things than Wyatt himself; indeed, they formed the very heart of the Tudor court. Their leader, Sir Anthony Denny, was chief gentleman of the privy chamber and all the rest of the faction were his subordinate officers there. Some of them – like Blage himself – came very near to being burned for heresy, but their place in the king's favour saved them from the flames. As Henry lay dying, in December–January 1546–7, this group entered into alliance with Edward Seymour, Prince Edward's uncle (who was later Duke of Somerset). In return for Seymour's promise of a further Protestant Reformation, the privy chamber doctored the king's will to make sure that the Council of Regency should be wax in his hands. The plot was successful. Somerset became Protector, and gave Cranmer and the Protestant bishops their head. Doctrinal reform followed, and Protestantism became so widespread that only the harshest and most sustained persecution could have rooted it out. Thus the crown lost control – especially at the local level – of the process of Reformation which it had itself begun. And the impetus for the destruction of Henry VIII's careful Erastianism had come, not from pressure from below, but from the court coup of 1546–7.

So the court of Henry VIII had nursed the ideas that were to challenge the royal supremacy that the court itself was designed to maintain. At the same time the material bases – political and economic – of the dominance of the royal household were undermined as well. Under Henry VII the great Tudor bastard feudal following had been remarkably united; but under Henry VIII factions reappeared. These were not localized factions, however, but divisions within the court itself. With the mounting religious disagreement that followed the Reformation, the lines of division became clear-cut. The result was that under the religiously partisan regimes of Edward VI and Mary there appeared for the first time since the fifteenth century groups of 'ins' at court and 'outs' in the country (or even abroad). The crown had lost its monopoly of politics. Elizabeth I did much to recover the lost ground, but even so the factional disputes between her two chief advisers, Burghley and Leicester, had become so bitter by 1569 that the whole stability of her government was threatened. Moreover, the erosion of the economic foundations of the Tudor affinity was no less dangerous than its internal divisions. Henry VII's bastard feudal power had been founded essentially on the crown lands: as we have seen, he was the biggest bastard feudal lord of all because he was the biggest landlord of all. By the early 1530s Henry VIII's wars and his general extravagance had diminished the royal landholding considerably, though not disastrously. The dissolution of the monasteries, however, in the later 1530s gave Henry VIII more land than his father could have dreamed of. And there is every sign that Thomas Cromwell – the king's chief minister – intended these broad acres to remain as a permanent landed endowment of the crown. But that was not to be. Renewed war and acute political weakness dissipated even the acquisitions of the 1530s. The result was that by the late sixteenth century the work of Henry VII was irretrievably destroyed. The balance of landholding between the monarchy and its greater subjects – which the first Tudor had tipped so decisively in his own favour – had now swung back almost to its mid-fifteenth-century position. So, re-endowed at the expense of both crown and church, the later Tudor nobility and upper gentry reclaimed commensurate political power. That power was exercised very differently from how it had been during the fifteenth century, but the difference of style must not obscure the fundamental similarity of strength.

This decisive change in politics impinged largely on the arts. Conventional comment on the difference between the earlier and later sixteenth century stresses two things: first, that the Reformation cut England off from the mainstream of artistic development in Catholic Europe; and, second, that royal patronage – predominant under Henry VIII – collapsed under his successors. Both points are true, but both are negative. There were in fact more positive changes as well. In architecture the revived prosperity of the nobility and gentry led to the great boom in country house building; in literature social groups outside the diminished court circle began to make their tastes felt. The result was that, though the household still dominated the social structure, it lost its old dominance of the world of ideas. Instead, there appeared an astonishing diversity of outlook. This means that talk of an Elizabethan world-picture misses the point: there was not one but several. In *Troilus and Cressida*, for example, no less than four different views emerge: Hector and Achilles subscribe to extreme versions of the knightly or household code of honour, self-regarding and selfish; Ulysses speaks for the ordered, hierarchical universe, in which the individual is subordinated to the common good; Troilus himself begins by imagining a world ruled by love and collapses into a violent nihilism when he discovers that it is not; while Thersites is a parody of a sixteenth-century humanist intellectual railing Erasmus-like against his social superiors because they are not as sharp-witted and well educated as he is. Of these four points of view, Ulysses' is generally assumed to represent the Elizabethan world-picture. But Shakespeare gives it no such primacy: all the systems of value – the knight's, the politician's, the lover's, the intellectual's – are shown as flawed and defective, and the play ends with their conflict unreconciled. The true test of what had happened in the sixteenth century lies in a contrast: between this bewildering variety on the one hand, and, on the other, Cavendish's simple certainty that Wolsey was above criticism because he was the greatest householder of his day.

Notes

Since the text of this chapter was finished in late 1977, two important books have appeared: Alan Macfarlane, *The Origins of English Individualism* (Oxford, 1978), and Lawrence Stone, *The Family, Sex and Marriage in England 1500–1800* (London, 1977), both of which bear directly on the core of its argument. We have, nevertheless, decided to let the chapter stand unaltered. For, though some points of detail need correction, the overall argument survives well enough and even, in fact, makes an independent contribution to the debate. The point is this. Macfarlane's study of the ordinary English family from *c.* 1200 to *c.* 1700 shows convincingly that England, unlike its continental neighbours, was not a peasant society.

From this, he goes on to claim that English society of this period was essentially 'modern': a 'capitalism without factories'. What we do, on the other hand, is to suggest that pre-modern England was neither 'peasant' nor 'modern', but a 'household' or 'servant' society. (After all, as Macfarlane himself points out, one-third of households had servants, while one-half of the population were servants at some stage or another.) This 'household' society is a distinct third type, with characteristic patterns of emotional, political and artistic experience which we explore at length.

1 A. R. Myers (ed.), *The Household of Edward IV* (Manchester, 1959), p. 86.
2 G. W. F. Hegel, *The Philosophy of Right*, trans. T. M. Knox (Oxford, 1965), p. 13.
3 Sir Thomas Smith, *De Republica Anglorum* (London, 1583), p. 18.
4 Ibid., pp. 18–19.
5 Ibid., p. 20.
6 Ibid., p. 27.
7 Ibid.
8 Ibid., p. 28.
9 See the link passage between the *Squire's* and *Franklin's Tales*, V (F), ll. 673 ff., and pp. 134–5 in Robinson's *Works of Geoffrey Chaucer*.
10 Quoted in C. Ross, *Edward IV* (London, 1974), p. 306.
11 E. K. Chambers, *The Mediaeval Stage*, 2 vols (Oxford, 1903), vol. 2, pp. 373–4; cf. S. Lee (ed.), *Dictionary of National Biography*, 22 vols (London, 1908–9), vol. 17, p. 1377.
12 Smith, op. cit., p. 13.
13 Quoted in H. S. Bennett, *The Pastons and their England* (Cambridge, 1968), p. 29.
14 Ibid., p. 30.
15 Ibid., p. 31.
16 Ibid., p. 33.
17 Ibid.
18 F. Procter and W. H. Frere, *A New History of the Book of Common Prayer* (London, 1901), p. 614.
19 J. Stow, *The Survey of London*, Everyman Library (London, 1965), p. 106.
20 H. Ellis (ed.), *Original Letters Illustrative of English History*, 11 vols (London, 1824–46), vol. 1, pp. 207–8.
21 Ibid.
22 *Wife of Bath's Prologue*, ll. 197, 526.
23 *Book of the Duchess*, l. 948.
24 *Piers Plowman*, C text, ed. W. W. Skeat (Oxford, 1886), Passus XI, ll. 202–3, 256–75, 279–83; ed. D. Pearsall (London, 1978), Passus X, ll. 200–2, 254–72, 276–80.
25 *Regement of Princes*, ll. 1618–87; in *Hoccleve's Works*, ed. F. J. Furnivall, EETS, 3 vols (London, 1892 and 1897), vol. 3, pp. 59–61.

26 J. Strype, *Ecclesiastical Memorials*, 3 vols (Oxford, 1822), vol. 1, ch. 2, p. 458.
27 R. Tottel (ed.), *Songes and Sonettes* (London, 1557; facsimile edn, London, 1970), sig. E.i.i.
28 *Knight's Tale*, ll. 1499–1500.
29 *Morte Darthur*, Bk 18, ch. 25, and Bk 19, ch. 1; in Malory, *Works*, ed. E. Vinaver, 3 vols (Oxford, 1947), vol. 3, pp. 1119 ff.
30 Public Record Office, London, PROB 11/40/19.
31 In H. Waddell (ed. and trans.), *Mediaeval Latin Lyrics*, 4th edn (London, 1933), p. 279.
32 'Merciles Beaute', ll. 14–15.
33 Ibid., ll. 27–8.
34 *Franklin's Tale*, l. 793.
35 Sir Thomas Wyatt, *Collected Poems*, ed. J. Daalder (Oxford, 1975), pp. 111–12.
36 K. Marx and F. Engels, *Manifesto of the Communist Party* (Moscow, n.d.), p. 47.
37 *Piers Plowman*, B text, ed. Skeat, Passus X, ll. 94–100; ed. A. V. C. Schmidt (London, 1976), Passus X, ll. 96–102.
38 *Winner and Waster*, ed. Sir Israel Gollancz (Oxford, 1921), ll. 20–1.
39 Myers, op. cit., p. 129.
40 Ibid.
41 Ibid., p. 136.
42 Ibid., p. 131.
43 Ibid., p. 132.
44 Tottel, op. cit., sig. X.i.v.
45 M. Airs, *The Making of the English Country House 1500–1640* (London, 1975), p. 161.
46 Marx and Engels, op. cit., p. 47.
47 F. J. Furnivall (ed.), *Manners and Meals in Olden Time*, EETS, 32 (London, 1868), p. 179.
48 Public Record Office, London, SP 1/47, fols 56–7.
49 Strype, op. cit., vol. 1, ch. 2, p. 458.
50 Society of Antiquaries, *A Collection of Ordinances and Regulations for the Government of the Royal Household* (London, 1790), p. 155.
51 Public Record Office, London, SP 1/125, fols 123–4.
52 Book of Common Prayer (1549 and later), The Second Collect: for peace, at Morning Prayer or Matins.
53 Tottel, op. cit., sig. K.i.i.
54 Ibid., sig. CC.i–ii.
55 Public Record Office, SP 1/241, fol. 285.
56 R. S. Sylvester (ed.), *Two Early Tudor Lives* (New Haven and London, 1962), p. 183.
57 J. A. K. Thomson (ed. and trans.), *The Ethics of Aristotle* (Harmondsworth, 1965), p. 125.
58 Ibid., p. 117.

59 Ibid.
60 *The Complete Poems of John Skelton*, ed. P. Henderson (London, 1966), p. 171.
61 Ibid., p. 242.
62 Sylvester, op. cit., p. 22.
63 Ibid., pp. 30, 51.
64 J. S. Brewer *et al.* (eds), *Letters and Papers of the Reign of Henry VIII*, 21 vols and Appendix (London, 1862–1932), vol. 4, 2, no. 3185.
65 *Morte Darthur*, Bk 12, ch. 9; in *Works*, vol. 2, p. 831.
66 Herald of Sir John Chandos, *Life of the Black Prince*, ed and trans. M. K. Pope and E. C. Lodge (Oxford, 1910).
67 John Lydgate, *Fall of Princes*, Book 1, ll. 92–8; quoted in D. Pearsall, *John Lydgate* (London, 1970), p. 7.
68 *Philip Sparrow*, in *The Complete Poems of John Skelton*, p. 83.
69 Myers, op. cit., p. 127.
70 W. W. Skeat (ed.), *Chaucerian and Other Pieces* (Oxford, 1897), p. 24.
71 *Mum and the Sothsegger*, ed. M. Day and R. Steele, EETS (Oxford, 1936), ll. 26–9.
72 *Morte Darthur*, Bk 1, chs 3, 4, 5; in *Works*, vol. 1, p. 12.
73 *Mum and the Sothsegger*, l. 36.
74 E. Hall, *The Union of the Two Noble and Illustre Families of Lancaster and York* [*The Chronicle*] (London, 1809), p. 599.
75 Quoted in J. R. Lander (ed.), *The Wars of the Roses* (London, 1974), p. 224.
76 Hall, op. cit., p. 712.
77 Ibid., p. 58.
78 Ibid., pp. 513–14
79 Brewer *et al.*, op. cit., vol. 2, 2, pp. 1490–2.
80 A. Barclay, *Bellum Jugurthinum* (n.d.), Preface.
81 *Lament for the Makaris*, ll. 1–4, 9–12, 49–52; in *Poems*, ed. H. B. Baildon (Cambridge, 1907), pp. 146 ff.
82 Wyatt, *Collected Poems*, pp. 185–6.
83 *Satire 1*, l. 100; in ibid., p. 104.
84 K. Muir (ed.), *Life and Letters of Thomas Wyatt* (Liverpool, 1963), p. 41.
85 B. Castiglione, *The Book of the Courtier*, trans. G. Bull (Harmondsworth, 1967), p. 284.
86 *Satire 3*, ll. 85–91; in *Collected Poems*, p. 112.

Select bibliography

For general history, see M. Keen, *England in the Later Middle Ages* (London, 1973).

A good introduction to the effect of family relations on English social structure is given by A. Wagner, *English Genealogy* (Oxford, 1960); while the development of the great house is brilliantly sketched in M. Girouard,

Life in the English Country House (New Haven, 1978). In contrast, there is no satisfactory history of either household or family, but various (and often conflicting) insights are offered by M. Jones, *Family, Lineage and Civil Society* (Oxford, 1974), P. Laslett, *The World We Have Lost* (London, 1956), A. Macfarlane, *The Origins of English Individualism* (Oxford, 1978), L. Stone, *Family, Sex and Society* (Harmondsworth, 1979). It is probably best, therefore, to turn to contemporary works, some of which are readily available: e.g. in A. R. Myers (ed.), *The Household of Edward IV* (Manchester, 1959) – the *Black Book* – and R. S. Sylvester and D. P. Harding (eds), *Two Early Tudor Lives*, for Cavendish's *Wolsey*.

On the peasantry, see R. H. Hilton, *The English Peasantry in the Later Middle Ages* (Oxford, 1975). On economic history, see M. M. Postan, *The Medieval Economy and Society* (London, 1972). Provoking thoughts on this subject (which is given short shrift in the text) are offered by A. Bridbury, *Economic Growth* (London, 1962); while an interesting outline of the political history is offered by J. R. Lander, *Conflict and Stability in Fifteenth Century England* (London, 1969). The same author's *Government and Community* (London, 1980) goes into more detail for the period 1461–1509, and 1509–59 is covered by the superb narrative of G. R. Elton, *Reform and Reformation* (London, 1977) – even if the interpretation is sometimes doubtful. (This last book is particularly useful in the present context as it contains a careful summary of my own analysis of the early Tudor court.) For earlier political history, see R. H. Jones, *The Royal Policy of Richard II* (Oxford, 1968), and A. Tuck, *Richard II and the English Nobility* (London, 1973). On bastard feudalism, see K. B. Macfarlane's article in *B.I.H.R*, 2 (1943–5) and the same author's *The Nobility of Later Mediaeval England* (Oxford, 1973). The political and artistic repercussions of later bastard feudalism are nowhere adequately worked out, but D. Starkey, 'Ightham Mote', *History Today*, 30 (1980), pp. 58 ff., represents a start.

On the world of heraldry itself the best beginning is C. Mackinnon, *The Observer's Book of Heraldry* (London, 1966). A useful introduction to Wyatt's life (as well as a reasonable working text of the poems) is given by R. A. Rebholz, *Sir Thomas Wyatt: The Complete Poems* (Harmondsworth, 1978), and standard accounts of his literary world are J. McConica, *English Humanists and Reformation Politics* (Oxford, 1968), H. A. Mason, *Humanism and Poetry in Early Tudor England* (London, 1959), and J. Stevens, *Music and Poetry in the Early Tudor Court* (London, 1961). There is no good general account of sixteenth-century rhetoric (the prime solvent of household culture), but P. Collinson, 'Sir Nicholas Bacon and the Elizabethan *via media*', *Historical Journal*, 23 (1980), pp. 255 ff., is a fascinating case study (if just beyond our period).

Epilogue: from *Troilus* to *Troilus*

STEPHEN MEDCALF

If we move back a half-century from Shakespeare's *Troilus and Cressida* to Cavendish's *Life* of Wolsey, we find, as at the close of the last chapter, a contrast between the play's 'astonishing diversity of outlook'[1] and the simpler world of the household, with its monolithic ideal of magnificence. But the comparison invites one to move another century and three-quarters further to *Troilus and Criseyde* and to Chaucer, whom we continually find elusive, unseizably ironic, and normally several moves ahead of his readers, modern or contemporary. Such a shift may contribute to solving the question we left hanging in Chapter 1 with a quotation from T. S. Eliot's 'East Coker': whether we should picture for the late fourteenth century an ordered cosmos, a culture all of a piece throughout and a society basically simple, whatever premonitory cracks and disruptions begin to disturb it.

For Eliot makes a similar point in relation to the play and the poem. Shakespeare's play, he says, is 'the passing fury of a prodigious and, for the moment, irresponsible Titan, working almost blindly through destruction towards his own ends'; Chaucer's story is 'the sober statement of a man who was a member of a spiritual (we do not mean ecclesiastical) community who had already arrived as far as he was to go'.[2]

Shakespeare continued the vehement condemnation that Henryson had passed on Criseyde in *The Testament of Cresseid* and extended it, setting his Cressida among people who share a chaos of flawed or abandoned values. The play can be read as a tragedy of

Troilus' disillusion and Hector's death or as a bitter Jonsonian comedy of the Renaissance, condemning every one of its characters.

'In Chaucer's poem', according to Eliot, 'there is no moral judgment either upon Criseyde, or upon Troilus, or upon Pandarus; only a high dispassionate view of the place of these persons in a fixed and firm moral order.'[3] Eliot's contrast is open to the danger that distance simplifies; and a nearer approach to Chaucer's idiom and context sheds an unfamiliar light on words like 'community', 'arrived' and 'fixed and firm order'.

Magnificence and authenticity

The material of the poem is certainly deeply dyed in the ideas and expressions of its age. The lovers are inextricably part of a servant and a household society. It is striking how much Chaucer accentuates the marks of such a society in his transformation of Boccaccio's *Il Filostrato*. On the metaphorical level – for example, the pervasion of love by the language of the household through the particular vocabulary of courtly love – Boccaccio makes his Troilo's continual thought after he first sees Criseida 'O clear light that wakens love in my heart',[4] which Chaucer turns to 'Good goodly, to whom serve I and laboure'.[5] So indeed Chaucer turns the whole poem into the history of a man who takes 'love heigh servise'[6] seriously. His Criseyde, too, much more deserves the name of 'lady' than Boccaccio's, fuller of 'daunger', fuller also of 'pitee', harder to be courted, concerned that a husband may be not only jealous but 'maisterfull'.[7]

On the most literal level, Chaucer repeatedly makes Troilus' difficulties in courting Criseyde, and Pandarus' solutions, touch on the household, and especially the absence of privacy in it – as in the complex arrangements for bedding at Pandarus' house.[8] At the end, when Troilus wants to look at Criseyde's house, Boccaccio only requires him to hide his misery, after he has left his own house, with 'different reasons', from those who were with him. Chaucer interprets this with the remark that even to leave his house

> . . . his meynee for to blinde,
> A cause he fond in toune for to go.[9]

All this is absent in Shakespeare's play, which is removed into a quite artificial period. A comparison of the styles of play and poem likewise emphasizes – even exaggerates – how Chaucer follows the aesthetic values and portrayal of psychology of his age: the magnificence, the leisurely and even relentlessly continuous beauty of narrative rhetoric, the unity of inner and outer. When Shakespeare's Troilus accuses Cressida of shaming all women, and Ulysses asks him 'What hath she done, prince, that can soil our mothers?',[10] he responds with his most moving line, metaphysical, paradoxical, broken and intensive: 'Nothing at all, unless that this were she.'[11] Chaucer gives him no such single line; perhaps the nearest are:

Who shall now trowe on any othes mo?
Allas! I nevere wolde han wend, er this
That ye, Criseyde, koude han chaunged so

. . . and I ne kan nor may
For al this world, withinne myn herte fynde
To unloven you a quarter of a day.[12]

Troilus' language as Chaucer gives it is conversational, direct, entire and extensive. So indeed is the poem itself: its painfulness masses up slowly like a wave.

The famous frontispiece to the Corpus Christi manuscript catches these features; first in its lower half by making the poem Chaucer's recital, almost his parody-sermon, to the great household, the court that is presumably King Richard's (his face obliterated, the easiest explanation of which is that it *is* King Richard, and the obliterator a Lancastrian). In the upper half it represents, Elizabeth Salter has suggested, the scene in which Criseyde is led out from Troy to be exchanged for Antenor and to meet Diomede.[13] This is plausible; for the company is descending into a curious valley between two fortresses, such as Chaucer invented for this scene out of Boccaccio's *vallo* (rampart); and behind the figure that would on this theory be Criseyde two men and two women seem to be attending to birds on their wrists, which may represent how Troilus, to cover his interest in escorting Criseyde, rode hawking. So the scene chosen as a symbol for the whole story is not one of the moments of dramatic emotional decision; but, on a functional and causal view of story, it is the crucial point, after which Criseyde will find she cannot return.

This is not simply a contrast of genre – that is, of recital and drama. It is also part of the poem's peculiar naturalism and perception. Chaucer knew as Dante did that we are normally 'full of sleep'[14] at the moment when previous lesser choices lead us past the irrevocable decision; the same is true of Gawain's fall in *Gawain and the Green Knight*, and may be part of the penitential awareness of self-love, with its concomitant blindness, as the ground of sin. It is one of the uses of Chaucer's perpetual appeal to authority that it enables him not to be too definite about Criseyde, psychologically or ethically. When Pandarus invites her to his house, intending the final stage of her seduction, perhaps she herself does not know how much she knows, for

> Nought list myn auctour fully to declare
> What that she thoughte when he seyde so
> That Troilus was out of toune yfare
> As if he seyde therof soth or no.[15]

Later, at the point of yielding, the decision has already been taken:

> Ne hadde I er now, my swete herte deere,
> Ben yold, ywis, I were now nought heere.[16]

Ben yold] Been yielded

The apparently flat narration works paradoxically to suggest both that reality is hard to determine, and that things could not have been otherwise.

In fact, the style of *Troilus and Criseyde* is not a monument, like some late medieval poetry, simply to magnificence. In contrast to the stress of Lydgate and Hawes on gorgeousness, on *amplificatio* to the neglect of *abbreviatio*, in this poem Chaucer gives explicit utterance to the claim that the procedures of rhetoric, *amplificatio* and *abbreviatio* alike, exist for the sake of authenticity: he begs 'yow that felyng han in loves art'

> To encresse or maken dymynucioun
> Of my langage . . .[17]

An examination of what he did with *Il Filostrato* shows that he follows this prescript – on the whole amplifying with all the colours of rhetoric when he speaks of the happiness, paring and simplifying when he speaks of the loss of love.

In one passage that owes little or nothing to Boccaccio this subtly mixed style produces a remarkable outer–inner effect; and the effect is supported by a moving in and out of public and private rooms, which was presumably novel and noticeable, and by a contrast of public and private in household service. Criseyde enters the extreme privacy of her closet for the double monologue instanced in Chapter 3,[18] and when it is over we move outward both psycho-logically and physically, downstairs with her to see her from outside, with company in the garden. There we hear Antigone's song, and the conversation between them following it, which carries us psycho-logically in, to find that Criseyde prints every word and that love is sinking 'in hire herte'.[19] We look out again, to see the light fading in the garden, then as they go in we repeat the movement inward both physically and psychologically, to be told that what she thought in bed, after her women bring her there, 'Reherce it nedeth naught, for ye been wise'.[20] Then, held between her inner and the outer world, we hear, outside her chamber, the nightingale's song. It is doubtless a specially Chaucerian comment that suggests it is 'a lay of love', for birdsong always suggests the problem of understanding to him, but the thought seems to become Criseyde's, 'that made hire herte fressh and gay'.[21] Then, as she falls asleep, this second song carries us into her very dream. Yet we are not at all violently aware of any change of consciousness. We slip from one surface to another, till the surface of her mind is spread out for us, but to the very end there is something that remains implicit.

In this kind of storytelling inner and outer, as we have so often observed, 'influence and dissolve into each other'.[22] In Troilus' poignant assertion that he cannot

> . . . withinne myn herte fynde
> To unloven you a quarter of a day[23]

Chaucer has removed even the suspicion of a contrast between the two: here Boccaccio had had 'I still keep the image of thy fair face'.[24]

Boccaccio's thought is a commonplace. But out of this common-place Henryson in the fifteenth century created a contrast between inner and outer as startling as Chaucer's fusion of them. His Troilus saw Cresseid again, diseased and deformed, and, not recognizing her, still was reminded enough for her image as she had been, 'sa deip imprentit'[25] in his imagination, to come before his mind and make him tremble. And this, John Bayley suggests, gave rise in Shakespeare's mind to Troilus' exclamation, 'This is, and is not, Cressid.'[26]

In Shakespeare's play, inner and outer are violently rent apart: for

Troilus 'a thing inseparate divides more wider than the sky and earth'.[27] Cressida is his, 'tied with the bonds of heaven';[28] but unless he can 'swagger himself out on's own eyes'[29] he must see that she is Diomede's. But Chaucer's Troilus simply 'nevere wolde han wend'[30] that Criseyde could change, and knows that he himself cannot.

Thus far, then, in style and in the presentation of consciousness, we find Chaucer more single in his view than Shakespeare and less disposed to develop certain contrasts, as of inner and outer, authenticity and gorgeousness. Even public and private are more subtly intermixed in Chaucer, and, in all three contrasts, Chaucer probably reflects the life of his age. In Chaucer's successors, it may be argued that as regards the first two contrasts, one limb of each, 'inner' and 'authenticity', tends to be suppressed; and that this was a prelude in either case to its reassertion as part of a violent contrast. But in Chaucer's own hands the single view was a wonderful means for exploring human potentiality without forcing it into the full daylight of consciousness.

Nevertheless, if we now turn to the background of ideas, we find that the single view goes with evident contrasts in Chaucer.

Love and medieval Platonism

When he sees inner and outer divided, Shakespeare's Troilus appeals to philosophy to unite them. The Platonism of the Middle Ages (mediated through Augustine and Boethius), to which Chaucer's Troilus appealed, has lapsed: the Renaissance Troilus turns to the fundamental intuitions of Plato himself, in what might be a quotation from the *Euthyphro*:

> If souls guide vows, if vows be sanctimonies,
> If sanctimony be the gods' delight . . .
> This was not she.[31]

If value exists, that is, Cressida is his, and is not the Cressida he can see, who is Diomede's. But since in the outside world Cressida is Diomede's Cressida, the argument serves only to set Troilus' gods, and Troilus' value, bound up as they are with his ideal Cressida, exclusively in his inner world. And even this subjectivized Platonism is only one of several philosophies presented by the play, which indeed over all presents a doubt as to whether anything in the outside world answers the expectations or gives ground for the values of selves, which are separated solipsistically from one another.

From the beginning in the play Troilus had, in fact, appealed not to absolute value but to a romantic and existential willed commitment. In neither Chaucer's nor Shakespeare's version are the lovers certainly – that is, publicly – married: the story relies on this. Canon law would probably have considered the marriage irregular but valid; public opinion and state policy have recognized this, or disapproved it as the wedding of a prince with a traitor's daughter. Shakespeare's Troilus takes the matter subjectively. In the great explicit debate on value, the debate on whether Helen should be surrendered, when Hector has spoken in favour of objectively recognizable value, Troilus cannot help thinking of the approaching consummation of his affair, and, though it is secret, it slips into his argument. 'I take today a wife',[32] he says and, having done so, cannot go back on his commitment. 'The bonds of heaven' *are* the permanence of this commitment, at variance with the objective mutability of the world and Cressida.

Chaucer leaves the question of marriage in such abeyance that it seems as ill mannered in his readers as it would have been in Troilus to raise it. His lovers have soon exchanged rings; and yet it was only 'pleyinge'.[33] He avoids even bringing to our attention the marriages of such of his characters as are married. We see Helen but not Paris, we see Hector but do not even hear of Andromache.[34] Religious law and state politics are left far in the hinterland. In the foreground and perfectly clear, as Thomas Usk saw, is love, something so nearly involuntary that the element of willed commitment comes out only in extreme circumstances, and yet absolute in its demands for truth. Chaucer's Troilus, like Shakespeare's, calls love 'a bond perpetuely durynge';[35] but, following Boethius and unlike Shakespeare, Chaucer means by this the love that exists whether or not men receive it, because it holds the universe together.

The certainty of love in *Troilus and Criseyde* is obscured for many readers by what is called the palinode. It seems as if Chaucer gives two explicitly authorial views of love. In the Prologue to Book 3 he not only endorses Troilus' opinion that love of man and woman is an aspect of the universal love but adds that it is like God's love.[36] Yet at the end of the poem he calls to lovers, avoiding 'feynede loves',[37] to love the best to love, who is God.

It is possible to feel that these represent the figural and the creatural forms of medieval feeling; or a world affirming secular enjoyment retracted at the thought of death and eternity; or at least two opposite sentiments necessitated by an intractable story.[38] In the poem's own epoch, according to their temperament or vocation, Usk read it as a 'tretis' praising the love that in many forms pervades the universe;[39] but in a copy of the treatise *Disce Mori* written for a nun of Syon called Dorothy Slyghe, someone has made a note recommending *Troilus* as a story about the 'sweet poison' that impedes our love of God.[40] The story itself makes convincing in turn the happiness of love that manifests the eternal, and the misery of love from which there is no refuge except the eternal.

But to the kind of Platonist that Chaucer was (at least during the years when he was writing *Troilus*, in virtue of his loving translation of Boethius) there is little or no inconsistency. Love, like any good thing, is a participation in the one good, which is God. But only the one good is eternal: only God 'to love wol nought werne'.[41] There is no more reason to deduce from participation that love will endure than that any particular good thing is perpetual. Nowhere, conversely, does the poem suggest that love is anything but a good, except in so far as it does not endure. When love exists, it manifests God; if it ceases, it falls away from God. Of course, some loves (Diomede's probably) are from the beginning 'feynede',[42] not real love. Shakespeare thought that love is not love if it alters and in conformity with this made Cressida's love doubtful and a matter of hours long. But to feel in this way would be to misread *Troilus and Criseyde*. We must not doubt – Chaucer has made it impossible to doubt – the reality of Creseyde's love, for something between fourteen months and three years, to Troilus. Yet Chaucer has also made both her, and Troilus' winning of her, such that we do not doubt either that, when different pressures assail her, her love simply is no more. Chaucer takes for granted what Galahad bid Lancelot remember, and what agonizes Shakespeare: that this world is unstable. As Julian thought, it would fall to nothing for very littleness except for love – God's love. In all this, it is hard to tell any difference between Chaucer's sublime Boethian awareness of eternity, and his regard – 'middle-aged',[43] as Burrow calls it – for time.

For all this, there is a real gap in the poem: not between the lovers' mutual and temporary love and God's, but between Troilus' betrayed and enduring love and God's. Chaucer does his best to

suggest that love may form a bridge between earth and heaven. At
the very start, he asks us to pray

> . . . for hem that ben in the cas
> Of Troilus . . .
> That love hem brynge in hevene to solas.[44]

And soon after he makes it clear that the proud Troilus of the
beginning is a better man for love: love 'worthi folk maad worthier
of name',[45] among them Troilus. Four of his quotations from Dante
seem to reinforce his Boethianism by suggesting a relation running
in his mind between the happiness of earth and the happiness of
heaven. To introduce Book 2, when Troilus' fortunes in courting
Criseyde begin to turn for the better, Chaucer uses Dante's lines on
leaving the inferno for purgatory;[46] while in Book 3, Pandarus uses
lines about the pain of the inferno to suggest the misery of losing
love,[47] and sixty lines afterward the joy of the united lovers is said to
be ineffable with a conceit from the *Paradiso*;

> Felicite, which that thise clerkes wise
> Comenden so, ne may nought here suffise;
> This joie may nought writen be with inke . . .[48]

Finally, the invocation of the close –

> Thow oon, and two, and thre, eterne on lyve,
> That regnest ay in thre, and two, and oon,
> Uncircumscript, and all maist circumscrive . . .[49]

– is a hymn of paradise of which Dante says that 'whoever laments
that we must die here to live there does not see what is the
refreshment of that eternal rain': its 'melody would be just reward
for every merit'.[50]

These thoughts, I think, were running in Chaucer's mind when
he added the three verses in which he makes them explicit by
showing Troilus hearing 'hevenyssh melodie' and comparing this
world's vanity with 'the pleyn felicite' of heaven.[51]

But if he is trying to make those connections he falters. Troilus is
convincingly shown as purified by the sufferings of his first 'sorwe'
to deserve the consummation of earthly love: he is not shown (as
Griselde and Constance in the *Canterbury Tales* are shown) purified
by his second 'sorwe' for heaven, only made miserable. The first
three Dantean echoes remain metaphorical; and the jump at the

end from Troilus' 'despitous'[52] death to the stars is too abrupt, the switch about from an immersion in the present time to Troilus' over-view after death too sudden. And in spite of the prayer at the beginning that love might bring suffering lovers to heaven, Troilus' suffering and truth are not shown to have any relation, such as Dante would have shown, to his fulfilled state in the other world: merely, Troilus laughed at his woe, emphasizing not the bridging of the worlds but their disjunction. His ultimate fate is hidden. (The shockingness, and therefore the suddenness, of the change in perspective from earth to heaven may well be deliberate, like that of the closing shifts by Boethius and others discussed in Chapter 3, or even of those in William Golding's novels. But the metaphysical discontinuity between Chaucer's worlds is not accounted for by that.)

Moreover, although Chaucer has that all-reconciling invocation out of the *Paradiso* to close with, he can scarcely bring himself to reach it. Even without the addition of the three verses of Troilus' ascent, his last pages read like a man's pushing himself over a series of barriers. It looks as if the only piece of cultural difference that Chaucer really emphasizes about Troilus' time – the worship of the pagan gods to whom he partly attributes Troilus' unhappy end – reminds him at the close of the poem of an aspect of the mysterious-ness of God's will which particularly exercised the fourteenth century: the salvation of the just pagan. Langland and Dante con-cluded that the good pagan could go to heaven, and Chaucer must have known Dante's treatment. Curiously, he mentions one of Dante's two pagans in heaven, though only in a list taken from Boccaccio. This is Ripheus, whom Boccaccio calls 'il troian Rifeo';[53] the phrase, unnatural in a list that includes Priam's son Polites, equally Trojan, proves that Boccaccio took the name from Dante's 'Rifeo Troiano' in the *Paradiso*.[54] Chaucer preserves the distinction 'the Troian daun Ripheo'.[55] But, even if the phrase stirred anything in his memory, he lacks the confidence about heaven to wade far into its mysteries.

Dante probably set Ripheus in heaven deliberately to counter Virgil's reference to him: 'the justest of men, as it seemed to men: the gods see things otherwise'.[56] Dante thinks that divine justice is beyond our understanding but not contrary to it. Chaucer is less sure. Troilus reaches the perfection of the medieval knights and their reconciliation of ethical paradoxes, 'lions in the field and lambs in the chamber'.[57] No doubt Usk would have had him in mind as one of love's servants in this phrase, and as such would probably have allowed him the grace of which love is a symbol. But Usk read *Troilus and Criseyde* only under one possible aspect. Chaucer, even with all the ways in which their common culture made it natural for him to do so, did not so easily read the universe symbolically as did Usk and Dante.

In contrast with all three, for Shakespeare inner and outer are divided and trying to be one. In Chaucer they are one, and there is no dispute about the absoluteness of value. But earth and heaven are divided. Chaucer is not troubled by the relation of our volitions to a world of chaos, but he is troubled by their relation to the will of God: by free will, salvation, predestination, grace and the knowableness of God. In this we recognize the disputes of his time, not only of Usk, Dante and Langland, but of Scotus, Ockham and Bradwardine.

In *Troilus and Criseyde*, in spite of Usk's reading of it, these disputes are not settled; and, in spite of Eliot, Chaucer has not arrived as far as he was to go. One can hear echoes, moreover, of the disputes of affirmative and negative, active and contemplative, and it does not seem as if he has decided for either side, or even more than tentatively taken the conclusion to which he seems nearest, that of the *Epistle of Discretion of Stirrings* that God is hid betwixt them. He is still working out a truth. His means, however, seem best expressed in Boethian terms, and do seem to guarantee him at least a perspective and a place to stand.

Eternity and types of perspective

Boethius' preferred metaphor for perception, as Chaucer renders it, is *unplyting*,[58] unfolding. Chaucer expounds in a gloss the opinion that Boethius rejects, 'that soul had been naked of itself, as a mirror or a clean parchment, so that all figures must first comen fro things fro without into souls, and been imprinted into souls.'[59] Rather, Boethius argues, when something strikes the senses from outside, thought calls up the 'species' that it holds within itself, and unites them with the sense impressions, mixing 'the images of things without forth to the forms ihid within himself'.[60] So what we see is affected by what we are, by our body – and time-bound existence. The intelligence of God alone sees the truth; for he is eternal and therefore sees all things past, present and future together in one moment. If we would see the truth, then, we should 'enhance us into the height of thilke sovereign intelligence' which is 'not enclosed nor ishet within none bounds'[61] – in Dante's and Chaucer's word, 'uncircumscript'.

The word almost concludes *Troilus and Criseyde*; and it is a plausible account of the poem that Chaucer is either consciously trying to achieve this view or is so steeped in Boethianism that he cannot help moving towards it. His reason 'unplytes' Boccaccio's story and reinterprets its events in the forms he understands. But among those forms, transcending all the rest, is the idea of eternity. Hence, first, come Chaucer's playing with distance in time, and the appropriate realization of alienness in culture, combined with immersion in the present sensations of Criseyde and of Troilus. Hence, secondly, while Chaucer shows us the two of them making their free and present choices, he continually appeals to an authority he cannot evade. And, thirdly, he continually searches for the reconciliation of free will and predestination. Together, these look like an attempt at seeing the world *sub specie aeternitatis*.

From Shakespeare's play, the sense of eternity is altogether gone, and with it Boethius – gone the more conclusively perhaps, as Ann Thompson suggests, through what can be felt as a 'bitterness . . . against Chaucer himself' for having a solution in his Boethianism which Shakespeare could not accept.[62] The play not only separates individual selves one from another but suggests even that there are no selves, only sequences of volitions. It is haunted by a sense of time as only a succession of presentational immediacies, offering no meaning but oblivion. (Of course, in this as in many other things, the variousness of *Troilus and Cressida* is only a part of the myriad-mindedness of Shakespeare; its fragmentedness is indeed untypical of him, and in his late plays, above all *The Winter's Tale*, something very like a Boethian sense of time and eternity reappears.)

In the bulk of his works, as G. T. Shepherd observes, Chaucer seems always haunted by the question 'How does a succession of events make any sense?'[63] But in *Troilus and Criseyde* time has a strong line of causal efficacy running through it, and Chaucer's strong but open sense of self keeps the notion of responsibility for ever in our attention – most particularly, perhaps, when he says that, if he could, he would excuse Criseyde 'for routhe'.[64] Even if in those most difficult passages which seem to have been added last,

Troilus' ascent to the stars and his meditation on free will, Chaucer seems to fail to show the gap between this world and eternity as being closed, none the less these two senses of responsibility and of causal efficacy still preserve the perspective of eternity.

It is a perspective reflected in his language and in the expression of his relation to the story. Where Shakespeare in *Troilus and Cressida* is paradoxical, multifold and full of evident warring contradictions, Chaucer offers something that is clear and simple when close at hand, shimmering, shifting and elusive in the middle distance, opening on an infinitely recessive profundity. It is a perspective he preserves even when in the *Canterbury Tales* he makes his book out of explicitly many voices, though not primarily by the Knight's rehandling of the Boethian themes of *Troilus and Criseyde*, nor by any of the individual tales. God's 'sovereign intelligence' is perhaps much more manifest by the way in which Chaucer's 'high dispassionate view' seems capable of taking in infinitely more pilgrims and tales without final moral judgement, only a sense of there being an order ready to receive them. And the gap between time and eternity seems most satisfyingly closed at the beginning and the end of the book, which with perfect appropriateness refer respectively to spring and to the end of time – at the end iron contrition for what is wrong and ascription of gratitude for what is right in the book to Christ; and new life with promise of universal meaning in that April, with the pilgrims running their course to the holy places along with the young sun, in the beginning.

Perhaps this perspective, which Chaucer shares with Langland and the author of *Pearl*, could not have outlasted the rigidifying of thought and authority of the fifteenth century, marked most hatefully by the statute *De Heretico Comburendo*. But perhaps for the writers of Chaucer's generation we may restate Eliot's description of *Troilus and Criseyde* to say that they are constrained at once to a tentativeness in their assertions and to a faith in the givenness of truth because in the end they expect to confront the very Truth:

Uncircumscript, and all maist circumscrive.

Notes

References to Shakespeare follow *The Complete Signet Classic Shakespeare* (New York, 1972).
1 See p. 286 above.

2   'Chaucer's *Troilus'* (unsigned), *The Times Literary Supplement*, 12 August 1926, p. 547.
3   Ibid.
4   Boccaccio, *Il Filostrato*, trans. R. K. Gordon, *The Story of Troilus* (repr. New York, 1964), p. 36.
5   *Troilus and Criseyde*, Bk 1, l. 458.
6   Ibid., Bk 3, l. 1794.
7   Ibid., Bk 2, l. 756; cf. *Il Filostrato*, trans. Gordon, p. 48.
8   H. M. Smyser, 'The Domestic Background of *Troilus and Criseyde*', *Speculum*, 31 (Cambridge, Mass., April 1956), pp. 297–315.
9   *Il Filostrato*, trans. Gordon, p. 98; *Troilus and Criseyde*, Bk 5, ll. 526–7.
10 Shakespeare, *Troilus and Cressida*, V. ii. 132.
11 Ibid., V. ii. 133.
12 *Troilus and Criseyde*, Bk 5, ll. 1681–3, 1696–8.
13 The frontispiece is best reproduced in the facsimile of Corpus Christi College, Cambridge, MS.61, published by D. S. Brewer Ltd (Cambridge, 1978), with introductions by M. B. Parkes and Elizabeth Salter; for the latter's interpretation, see p. 22.
14 Dante, *Divine Comedy, Inferno*, I, l. 11.
15 *Troilus and Criseyde*, Bk 3, ll. 575–8.
16 Ibid., Bk 3, ll. 1210–11.
17 Ibid., Bk 3, ll. 1333, 1335–6.
18 See p. 110 above.
19 *Troilus and Criseyde*, Bk 2, ll. 900, 902.
20 Ibid., Bk 2, l. 917.
21 Ibid., Bk 2, ll. 921–2.
22 A. C. Spearing, *Chaucer: Troilus and Criseyde* (London, 1976), p. 49.
23 *Troilus and Criseyde*, Bk 5, ll. 1697–8.
24 *Il Filostrato*, trans. Gordon, p. 122.
25 R. Henryson, *The Testament of Cresseid*, l. 508.
26 *Troilus and Cressida*, V. ii. 144.
27 Ibid., V. ii. 147.
28 Ibid., V. ii. 152.
29 Ibid., V. ii. 134.
30 *Troilus and Criseyde*, Bk 5, l. 1682.
31 Plato, *Euthyphro*, 6e; *Troilus and Cressida*, V. ii. 137–8, 140.
32 *Troilus and Cressida*, II. ii. 61.
33 *Troilus and Criseyde*, Bk 3, l. 1368.
34 See M. Salu (ed.), *Essays on Chaucer's Troilus and Criseyde* (Cambridge, 1979).
35 *Troilus and Criseyde*, Bk 3, l. 1754.
36 Ibid., Bk 3, l. 12.
37 Ibid., Bk 5, l. 1848.
38 Among many others, see E. Salter, '*Troilus and Criseyde*: a reconsideration', in J. Lawlor (ed.), *Patterns of Love and Courtesy*

(London, 1966); also the essays in R. J. Schoeck and J. Taylor (eds), *Chaucer Criticism* (Notre Dame, Indiana, 1960), vol. 2.
39 Thomas Usk, *Testament of Love*, Bk 3, ch. 4; in *Chaucerian and Other Pieces*, ed. W. W. Skeat (Oxford, 1897), p. 123.
40 *A Book of Showings to the Anchoress Julian of Norwich*, ed. V. E. Colledge and J. Walsh (Toronto, 1978), vol. 1, p. 40.
41 *Troilus and Criseyde*, Bk 3, l. 12.
42 Ibid., Bk 5, l. 1848.
43 J. A. Burrow, *Ricardian Poetry* (London, 1971), pp. 126–9.
44 *Troilus and Criseyde*, Bk 1, ll. 29–31.
45 Ibid., Bk 1, l. 251.
46 Ibid., Bk 2, ll. 1–3; Dante, *Purgatorio*, I, ll. 1–3.
47 *Troilus and Criseyde*, Bk 3, ll. 1625–8; Dante, *Inferno*, V, ll. 121–5.
48 *Troilus and Criseyde*, Bk 3, ll. 1691–3; Dante, *Paradiso*, XIX, l. 8.
49 *Troilus and Criseyde*, Bk 5, ll. 1863–5; Dante, *Paradiso*, XIV, ll. 28–30.
50 Dante, *Paradiso*, XIV, ll. 26–8, 33.
51 *Troilus and Criseyde*, Bk 5, ll. 1813, 1818.
52 Ibid., Bk 5, l. 1806.
53 Boccaccio, *Il Filostrato*, IV, l. 3.
54 Dante, *Paradiso*, XX, l. 68.
55 *Troilus and Criseyde*, Bk 4, l. 53.
56 Virgil, *Aeneid*, II, ll. 426–7.
57 Usk, *Testament*, Bk 1, ch. 5, p. 24.
58 Chaucer, *Boece*, Bk 5, metrum 4.
59 Ibid.
60 Ibid.
61 Ibid., Bk 5, prosa 5.
62 Ann Thompson, *Shakespeare's Chaucer* (Liverpool, 1978), p. 165.
63 Geoffrey Shepherd, 'Religion and philosophy in Chaucer', in D. Brewer (ed.), *Geoffrey Chaucer* (London, 1974), p. 273.
64 *Troilus and Criseyde*, Bk 5, l. 1099.

Index